The Phyllis Thompson Trilogy

The Phyllis Thompson Trilogy

Madame Guyon
A London Sparrow
Pilgrim In China

OM
publishing

The Phyllis Thompson Collection first published 2001 by Alpha

Alpha is an imprint of Paternoster Publishing, PO Box 300,
Carlisle, Cumbria, CA3 0QS, UK
And Paternoster Publishing USA
PO Box 1047, Waynesboro, GA 30830-2047

Madame Guyon
First printed 1986 by Hodder and Stoughton Ltd.

A London Sparrow
First published 1971 by Word (UK) Ltd.
Reprinted 1972 by Pan Books Ltd.

Pilgrim In China

First published in the UK By Highland Books

British Library Cataloguing in Publication Data
A catalogue record for this book is available
from the British Library
1-85078-379-9
Cover design by Diane Bainbridge

Printed in Great Britain by
Cox & Wyman Ltd., Reading, Berkshire, RG1 8EX

Madame Guyon

Also by Phyllis Thompson

TO THE HEART OF THE CITY
THE GIDEONS
AN UNQUENCHABLE FLAME
MR LEPROSY
THE RAINBOW OR THE THUNDER
CHINA: THE RELUCTANT EXODUS
CAPTURING VOICES
MINKA AND MARGARET
WITHIN A YARD OF HELL
THE MIDNIGHT PATROL
A LONDON SPARROW
FIREBRAND OF FLANDERS
FAITH BY HEARING
PROVING GOD
MATCHED WITH HIS HOUR
DAWN BEYOND THE ANDES
GOD'S ADVENTURER
CLIMBING ON TRACK
NO BRONZE STATUE
DESERT PILGRIM
BEATEN GOLD
AFLAME FOR CHRIST
THERE CAME A DAY
THEY SEEK A CITY
OUR RESOURCES
COUNTDOWN FOR PETER
EIGHT OF GOD'S AGENTS
BIBLE CONVOY

Books for children

TEACHER JO LIKES LITTLE CATS
KING OF THE LISU

Madame Guyon

Martyr of the Holy Spirit

by

Phyllis Thompson

Acknowledgements

My thanks are due to Mrs Stanley Rowe, the Rev. Paul Bassett and to all those who have encouraged me in the writing of this book, especially Miss Stephanie Wright of the Evangelical Library. Also to Miss Mollie Robertson for typing the manuscript so meticulously, and the Dr. Jonathan Chao of the Chinese Church Research Centre for permission to use the poem at the end of the Epilogue.

Contents

Prologue — 9

1. The Irrevocable Step — 15

2. Start of the Pilgrimage — 25

3. Vanity — 37

4. Dark Night Ended — 51

5. Into the Unknown — 73

6. Thonon to Turin — 89

7. Exodus from Grenoble — 99

8. Imprisoned in Paris — 119

9. Enter Fenelon — 133

10. Pilloried — 143

11. To the Bastille — 157

12. It does not end here — 173

Epilogue — 189

He made me understand the He did not call me, as had been thought, to the propagation of the external of the Church, which consists in winning heretics, but to the propagation of His Spirit, which is no other than the interior Spirit, and that it would be for this Spirit I would suffer.

He does not even destine me for the first conversion of sinners, but to introduce those who are already touched with the desire of being converted, into perfect conversion, which is none other than this interior Spirit.

Jeanne de la Mothe Guyon

Prologue

It was T. C. Upham who set me thinking. I'd never heard of Madame Guyon until I read his book about her. If it had not been given to me with a personal inscription in the flyleaf by a young woman dying of TB, I doubt whether I should have got any further than the title page. *Life, Religious Opinions and Experience of Madame Guyon* held little appeal, and the opening sentence would have put me off altogether.

'The subject of this Memoir was born on April 13th, 1648, and baptized on the May 24th.'

1648 – three hundred years ago! But the book had been given to me in touching circumstances, so I read on, and the more I read, the more relevant I found it to be. The outward conditions of that young aristocrat living in the glittering reign of the Sun-King, Louis XIV, were vastly different from those of myself, a rather humdrum missionary on furlough from China, but the inner experiences had a significance I could not ignore. True, some of them were quite beyond me, but if I could not understand them all, or the writer's interpretation of them, two spiritual principles emerged which I never forgot.

One was accepting the will of God in the vicissitudes of life, and the other the necessity of dying to self.

The processes by which they were worked out in Madame Guyon's life were instructive and challenging when applied personally. And I have since discovered that I am not alone in finding them so. 'Madame Guyon! She's my favourite character!' said one friend enthusiastically, adding more quietly, 'Mine weren't the same as hers, of course, but I could relate to her sufferings.'

'She helped me more than anything else in a situation in South America in which I found myself trapped,' reflected another. She did not go into details. Some experiences are too

9

personal to be shared, but, 'It was like being in prison and what she had written when she was actually there was what spoke to me – especially that little poem about a bird in a cage, singing . . .'

'Madame Guyon?' exclaimed a Canadian visitor when I mentioned her. 'Why, she was a compulsory study in the Prairie Bible Institute when I was there. L. E. Maxwell, the founder, wanted all his students to know the reality of her teaching on death to self.'

'Death to self – we don't hear much about that in these days, our minister says,' remarked an old friend, living now in Leicester. 'He's always quoting Madame Guyon . . .' He had been introduced to her when reading Dr. A. W. Tozer's biography. She was more widely known than I had realised.

Then someone reminded me that her story was the last book Watchman Nee produced before the Communists gained complete control in China. Mary Wang, Director of the China Overseas Christian Mission, had been greatly moved by it at that time, and told me, 'It was her willingness to suffer that so inspired and challenged us young people in those days.' She herself had eventually escaped from China, but most of those young people had had to remain, and it meant suffering if they were to remain loyal to Christ. The Frenchwoman who had lived three hundred years before had nerved those young Chinese Christians for what lay ahead of them in the grim second half of the twentieth century.

Madame Guyon evidently ranked among those who, being dead, continue to speak, for the message she proclaimed does not alter with the times.

Someone in the 1970s suggested that I might write her biography for the present generation, and the idea held a strong appeal, but it was not until early in 1985 that I signed a contract to do it, and set about my research. The book by T. C. Upham was all I had to go on, and I realised that he had interpreted her from his own point of view, all but making a Protestant of her. Although it had inspired me, it was an insufficient source from which to obtain as unbiased an account of her life and character as possible, seeing she had lived so long ago. References made to her in historical books were sketchy and mainly derogatory, depicting her as a rather silly religious fanatic, not clever enough to be really dangerous, but attractive enough to be disturbing, who made a short-lived appearance on the stage of world history. I was not likely to glean much from them.

Then I applied for help to the Evangelical Library, and in their archives was found just what I needed. Not only had they *Bossuet* by H. L. Sidney Lear, *The Archbishop and the Lady* by Michael de la Bedayère, a booklet by Mrs. Jessie Penn Lewis, and three devotional books by Madame Guyon herself. *A Short Method of Prayer, Spiritual Torrents* and a little book of poems. But they had something else, which far exceeded them all in value for my purpose. There before me was *The Autobiography of Madame Guyon,* fully translated from the French by Thomas Taylor Allen of the Bengal Civil Service, and published by a firm in Charing Cross Road in 1898.

Mr. Allen made it quite plain in his preface that he took a very dim view of 'Upham's defective and misleading *Life,* where her catholic spirit appears bound in the grave clothes of so-called Evangelical dogma'. As for himself, he had translated Madame Guyon's autobiography word for word from the French, omitting nothing. Let it speak for itself.

What better source for a biographer than the subject's own life story as related by herself? I plunged into it with enthusiasm and expectancy – and found myself again and again quite out of my depth as I tried to follow the thread of narrative in the welter of words that flowed from the pen of a mystic. Madame Guyon wrote impulsively, just as she saw and felt things, with very little thought as to what it would all convey to the reader. In fact, the earlier part of the autobiography was written on the understanding that it would never be published at all. It was intended only for the eye of her spiritual director, at whose command she wrote it. The latter part was more evidently written with the view of vindicating not only herself but others who were connected with her. But whatever was her motive for writing, the subject matter remained the same. With her introspective nature she could not refrain from relating her 'religious opinions and experience' and they sometimes made heavy reading, especially as they were couched in the archaic language of a former generation. But through them all certain facts emerged which surprised me.

One was that the Bible was evidently accessible, at any rate to the educated classes, in the reign of Louis XIV. Madame Guyon's autobiography throughout is permeated with Scriptural references, and she wrote and had published commentaries on some of the Old Testament books. To whatever extent it has been suppressed in other places and ages, there is no suggestion that it was forbidden reading to her and her contemporaries.

Another fact that emerged was that she was not without friends who were willing to stand by her even when she was most decried. She sometimes referred desperately to being 'abandoned by all', but it was an exaggeration unsupported by evidence. One of the moving things about her story is the loyalty displayed, not only by her to her friends, but by her friends to her. They were impelled by the same Spirit towards the same end – perfect union with God Himself.

And this leads to the supreme theme of Madame Guyon's story, which is none other than the effect of the activity of the Holy Spirit in the depths of a human soul, and a very complex human soul at that. The effect was two-fold. On the one hand there was the devastating revelation of the iniquity within, the SELF which she saw and loathed, which writhed under the blows showered upon it, but which she agreed had to die. On the other hand there was the ineffable peace and joy brought by the indwelling presence of God, and an increasing knowledge, not only of the Man, Christ Jesus, but of the power of His resurrection, and the fellowship of His sufferings – those sufferings which because of her love for Him, she longed to share.

It is the story of an inner life, lived in the context of circumstances very different from those of the twentieth century, and as such it can only be told with the imperfection of the writer's own limitations. But it is a story which does not end with her death. The thread of apparently incidental events which links it with the present day was so tenuous at times that the marvel is that it did not snap, yet the fact remains that her autobiography and some of her writings are still being produced in various forms today. As she herself predicted when she wrote in her prison cell, 'I have confidence that, in spite of the tempest and the storm, all You have made me say or write will be preserved.'

To trace her story, as best I can, has been a fascinating and enriching task, taking me back in time to the mid-seventeenth century, to the town of Montargis, south of Paris, where a teenage girl had just been married . . .

By sufferings only can we know
   The nature of the life we live;
The trial of our souls, they show,
   How true, how pure, the love we give.
To leave my love in doubt would be
No less disgrace than misery.

I welcome, then, with heart sincere,
   The cross my Saviour bids me take;
No load, no trial is severe,
   That's borne or suffered for His sake:
And thus my sorrow shall proclaim
A love that's worthy of the name.

Jeanne de la Mothe Guyon, aged nineteen

1

The Irrevocable Step

The young bride was in tears. It was the day after her wedding, when the pageantry and the music and the crowds of fashionable guests had carried her through the solemn ceremony in which she and the man beside her had been pronounced man and wife. Even then a sense of foreboding had robbed the occasion of the gratification she would otherwise have experienced at knowing herself to be the most beautiful bride of the season. As it was, she had found it hard to retain her poise, to smile back brightly at everyone who nodded or spoke to her. But now, the day after, when the realisation of the irrevocable step taken had dawned on her, she could control her dismay no longer. Jeanne de la Mothe had become Madame Guyon, and there was no going back on it.

It was not that her husband had treated her roughly, or that her natural modesty had been unduly affronted. It was not because the marriage had been arranged by her parents without even consulting her. That, after all, was quite customary, though she had been a little surprised when she discovered that she had signed the articles of marriage without even being told what they were. When she had met her fiancé for the first time, only three days before the wedding, she had felt he compared very unfavourably in appearance with one or two of her other suitors. In the eyes of a teenager who had been feeding her mind on romantic novels, his great wealth and good reputation scarcely compensated for his being twenty years her senior and not particularly good-looking. But the reason for her tears lay deeper than a merely natural reaction. Her desperate answer to the question, 'Whatever are you crying about?' summed

15

up the inner conflict of her young life, for there had been times when she had seriously decided to take the veil, to be wholly dedicated to God. And now –

'Oh, I had once so desired to be a nun! Why am I married? How has this happened to me?' She had gone back on her secret vow, and now it was too late.

This pious desire had been born in her early, for from the age of two-and-a-half the greater part of her life had been spent in convents. Both her parents had been married before, already had older children, including a daughter apiece, and her mother in particular had little inclination for looking after a small girl. She preferred boys. The easy way out was to put her in the charge of the nuns whose job it was in life to look after other people's children. So to the convent of the Ursulines little Jeanne de la Mothe was sent, and there is no doubt but that she was better off with them than she was at home. The determination to be a nun was conceived in her through their example, and being of an ardent nature, on hearing some of the stories of martyrs, she asserted her willingness to become one, too. Thus early in life her sights were set on sacrifice.

It is quite probable that some of the nuns took her seriously, but schoolgirls in convents being not so very different from schoolgirls elsewhere, a few of the older girls decided to play a practical joke on this devout child.

Was she really willing to be a martyr? They would put her to the test. So one day they approached her with the solemn announcement that the time had come. God was calling her to forfeit her life for His sake. They would give her time for her last prayers, then lead her away to her execution.

On the whole Jeanne did very well. Firmly believing that her last hour had come, she knelt in prayer, then unquestioningly followed her executioners to the room they had prepared for the occasion, where a white cloth was spread on the floor to receive the blood that would be shed when her head was chopped off. But when she got there and saw one of the girls with a cutlass, with which the deed was apparently to be done, her courage failed her.

But not her pride. Unwilling to admit she feared to die, she avoided doing so by announcing with a resourcefulness unusual in one so young, that she could not be a martyr yet, since she had not asked her father's permission. Without that, it would not be right to proceed.

The howl of derisive laughter that greeted this explanation no doubt had an element of relief in it, for the jokers were fast approaching the point where they themselves would have been compelled to give up. But for Jeanne the sense of humiliation was not only that she had failed in the eyes of her companions, nor was it only that she had let herself down. There was the uneasy fear that she had come short in the eyes of God, and was no longer in His favour. That unseen Being of whom she was daily reminded in the religious services in the convent set very high standards . . .

Her failure as a martyr worried her more than the lies she told quite fluently, which could be duly disposed of in the confessional box.

All the same, she was happy while with the nuns, most of whom treated her very kindly. In the convent she was spared the peculiar grief experienced by a child at home who knows herself to be the one unloved. Her brother, not she, was their mother's favourite. He, it seemed, could do no wrong, while she could do nothing right. He was indulged, she was reprimanded. If he wanted something of hers, it was taken from her and given to him. Her childish efforts to win approval, to do something that would bring a smile to her mother's face, and a kiss and a hug, were in vain. A cold look of disapproval greeted her instead.

Her happiest times were when she was in the Ursuline convent where her paternal half-sister, who really loved her, was put in charge of her. 'Oh, I enjoy teaching you more than doing anything else!' exclaimed the young nun one day. She spent every spare moment allowed her with her little sister. Under her tuition the child developed well, with charming manners and a ready wit which so attracted the exiled Queen of England, widow of Charles the First, that she wanted to adopt her. She was staying in the de la Mothe home at the time, and Jeanne had been brought back on a visit.

'Let her come to me. I'll train her as Maid of Honour to the Princess,' she said. But Jeanne's elderly father, who was very fond of his little daughter, though he did not often see her, refused to part with her. For various reasons, however, he was persuaded to remove her from the convent of the Ursulines and place her in one of another order – the Dominicans this time. And it was here that she found the Vulgate version of the Bible.

How it came about that the book had been left in the little room allotted to her is a mystery, but there it was, and as she was quite often ill and confined to bed, she had ample opportunity to read it.

She was fascinated. At that age it was naturally the narratives that appealed to her most, and being alone for hours on end – when she was ill, she learned many of them off by heart.

'I spent whole days in reading it,' she wrote in her autobiography years later. 'And having great powers of recollection I committed to memory the historical parts entirely.' The self-imposed task occupied her mind and gave her vivid imagination the opportunity to reach out far beyond the restricted world in which she lived. Abraham the nomad with the flocks and his herds, Joseph sold by his brothers into slavery, Moses defying Pharaoh in the name of the God of Israel, David hounded by the jealousy of Saul – she knew them all, and felt herself at one with them. Her familiarity with the Scriptures, which revealed itself later in so many of her writings (she produced commentaries on the whole Bible at one stage) had its roots in those lonely hours as a child in a sick room in a Dominican convent.

Nor was the Bible the only book she read during those impressionable years of her disrupted and rather unhappy childhood. The writings of St. John of the Cross and other Christian mystics appealed to her. Particularly what she

read of St. Francis de Sales and Madame du Chantal
influenced her thinking.

It was these two, whose lives had been so strangely
entwined in a mystical union, who attracted her most. After
all, it was less than a hundred years ago that they had lived
and laboured in the north of the country, not far from
Geneva, that hot-bed of Calvinism. It was claimed that St.
Francis had converted thousands of Protestants back to the
Church of Rome, sometimes, it was inferred, at the risk of his
life, in addition to founding with Madame du Chantal the
Order of the Visitation. Scores of communities had been
established, and their black-robed nuns were a common
sight on errands of mercy to the poor.

The practical achievements of Francis de Sales and
Madame du Chantal were matched by the spiritual quality
of their lives. Their love for God, their teaching on the will of
God and the crucifixion of the self-life had been duly
examined and pronounced pure by the hierarchy in Rome.
What they had written could therefore be relied on, and the
ten-year-old girl, perusing their books, discovered something
new.

She learned that they prayed.

This secret activity of theirs awakened within her a vague
awareness of a realm about which she knew nothing. Their
prayer was apparently different from the incantations and
recitals, the versicles and responses, to which she was
accustomed. It went much deeper. She wished she could
pray, and made some attempts to do so, without any
apparent result. But desire had been born, a conscious
vacuum waiting to be filled

So passed the earlier years of her life, with fluctuating
aspirations after higher things which were largely condi-
tioned by her circumstances, by the examples she admired,
and by the books which she read.

The influence of those books, read in the impressionable
years of her childhood, was incalculable. Because she was
often alone, her imagination had freedom to stretch out and

expand, and the writers of the books became as real to her as the people she met in ordinary life. Madame du Chantal was her heroine. 'All the vows she made, I made also, as aiming always at the perfect, and doing the will of God in all things.' Reading that in her ardour Madame du Chantal had branded the name of Jesus on her breast with a red hot iron, she wished she could do the same. 'Jesus.' That was the name Madame du Chantal had chosen, not Mary or one of the saints. How could she, a little girl in a convent, obtain the necessary means to brand the name on her own skin? Eventually she had to give up that idea, but decided on the next best thing. She would write the name carefully on a piece of paper, then pin it to her skin. It must have been a very painful operation, but she went through with it, and 'it continued for a long time fixed in this manner'.

'My only thought was to become a nun, and I went very often to the Visitation to beg them to be willing to receive me, for the love I had for St. Francis de Sales did not allow me to think of other convents.' The mystical union between St. Francis de Sales and Madame du Chantal, joint founders of the Order, she accepted without question. They were knit together by a spiritual, not a natural affinity, altogether in keeping with the religious life they had chosen. It was the only sort of union that made any appeal to her.

However, this excess of ardent piety later swung to the opposite extreme. As she entered her teens it was romantic novels, not the writings of the mystics, that kept her reading into the early hours of the morning. Her own reflection in the mirror, viewed from as many angles as possible, gave her a much more animated and attractive object of adoration than the image of the Virgin Mary. In her mirror she saw a beautiful girl, with lustrous eyes and a flawless fair skin, soft curls and a well-formed mouth. Much prettier, she knew, than most of the other girls and young women in the social circles of Montargis, and she thought with secret scorn of their defects, although she was careful never to reveal it. Jeanne de la Mothe had a charmingly modest manner which enhanced her still further in the eyes of her admirers – of whom she herself was the most fervent. When she went out she was, of course, always accompanied by her mother or a chaperone, but that did not deter her from noticing the glances of warm admiration in her direction from members of the opposite sex – nor of envious dislike from her own! She was equally gratified by both.

Nevertheless: 'I did not fail every day to say my vocal prayers,' to make confession pretty often, and to communicate almost every fortnight. I was sometimes in church weeping and praying to the Holy Virgin to obtain my conversion . . . I was very charitable. I loved the poor.' In this her mother had set her a good example, for Madame de la Mothe was very generous to needy people in her neighbourhood, as her daughter readily admitted.

Then, when she was in her mid-teens, her parents took her to Paris.

Paris! Capital of the nation fast becoming the greatest power in western Europe, centre of art and culture, fashion and frivolity. Paris with its boulevards and its magnificent buildings, the Louvre and Notre Dame, its bridges over the Seine, its tall, sharp-roofed houses with their diamond-paned mullion windows and little iron balconies. Paris with its elegantly dressed ladies bowing and smiling from sedan chairs on the chivalrous gentlemen in their richly embroidered cloaks who swept off their hats with a flourish and bowed low in homage. Paris with its animated visitors in the salons, its fêtes and its hunting parties led by the virile young King, glad to be in the saddle with his mistress beside him after hours at his desk studying reports.

Paris with its preachers, too. If the King had made adultery the fashion, he also set the example of outward piety, attending Mass regularly and listening with apparent approval to the forthright sermons of men like Bossuet, who pulled no punches, even in the presence of His Majesty. There were few public entertainments in the seventeenth century, and eloquent preachers could always draw a crowd.

The confessional boxes provided a different sort of outlet, where those who were uneasy about their souls could acknowledge their sins and misdemeanours with the assurance that the priest behind the grill was pledged to secrecy, and would not betray their confidences. To go to Mass, to go to confession, to observe the feast days of the saints, was all part of the fashionable round, and in addition it was quite the right thing to have your own personal spiritual director, who gave you good advice, writing letters on occasion to point out your faults, making suggestions for your spiritual improvement, and generally taking an interest in you.

Religion was something to be donned and doffed, as occasion served, but not to be taken too seriously, except by those who were called to it, and saw it as their vocation. Or, in some cases, as the only way out. To women it was the one alternative to marriage – that is, to the women born into the fortunate ten per cent of French families who lived in affluence; the aristocrats, the nobility, the wealthy landowners. The remaining ninety per cent, including the indiscriminate rabble responsible for the Bread Riots, were of course in an entirely different category, about which the ten per cent knew very little, except that those who happened to live near enough to them provided objects of charity to whom gifts of food and clothing and money could be given from time to time. Charity was a Christian virtue to be cultivated, as it offset failings in other directions.

Jeanne de la Mothe belonged to the privileged ten per cent, and as she was developing into a very attractive girl, with every prospect of making a good match, her parents saw no reason for her to take the veil.

Neither, at this time, did she.

What she saw of life in Paris, the gaiety and the intellectual pursuits, the lavish entertaining and the elegance, delighted her. This was what she wanted – the opportunity to display her charm and her beauty, 'to make myself loved without loving anybody', and to be free from the domination of her mother. Marriage, it seemed, would be the open door to the gratification of all these desires. She began to have her doubts when she learned to whom she had been affianced and realised that his wealth rather than his rank was the attraction in her father's eyes, and the fact that he spent most of his time in her own home town, Montargis, and would not be likely to take her to live far away, or abroad. As the time drew near for the wedding there was also the natural shrinking from the unknown mysteries of the bed, to be shared with a strange man. But it was not until the wedding day itself that the oppressive cloud descended so heavily on her spirit that she could not eat. She had a presentiment then that she was entering gloom, not brightness, and the presentiment proved to be true. The full realisation of it broke when her husband took her back to Montargis, to the home where his mother was in unchallenged control. Her own mother's attitude had been strangely lacking in love, but now she was to be plunged into an atmosphere of suppressed hostility.

My husband was reasonable and loved me. When I was ill he was inconsolable to a surprising degree, and yet he did not cease to get into passions with me. I believe that, but for his mother and that maid of whom I have spoken, I should have been very happy with him; for as to hastiness, there is hardly a man who has not plenty of it, and it is the duty of a reasonable woman to put up with it quietly without increasing it by sharp answers.

You made use of all these things, O my God, for my salvation. Through Your goodness You have so managed things that I have afterwards seen this course was absolutely necessary for me, in order to make me die to my vain and haughty natural character . . . an altogether wise dispensation of Your providence.

Jeanne de la Mothe Guyon, in her autobiography.

2

Start of the Pilgrimage

'I was no sooner at home with my new husband than I saw clearly it would be to me a house of sorrow,' she recorded in her autobiography years later, and so it proved to be. Her mother-in-law was an austere, uncultured woman, and one in whom thrift had become such an obsession as to make life a misery. The young Madame Guyon, whose parents were not nearly so wealthy as the family into which she had married, found herself in a dark, heavily furnished home which lacked all the brightness and elegance to which she had become accustomed. Gone was the atmosphere of refinement and culture, the intelligent discussions and the witty sallies, the hum of conversation and the chuckles of laughter, the music and the colour of the salons of Paris. The upbringing and temperament of Madame Guyon senior precluded such frivolities, and she would have none of them.

What was worse, from the point of view of the newly arrived young mistress of the home, was that the manners of the household were different. If her own mother had chided her unduly when she was a child, she had treated her with courtesy in the presence of others as she grew older, while her father, pleased to see his attractive young daughter cultivating charming manners and obviously delighting the guests who came frequently to their home, had encouraged her to join in their conversations and express her opinions.

Now all that was changed. The natural charm that had been one of her greatest assets was repulsed. She was no longer a centre of admiration, moving easily among those whose interest and approval brought out all her social graces. Her mother-in-law, it soon became evident, resented her presence, was angered by her refinement, and suspected her motives. The young girl's cultured voice and polished manners were in sharp contrast to her own rather uncouth ways, putting her at a disadvantage against which she fought angrily.

Right from the start young Madame Guyon realised that there was no doubt as to who reigned supreme in the Guyon household. The hopes she had entertained of freedom to reign as mistress in her own home were dashed completely. The cooks and the coachmen, the maids, the valets and the footmen, even her husband himself, were under control of the older Madame. Her own position was virtually that of a captive, and a despised one at that. She was accustomed to being accompanied by a maid or a footman when she went out, and they had been with her to protect her from embarrassments, and generally ease things for her. She very soon found that the maid or the footman who now went with her was expected to report when they got home on everything she had done, and everyone she had spoken to. There was a subtle difference in their attitude towards her, too. They knew it was the old Madame who held the reins, not the newly-arrived young bride, and that to win favour with the one, the other could be slighted. One maid in particular, who was in the confidence of her mother-in-law, was quite insolent, and the teenage girl scarcely knew how to control her indignation. On a few occasions she flared up, but that only made matters worse. Her mother-in-law sided with the maid.

It would not have been so bad if at least in the presence of guests and relatives her mother-in-law had shown a semblance of respect towards her, but she did not. If she entered into a discussion at the table or in the salon, she was snubbed. If she remained silent, she was accused of being sulky.

'She spoke disparagingly of me to everyone, hoping thereby to diminish the esteem and affection each had for me, so that she put insults upon me in the presence of the best society.' She longed for someone in whom she could confide her distress, someone who would comfort her and give her some moral support, but the one person to whom she could have poured out her sorrows without fear of being misunderstood, her half-sister the Ursuline nun, had just died. When others spoke to her own mother about the indignities she suffered she was reprimanded sharply for being so poor-spirited as to put up with it.

'You forget your rank!' she was told. 'You should not allow yourself to be spoken to like that. Nor should you allow your social inferiors to be placed above you at table and in the salon. That a de la Mothe should give precedence to such persons! Have you forgotten that your father is Seigneur of Montargis?'

Young Madame Guyon, so eager to please everyone, found she could please no one. Even her husband, who was very fond of her in his way, did little to defend her. He was almost completely under the influence of his mother and the maid in her confidence, who, being a good nurse, was the one who tended him when he was ill. And as it soon appeared, the man had his own troubles, one of which came to light four months after the marriage.

He had developed gout.

Now gout, with the limited medical remedies available in the seventeenth century, could be a very painful disease, and in its way rather humiliating into the bargain. The unfortunate Monsieur Guyon took to his bed with it for weeks on end, during which time his young wife waited on him assiduously. For this she got into trouble with her mother. 'You are very foolish to spend so much time with him,' she was told. 'You are laying up trouble for yourself. What you are doing out of kindness he will take for granted, and you'll find yourself more and more tied to him, and get no thanks for it.' Then she complained that her daughter never came to see her own parents, and had obviously ceased to love them.

Her friends argued with her, too. 'A girl of your age to be wasting your talents, nursing a sick man! It's disgraceful.'

'As I have a husband, I ought to share his troubles as well as his wealth,' she answered mildly. There was a stoical streak in her nature, and she always managed to put on a brave face, however she was feeling. They might have thought her very happy with her husband if it had not been for the bad temper he sometimes showed towards her, even in the presence of others. She was determined to be dutiful, and on the occasions when he was evidently appreciative of her presence she was relieved, even satisfied. More often, however, he was thoroughly irritable, and what with the fault-finding of her mother-in-law, and the unrestrained insolence of the maid-servant, she became so cowed outwardly and so desperate inwardly that she was in despair.

One day, all her efforts to say the right thing having been snubbed or ridiculed or indignantly repudiated, she escaped to her room in such an overwrought state that she had to do something to give vent to her feelings. An extrovert would have screamed, lashed out, smashed some furniture, but it was typical of Madame Guyon that she turned in on herself. Grasping a sharp knife she thought wildly, 'I'll cut out my tongue! Then I shan't be able to speak, I shan't be able to say the wrong thing. I'll cut out my tongue!' Reason triumphed over the madness of the moment, and she did not do it, but the thought of becoming dumb persisted, and she prayed constantly that she might lose the power of speech. 'I even communicated and had Masses said that I might become dumb, such a child was I still.'

The effect of this daily hostility from which she could rarely escape, for she was required to spend all her time in her mother-in-law's apartment, was to crush her vivacity and drive her into silence. Before her marriage she had been an animated girl, with exceptional conversational powers and a ready wit. Now she was quiet, timid, with nothing to say for herself. She seemed almost stupid, and was certainly very unhappy. What made things worse for her was the remembrance of two or three of the young men who had sought her hand in marriage earlier. Young, charming, well-bred – how much happier she would have been had a marriage been arranged with one of them!

But it was the very misery of the circumstances in which she found herself that forced her back to God.

'These severe crosses made me return to you, O my God. I commenced to deplore the sins of my youth . . .

'I endeavoured to improve my life by penitence and a general confession . . .

'I gave up at once all romantic novels, although they were at one time my passion . . . though it had weakened some time before my marriage by the reading of the Gospel . . . I found it so beautiful, and I discovered in it a character of truth that disgusted me with all other books . . .

'I resumed prayer, and I endeavoured not to offend you, O my God. I felt that little by little your love was regaining the supremacy in my heart.'

Suffering was the pathway leading her to God.

*　　　*　　　*

'While you are brushing my hair I'll read aloud from this book,' said young Madame Guyon pleasantly to the maid who was standing, brush in hand, behind her. 'It's by St. Francis de Sales, and it's called *An Introduction to the Devout Life*. It is written for people in all walks of life, and it shows us how we can all be devout, whatever our circumstances. I've got to the part about mental prayer,' and picking up the book she started to read.

' "Perhaps you do not know how to pray mentally – that is, in your heart. Unfortunately, this is a thing that few in our age know how to do. For this reason, I give you a short and plain method" . . . Oh!' She gave an involuntary exclamation of pain as the maid brushing her hair pulled at it too hard, but quickly resumed her reading. She wanted her maid to profit by what she was reading, as well as herself, even though she really did not understand what was written.

' "Place yourself in His sacred presence. Reflect that God is not only in the place in which you are, but that He is, in a most particular manner, in your heart, and in the very

centre of your being . . . Heart of your heart. Spirit of your
spirit. . . !" '

In years to come she was to use almost exactly the same
words when she set out to teach people how to pray. They
were sown in the fertile soil of her mind, though the time had
not yet come when she would know their reality. These
writings of St. Francis de Sales attracted her because they
were intended, not only for monks and nuns and those whose
lives could be so ordered as to put devotional exercises first,
but for people in the workaday world where the claims of
home and employment left little time for such occupations.
What she read aroused desire for what St. Francis evidently
possessed, and in order to obtain it she decided it was
necessary to be a devout person. For this reason she had
resolved to pray twice every day, to go frequently to
confession, and to check carefully on her faults. How that
vanity of hers asserted and reasserted itself! She deliberately
had her hair dressed very simply, refrained from looking in
the mirror, and tried to think of something else when she
went out, but try as she would she could not help being
gratified by the glances cast in her direction which told
her that she looked very, very pretty. Even in church she
was conscious of her attractive appearance, thinking more
about it than about the prayers and the responses and all that
ought to have been absorbing her mind. She wrote these and
other failings honestly in a book, going over the records each
week to see how well she was succeeding in eliminating
them.

'Alas! This labour, though tiring, was of but little use,
because I trusted in my own efforts. I wished, indeed, to be
reformed, but my good desires were weak and languid.'

All the same, as time went on, there was some improvement, and on the practical side she developed a virtue
which had been set by her own mother, who had recently
died. She had been particularly charitable to the poor, so
now young Madame Guyon, following her example, went
personally to visit the poor in her own neighbourhood, to

give them material help when necessary, and to do something to alleviate their sufferings when ill. She had been an intelligent child with an interest in medicine and in the course of her sojourns in various convents besides picking up simple remedies for common complaints, had learned to compound some very effective ointments. She began putting some of her skills into practice, and her happiest hours were those employed in this way.

It was not only the useful employment that satisfied her. Such meritorious acts also provided her with practically the only reason whereby she could escape the confinement of the house and her mother-in-law's criticisms. There were, however, occasions when she was able to visit her father, to whom she was devoted, although she stood somewhat in awe of him. It was through him that she was brought in touch with three people who played a decisive part in her spiritual pilgrimage at that time.

The first was the Duchess of Charost, whose father, a prominent court official, had been imprisoned by the King, so his daughter, temporarily in exile, had found a refuge in the de la Mothe household. Young Madame Guyon, on meeting her, had been impressed by the tranquil expression on her face, and also by her readiness to talk about prayer and the inner life and God, the God of whom St. Francis de Sales wrote so intimately.

'I want to please God,' Madame Guyon confided simply to this new friend, and related some of her efforts to do so, to which she received a rather perplexing reply.

'Yes, I can see you live a bustling, active sort of life,' said the Duchess of Charost. 'That is good. But your prayer life seems very complicated. For me, prayer is much simpler.'

Much simpler, and much more satisfying, Madame Guyon reflected, and wondered why there was such a difference. She looked with admiration at the beatific appearance of the Duchess of Charost's face, and tried to emulate it, tried to cultivate an inner composure which would result in an equally peaceful expression.

Inner composure, in her case, took the form of resignation
at best, and a bottled-up rebellion at worst, neither of which
is conducive to genuine tranquillity.

There was something else about the Duchess of Charost's
demeanour, however, which quickened her interest and
curiosity. It was revealed when Monsieur de Chamesson, a
nephew of de la Mothe, returned from Cochin China, and
paid a visit to his uncle.

Monsieur de Chamesson had gone to Cochin China as a
missionary, some years before, and Madame Guyon, as a
child, had heard about him and his reputation for zeal and
piety. She had wept bitterly because, when he passed
through Montargis on his way to Cochin China, she had not
seen him. Now that he had returned she was thrilled to be
able to meet him, and was touched at his evident concern for
her, his ardent young cousin. But what impressed her more
than anything else was the way in which he and Madame de
Charost seemed to understand each other right from the
start. They had never met before, but within minutes of
being introduced they were talking with the unihibited
intimacy of those who have known each other for a very long
time, and are held together by a strong mutual attachment.
Madame Guyon had never seen anything quite like it before,
and she knew instinctively what was that invisible bond of
union.

They both loved God. Devout Roman Catholics as they
were, they were punctilious in their observance of various
acts of piety, attending Mass and confession, fasts and feasts,
but she knew that their inner satisfaction was rooted in
something deeper than outward rites could provide. They
tried to help her to understand, to teach her a simpler form of
prayer. When her cousin told her that there were times at
prayer when he thought of nothing, she was mystified. Silent
communion of man's spirit with God was beyond her. She
depended on her own mental activities, forcing herself to
meditate on some aspect of God's goodness or Christ's
sacrifice, uttering ejaculations and repeating prayers when

alone, bemoaning her shortcomings and castigating herself
for her sinful tendencies.

And she seemed to be getting nowhere. The efforts of her
two friends to enlighten her were apparently useless. As she
herself observed later, their prayers were more efficacious
than their words, and prepared the way for the divine moment
in which the revelation of what she was blindly seeking came
to her. The fullness of time had come for her at last.

Years later she wrote of it in the words, 'O, my divine
Love, the desire I had to please You, the tears I shed, my
great labours and the little fruit I reaped from it, moved Your
compassion. You gave me in a moment, through Your grace
and through Your goodness alone, what I had been unable to
give myself through all my efforts.'

The revelation came to her through the lips of a Franciscan monk who, after living in solitude for five years, had
recently come to the neighbourhood of Montargis with a
deep conviction that God had something important for him
to do there. The idea in his own mind was that it would lead
to the conversion of an influential man in the neighbourhood,
but as a matter of fact, nothing came of his efforts in that
direction. He little thought that the object of his mission
might be a girl in her teens. Such an idea never entered his
head. Had he not vowed that he would avoid women
altogether, unless God very clearly showed him otherwise?
And since he had received no special intimation that such a
thing might happen, on the day when he saw two women
approaching him, one a singularly beautiful, fashionably
dressed young woman, he wondered if he were dreaming.
And when she started talking to him, he felt thoroughly
embarrassed.

She introduced herself as the daughter of the Seigneur de la
Mothe, and said that her father had sent her to him to ask his
help. She was in spiritual difficulty. She could not pray as she
ought. She tried to concentrate, but her mind wandered. Her
vanity, her many faults, hindered her devotion. She tried to
live always in the presence of God, this was her aim, but she

could not achieve it. She went frequently to confession, to Mass, observed all the ordinances, repeated prayers, did everything she knew, but still she could not find what she wanted – the continual presence of God. What must she do?

The Franciscan monk was silent, so she went on talking, trying to explain her difficulty, feeling that she was not making herself intelligible to him. His quietness slightly disturbed her, and the fact that apart from the elderly woman she had brought as a chaperone, she was alone with a man. She was a very circumspect young woman, determined that on no account would she give occasion for gossip or scandal. Indeed, had it not been that her father, to whom she had confided her spiritual longings, had urged her to seek the Franciscan's help, she would not have come to him. And now that she had come, he seemed to have nothing to say.

Had she but realised it, he himself was at a loss to know what to do. Not having spoken to a woman for five years, he would gladly have escaped from what he felt was a potentially inflammable situation, but there was no way out. Her questionings demanded an answer, and gradually it dawned on him that behind that dangerously attractive exterior was a soul seeking desperately to find God. And God was so very, very near! All that was necessary was to tell her so.

'Madame, it is because you seek outside what you have within,' the monk said at last. 'Accustom yourself to seek God in your heart, and you will find Him there.' And then, without another word, he left her.

The effect on the girl of those two short sentences was amazing. 'They were for me like an arrow that pierced my heart through and through. I felt in that moment a very deep wound, delicious and full of love, a wound so sweet I desired never to be healed of it.' All her life she remembered that occasion as the time of her conversion. Yet there was nothing new in what had been said. Had not St. Francis de Sales said the same thing? And had she not read in the Gospel itself 'The kingdom of God is not here and there, but the kingdom of God is within you'? She had read it without understanding it, but in that moment of revelation she saw the true meaning at last. Her heart was the kingdom over which God had come to reign. He was there. He was with her. And the effect of His presence was not to shame or terrify her, but on the contrary, to fill her with an indescribable ecstasy of love.

'Your love, O my God, was not only for me like a delightful oil, but also like a devouring fire, which kindled in my heart such a flame that it seemed bound to devour everything in an instant. I was no longer recognisable either by myself, or by others.' All consciousness of the faults that had worried her was swallowed up in the bliss of being accepted without question and loved unconditionally.

'I don't know what you've done to me,' she said excitedly to the Franciscan when she went again to see him. 'My heart is quite changed. I love God. Oh, I love Him! I love Him!'

Happy Solitude - Unhappy Men

My heart is easy, and my burden light;
I smile, though sad, when Thou art in my sight;
The more my woes in secret I deplore
I taste Thy goodness and I love the more.

There, while a solemn stillness reigns around,
Faith, Love and Hope within my soul abound;
And while the world suppose me lost in care,
The joy of angels, unperceived, I share.

Thy creatures wrong Thee, O Thou Sovereign Good:
Thou art not loved, because not understood;
This grieves me most, that vain pursuits beguile
Ungrateful men, regardless of Thy smile.

Frail beauty and false honour are adored;
While Thee they scorn, and trifle with Thy Word;
Pass, unconcern'd, a Saviour's sorrows by;
And hunt their ruin with a zeal to die.

Jeanne de la Mothe Guyon

3

Vanity

'She's under a delusion,' announced Madame Guyon's confessor, and her mother-in-law agreed. So did her husband. Her manner was most peculiar, they considered. It was not that she had become argumentative or arrogant, or that she behaved badly. She was, in fact, even more docile than she had been before going to see that Franciscan monk who had had such a strange effect on her. There had been times in the past when she had flared up in temper, especially when one of the maids had been impertinent. But now that never happened, even under severe provocation. She was not so finicky about what she ate, either. Indeed, she seemed deliberately to choose the things she had formerly disliked.

What irritated them was a change that had taken place within her which was hard to define, except that she seemed to have some secret source of satisfaction which they could not fathom. She would close her eyes and sit quietly while others were talking, and when spoken to often did not hear until shaken or addressed again sharply. Then she would open her eyes and look round almost in bewilderment before speaking, as though she had been dragged back from another world.

She herself might well have described it in that way. There was a world unseen, into which she could retreat and experience peace and joy, a world in which the love of God so enfolded her, transported her, that speech was almost impossible.

'Nothing was now more easy for me than to pray. Hours were to me no more than moments, and I was unable not to do it.' But her prayer was quite different from what she had been taught and had recited so painstakingly. It was no longer an exhausting mental activity, but rather an awareness of God's presence that was overwhelming. 'Nothing of my prayer passed into my head, but it was a prayer of enjoyment and possession of the will, where the delight of God was so great, so pure, and so simple . . . Everything was absorbed in a delicious faith, where all distinctions were lost to give love room for loving without motives or reason for loving.'

For all her unusually analytical mind, when it came to defining love, young Madame Guyon could find no words beyond those 'loving without motives or reasons for loving'. It was not the holiness and the justice, not even the love and the mercy revealed through the sacrifice of His Son, that ravished her, but God Himself. 'I love Him because I love Him,' was her simple explanation, and in her wildest imagination she could conceive of no circumstance or condition in which she would cease to love Him. Hers was essentially the religion of the heart, and this is what her enemies and detractors could never understand. They found themselves up against something which went beyond intellectual apprehension, a living force stronger than the determination of the will.

In those early days, when she was at the mercy of her husband's household, her ardent desire for silent communion with God was viewed with disapproval. They thought she was going mad, and decided to put a curb on this incessant praying. If she was absent for half an hour, and was found to be praying, she was called peremptorily away, and made to sit with her mother-in-law, or by the bedside of her husband when he was ill. The effort to concentrate on things around her, to make appropriate responses in idle conversation, was such a strain that there were times when she was incapable of acting normally. To make matters worse, there was the increasing insolence of the particular maid whose position in the Guyon household was so firmly entrenched. On one occasion the woman created such a scene, asserting that she was being badly treated by her young mistress, that Monsieur Guyon threw his crutch at his wife, and insisted that she should apologise. The principle of obedience to authority was so deeply ingrained in her that she obeyed without a moment's hesitation, although she knew she had done no wrong. She went even further. She gave the maid a present. The only effect this gentleness had on the woman was to elicit the remark, 'There you are. I knew I was in the right!' and the insolence continued.

Worst of all, perhaps, was the attitude of her eldest child towards her. The little boy was spoiled by his grandmother, and when Madame Guyon tried to correct his faults, he knew where to go for support.

'Grandma says you used to tell far worse lies that I do!' he told her defiantly when she had found him out in a falsehood. She did not deny it – lying had been one of her besetting sins, as she acknowledged.

'It's because I know how wrong it was of me to tell those lies that I want to stop you doing the same thing,' she replied, and she was grieved to see the expression of defiance on the little face. He referred to her contemptuously as 'she' sometimes when he spoke of her, she knew, and was not reprimanded for it. The attitude of her own child towards her was the hardest of all to bear, but she accepted even this as a cross that she must carry for the sake of her love for God.

Her crosses. All the afflictions and reverses of this mortal life were the crosses she was called upon to bear, and the heavier the cross, the deeper was the inner consolation, the consolation of fellowship with Christ. Had not His been a life of suffering, crowned with the crucifixion?

'. . . You taught me so well a Jesus Christ crucified, that I madly loved the cross, and all that did not bear the character of cross and suffering failed to please me.'

This love of suffering drove her to strange extremes. She scourged herself, wore girdles of hair with iron nails, lay on nettles and brambles and thorns. She put stones in her shoes, so that even walking was painful. Whether these self-inflicted penances achieved anything beyond adding to her already overwrought condition is open to doubt, but her stern handling of her natural appetites soon had a very salutary result. By abstaining from the things that she most enjoyed, and eating what was most distasteful, she completely overcame her fastidiousness, and in less than a year she could eat whatever was put before her with imperturbability.

In addition to controlling her appetite, she entered into situations which she would formerly have found intolerably revolting. Pus-filled wounds and bleeding sores would have horrified her, but now, when injured or sick people were brought into the house she personally attended to the dressings, and used ointments she had made. Her activities along this line, and in visiting and helping the poor, were evidently tolerated, even approved, by her mother-in-law, for while so employed she could obviously not be indulging in that secret passion for silent prayer. What the older woman probably did not realise was that her young daughter-in-law was gaining a reputation in the town for piety and good works. It was a reputation which was to stand her in good stead when she became the object of slander in later years.

Even at that time, however, she was becoming a controversial figure in her home town of Montargis. The treatment she received at the hands of her mother-in-law, and the patient way in which she accepted it did not pass unnoticed, and there were some who said she was a saint. On the other hand, her own confessor asserted that she had gone astray, and the monks of his order even referred to her openly as being completely deceived.

As for Madame Guyon herself, she did not know what to think. Something was happening within her which she could not understand. For instance, she had become so acutely aware of her own shortcomings that she went to church one day in order to obtain the remission of the temporal punishment due to her sins. The guilt had been dealt with, she knew, for she had confessed each one and been absolved, but the debt of temporal punishment remained, and the way to get rid of it was to obtain indulgences. She had been taught that a sort of spiritual treasury had been formed by the surplus merits of Christ, and the Virgin Mary, and all the saints, and from that treasury a sinner like herself, unable to do sufficient penance to expiate all her sin, could draw. This principle of vicarious satisfaction was one with which she had been familiar from childhood, and she accepted it without question, as she accepted all the dogmas of the church to which she belonged. But when she entered the church building that day, intent on obtaining the necessary indulgences from the priest, whatever the penance imposed required, she was so overcome by the sense of God's love, she could not do it. She wanted to take her own punishment at His hands, whatever it might be, as a child accepts its father's strokes, knowing they are merited. As the prophet Micah said, 'I will bear the indignation of the Lord, because I have sinned against Him, until He plead my cause, and execute judgment for me.' Indulgences were all very well for those souls who did not know the value of suffering, nor desire that divine justice should be satisfied; who were more afraid of the penalty that follows wrong-doing than displeasing a holy God. But as far as she was concerned, she preferred to suffer when she had done wrong.

So she obtained no indulgences that day and went home. However, not being quite sure that her attitude was right, not having heard or read of anyone else holding her views, she went along to church another day with the same object in view, but again she found she could not ask for indulgences, and gave up the idea. She wrote to the Franciscan monk, telling him what she thought about indulgences, and expressed herself with such freedom and clarity that he incorporated her words in his sermon the following day.

The matter of indulgences was not the only one which, as far as she was concerned, she felt she could dispense with.

There was the habit of praying to the Virgin Mary or St. Mary Magdalene, or one of the saints, asking for their intercession on her behalf. Somehow, she now found herself instinctively by-passing them, so to speak, and going direct to God Himself. This perplexed her. She had the utmost veneration for the saints, and for the Virgin, and all her life had been taught to invoke their aid. Why did it no longer seem necessary to do so? She eventually came to a conclusion that satisfied her. Jesus Christ was the bridegroom of her soul, and with that relationship, what need had she for the kindly intermediacy of others? It was quite logical to need their services no longer, however deeply they were to be admired and commemorated, since a bridegroom would care for the needs of his bride without being prompted by others. Having thought the matter through on these lines, she had no further compunction about not praying to the saints.

There was one thing that really worried her, however, and this was her vanity. She was not particularly aware of it in Montargis, but when she accompanied her husband to Paris for a time it flared up again, although it was apparent to no one but herself. Indeed, the priests whom she met when she went to confession were astonished that one so young and attractive should have so little of a serious character to confess, and they told her so.

'They said to me that I could not sufficiently thank God for the graces He had bestowed on me; that if I knew them I would be astonished. Some declared they did not know a woman whom God kept so close and in so great a purity of conscience.

'What made it such was that continual care you had over me, O my God, making me experience your intimate presence, as you have promised us in your Gospel, "If any one does My will, We will come unto him and make our dwelling in Him."' This she wrote in her autobiography years later, and with hindsight added the significant words, 'But alas! My dear Love, when You ceased Yourself to watch, how weak I was, and how my enemies prevailed over me. Let others attribute their victories to their own faithfulness; for me, I will only attribute them to Your paternal care. I have proved my weakness too well, and had such a fatal experience of what I should be without You, to presume anything was due to my own care.'

Her weakness, to the average person, would have seemed innocent enough. The gaiety of Paris was infectious, and it was natural that a young, beautiful woman should be affected by it. As far as she was concerned, she behaved with restraint and decorum outwardly, but inwardly found herself yielding again to that vanity of hers, with its gratification at being seen and admired, its willingness to be loved without loving in return. When she took a turn on the promenade it was as much to be looked at as for the exercise. '. . . I knew the violent passion certain persons had for me, and I allowed them to show it,' she wrote, although she was careful never to be alone with them. 'I also committed faults in leaving my neck a little uncovered, although it was not nearly so much so as others had it. I wept because I saw I was growing slack, and it was a very great torment for me.'

Since the memorable conversation with the Franciscan monk she had never been without the powerful attraction of God's love in her heart. Now that seemed weaker, and the instincts of nature were reasserting themselves. It was a time, as with King Hezekiah, when it is recorded that 'the Lord left him, that he might know what was in his heart'. The diminishing sense of God's presence was giving young Madame Guyon a practical revelation of what she would be like if left to herself, and it was very alarming. When some of her admirers arranged a special party for her at Saint Cloud, where Monsieur, the King's brother, had his residence, she accepted their invitation although very uneasy about doing so. It was a magnificent affair, with entertainments and a banquet, everything done on a lavish scale, and the guests all behaved admirably, doing and saying nothing that could give offence to the young woman who was noted for her piety. All the same, she was thoroughly miserable. She was wise enough to realise where this sort of thing could lead her, for she was not ignorant of the moral laxity of Paris at that time. Knowing that her own vanity and weakness had led her into this fashionable, extravagant set, she felt she had deeply offended God. All sense of His presence left her, and it was three months before her peace of heart was restored.

While in Paris she had a strange experience which left an indelible mark on her memory. She had decided to go to Notre Dame on foot rather than in a carriage, and accompanied by a lackey, was crossing one of the bridges when a very poorly-dressed man approached her, whom she thought to be a beggar. She drew a coin from her pocket and offered it to him, but he politely refused it, and explained that he was not asking for money. Then he started to speak about God, very reverently but very ardently. Madame Guyon listened with surprise, her heart responding to all that he said, and when he went on to enlarge on the Holy Trinity it was as though she were hearing it for the first time. He spoke of the Mass, and of the care that should be taken by any who take part in it. Again she found herself agreeing with all that he said.

At last he spoke more personally. She had never met him before, and as her face was veiled he could not have known who she was, yet what he said revealed an intimate knowledge of her.

'I know, Madame, that you love God, that you are very charitable and give many alms to the poor,' he said, and went on to enumerate other virtues which had been developed in her. But then he went on, 'Yet you are very much astray. God desires something else from you.' He paused for a moment, then said clearly, 'You love your beauty.'

She walked silently on beside him, listening attentively to what he said, acquiescing with what he said about other faults of which she was aware, although it was the reference to her pride of appearance that impressed her most deeply. In later years she recalled his words about not merely being content to avoid the pains of hell, but arriving at such a state

of perfection in this life that she would even avoid the pains of
purgatory.[1] It was not so much fear of the pains of either hell
or purgatory that worried her, however, but fear of grieving
God. At that time in Paris, and later in Touraine where she
also accompanied her husband, the consciousness of her
attractive self was at once her source of natural pride and
spiritual shame. And the two were in violent conflict.

'On this journey my vanity triumphed . . . I received many
visits and much applause. My God, how clearly I see the folly
of men, who let themselves be caught by a vain beauty! I
hated passion,' she added. She admitted this more than once,
and her husband easily detected it, petulantly telling her that
since she loved God she had ceased from loving him. But
although with him she had to fulfil her conjugal duty, she was
under no such obligation to anyone else, and could enjoy
seeing desire light up in amorous males who were stirred by
her feminine charms. 'I hated passion . . . but I could not hate
that in me which called it to life.' That in her which aroused a
man's desire fed her pride, her self-love. She was ashamed of
it, but try as she would she could not overcome it.

This particular form of vanity lay dormant when there was
nothing, or no one, to stimulate it. She longed to go into a
convent, where she would be completely shielded from all
temptations to indulge that peacock-like propensity to
display her charms. She talked it over with Mother Granger,
Prioress of a Benedictine convent, who was the one person in
whom she could confide, and to whom she went whenever
she had the opportunity. As two of her sisters-in-law were
nuns in the convent, it was easier for her to do so than would
otherwise have been the case, although when her confessor
and her mother-in-law realised the closeness of the friendship that had developed, they did everything in their power

[1] According to Roman Catholic theology eternal punishment and the guilt of
mortal sin is absolved by the sacrament of penance, but if appropriate
satisfaction has not been made for sins committed and absolved in life,
satisfaction must be made after death, in purgatory, where the duration of
time is limited, not in hell, where it is eternal.

to put an end to it. She discovered that Mother Granger too had had her problems with the Guyon family.

'I've been trying to please them for twenty years,' she said with a wry smile when Madame Guyon told of her vain attempts to win her mother-in-law's approval. 'Trying for twenty years without succeeding! So how can you expect to succeed in less than half that time!' Then she went on to give what advice she could. 'Give yourself up to God. Offer yourself to Him. Then, if He gives you this cross, carry it for love of Him,' was the gist of what she said. But in the case of the fight against natural vanity, all she could do was to give advice that was practical. Looking at the fashionably-dressed, beautiful woman in her full billowing skirts, her tight bodice and low-necked blouse, she remarked:

'I know your husband wishes you to be well-dressed, so you must follow the fashion – but is it necessary to expose so much of your neck and bosom? Wear a kerchief round your neck to cover it up. That will be much more modest and will attract less attention.' It was a simple enough thing to do, and did not deal with the basic problem, but at any rate it was a step in the right direction. Madame Guyon always wore a kerchief over a low-necked garment after that. Nor was it the only matter in which she followed the advice given by her mentor. Mother Granger was an unusually spiritually-minded woman for her day, completely loyal to the Roman Catholic church to which she had belonged all her life, with a suitable veneration for the saints who had worn hair shirts next to their skin, and in other ways demonstrated their devotion by inflicting pain upon themselves. All the same, her feet were on the ground. When she learned of the physical sufferings to which her young friend subjected herself, she wisely advised her to desist from doing anything that was harmful to her health. Her advice on all matters was followed implicitly, both the simple practical suggestions regarding the outer life, as well as the deeper inner lessons to be learned in trusting oneself totally to the will of God, come what may.

At that period of her life, the Benedictine Prioress was the closest friend Madame Guyon had, the one who more than any other encouraged her in the pilgrimage of her soul. But even the godly Prioress could not point the way to the deliverance from vanity that she longed for.

'I lamented my weakness. I made verses to express my trouble, but they served only to augment it. I prayed You, O my God, to take away this beauty, which had been so disastrous to me. I desired to lose it, or cease to love it.'

She felt as though she were being dragged in opposite directions. 'I was as if torn asunder, for on the outside my vanity dragged me, and within, the divine love. . . . As soon as I had the opportunity of exhibiting my vanity, I did it. And as soon as I had done it, I returned to you.' She could not lose her vanity, nor could she cease to love it. In her desperation she almost challenged God, 'Are You not strong enough to stop this?'

It was a cry from the heart, and the answer came quite soon, but in a form from which she would have shrunk if she had been told of it beforehand.

On arrival home from Touraine she was greeted with the news that her youngest child, a little girl, was down with smallpox. Intuitively Madame Guyon knew that she would be stricken with it, too. And so it happened. Her mother-in-law's stubbornness in refusing her the medical aid she needed nearly cost her life, but the providential appearance of a doctor who insisted on treating her saved it – but nothing could save her beauty. When the weeks of illness were drawing to a close and she was sufficiently restored to wonder what she looked like, the mirror revealed that her prayer 'take away this beauty' had been granted. The eyes that gazed back at her were the same, but the lids were inflamed and swollen. The contours of the cheekbones, the straight nose, the well-shaped mouth and chin had not changed, but the skin that covered them was like discoloured parchment, lifeless and pitted with pockmarks. Gone for ever was the fair, transparent complexion with its soft colourings,

the faint blue shadings under the eyes, the rosy lips, the pink
cheeks, the white forehead. Never again would men's eyes
rest admiringly on her face – and never again would envious
women whisper together that she was very skilful in applying
make-up.

And never again would that peacock-like vanity that had
drawn her attention away from God to herself have the
power to do so.

It is impossible to delve the depths of that twenty-two-
year-old girl's emotions as she faced the end of an era in her
life. She would not have been human if she had not regarded
that strangely unfamiliar-looking face with dismay, or have
wondered what would be the reaction of others when they
saw her. But beyond all that was the determined acceptance
of what had happened as being the means of her deliverance.
She would even further the work of destruction! She did
nothing to alleviate the condition of her skin. She did not
even try to protect it from further depredations. She refused
to apply the herbal remedies that others had found effective,
and went out of doors in all weathers even in bitingly cold
winds which aggravated the pockmarks and inflamed them.

> 'To my God a heart of flame . . .
> To myself a heart of steel.'

'To myself a heart of steel.' It summed up her attitude, and
the heart of steel refused to be moved by the piteous cries of
despoiled nature. Madame Guyon's beauty, the cause of her
vanity, had gone, and she would not bemoan it. Indeed, she
could not bemoan it, for the contentment within her soul was
deeper than it had ever been before. As she herself expressed
it, 'The devastation without was counterbalanced by the
peace within.'

Even the death of her second child, a little boy whom she
loved dearly, could not disturb it, for although the blow
overwhelmed her in one way, she found herself saying, as Job
had said thousands of years before, 'The Lord gave. The
Lord has taken away. Blessed be the name of the Lord.' And

in some mystical way which she did not fully understand, came the assurance that a spiritual son would be given her in his place.

About eight months later she first met Francis La Combe, with whom her life was to be so strangely, even fatally, entwined.

A Benedictine nun, who is a most holy woman, in their refectory saw our Lord on the cross and the Holy Virgin near Him, and they appeared in great pain. They made movements which seemed to mark their sufferings and the desire they had to find someone who would be willing to share them. She ran to inform the Prioress. She said she was busy and could not go. In fact, she was amusing herself with flowers and trees. Not finding anyone who was willing to go, in great trouble she met and told me. I at once ran there, and our Lord appeared very pleased. He received and embraced me as if to associate me in His sufferings. . . .

Jeanne de la Mothe Guyon, while still in Montargis

4

Dark Night Ended

Francis La Combe was born in Thonon in Savoy, on the banks of Lake Geneva. He was a religious little boy, and early in life joined the Order of the Barnabites, with whom his natural talents were developed by a good education. By the year 1671 he was a tall, well-set man in his early twenties, and his first meeting with Madame Guyon was as the result of a letter he carried to her from her half-brother, Father de la Mothe.

Madame Guyon stood in some awe of Father de la Mothe, and not without reason. In the first place, his relationship as an elder brother put him in a position demanding her respect. Secondly, he was an ordained priest of the Church, and therefore to be venerated by all good Catholics. Thirdly, as later events were to prove, he was a clever and unscrupulous man whom it was wiser not to cross. So when she received a letter from him, urging her to receive the bearer of it and treat him as one of his most intimate friends, she had no option but to comply, although at the time she was in no mood to make fresh acquaintances.

Francis La Combe was therefore invited to the Guyon home, and there he met a pockmarked woman, some years his senior, simply dressed, graceful, courteous, and with whom he felt unusually free to talk about spiritual matters. This was surprising since she was a woman in the everyday world, married and with children, and not even a nun from the cloisters. But he had heard that two or three other Barnabites had been influenced by her, to the vast improvement of their spiritual lives, and had wondered why. Now, on meeting her, he began to understand.

'I have never seen a woman like this before,' he thought.

51

She seemed to be the possessor of an inner life which he could not define, and even as he talked to her husband, he was conscious of her. Yet not so much of her, as of an awareness of the presence of God. There was a quality of tranquillity in her silence which made him long to know its source. He therefore decided to call on the Guyons again, in the hope of having an opportunity to talk to her. That opportunity came quite inadvertently, for while he was chatting with her husband he suddenly felt faint and, excusing himself, went out into the garden to recover.

'Go and see if he's all right,' said Monsieur Guyon, crippled with gout, to his wife, and obediently she went. This was the very opportunity La Combe had desired. There was only a short time to talk, but it was sufficient for him to enquire and for her to explain the reality of what she called 'the inward way'.

God comes to dwell in the heart. He makes it His kingdom, bringing everything under His control. Jesus Christ had said, 'If a man loves me, he will keep my words and my Father will love him, and we will come unto him and make our abode with him.' It is there that He communes with us, speaks to us, reveals Himself. It is there, too, that the ego, the SELF, has to be dethroned, put to death.

She had little enough time for explanation, but little time is enough for divine revelation. Just as the Franciscan monk's two sentences to her had answered in a flash her questionings of years, so that conversation now answered La Combe's. He went away, as he said afterwards, changed into another man. God, the source of all spiritual power, was dwelling within him, and he returned to his native Savoy outwardly the same, but inwardly with a peace he had never known before. As for Madame Guyon,

'I preserved a root of esteem for him, for it appeared to me he would be God's. But I was very far from foreseeing that I should ever go to the place where he would be.'

They were not to meet again for nine years.

For him, those years were outwardly uneventful. A sincere

and earnest man who had early taken the vows of celibacy, he devoted himself to the religious life, developing into an unusually eloquent preacher, with administrative ability into the bargain.

He knew what was going on in the ecclesiastical world – the rise of the forthright Bossuet to a place of eminence at court, with his appointment as tutor to the Dauphin; of the problems connected with the status of the King's illegitimate children; of the tensions beginning to rise between the King and the Pope as to how far the divine right of each entitled them to supremacy in matters of earthly policy; and of the suspicion with which the King was viewing the increasing power of the Protestant nations, and, as a result, his changing attitude towards the Huguenots in his own realm. La Combe himself was by no means favourable to the Protestant faith, and viewed with disapproval its established position in Geneva. The movement towards reformation within Roman Catholicism itself was a different matter, in his view, and the emergence of Port Royalists, the Jansenites, the Quietists, commanded his respect if none of them claimed his allegiance. His deepest conscious desire was to please God, and he believed the way to do that was within the Order of the Barnabites, by adhering to their basic principles and practices, and cultivating his own inner life along the lines indicated in that illuminating interview with Madame Guyon.

For Madame Guyon herself, life was very different, and lived in a much less congenial atmosphere than that of a well-run monastery. The situation at home remained the same, with constant criticism and suspicious surveillance. Her happiest periods were when she was sufficiently ill to be left to herself. Then she could enter and enjoy the peace of that unseen world where, without interruption, she could listen to and speak to God. Even when, in July 1672, she suffered the double bereavement of her father and her little daughter, the inner peace balanced the natural grief, deeply as she felt it.

It was at this time that Mother Granger wrote to her, giving some instructions which she was expected to obey. She was to fast on St. Magdalene's Day, go to church wearing her signet ring, and on returning home go to her private closet, and there read a contract that had been prepared for her. This Madame Guyon did, and kneeling before an image of the child Jesus in the arms of his mother, she read the contract. It was very simple. It ran: 'I . . . promise to take for my spouse our Lord, the Child, and to give myself to Him for spouse, though unworthy.'

Kneeling there in the silence of her room with the contract before her, she made the deliberate, considered consecration of her life, her soul, her will, all that she was in herself, to Christ.

In one way it merely involved the ratification of the decision she had already made. Ever since the never-to-be-forgotten experience of realising the indwelling of God within her, her only ambition had been to belong unreservedly to Him. By putting her signature to that contract she was committing herself as irrevocably to Christ as the husband of her soul as when she signed the marriage contract which made Monsieur Guyon the husband of her body. And with her deep awareness of suffering as being the symbol of the Man, Christ Jesus, she prayed, not for blessing, not for fruitfulness, far less for spiritual gifts – and as for earthly prosperity, such a desire seems not to have entered her head. No, what she prayed for was 'crosses, scorn, confusion, disgrace and ignominy', and the grace to bear them all with the meekness of Christ.

She sealed the contract with her ring, on July 22nd, 1672.

It was to her a sacred festival, alone there in her room. 'O Divine Spouse, it seems to me that you then made of me your living temple, and that you yourself consecrated it as churches are consecrated.' With her colourful imagination she applied the signs used in the consecration of churches to herself. 'As churches are marked with the sign of the cross, you marked me also with the same sign. . . . And as at the consecration of churches there are candles, which are lighted in the place for the crosses, and the candle represents faith and charity, so I have ground to believe that you have not permitted those virtues to abandon me since that time. But as the characteristic of the candle is to gradually consume itself by its own fire, and to destroy itself by the light and heat which make it live, so it seemed to me that it was necessary for my heart to be perfectly destroyed by this fire of love.'

This experience, while deepening her inner sense of security, also made her much more sensitive. There were times when the awareness of God's presence was withdrawn, and she usually found that the reason for it was self-pity, or a subconscious rebellion against circumstances, or even a secret complacency in her own faithfulness. Self dies hard. It has so many subtle forms of apparent virtue that when one appears to have been dealt with, another rears its head. She hated them all as they were revealed to her in their true light. The Spirit of God was working deeper and deeper within her, and with the decreasing satisfaction in her own virtues there came, unknown to herself, an increasing evidence of His presence in her. Others noticed it. 'I have seen your niece,' said a worldly-minded man to an aunt of her husband's, and added, 'One can see she never loses the presence of God.' She was very surprised when this remark was reported to her, not only that she should have been the subject of it, but also because, 'I did not think he understood what it was to have God present in this way.' She was surprised, too, when the wife of the governor of the town, whom she met from time to time socially, came to her one day and said, 'God drew me so powerfully yesterday that I cannot hold out against Him. I've come to tell you so.'

They had been together when another woman had entered into conversation and spoken in a very learned way about spiritual things, having studied the Fathers and arrived at certain conclusions about God which she aired authoritatively. She had spoken with finality, evidently feeling there was nothing more to be said. She had spoken with such assurance that Madame Guyon was repelled, but had remained quiet, feeling grieved at hearing God discussed in such a way. But evidently what the woman had said had impressed the governor's wife? In some way, God Himself had drawn her through that conversation. So she assumed, but she was wrong.

'Oh, it wasn't what *she* said,' explained the governor's wife quickly. 'It wasn't her talking – it was your silence. It was your silence that spoke to me, in the depths of my heart. I could not enjoy what she was saying to me at all.'

Her silence. There had been a greater eloquence in it than in the flood of words gushing from the woman who seemed to know everything, and she knew whose voice had reached the heart of her friend. It was the voice of her divine Bridegroom. 'I stand at the door and knock. If any man hear my voice and open the door, I will come in. . . .' All that was needed was to explain to her that God had come to make His kingdom within her, and all she had to do was to let Him in. The transformation in the life and character of the governor's wife was lasting after that – as for Madame Guyon, she began to realise how her own death to self was resulting in life to others.

*   *   *

Monsieur Guyon was often ill, and he began to be very worried as to what would happen to all his great wealth when he died. 'As he had no children but my eldest son, who was often at the gates of death, he wished extremely to have heirs.' He therefore made a special journey to obtain the intercession of St. Edme on his behalf, and 'he was heard, and God gave me another son'.

Those months were the happiest she had yet experienced. She knew such uninterrupted peace and joy of heart that it was like entering a new life. Even the suffering of the difficult confinement was more than compensated for by the fact that she was so ill she had to be kept quiet and undisturbed, free from all distractions. The solitude was a relief. 'I endeavoured to compensate myself for the little leisure I had at other seasons for praying, and remaining alone with God.' As for the pain and the weakness, was this not just what she had prayed for? Her ardent soul would not have been fully satisfied without it.

But this halcyon period was not to last. It proved to be the preparation for the darkest years of her life, years in which all the delicious feelings that had supported her inwardly subsided, dissolved, vanished altogether, leaving her bewildered like a child in the dark, who has suddenly been forsaken.

It started with the death of the woman who had been to her a spiritual mother – Mother Granger, the Prioress. When she heard of it, she was overwhelmed. The one person who really understood her, the one person to whom she knew she could safely reveal all that was in her mind, had gone. 'I declare that this blow was the most severely felt of any I yet had.' What made the blow the more acute was that it was totally unexpected, and that she had had no intimation of her friend's condition. This distressed her. That invisible bond between them had been so strong that on several occasions they had been aware of each other's thoughts and feelings, even though separated by long distances, and without opportunity for verbal communication. When her own father was taken ill she had known of it intuitively before the news reached her. Why then had she been left without that mystical enlightenment that Mother Granger, who was spiritually closer to her than anyone else, was dying? Had she but known, she might have had the opportunity to go and see her, to receive some last loving message or exhortation that would support her in her loss and give her direction for the future. But as it was, 'I felt myself utterly deserted, inwardly and outwardly. I thought only of the loss I sustained in a person who would have conducted me on a road where I no longer found track nor path.'

That trackless way was already spreading out before her,

for she realised that her reaction to the death of Mother Granger was quite different to that when her father and her little daughter had died within days of each other. Her grief then had been balanced by an inexplicable inward peace. Now there was no such comfort. There was only a deadness. It was as though God had withdrawn himself. And as time went on, she was dismayed to find how different she herself was from what she had been. She seemed to be disinclined for all she had formerly longed for. That fervent love for God was there no more. She felt there must be something terribly wrong with her, and in order to rectify this state of affairs she reverted to some of her former practices. 'I used all sorts of penances, prayers, pilgrimages, vows.' But they were useless. The heavens seemed like brass. She had long since ceased praying to the saints, but now she would have besought the Virgin Mary to intercede on her behalf if she could have believed she would hear her.

'The Holy Virgin, for whom I had had a very great and tender devotion from my youth, appeared to me inaccessible. I did not know whom to turn to for help, either in heaven or earth. If I tried to find God in my heart, to find Him who once had possessed it so powerfully, not only did I find nothing there, but I was even repelled with violence.' Her own heart condemned her. She was the worst of sinners.

The time was to come when she would write, '. . . I saw there was no salvation for me in myself . . . I was, O divine Jesus, that lost sheep of the house of Israel that You were come to save. You were truly the Saviour of her who could find no salvation out of You,' and then add recklessly, 'O men, strong and holy, find salvation as much as you please in what you have done, that is holy and glorious for God; as for me, I make my boast only in my weaknesses, since they have earned for me such a Saviour!'

But that time had not come yet, and years were to pass before she could assert it with such freedom. Now she was only conscious of feeling devoid of God's presence, of being without those ecstatic feelings that had buoyed her up, and of being oppressed by the sense of her own intrinsic sinfulness, which had soiled even the good she had tried to do.

Gone were the periods of ecstatic joy when it seemed she was transported to realms far beyond human telling. Gone was the ineffable sense of God's presence, stirring her to love and adoration, quickening her desire to please Him, sacrifice for Him, suffer for Him. The spiritual darkness into which she found herself slipping left her without any urge either to worship God or befriend man. She was only oppressed by the sense of her own sinfulness. Yet the sinfulness of which she was aware was not that against which she had battled earlier. The faults of vanity, the propensity for lying, the secrets of lusts – these had been dealt with through genuine confession and sincere repentance. What oppressed her now was the sense of her inbuilt sinfulness which had soiled even the good she had tried to do.

Even her apparently righteous acts now appeared filthy. 'All appeared to me full of defects; my charities, my alms, my prayers, my penances, all rose up against me as objects of condemnation. My conscience was a witness I could not appease, and yet strangely, it was not the sin of my youth that caused my pain. It was not they that bore witness against me; it was a universal witness that in all the good I had done there were sentiments of evil.' The inexplicable thing was that she could not put her finger on any specific sins or faults. 'As a consequence I did not find any remedy for my ills in confession.' What a relief it would have been to have enumerated her iniquities and shortcomings in the confessional box! Any penances imposed would have been welcomed, however harsh. But she knew that if she tried to explain her guilt to her confessor he would have commended her on her humility. He would not have understood.

No one, it seemed, could understand her state. There was no one to tell her that others had passed that way, experiencing what some of the mystics referred to as 'the dark night of the soul'. Even the Franciscan monk, who had first spoken to her of God making His kingdom in her heart, gave her no help now. The flood of words that poured from her pen was as bewildering to him as her own state was to her, and she did not express herself clearly. Eventually he told her to stop writing to him – he had had enough of it. Likewise the Jesuit Father, formerly very sympathetic towards her. Another cleric, a Jansenist, offended that she did not respond to his special line of teaching, openly preached about her, saying that she who had once been an example to all the town through her good works, was now a scandal. Certainly, the urge to help the poor had left her, and if she forced herself to go and see them, she had nothing to say. She seemed powerless to do anything for anybody. Before the birth of her fifth child, a girl, she gave way to such paroxysms of sobbing when alone that she marvelled there was not a miscarriage. It was as though she was deranged at times. If she had lived in the twentieth century she would probably have been sent to a psychiatric hospital. As it was, she felt forsaken by God and man, for everybody seemed to disapprove of her, and when by chance anyone praised her, she blushed with shame – they did not know what a hypocrite she was! 'If I endeavoured to exhibit an outward righteousness by the practice of some good, my heart secretly gave the lie to my action; I saw it was hypocrisy to appear what I was not.'

Although she remained in this state, on and off, for seven years, there were occasions when a certain practical ability was made evident that surprised everyone, herself more than all. One had to do with no less a person than Monsieur, the King's brother. One of the most notorious characters in French history, Monsieur was often in need of money, and had no scruples as to how he obtained it. It was not difficult, therefore, for someone to concoct a story, in his name, to the effect that Madame Guyon and her brother owed him two hundred thousand livres. Her husband angrily washing his hands of the whole affair, she had no one to whom to turn for help, and it was not until the very day when the case was to be decided that, after Mass, she felt strongly urged to go to see the judges herself. So to the judges she went.

'I was extremely surprised to find that I knew all the twists and turns of this business, without knowing how I had been able to learn it. The first judge was so surprised to see a thing so different from what he thought, that he himself urged me to go and see the other judges.' The upshot of that affair was that, since the face of Monsieur had to be saved, judgment was given in his favour – but to the tune of one hundred and fifty livres, instead of two hundred thousand demanded.

It was one of the few occasions when Madame Guyon's husband expressed himself very pleased at what she had done. He had no cause for complaint, either, when at the instigation of his mother, he demanded that she should give account of the money entrusted to her for housekeeping. It was suggested that she gave so much to charity, she was almost certainly running into debt. Once again, she acquitted herself well.

'I did not write any of my alms, and my expense was found right without a franc more or less. I was amazed, and saw that my charities were given out of God's capital.' She learned through that experience what many of God's servants have learned down through the ages – that He is no man's debtor. 'Oh, if people only knew how charities, far from inconveniencing, bring plenty!' she wrote. 'What useless extravagance there is which might maintain the poor, and which God would repay. . . .'

Not long after that incident her husband was taken seriously ill, and eventually died, but not before his attitude towards her had changed completely. As she knelt beside his bed one day, and asked his forgiveness for any way in which she had displeased him, he was evidently deeply moved, and said, 'It is I who ask your pardon. I did not deserve you.'

From that time on, knowing he was dying, he showed he was glad to have her with him, and gave her advice as to what she should do after his death. He died on the eve of St. Magdalene's Day. It was a significant date for her.

Exactly four years had passed since she had signed the contract Mother Granger had given her, in which she

consecrated herself to Christ. Now she was free, and had it
not been for her children, she would have entered a convent
and become a nun. This is what she would have desired, but
as it was, instead of the peace of a convent, she found herself
plunged into business affairs for which she had little
preparation, and no experience. Her husband's affairs were
in rather a chaotic condition and it took her days to sort them
out. Then, among his securities, she found papers belonging
to other people. These had evidently been deposited with
him for safe keeping and must now be returned.

'I made an exact inventory for each person with my own
hand, and sent them to those to whom they belonged. This
would have been very difficult for me, O my God, without
Your help, because, owing to the long time my husband had
been ill, everything was in great disorder. This got me the
reputation of a clever woman,' she commented naively, 'as
well as another affair which happened.' And she went on to
relate it.

'A great number of persons, who were mutually litigating
for more than twenty years, applied to my husband to
reconcile them. Although it was not the business of a
gentleman, they entreated him because he had uprightness
and a good intellect; so, as there were among those persons
some he loved, he consented to it.

'There were twenty suits, one against the other, and there
were twenty-two people who were litigating in this way,
without any one being able to end their difference, owing to
new incidents that arose every day. My husband undertook
to engage advocates to examine their papers, but he died
without having done anything. After his death I sent to fetch
them to give back their papers, but they would not receive
them, and begged me to reconcile them and prevent their
ruin. It appeared to me alike ridiculous and impossible that I
should undertake so serious a business, and one so long in
dispute. Yet, supported by Your strength, O my God, I
followed the movement you gave me to consent. I shut myself
up for more than thirty days in my closet on this business,

without leaving it save for Mass and meals. These worthy people all blindly signed their compromise without seeing it. They were so pleased about it they could not help publishing it everywhere.'

Little wonder that young Madame Guyon, not yet thirty, was becoming a well-known personality in Montargis. Little wonder, too, that those who were her friends, some in influential positions, urged her, now that her husband was dead, to separate from her mother-in-law. The older woman's bad temper, and rudeness to her daughter-in-law, was well known.

'I answered them I had no ground's to complain of her, and that I counted on remaining with her if she would allow me. It was the view You from the first gave me, O my God, not to descend from the cross, as You yourself had not descended from it. For this reason I resolved not only not to leave my mother-in-law, but even not to get rid of the maid of whom I have spoken.'

And so, for the next three years, she remained in the house with her mother-in-law until at last, following a visit she made on business to a neighbouring town, things came to a head.

It so happened that in that particular town there lived some relatives of her mother-in-law, who had always treated her with warmth and courtesy, vying with each other to entertain her. Now, to her astonishment, their attitude had changed completely. So far from being cordial, they were quite antagonistic, and then it was that she heard that her mother-in-law had complained to them about her, telling them how unkind she was to her, and how unhappy she made her.

Poor Madame Guyon! She had always thought of herself as being the one who was ill-used, and undoubtedly she was, but it had never occurred to her that her mother-in-law might be feeling the same. It is given to few, if any of us, to know the effect we have on other people, 'to see ourselves as others see us.' It had never crossed her mind that to an outspoken woman like her mother-in-law her docility might have been taken for contempt, her well-meant efforts to please for derision, and that the very suppression of her natural instincts almost certainly created an indefinable atmosphere of pent-up forces which might erupt violently at any time. On her own showing she behaved very strangely at times, with eyes wide open looking around in church when everyone else was reverently bowed, retreating silently into herself in company, seeking spiritual help from well-known ecclesiastics then withdrawing when they offered it. As she herself admitted many years later, she may have unwittingly irritated her mother-in-law beyond what a quick-tempered woman could endure. 'She had a very good heart, but her temper was perhaps there in spite of her . . . She had virtue and intelligence, and putting aside certain failings, which people who do not use prayer keep ignorant of, she had good qualities.'

However, she saw nothing else but her own pitiable situation at the time, and when she got home, determined to have the matter out.

'People are saying I make you unhappy,' she said. 'I am sorry. I have tried to please you, I really have. You know I don't like this house. I've only stayed because I thought you wanted me to. But I've no intention of living with you if it only gives you trouble. I'll leave, and go somewhere else rather than make things difficult for you.'

'Do what you like,' said her mother-in-law coldly. 'I haven't spoken of it to anyone, but I've made up my mind to keep house separately now.'

So that was that. 'This was fairly giving me my dismissal.' The relief of feeling free at last to move away was tempered by the consciousness that it was the dead of winter, and she had nowhere to go. 'I did not know what to do. I saw myself obliged to turn out in the depth of winter with the children and their nurse, without knowing what would become of us.' But she was a very wealthy woman, and although there was no suitable house in the town for her then, the Benedictines provided her with an apartment until she found a place in the country – and then the tide began to turn.

*   *   *

It was during this long unhappy period of spiritual darkness that one of her footmen came to tell her that he wanted to become a Barnabite. She wrote to her brother, Father de la Mothe, about it, and he told her she should get in touch with Father La Combe, who was now Superior of the Barnabites in Thonon.

Father La Combe! That young Barnabite who had shown such a desire for the same personal relationship with God as she had been enjoying at the time when they met, years ago! So now he had advanced so far in his Order as to be a Superior, while she was so debased that she doubted whether there was any hope for her. She seemed to be past caring whether she did wrong or not. 'I found myself hard towards God, insensible to his bounties. There was not shown me any good that I had done in all my life. The good appeared to me evil, and what is frightful is that this state appeared to me bound to endure eternally . . .' That was her inward condition when her footman's request and her brother's instruction made it necessary for her to write to Father La Combe.

'I was very glad of this opportunity of asking him to pray for me. I wrote to him that I had fallen from the grace of God, that I had repaid God's benefits by the blackest ingratitude; in short, that I was abjectness itself, and a subject deserving compassion; and that, far from having advanced towards my God, I had entirely alienated myself from Him.'

She was slightly eased after writing that letter. It had alleviated the strain to expose her innermost thoughts to someone who she felt might understand, although, about the same time, she was horrified to find that the city of Geneva came repeatedly to her mind. Geneva! Hotbed of the Calvinistic heresy! It would be the end of all hope if she drifted so far as to quit the true faith for apostasy!

Then came a reply from Father La Combe. It was infinitely reassuring. Far from rebuking or condemning her, as had others, he assured her that she had *not* fallen from grace. The fact that she was so stricken with the consciousness of her sinfulness was evidence of that. He went on to tell her something of his own spiritual experiences, some of which were very similar to her own. The effect of this letter was to bring peace of mind, and a calming of spirit, and a renewal of hope that perhaps, after all, she was not damned. A dream she had was strangely comforting, too, as it seemed to contain a message from God. She saw a little nun with a beatific expression, who came to her and said, 'My sister, I come to tell you that God wishes you at Geneva.' That set her mind at rest. If God sent a message to tell her He wanted her there, He must have a purpose in it, though she did not know what it could be.

It was the month of July, and St. Magdalene's Day was approaching. Every year, in spite of her spiritual depression, she had commemorated her contract of spiritual marriage on that day, and the thought came to her that she would like Father La Combe to say the Mass for her on that day. So she wrote to him and asked him to do so, although she doubted whether the letter would reach him in time.

The day dawned – St. Magdalene's Day, 1680. It was a day she would never forget, imprinted indelibly in her memory. 'It was this happy day of the Magdalene that my soul was perfectly delivered from all her troubles,' she wrote, although how and where it happened her diary did not divulge. The dark cloud of depression was lifted completely, all the peace and joy and love she had known before returned, but with a difference. 'My trouble and my pain were changed into a peace such that, the better to explain, I call God-peace. The peace I possessed before this time was indeed the peace of God – peace, the gift of God – but it was not God-peace; peace which He possesses in Himself, and which is found only in Him.'

She was not able to express clearly the joy that was now

hers. 'One day of this happiness would be indeed the recompense with usury for many years of suffering. O Paul! You say that the sufferings of this life are not worthy to be compared with the glory that is prepared for us!' she continued ecstatically. 'It is true even in this life, I can say from actual experience.' She felt it was too good to last, but as time went on she found that the inner stability and liberty and peace increased rather than diminished, and that all her former conscious love for God and desire to help others, especially the poor, had returned.

She had changed outwardly, too. She was still the same person, yet there was a simple, unaffected spontaneity about her which had been lacking before. The self-consciousness which had revealed itself in a variety of ways, sometimes an awkward reserve, sometimes an excess of zeal or piety, that had robbed her personality of simplicity, had gone. She was perfectly natural in her behaviour, going about the ordinary affairs of life cheerfully and without affectation. Yet, with her analytical mind, she realised that something had happened that she could not altogether account for.

'That intellect which I once thought I had lost in a strange stupidity, was restored to me with additions. I was astonished at it myself, and I found that there was nothing for which it was not able, and in which it did not succeed. Those who saw me said I had a prodigious intellect. I know well that I had but little intellect, but that in God my mind had taken a quality which before it was without. It experienced, it seemed to me, something of the state in which the apostles were after having received the Holy Spirit.'

She heard from Father La Combe soon afterwards. Yes, her letter had arrived in time, and to his surprise, as he was bringing her before God during the Mass, an inner voice had said to him three times, 'You shall both dwell in the same place.' Furthermore, God had told him He had great designs for her. That was all he knew but he passed on to her what he had been told.

She did not pay too much attention to it at the time. It seemed very unlikely that God had anything special for her to do, a pockmarked widow with three children, and with only a sketchy sort of education obtained in convents in a provincial town. But there were some things she could do, and she set about doing them with vigour, renewing her charitable acts to the poor, setting some of them up in business, and especially ensuring that pretty girls were taught a skill that would provide them with an honest livelihood. She knew the temptations that would otherwise assail them. She tended a number of sick people, too, with such success that she gained a reputation for healing those whom the surgeon had given up as incurable.

She was free now as she had never been before, free to worship as well as to work. 'What happiness did I not taste in my little solitude and my little household, where nothing interrupted my repose! My young children did not require too much of my attention, as they were in good hands, so I went into the woods where I spent as many happy days as I had spent months of grief.'

She could happily have spent the rest of her life in that place, bringing up her children, doing all the good possible in the neighbourhood, attending church and retreats and festivals to her heart's content. Everything was turning out well. Amazingly, even her mother-in-law's attitude towards her changed. What brought this about it would be difficult to say, but it was partly, at any rate, a discovery the old woman made concerning her daughter-in-law's opportunities for re-marriage. Three men in high social positions had proposed marriage, and she had refused them all, but had said nothing about it to anyone. Old Madame Guyon had sometimes taunted her about her lack of suitors, telling her friends that her daughter-in-law hadn't re-married because she had never had the chance. When she learned from other sources what the true situation was, she was rather abashed, and although she never apologised, she began to speak so highly of her daughter-in-law, and to show her such affection, that Madame Guyon observed of that period that she had no crosses to bear at all.

Nevertheless, she was careful not to settle down into this congenial form of existence, as though it would continue indefinitely. 'I kept myself in expectancy, with a firm will to execute God's orders at the expense of my own life when He should make them known.' All the same, when the intimation came, it was unexpected, and took her by surprise.

She had gone to Paris on business, and, as was her custom, entered a church to make her confession. She went to the first confessor to be found, made her confession, which was a very short one, and was prepared to be dismissed when the man said to her, 'I don't know who you are. I don't know whether you are married or single, or a widow. But I feel very strongly that I should tell you that you must do what our Lord has made you know He desires of you. That is all I have to say.'

'But Father, I am a widow,' she answered. 'I have three children, two of them under six. What else could God desire of me, but to bring them up?'

'I know nothing about that,' was the answer. 'You know whether God has made you recognise that He wishes something of you. If it is so, there is nothing that should hinder you from doing His will. One must even leave one's children to do it.'

She made no answer, and went away, but in her heart, she knew what it meant. Geneva. She should go to Geneva.

Just about that time a Dominican monk who was a friend of hers came to visit her, and she talked it over with him. He told her he would pray about it for three days, and then give her his opinion. At the end of the three days he told her he believed it was God's will she should go there, but in order to be sure, she ought to see the Bishop of Geneva. After all, she would be going into his diocese and it was only right that he should be consulted. He also advised her to write to Father La Combe, to ask for his prayers, since he was also living in that area.

It was at this point that she ran into difficulties. Father La
Combe not only prayed about it himself, but invited some
godly women of his acquaintance to do so too. They all
agreed, unanimously, that she should go to Geneva. In
addition, a Benedictine nun, a nun of the Visitation, and a
Father Claude Martin all gave the same opinion, independently of each other. With so much evidence to confirm
her own conviction, there seemed no reason to change her
course – except for one thing.

The Bishop of Geneva did not agree with them.

He was not unsympathetic. Quite the reverse, in fact. He
thoroughly approved of her resolve to come into his diocese,
wealthy woman that she was, and with a reputation for piety
and good works. The only thing in which he did not agree
was the exact whereabouts of her calling. He did not think
Geneva itself was the right place – she should go to Gex,
where the New Catholics were starting a work. She should go
and join them.

'But I have no call to Gex,' she remonstrated. 'God has
called me to Geneva.'

'There is nothing to stop you visiting Geneva,' he replied.
'It is only a few miles from Gex. It is to Gex I think you
should go.' So with her invariable habit of bowing to
authority, she agreed to go to Gex – but not to join the New
Catholics, as he urgently suggested. She could not deny her
inner conviction to that extent. She would go to Gex, she
would give all her money to the New Catholics for their work
there, she would live with them, but she would not become
one of them. The idea she had had of going quietly to the city
of Geneva, getting a small apartment there, and commenc-
ing to do simple medical work, using her skills in that way to
help people, and especially to strengthen the few Catholics
who were there, had to be abandoned. She would go to Gex,
as the Bishop insisted, and there she would commit her way
to God, to show her what she should do. So she sold her
home, left her two older children, boys, in the care of
guardians ('although I was extremely grieved to leave my

younger son, the confidence I had in the Holy Virgin, to whom I had vowed him, and whom I looked on as my mother, calmed all my griefs'), gave a huge sum of money to the New Catholics, and with her little daughter, a nun and two maids, set out for the unknown.

The Soul That Loves God
Finds Him Everywhere

Oh Thou, by long experience tried,
Near whom no grief can long abide;

My Love! How full of sweet content
I pass my years of banishment:

All scenes alike engaging prove
To souls impressed with sacred Love:
Where'er they dwell, they dwell in Thee;
In heaven, in earth, or on the sea.

To me remains no place nor time
My country is in every clime;
I can be calm and free from care
On any shore, since God is there.

While place we seek, or place we shun
The soul finds happiness in none;
But with a God to guide our way,
'Tis equal joy to go or stay.

Could I be cast where Thou art not,
That were indeed a dreadful lot;
But regions none remote I call,
Secure of finding God in all.

My country, Lord, art Thou alone;
No other can I claim or own;
The point where all my wishes meet;
My Law, my Love; life's only sweet:

I hold by nothing here below;
Appoint my journey, and I go . . .

Jeanne de la Mothe Guyon

5

Into the Unknown

When wealthy young widows, noted for piety and good
works, suddenly steal away, apparently deserting their
children, and make for some remote destination with the idea
of serving God there, it is inevitable that people will talk.
Madame Guyon had slipped off very quietly, rather fearful
that attempts would be made to stop her, but when it was
realised that she had placed her six-year-old son with her
cousin, a counsellor of Parliament, whom she had made her
children's guardian, and that she had given an enormous
sum of money to the New Catholics, there was quite a furore
among those who knew her. Opinions were sharply divided
as to the rights and wrongs of what she had done. There were
those who asserted that her duty was to stay in Montargis
and bring up her children. There were others who were
overcome with admiration at the sacrifice she was making
and the dedication she showed. Some of these, like the
Duchess of Charost, had friends at Court, where religion had
taken a new turn, with one of the King's mistresses taking the
veil, another departing in high dudgeon to her estate in the
country, and the King himself, a reformed character, having
only a platonic friendship with his children's demure and
pious governess, Madame de Maintenon. A mild interest in
the provincial heiress was being aroused in Paris.

All of which was intensely provoking to Father de la
Mothe. After all, when one's young half-sister has been
successfully married off to a very wealthy man, and then
been left a widow, one expects to derive some personal
benefit, and to have an authoritative voice in the disposal of
her money. Instead of this, the self-willed creature had not
only not given him the annuity he was expecting, but had

donated what he had hoped would be coming his way to an organisation with which he was not even connected.

His reaction to the news he got about her boded no good for Madame Guyon who, by this time, was well on her way to Gex.

The journey there was punctuated with various dangers, through which she and her little party came without serious injury, and 'the external gaiety' she preserved reassured the fearful among them. As for her, she was so happy and carefree that she sang aloud, glad to be done, as she thought, with the entanglements of wealth and worldliness, feeling that, like the Israelites of old, she was being led by a pillar of cloud by day and a pillar of fire by night.

It was not that she expected things to be easy, or that she was left in ignorance that trials awaited her. Her own little girl was an unconscious prophet during that journey, her childish occupations containing a significance which Madame Guyon herself recognised.

'What was astonishing was that in the boat my daughter, without knowing what she was doing, could not help making crosses. She kept a person employed in cutting rushes, and then she made them into crosses and quite covered me with them. She put more than three hundred on me. I let her do it, and I understood inwardly that there was a mystery in what she was doing. There was given to me an inward certainty that I was going there only to reap crosses, and that this little girl was sowing the Cross for me to gather.

'Sister Garnier, who saw that whatever they did they could not prevent the child from loading me with crosses, said to me, "What this child is doing is very mysterious," then said to her, "My little lady, put crosses on me also." She answered, "They are not for you; they are for my dear mother." She gave Sister Garnier one to please her, then she continued putting them on me. When she had put on a very great number she had river-flowers given to her, which were found on the water, and making a wreath with them she placed it on my head and said to me, "After the

Cross you will be crowned." In silence I wondered at all this . . .'

And sailing along on the quiet waters she offered herself afresh to her Lord for whatever He might call upon her to suffer. He had suffered, and she wanted to enter into that fellowship with Him. It was a further step, taken deliberately, of conformity to His will.

About the same time a friend of hers, a nun, had a vision about her, which was related to her later. 'She saw my heart in the midst of a great number of thorns, so that it was quite covered with them, and said that our Lord appeared in this heart, very well pleased; and she saw that the more strongly the thorns pricked, instead of being disfigured my heart appeared more beautiful, and our Lord was more pleased.'

So she travelled on, and events were so timed that she arrived at Annecy on the even of St. Magdalene's Day. Annecy! It was always associated in her mind with St. Francis de Sales. She had reached the very place where was the tomb of the man whose life and writings had so inspired her, on the very day when she always renewed the vows she had made to Christ. It was a notable experience. The Bishop of Geneva met her there, and said a Mass for her, and the words 'I will espouse thee in faith, I will espouse thee for ever' were deeply impressed on her mind.

'I honoured the relics of St. Francis de Sales with whom our Lord gave me a particular union. I say union, for it appeared to me that the soul in God is united with the saints more or less as they are conformed to her, and then those saints are rendered more intimately present to her in God Himself.' To her these saints were friends, united by God in an immortal bond. Her spiritual friendships were not limited to those she had known in the flesh, like Mother Granger. 'The whole family, in heaven and on earth' contained those whose experiences she could relate to, whose examples and words had reached her heart. St. Francis de Sales, though he had died before she was born, was one of them. He, too, had been drawn to Geneva, he too believed that ordinary people like herself could know and love God. She felt she was in the right succession.

But she did not stay more than twenty-four hours in Annecy. The next stop was Geneva itself, and another Mass, at the house of the French Resident. 'I had much joy in communicating, and it seemed to me that God bound me there even more strongly to Himself.' But she did not stay there, either. That very day she travelled on to Gex, arriving at her destination late in the evening, and it was there that everything suddenly began to go wrong.

No preparation had been made for them. An empty apartment awaited them, just four bare walls. There was not even a bed, although the Bishop had assured her that it was furnished.

'Apparently he thought so. We slept at the Sisters of Charity, who had the kindness to give us their beds. . . .' But Madame Guyon could not sleep. 'I suffered a pain and agony which can be better experienced than described.' For she became aware that her little girl was not well. She had evidently not noticed it before, for the child had been very lively on the journey, but now she was weak and listless, and Madame Guyon was overwhelmed with self-accusation. Why had she brought the child to such a place, forcing her to share the privation she was quite prepared to endure herself? All confidence that she had done the right thing deserted her that night, and lying in her narrow bed she could not restrain her tears. The whole thing had been a mistake! She ought never to have left home. Suppose her little girl died! It would be her fault. 'I saw her as a victim whom I had sacrificed by my imprudence.' Then she rememberd that there was an Ursuline convent in Thonon, about twenty miles away. The child would be better off with the Ursulines, who specialised in training and caring for little girls. She would take her there the very next day!

But next day, when she explained her plan, she found herself unexpectedly opposed. She was not helped, but deliberately hindered, in making arrangements to go to

Thonon. She was in a strange neighbourhood where she knew no one, she had given away her money, and now was more or less at the mercy of the New Catholics to whom she had given it. They were determined to keep her within their own community. She was at her wits' end when suddenly she thought of the young Barnabite in whom she had always taken an interest since the time he visited her home years ago – Father La Combe. Father La Combe was in Thonon. She would write to him. This she did, begging him to come and see her and advise her, for she was terribly anxious about the health of her little girl. And as he had a letter from the Bishop of Geneva about the same time, urging him to go and see Madame Guyon who had just arrived from Paris and was rather upset, he went promptly.

It was in these circumstances that the two met again. Although their first and only personal conversation had taken place years before, as soon as they saw each other they were conscious of an affinity of spirit difficult to describe, but of which both were aware. 'There was in it nothing human or natural,' Madame Guyon wrote later. The very absence of personal attraction enabled them to speak freely, not only of their personal spiritual experiences, but of the immediate problem confronting her. To her relief he told her at once that she should take her little daughter to Thonon, where she would be well looked after by the Ursulines. Then she confided in him that she did not feel at all easy with the New Catholics, and that others had warned her not to join them.

'I don't believe God requires it of you, either,' he said. 'But I think you should remain with them, without committing yourself to anything, until God makes it plain, perhaps through circumstances, whether you should leave or stay.' So with Father La Combe as an escort she took her little girl to Thonon, and remained with her for a fortnight at the Ursulines. The child did not get on as well there as she expected, and Madame Guyon who, in spite of her own readiness to take the vows of poverty, chastity and obedience, had no intention of imposing them on her children, was dismayed to realise that the child's education would suffer there.

'With her natural disposition it seemed she would have done wonders if educated in France, and that I was depriving her of all this, and putting it out of her power to do anything, or to find in the future proposals of marriage such as she might hope for.' A good marriage to a man of rank was what it was her duty to provide for her daughter – what else was there in life for a young woman? But a girl brought up in Savoy, with a provincial accent and provincial manners, lacking finesse and social poise, would be at a disadvantage, as Madame Guyon very well knew.

'For thirteen days I suffered a trouble inconceivable. All that I had given up seemed to have cost me nothing in comparison with what the sacrifice of my daughter cost me.' But through it all she began to see there was a purpose of sanctification in her own soul. 'I believe, O my God, that You caused this to purify the too human attachment I had for her natural gifts.' There remained a streak of worldly pride, known to a later age as snobbishness, if not for herself at least for the child she loved, and it had to go. Not without a struggle did she reach the point of renunciation, and, leaving her child in Thonon, return to Gex. Incidentally, as soon as she left, the child's health began to improve.

The fortnight in Thonon had been fraught with some traumatic experiences, one at least of which was connected with Father La Combe. She met a hermit living in the neighbourhood, a man renowned in the vicinity for his holiness, whose life-style resembled that of John the Baptist. He told her that God had revealed to him that He had great designs for her and for Father La Combe, that their destiny was to help souls – but that strange trials awaited them both. He did not try to minimise their intensity, though he did not know what they would be. As far as she was concerned, an unexpected one awaited her on her return to Gex.

A letter awaited her from her half-brother, Father de la Mothe, and as she read it she realised he had not been idle.

All the best people, he told her, the pious, the professionals, the gentlemen, were united in condemning her for the course she was taking. Furthermore, her mother-in-law had been so shocked by her departure that she had suddenly become senile, and therefore the children's inheritance was in jeopardy. (This turned out to be quite untrue, but she had no reason to doubt it at the time.) See what she had brought upon her family! His was not the only letter that reached her. Others came from various sources, some accusing her quite violently, and there were times when she felt submerged by it all. Yet somehow, there was a deeper peace of heart than she had known before. Perhaps it was this that enabled her not to show outwardly what she was suffering inwardly – for there was no doubt about her suffering.

'I shut myself up as much as I could, and there I allowed myself to be penetrated by the pain, which appeared to me very profound. I bore it very passively without being able, or even wishing, to alleviate it . . . It appeared to me that I then commenced to bear troubles in a divine manner, and from this time forward, without any sentiment, the soul could be at the same time very happy and very pained, afflicted and beatified.

'It was not in at all the same way I had borne my first griefs, nor as I had borne the death of my father, for then the soul was buried in peace, not delivered over to pain. What she suffered then was only a shock to nature.' As always, she analysed her feelings in order to discern wherein her present suffering differed from that which she had known earlier. Her present suffering was intense, and she felt every pang of it – but she bore it with a strength that was not her own. This was the conclusion she came to. 'These sufferings were impressed on me by God Himself, as in Jesus Christ; He suffered as God and man; in short, God-Man, suffering and rejoicing, without the beatitude diminishing anything of the pain, or the pain interrupting or altering the perfect beatitude.'

The most learned theologian could scarcely have expressed it better than the widow who, having given away the bulk of her personal fortune, was doing jobs of sweeping and washing in the very establishment her wealth was supporting. She managed the sweeping without much difficulty. 'What troubled me most was that I had never done washing, and it was necessary for me to wash all the linen of the sacristy . . . I spoiled everything!' she added ruefully. She had to request one of the servants she had brought with her, now under the authority of the Superior, to help her out.

When her domestic duties and the religious services of the House did not claim her attention she retreated to her room, and there she replied to the denunciatory letters she was receiving. She was evidently better at writing than at washing, for those letters had a surprising effect on the recipients, turning them in her favour, as she learned later.

For her the one comforting factor in those bewildering days was that Father La Combe had been appointed by the Bishop of Geneva to be her spiritual director. 'He is a man enlightened by God, and understands well the ways of the spirit,' the Bishop had said, adding with a flash of insight, 'and he has a singular gift for calming souls.' Perhaps he saw that that gift would be needed in her case. It was a relief to her to have this authorised connection with the only person in the neighbourhood whom she knew and could trust. From time to time Father La Combe travelled from Thonon to Gex to see her, and on one occasion walked all night in response to an urgent summons from the Sisters. Madame Guyon had been taken ill, it appeared that she was dying, and the doctors could do nothing for her. They begged him to come immediately, and receive her confession, before it was too late.

'But as soon as he entered the house, without my knowing it, my pains were alleviated. And when he came into my room and blessed me, with his hands on my head, I was perfectly cured. . . . The doctors were so surprised that they did not know how to account for my cure. Being Protestants,' she added artlessly, 'they were unable to recognise a miracle.'

Whatever may have been the view of the Protestant doctors, she was not alone in thinking that Father La Combe had been the means of working a miracle.

'My miraculous cure was written about to Paris, and made a great sensation. . . . Almost all the persons then in repute for holiness wrote to me. The Demoiselles of Paris, who were renowned for good works, congratulated me.' One wealthy lady wrote to her, sending a large gift of money with the assurance that more would follow whenever she chose to apply for it. So the tide of opinion was turning in her favour. 'At Paris they talked only of the sacrifice I had made. All approved and praised my action, so that they wanted an account of it printed, together with the miracle which had taken place. I do not know who prevented it.'

The probability is that Father de la Mothe had a hand in preventing the publication of that pamphlet eulogising his sister, just as he was behind the proposal that she should relinquish her rights to her property in favour of her children, giving power of attorney to relatives, and retaining only an annuity for herself. She was in the New Catholics' House in Gex when the suggestion reached her. She read through the legal documents that had been prepared, and although there were clauses inserted wholly to her disadvantage, they did not worry her. In her guilelessness she did not even notice them. She had taken the vow of poverty, had desired to be conformed to her Master, and she had meant what she said – and God had accepted her vow. She knew what she had to do. With the stroke of a pen as she signed her name to the document, she who had been rich became poor – so poor that on one occasion all she had to give to a beggar was some buttons.

Poverty she had asked for, and nakedness and stripping. They were to follow. She believed herself ready for them, anticipating sufferings of a general nature without realising the means by which they would come. If she had known the form in which they would be inflicted, she would have shrunk

from them. One of God's many mercies is that the future is
veiled.

*   *   *

The habit of a nun, it is generally agreed, is not one designed
to set off feminine charms, but rather the reverse, and it
usually succeeds in its purpose. However, there are some
faces, especially when young and fresh, which are so
moulded by nature that even the habit of a nun cannot
conceal their beauty, and there was one such face which fell
into that category in the New Catholic convent in Gex. The
young novice who owned it caught the eye of the ecclesiastical
gentleman who heard confessions in the House, and the more
she caught his eye, the more confessions he encouraged her to
make. 'The little Bishop', as he was called behind his back,
then set out to persuade her that what she needed was a private
retreat, which he offered to conduct for her personally.

What it would all have led to must be left to the
imagination, for that is as far as it got, much to the chagrin of
'the little Bishop'. Things would have gone for him just as he
planned had it not been for the influence of that woman from
Paris – Madame Guyon. It was she who observed what was
happening, got the ear of the young novice, started teaching
her to pray personally in addition to repeating the usual
offices, and persuaded her not to enter into a private retreat
with him, but rather to wait for Father La Combe. He was
due to arrive shortly for the purpose of conducting retreats in
the establishment.

'Our Lord gave her such blessing in her prayers that this
girl gave herself to God in earnest and with all her heart. The
retreat completed the victory. Now, as she apparently
recognised that to connect herself with that ecclesiastic was
something imperfect, she was more reserved,' observed
Madame Guyon, adding that the little Bishop was very put
out over the whole affair, and very embittered against her
and Father La Combe. There was little enough he could do
to regain control over the young novice, but there was quite a

lot he could do to make things uncomfortable for Madame Guyon.

It was an awkward situation for her since she, like everyone else, went to him for confession, and the difficulty was that she had so little to confess. This amazed him, but as she explained, her present manner of life provided few opportunities for committing faults. There was one sin of her past life for which she could not forgive herself, though she had confessed it before, but when she told him of it he was not satisfied. She must be hiding something. He jeered at her covertly, and went so far as to preach against her, without actually mentioning her name. There were some people who were so proud that instead of confessing gross sins, they confessed only peccadilloes, he said, and then repeated word for word what she had said in the confessional box. Such trivial matters! Eventually Madame Guyon wrote to Father La Combe and asked him if it would be all right to confess some of her past sins, just to satisfy the little Bishop.

Father La Combe's reply in the negative was prompt and unequivocal. 'He told me, no! That I should take great care not to confess them except as past, and that in confession the utmost sincerity was needed.' The little Bishop continued dissatisfied, and said so.

He was not the only enemy she made while in the convent at Gex. Female hearts, she observed, even in such secluded places, can prove very vulnerable. Marriage being out of the question, the instinctive desire for relationship with a man can take another form, apparently entirely spiritual. Madame Guyon recognised this. She had read in St. Francis de Sales' *Devout Life* the warning to discern between true and vain friendships, the danger of mistaking the one for the other, and the need to be on one's guard. 'This is particularly true when they are contracted between persons of opposite sexes, under no matter what pretext, for Satan very often touches those that love. They begin with virtuous love, but if they are not very prudent fond love will begin to insert itself, then sensual love, and afterwards carnal love.' This she had read and noted, so when one of the nuns confided in her that God had revealed to her that Father La Combe was a saint, something in the woman's attitude disturbed her.

'He is a saint, and I am going to take a vow to obey him in everything,' the nun went on ardently, and was evidently on the verge of pronouncing the vow, then and there, but Madame Guyon stopped her.

'You mustn't do that!' she said. 'These things cannot be undertaken lightly – besides, it would not be right to do it without first consulting the person concerned, to find out whether or not he would accept the responsibility.'

This seemed reasonable, and the nun agreed to write to Father La Combe, affirming that God had revealed to her that he was a saint, and that she wanted to take a vow of obedience to him.

'I believe she was then quite sincere, for she had ups and downs of weakness, which are common enough to our sex and ought to make us very humble,' wrote Madame Guyon later. 'Father La Combe answered her quickly, and she showed me the letter. He told her she should never make a vow to obey any man; that he would never be her adviser; that the person who is suitable at one time is not so in another, and that as for himself, he had never received such a vow from anyone, and never would; that it was even forbidden him by their rules.' He added, however, that he would serve her to the best of his ability, and as he was coming to Gex in the near future to conduct retreats he would have a talk with her.

The outcome of that conversation was disastrous. The nun flew into a rage at what he said to her, went to the little Bishop with her grievances, and together they joined forces to bring about the downfall of both Madame Guyon and Father La Combe.

They started on Father La Combe. The nun asked him to preach a sermon on the inner life, which he did, taking as his text, 'The beauty of the King's daughter comes from within.'

He explained what the inner life is, and how one should act from it. When he had finished the little Bishop angrily asserted that it was preached against him, and had been done deliberately to offend him.

Father La Combe assured him that it was not so, and that he had already preached the same sermon in a number of other places. As it happened, being a methodical man, he had kept a list of places where he preached it on the sermon notes, and so was able to produce them on the spot, as evidence. Instead of being appeased the little Bishop was further infuriated. Father La Combe, well instructed in humility, quietly got down on his knees without saying a word, and while the little Bishop raved on remained there with head bowed. It won for him the approval of most of the onlookers, enhancing his reputation for holiness, though they wisely kept quiet about it at the time. Meanwhile, the little Bishop, not content with abusing him, said his sermon was full of errors, and that he would write to Rome about it. He wanted what Father La Combe had said to be examined by the Sacred College and the Inquisition.

When the tirade was over Father La Combe rose to his feet and went on his way little realising what further trouble was brewing for him. He went to Annecy, where lived the Bishop of Geneva, as he had to see him about some affairs in Thonon. But the Bishop was not interested in affairs in Thonon. What was occupying his mind was Madame Guyon. That lady had already given a great sum of money to the New Catholics in his diocese, but she still had an income of her own, and the Bishop did not like the idea of it going elsewhere. Furthermore, the lady had some influential friends in Paris. Who could tell how much more money might be directed into the coffers of the New Catholics in Gex if only Madame Guyon could be persuaded to bind herself to them? So with the idea of keeping her permanently in Gex he had made the proposition to her that she should be installed in the House where she was residing as its Superior. She was already having a splendid influence on its inmates, he had told her – how greatly that could be extended if only she would agree to becoming Superior!

Madame Guyon had promptly rejected the idea. Very reasonably, she had pointed out that she had not even served a two-year novitiate, so how could she become Superior of a House? In any case, she was not prepared to bind herself, as she believed her vocation to be elsewhere. But the Bishop would not take no for an answer, and with the arrival of Father La Combe, whom he had appointed as her director, he thought he saw a way of making her change her mind.

'Father La Combe, it is absolutely necessary to bind Madame Guyon to give what she has to the House of Gex, and to become its Superior,' he said. 'And I want you to help me to persuade her to do so.'

'My lord, she had already told you of her vocation, both when you met her in Paris and here,' remonstrated Father La Combe. 'I don't believe she will bind herself. It is not likely that, having given up everything in the hope of going to Geneva, she should bind herself elsewhere. By doing that she would make it impossible for her to fulfil God's purposes for her. She is ready to remain with the Sisters as a lodger, if they will have her. If not, she will go to some convent, and wait there to see how God directs her.'

'My Father, I know all that,' said the Bishop impatiently. 'But I also know that she is very obedient. You are her director, and if you instruct her to do it, she will obey.'

'All the more reason, since she is so obedient, to be very cautious how one commands her,' retorted Father La Combe. 'It is not likely that I will urge a foreign lady, who now has only the little income she has reserved for herself, to give that to a House which has not yet been founded. Which, perhaps, never will be founded! If this House fails, on what will the lady live? Shall she go to the almshouses?'

The Bishop got really angry at this. 'All these reasons are good for nothing,' he snapped. 'If you don't make the lady do it, I will excommunicate you.'

Father La Combe was taken by surprise. He knew the rules of the interdict, and that the Bishop was going beyond his measure. But he answered readily enough that whatever happened, he would rather die than do anything against his honour and his conscience, and bowed himself out. He left behind him an infuriated man in whom the little Bishop in Gex could find inflammable material on which to work.

Extracts from 'The Nativity'

But I am poor; oblation I have none
None for a Saviour, but Himself alone:
Whate'er I render Thee, from Thee it came:
And, if I give my body to the flame,
My patience, love, energy divine,
Of heart and soul and spirit, all are Thine;
Ah, vain attempt to expunge the mighty score!
The more I pay, I owe Thee still the more.

Upon my meanness, poverty, and guilt,
The trophy of Thy glory shall be built;
My self-disdain shall be th' unshaken base,
And my deformity its fairest grace;
For destitute of good and rich in ill,
Must be my state and my description still.

Jeanne de la Mothe Guyon

6

Thonon to Turin

Madame Guyon was not happy in Gex. If personal inclination had prevailed she would have remained in Thonon with her daughter in the Ursuline convent, and not returned to Gex at all. Her obedience to ecclesiastical authority had taken her there in the first place, rather than to Geneva itself, and then La Combe's advice to stay there until God showed her, perhaps through circumstances, that she should move away, had confirmed her in doing so. The harshness with which she was treated by the nuns, allied to some strange experiences of occult forces, with noises in her room at night, and once a mental picture of Satan himself, his face horrible in a bluish light, made the place sufficiently uncongenial for her to want to get away from it. However, that very fact was, for her, a reason for staying. Also, there was the apparent need to give moral and spiritual support to the young nun who was being harassed by the little Bishop. She therefore made no attempt to move until the circumstantial guidance came to which La Combe had referred.

It came in the form of two letters. One was from La Combe himself, written immediately after his interview with the Bishop of Geneva, telling her exactly what had passed between them, warning her what to expect that she might act accordingly. The other, providentially, came from the Ursulines in Thonon, urging her to come, as the sister who was looking after her little daughter was ill. This second letter was all that she needed. Showing it to the nuns she announced her intention of going at once, and there were obviously no grounds on which they could stop her. Thus she was extricated from the New Catholics at Gex, and never returned.

Meanwhile, Father La Combe had been summoned to Rome. His doctrine was being called into question. He had become widely known in the region of Thonon for his powerful preaching, and for the influence of the missions he held. That was all very well, but now there were suggestions that what he was saying might be heretical, and due examination of it must be made. The very day after Madame Guyon arrived at the convent of the Ursulines in Thonon, he left the city, first to preach the Lenten sermons in the Valley of Aost, then to proceed to Rome. He managed to fit in a visit to her, however, to warn her that trouble was brewing, and that he himself would not be at hand to stand by her. He was sorry to leave her in a strange country without help at such a time, he told her.

What he did not tell her was that rumours were being spread about his association with her, that it was insinuated they were having illicit relations under the cloak of religion. He had not missed the covert glances and remarks dropped by one or two of the ecclesiastics who he knew disliked him, and who resented his popularity as a preacher. In one way he was not sorry to be going to Rome. At any rate he could not be suspected of carrying on with a woman and meeting her privately if he were so far away. But he wondered how she would feel, left alone to face the music.

Her reaction to the unexpected information of his immediate departure for Rome was reassuring. On the human level it must have been a disagreeable shock to her, especially when he explained that he might be detained there for a very long time. He was undoubtedly her closest friend in the neighbourhood, and the only one to whom she could turn for advice. But she showed neither alarm nor dismay. When God withdrew human supports, she said, she managed very well, for He did not withdraw His mercy. In fact, if they never met again, she would not be upset, she assured him. God's will was what mattered. If it was His will they should be separated, she not only acquiesced to it, but accepted it gladly. He could go to Rome with an easy mind on that score. So they parted, conscious that for each of them the way ahead was likely to be a difficult one.

As things worked out, their apprehensions over La Combe

proved groundless. So far from being condemned, his doctrine was praised at Rome. 'He was received with so much honour, and his doctrine so esteemed that the Sacred Congregation did him the honour of taking his views on certain points of doctrine, and found them so sound and clear that it followed them.' When he eventually returned to Thonon he was cleared of all fault by Rome. He could continue his activities of conducting missions and receiving confessions as before, to the disappointment of those who had been spreading reports about his heresies.

For her, things did not go so smoothly. The Bishop and her half-brother, Father de la Mothe, ganged up to get her back to Gex, she knew that the little Bishop was implying that she had had a lesbian relationship with the young nun there, and in addition, her letters were being intercepted. For months she was without the remittances due to her, and this could have been serious, but for some encouraging evidences of God's overruling. She related some of them to Father La Combe, on his return from Rome.

'After having been many months without any news of my papers, and when people even pressed me to write, blaming me for my indifference, an invisible hand held me back . . .' It was an exercise in patience, although action would have been easier. But she waited, and, 'Some time after I received a letter from our domestic ecclesiastic, telling me he was ordered to come and see me, and bring my papers.'

There were other occasions, too, when she was conscious of God's hand in her affairs. 'I had sent to me from Paris a considerable package for my daughter. It was lost on the lake, and I could get no news of it, but I gave myself no trouble. I believed still it would be found. At the end of three months a person had it brought to us. It was found – the house of a poor man. He had not opened it, and did not know who had brought it there.

'Once when I had sent for all the money which had to supply my wants for an entire year, the person who had been to cash the letter of exchange, having placed the money in two bags on a horse, forgot that it was there, and gave his horse to a boy to lead. He let the money fall from the horse in the middle of the market-place of Geneva. I arrived at that moment, coming from the other side, and having got out of my litter, the first thing I found was the money, over which I walked; and what is surprising is that, though there was a great crowd on that spot, no one had seen it. Many similar things happened to me, but I won't mention them all, for fear of becoming tedious.'

Here in Thonon she was often ill, at one period for about eight months on end. It was during those times of physical weakness, often lying prostrate on her bed, that she entered into new dimensions of spiritual experience, interpreting them as she understood them. She arrived at all her conclusions in this way. As she expressed it:

'Our Lord instructed me by experience. It is the way He has always acted with me. He has not enlightened me by illumination and knowledge, but while making me experience the things, He has given me the understanding of what I experienced.'

Whatever may have been the reason for her veneration of the Virgin Mary when she was young, it now stemmed from the fact that through her the Child Jesus had been born. And in a spiritual sense she could relate to her, for had not Jesus Christ said that whoever did the will of His Father, the same was His mother, His brother, His sister? 'I understood also the maternity of the Holy Virgin, and in what manner we participate in her maternity . . . producing Him in souls.' This, it began to dawn on her, was to be her role—a spiritual mother.

Page after page of her autobiography deals with the flights of her spirit during those months in Thonon. The Last Supper became real to her.

'In an ineffable silence I understood the manner in which Jesus Christ communicated Himself to His intimates, and the communication of St. John on the breast of our Lord at the Last Supper. . . . It was then there was communicated to him that wonderful secret of the eternal generation of the Word, because he was rendered a participator in the ineffable intercourse of the Holy Trinity. . . . It was then he learned the difference of being "born of the flesh, of the will of man, or of the will of God".'

She learned secrets of silence. 'You made me conceive, O Divine Word, that as You are always speaking and working in a soul, although You there appear in a profound silence . . . I learned then a language unknown to me before . . .'

She had confrontations with the prince of darkness, too, as well as revelations concerning the woman in the Apocalypse, who had the moon under her feet, was encircled with the sun, had twelve stars on her head and cried in the pains of childbirth. From this she understood that the moon under her feet signified that her soul would be above the vicissitudes of mortal life, since she was surrounded by the sun, representing God Himself, and that the pregnancy indicated spiritual children, and the dragon was the Devil who would seek, unsuccessfully, to devour them. Spiritual motherhood again, with its birth-pangs and pain, and an enemy ready to attack . . .

It was during this time of constant illness that she developed the ability which was to bring her into the public eye, and preserve her name for posterity. She started to write.

For several years she had written poetry, on and off, but this was different. She told Father La Combe that she felt strongly urged to write, and he told her the same thought had been impressed upon him. But what did she want to write? he asked. She had no idea, she answered. So he told her to write as the spirit moved her, and that is what she did. Words poured from her pen without any reflection on her part, and within a short time she had written a whole treatise on three classes of souls, as she saw them – souls that have turned to God and known His life within them, but who respond in varying degrees of fervour. With the analogy of streams and rivers, she likened some to the slow and sluggish that meander along and get nowhere, some to those that flow more rapidly, gathering rivulets to join their progress towards the ocean, and some to mighty torrents that pour down with an impetuosity that nothing can hinder. When she had finished writing, she thought no more of it. She just knew that she felt relieved, and her health improved.

However, La Combe demanded that she continue writing. Let her write to him everything that came to mind, all her experiences, the things that had happened to her, her spiritual growth. He was frequently away conducting missions, so he could not see her often, and as her spiritual director he wanted to know how she was getting on. It is possible that he not only wanted to learn from her but also to rectify what might be wrong thinking! There were times when the two of them got on each other's nerves. Something she told him 'irritated him against me several days. When I told him anything, this produced in him disgust for me and alienation.' She put this down to his spiritual immaturity, and as she felt as great a responsibility for his soul as he felt for hers, she 'suffered a martyrdom exceeding anything that can be told, and which has been very protracted'. After all, he might have been appointed her spiritual director by the Bishop, and this she gladly accepted, but they both of them took the view that she was, to him, his mother in Christ. And as such, she watched for his soul.

'I had so strong an instinct for his perfection, and to see him die to himself, that I would have wished him all the ills imaginable, far from pitying him.' Death to self was the only way to perfection, and dying could be painful, but it was necessary. 'When he was not faithful, or took things so as to nourish the self-life, I felt myself devoured . . .'

By and large, however, they got on very well, for they both had the same object in view – perfect union with God, and what she referred to as 'annihilation' of the self-life in order that His will might have unhindered sway.

Although their influence in the neighbourhood was mainly through their teaching, they were also noted for improving social conditions. Madame Guyon had always visited and helped the poor in practical ways, and when she was well enough she continued these activities. But it was during one of her periods of sickness that Father La Combe, stirred to action by what he saw of the plight of the poor, conceived the idea of establishing a little hospital for them. He got the cooperation of the local authorities to the extent of obtaining from them the use of some rooms they did not require, and Madame Guyon, as soon as she heard about it, donated some beds. Others followed her example, and in a very short space of time the hospital was a going concern, with twelve beds, and a voluntary staff of workers to run it. At this point Madame Guyon's flair for compounding ointments proved of very practical value. She taught the staff how to make them, and instructed them to sell them to the rich, so obtaining an income for the running of the hospital, while the poor who needed them were to receive them free of charge.

'The Dames of Charity were so well disposed that through their charity, and the care of the nuns, this hospital is very well maintained,' she wrote years later. 'Those Dames formed a union also to provide for the sick who could not go to the hospital, and I gave them some little rules I had observed when in France. They have kept this up with love and charity.' Then followed a simple note which revealed the centrality of Christ in her thinking, and the significance with which she regarded dates and anniversaries. 'We had also the devotion to cause every twenty-fifth of the month a service of blessing to be celebrated in the chapel of the Congregation, which is dedicated to the Holy Child Jesus; and for this we gave a complete outfit to the chapel.'

The effect of this quiet manifestation of charity and devotion was two-fold. It gained the approbation of the people of Thonon, but infuriated the Bishop of Geneva, who angrily told her that she was winning over everyone to her way of thinking, and that he did not want her in his diocese. The Prioress of the Ursulines who had become her friend had a hard time of it at his hands – or, to be more accurate, his tongue. And as Madame Guyon was so often ill, and the physicians said the proximity of the convent to the waters of the lake was bad for her, she decided to move away to a more secluded spot.

'I left the Ursulines, and a house at a distance from the lake was sought for me. The only empty one available had every appearance of the utmost poverty. There was no chimney except in the kitchen, through which we had to pass to reach the room. I took my daughter with me, and gave the largest room to her and the maid who attended her. I settled in a little hole with some straw, which I went up to by a wooden ladder. As I had no furniture but our bedsteads, which were white, I bought some rush-seated chairs, with plates and dishes of earthenware and wood.

'Never have I tasted such contentment as I found in this little spot,' she continued, remembering vividly the simplicity of those days. 'It seemed to me so in harmony with Jesus Christ. I relished everything better on wood than on silver. I can say that I have never tasted an equal pleasure to that in this poor and solitary little place where I lived. I was happier than kings!' Her companions were her little daughter, a lively, adaptable child, and her maid.

This young woman, the maid, had been brought to Thonon by a relative of Madame Guyon who had come from Paris to visit her, and the girl remained in Madame Guyon's employ. Madame Guyon always believed that God had inspired that visit for the sole purpose of bringing the girl to her. She was to prove a loyal and devoted servant and companion through all the trials that lay ahead.

The trials were soon encountered. The peace of the tiny home, not much better than a hovel, was shattered when rioters came, throwing stones through the windows, shouting abuse, and then one night tearing up all the trellis work in the little garden that had been so carefully put in order, overturning pots and plants, leaving it looking as though an invading army had gone through it.

She learned later who had set the rioters on to these unprovoked assaults – the little Bishop at Gex. However, there was nothing she could do about it. There was no civil authority to which she could turn for help or protection, for the Bishop himself had made it quite plain that he did not want her any longer in his diocese. In any case, she was always reluctant to plead for help from man, and at this time she seemed benumbed. 'I was so lost that I could neither see nor regard anything, taking all that came as from the hand of God. During all this time I never felt grief or regret at what I had done in giving up all.' Nor was she plagued with fears that she might have made a mistake. She had committed her way to God, and was confident that He had her affairs in hand.

So it proved to be. Unknown to her, someone was working quietly on her behalf, away in Italy. The godly Marquise de Prunai, sister of the chief State Secretary, living in the city of Turin, had heard about her and the difficulties she was encountering, and sent her a warm invitation to come and stay with her. Then she felt impelled by a superior power, God Himself she believed, to take further action. She obtained a *lettre de cachet* instructing Madame Guyon, accompanied by Father La Combe, to proceed to Turin.

This came as a complete surprise to both of them, but its arrival was certainly opportune as far as Madame Guyon was concerned. They both saw in it the hand of God, and accepted it unhesitatingly.

Knowing the rumours that were being spread about them, however, they took the precaution of ensuring that they did not travel together unaccompanied. A monk who had been teaching theology, and a boy Madame Guyon had brought from France and had trained as a tailor, went with them. The men rode on horses, Madame Guyon and her little girl and the maid in a litter. Nothing could have been more decorous, since the presence of an ecclesiastic travelling as escort was sufficient to lend an air of respectability to any company.

So they arrived in Turin. Once again she had been extricated from a situation in which she was helplessly entangled – but once again it was seen to be Father La Combe who was with her, and the rumours linking their names together persisted. She had prayed for ignominy and shame, and she was to get what she had asked for.

Prayer is the key of perfectness and of supreme well-being. It is the effectual means of delivering us from all vices and of acquiring all virtues; for the great means of becoming perfect is to walk in the presence of God. This He said Himself, 'Walk in My presence, and be perfect.' (Gen. 18.1) 'Tis prayer alone that can give you this presence, and that can give it you continually . . .

This is not the prayer of the head, but the prayer of the heart. It is not a prayer of thought only, because the spirit of man is so bounded that while he thinks on one thing he cannot think on another; but it is the prayer of the heart, which is not at all interrupted by all the occupations of the mind; nothing but irregular affections can interrupt the prayer of the heart . . .

Jeanne de la Mothe Guyon, from "A Method of Prayer"

7

Exodus from Grenoble

The Marquise de Prunai spoke very little French. She had heard about Madame Guyon, and the harsh treatment she had received in Gex and Thonon, and her heart had been touched. The circumstances of her own life had been similar in some respects, for she, too, had been left a widow in her twenties, and had decided against remarrying in order that she could devote herself, devotionally and practically, to religious exercises. She was glad to welcome into her home this Frenchwoman whose reputation for piety, and an unusual spirituality, had reached her.

But Madame Guyon spoke very little Italian. Furthermore, she was exhausted after the strain of the past months, and could not adapt quickly to her new situation. She was often silent, and sometimes felt so ill that she took to her bed. Then her elder son arrived, with news of her mother-in-law's death and complications that had arisen regarding her property. Madame Guyon did not divulge what were her feelings towards the son who had been so heartlessly estranged from her when a child. She merely wrote in her autobiography, 'My elder son came to see me on the subject of my mother-in-law's death, which was a very serious addition to my crosses; but after we had heard all his reasons – seeing without me they had sold all the movables, elected guardians, and settled everything independently of me – I was quite useless.'

The marquise, not surprisingly, found it hard to understand her guest. She seemed spiritless and rather stupid. The only person who appeared to have any influence over her was Father La Combe, who had left her in Turin and gone on to Verceil, thirty or forty miles away, at the invitation of the Bishop there. The marquise began to lose patience.

For Madame Guyon, a stranger in a strange land, Father La Combe was again the only one with whom she felt she could communicate freely. She wrote to him frequently, and he came to Turin occasionally, as her spiritual director. It came as an unpleasant shock, like a douche of cold water, to find that time and time again he apparently failed to understand her. When she turned to him for guidance as to what she should do, he told her he had no light on the matter. She must do what she believed to be right. They often disagreed, usually in their assessment of others. Limited as she was, with no household or social responsibilities, with inadequate language and generally poor health, she became excessively concerned about the spiritual condition of those whom she met, and who went to him for confession. When she told him that this one and that one was still full of SELF, he would accuse her of pride, and rash judgment, while she would grieve that he was so lacking in discernment. They knew each other well enough, and had sufficient humour to agree that if their association had been the natural one of which their detractors accused them, it would have broken up long ago.

'He who to everyone else was gentle, often had for me an extreme hardness,' she wrote. It pained her, but through it all she believed it was the will of God, that she might be left with no support but in God Himself. As for Father La Combe, he found that when he was at odds with her, he was uneasy. It interrupted his communion with God.

'When I am well with God I am well with you, and as soon as I am ill with God I am ill with you,' he told her more than once. The deep union of spirit they had always known was not without its testings.

Her spiritual relationship with La Combe was not the only experience of those months in Italy. Although she felt unusually helpless, 'childlike' as she expressed it, she found to her own surprise that when confronted with people who had a particular need, unknown to themselves, she could put her finger on it. '. . . Our Lord made me utter oracles; for when it was a question of helping anyone, or of anything our Lord wished for me, He gave me a divine strength.' Discernment of spirits was being given to her, and the time for the exercise of it was soon to come. As so often happens, guidance came as the result of outward events.

The marquise announced that she had to leave Turin for her estate in the country. This threw Madame Guyon into a state of uncertainty. What should she do? What about her daughter's education if she took her to the marquise's place in the country? She had to make a decision, but seemed unable to do so until one day, quite unexpectedly, Father La Combe arrived from Verceil, and for once he took a determined line with her. He told her what to do. Speaking quite firmly, he said she was to leave Turin immediately, and proceed to Paris.

To Paris! To the place where Father de la Mothe had been spreading rumours about her, asserting that she was running after Father La Combe, that she had left home on account of him, and that they had been seen in all sorts of compromising situations together! But such was her state of bewilderment and personal indecision that without a demur she started making preparations to leave Turin with her little daughter and the maid, the very next day.

Father La Combe accompanied her, much against his own will (he did not want to give occasion for any more scandals about him and this lady) but because the Father Provincial of Turin ordered him to. 'She can't be allowed to travel through those mountains without someone she knows to accompany her – especially as she has her child to look after. You must go with her,' he said. 'Go with her as far as Grenoble. She'll be in her own country then. You can leave her there, and come back here immediately.' So off they went, arrived safely in Grenoble, a town a couple of hundred miles south of Geneva, and there La Combe left her with a friend who lived there. But he spoke no more of her going on to Paris.

'I believe God has a work for you to do here,' he told her. 'I think you should remain here.' Accommodation was found for her in a widow's home, her little girl, about whose lack of a suitable French education she had been worried, was placed in a convent, and she herself settled down to what she expected to be a quiet and secluded life. It was what she always longed for.

But solitude did not last long. Unknown to herself, her reputation had gone before her, and when it was known she had come to Grenoble the city was agog with the news. She was actually here, this wealthy widow who had given away a fortune, helped to found a hospital in Thonon, and whose personal conversations with a variety of people were said to have brought them in touch with God! To her great surprise she started receiving calls from those who had heard of her, and wished to meet her. Then it was that she realised what was happening to her.

'I at once became aware of a gift of God, which had been communicated to me without my understanding it, namely, the discernment of spirits, and the giving to each what was suitable to him. I discerned the state of the souls of the persons who spoke to me, and that with such facility that they were astonished and said one to the other that I gave each that of which he was in need.

'It was You, O my God, who did all these things!

'They sent each other to me. It reached such a point that ordinarily from six in the morning till eight in the evening I was occupied in speaking of God. People came from all sides, from far and near – monks, priests, men of the world, girls, women and widows – all came, the one after the other, and God gave me wherewith to satisfy all in an admirable manner, without my taking any thought, or paying any attention to it.'

The effect of what she said to them, sometimes even her silences, was evident.

'God gave them great graces and worked marvellous changes . . . I saw monks of different orders and priests of merit, to whom our Lord gave great graces; and God gave grace to all, without exception – at least, to all who came in good faith.'

Inevitably there were some who did not come in good faith. One day a little group came to catch her out in her words. Although she did not know who they were, or what were their motives, she found herself unable to say anything to them, and they eventually went off to report that the woman was quite stupid, she hadn't a thing to say. Some time later one of her friends arrived in a hurry, and exclaimed, 'Oh, I couldn't get here soon enough! I wanted to warn you not to say anything to those people. They were sent to spy on you.'

'Our Lord has been beforehand with your kindness,' replied Madame Guyon with a twinkle. 'I wasn't able to say a word to them!'

She was in Grenoble for about two years, and it was a golden period in her life. She was the centre of a spiritual revival, the effects of which were evident in many circles of society.

'I have never in my life had so much consolation in seeing in that little town so many good souls who vied with each other in giving themselves to God with their whole heart. There were young girls of twelve or thirteen years of age, who worked all day in silence in order to converse with God. As they were poor girls, those who knew how to read out something to those who could not. It was a revival of the innocence of the early Christians.

'There was a poor washerwoman who had five children and a husband paralysed in the right arm, but more halt in his spirit than in his body; he had no strength except to beat her. Nevertheless this poor woman, with the sweetness of an angel, endured it all, and gained subsistence for that man and her five children. This woman had a wonderful gift of prayer, preserving the presence of God and equanimity in the greatest miseries and poverty.'

It was not only among the lower classes of society that Madame Guyon's emphasis on personal and private prayer was having its effect. Among the members of the upper classes in Grenoble, too, were many who came to her, and among them one, a counsellor of the Parliament, who remained her staunch friend and who was instrumental in bringing her teaching before a much wider public. It all happened in quite a casual way. He came to see her one day, noticed a manuscript entitled *A Method of Prayer* on her table, and glancing through it, asked if he might borrow it. She had written it months before, she told him, and used it to help some of the people who came to her. He brought it back to her a short time later, telling her that he had shown it to several of his friends, all of whom wanted a copy of it, and he asked her permission to have it printed. Nothing could be printed without royal consent, but this approbation was duly obtained, and she was asked to write a preface to it. So her first book was published, and the first edition ran out in no time. Some of the monks she had been in touch with took fifteen hundred copies outright, and the little publication found its way into the hands of people she had never heard of, and to places she never expected to visit. It was a great success.

No one could have foreseen the troubles it would cause her. Private and personal prayer was seen by some as a threat to the Establishment. There is something almost ludicrous in the fact that the trouble started in Grenoble, not because of the little book, but because of the washerwoman who was known to pray.

It came about in this way. The washerwoman had two friends, one the wife of a shopkeeper, the other of a locksmith, and when there was an opportunity they used to read aloud to her from the Bible. They were amazed at her grasp of what she heard, of the deep insight she had into the

Scriptures that were read to her, and her eloquence in speaking of it. Somehow this reached the ears of a group of monks of a certain order who were all against private prayer.

'These monks sent for this woman, and threatened her if she would not give up prayer, saying it was only for monks, and that she was very audacious to use prayer. She answered them – or, rather, He who taught her, for she was in herself very ignorant – that our Lord had told all to pray; and that He had said, "I say unto you *all*," not specifying either priests of monks; that without prayer she could never support the crosses, nor the poverty she was in; that she had formerly been without prayer, and she was a demon; and that since she used it, she had loved God with all her heart; and therefore to give up prayer was to renounce her salvation, which she never could do.

'She added, let them take twenty persons who have never used prayer, and twenty of those who use it; then, said she, make yourselves acquainted with their lives, and you will see if you have reason in condemning prayer.'

Such a reasonable argument infuriated the monks. They threatened her that she should be refused absolution unless she promised to give up praying. Even that did not shake her. The Lord was her Master, she said, and He would communicate with her in whatever way He pleased.

Highly incensed, they refused her absolution, went on to abuse a tailor who was known as a very godly man and who also prayed, then demanded that all books on prayer should be brought out and burned. They made a great bonfire of them in a public square. They were very pleased with themselves over this. Then they went too far. A Father of the Oratory, well-known in the town and well-liked, was known to pray at evening, and on Sundays made a short and fervent prayer which helped others to learn how to pray, too. The monks beat him up.

That was too much for the townsfolk. If the monks went around terrifying members of the lower orders, it did not matter much, but to attack with sticks a Father of the Oratory! Public opinion was aroused to such an extent that the authorities had to do something about it. They sent for the Bishop of Geneva, who came and protested from the pulpit that he had no part in what had happened, that the monks, in their false zeal, had gone beyond their measure. Things quietened down after that for a time, but inevitably word got around that something was happening in Grenoble. People were praying privately.

Meanwhile, Madame Guyon was brought in touch with some monks of the very order that had created the sensation by their burning of books and beating of prelates. It started with the visit a friar paid her. He had come begging for money, that being his job, but when he discovered that she was ill, he gave her some of his medicines, medicine being a sideline of his. She recovered very quickly, and when they got into conversation, she, as usual, spoke about God, and in a very short time he was explaining to her that he did have a love for God, but that he was so busy he hadn't the time to develop it.

We don't need *time* to love God, she explained. We can love Him and think of Him, whatever we are doing. The friar's attention was arrested. There was that about her which had the same effect on him as on the many others that she met — something which quickened the desire for the spiritual life that she obviously enjoyed. He opened up, confiding in her his feelings, and as she talked to him, gently reminding him of the simplicity of speaking to God in the heart, his spirits revived, and he eventually left her saying, 'You are my true mother.' There were many who called her that, confirming the vision she had had in which she had been told she would be the spiritual mother of multitudes.

The friar did not keep quiet about what had happened. Back in the House to which he was attached, he told some of the monks there about his experience, and they, too, went to Madame Guyon. This reached the ears of the Superior of the

House, and the Master of the novices. That there was an improvement in the dispositions and general behaviour of the monks in question they could not deny, but they were annoyed that it should all have come about through a woman.

'They were vexed that a woman, they said, should be so sought after . . . they only had scorn for the gift which was contained in so miserable a vessel, in place of esteeming only God and His grace, without regard to the baseness of the subject in which he pours it out.'

However, as Madame Guyon gave a great deal to charity, the Superior of the House eventually came to thank her, and in talking with her was so completely won over that he distributed quantities of her little book, for which he and the monks paid themselves. 'It was, then, monks of this same order of whom our Lord made use to establish prayer in I know not how many places, and they carried a hundred times more books on prayer into the places where they went than their brothers had burnt. God appears to me wonderful in these things.'

Meanwhile her personal conversations continued. Some of the confessors complained that their penitents confided more in her than in themselves, while others applauded her. 'It was here one might easily see the difference between those confessors who sought only God in the conduct of souls, and those who sought themselves. The former used to come to see me, and were delighted with the graces which God bestowed on their penitents, without paying attention to the channel of which He made use. The others, on the contrary, secretly moved to stir up the town against me.' Some came to her to argue with her on theological matters, of which she confessed herself to be ignorant. 'Although they were matters beyond my scope, our Lord made me answer with as much correctness as if I had studied them all my life. . . . They went away not only convinced and satisfied, but smitten by God's love.'

When night came and her stream of visitors ceased, she

started writing. She was soaking herself in the Scriptures
now, and could not refrain from passing on what she
discovered.

'I had no book except the Bible, and that alone I used
without searching for anything. When, in writing on the Old
Testament, I took passages from the New to support what I
was saying, it was not that I sought them out but they were
given to me at the same time as the explanation . . . and
exactly the same with the New Testament.

'I wrote with incredible quickness, for the hand could
hardly follow the spirit that dictated.' It took the copyist five
days to copy what she wrote in a single night. A flow of inner
strength sustained her in a remarkable way during that
period in Grenoble. She mentioned having written a commentary on the Song of Solomon in a day and a half, in
addition to interviewing the usual flow of visitors. She was
becoming known as a writer as well as a spiritual counsellor,
and among her other activities was the founding of another
hospital, on similar lines to that in Thonon.

'My enemies have made use of this subsequently to
calumniate me, saying that I had spent my children's
property in establishing hospitals, although the truth is that,
far from having expended their money, I have even given
them my own, and that these hospitals have been established
merely on the capital of divine providence, which is inex-
haustible.' She would have subscribed heartily to the maxim
of a later age that 'God's work, done in God's way, never
lacks God's supplies.'

But she was not to be left in peace in Grenoble. Rumours
began to circulate, letters were received which asserted she
was a sorceress, that she attracted people by magical means,
that she was in league with the devil. Others whispered that
she was an immoral woman, and that as for her gifts to
charity, she used false money. The absurdity of the accusations could not prevent people from talking about them, and
things got to such a pass that some of her friends advised her
to move away from the district for a time, until the storm had

subsided. Without the support of the Bishop of Geneva, in whose diocese Grenoble was situated, she was in a vulnerable position, and the Bishop would do nothing to protect her.

So where was she to go?

Gex, Thonon, Grenoble — she felt like a hot potato in them all. There was just one place where she would be welcome, and that was in Italy. Her friendship with the Marquise de Prunai had revived, and she was receiving warm invitations from her to go back to Turin, as well as from the kindly Bishop of Verceil, urging her to return to his diocese. The obvious thing was to accept this opening, so providentially made again at the time when she needed it. There was only one obstacle in the way of her accepting it.

Father La Combe was still in Verceil. If she went again into the diocese where he was living it would look as though she were running after him, and for the sake of her own reputation as well as his, she was determined to give no occasion for further gossip. So when a leading ecclesiastic suggested she should go to Marseilles, where he assured her there would be a welcome for her, and that he himself would accompany her on the long journey south, she fell in with the idea. She would leave her daughter in the convent, where her education would not suffer through further travels, she would leave the maid from Paris, who was already proving a true colleague, in charge of the child, while she herself would go on to Marseilles.

Humanly speaking, the decision was disastrous. Her little book on prayer had reached Marseilles ahead of her, and had got into the hands of the disciples of Monsieur de St. Cyran the Jansenist. The disciples of Monsieur de St. Cyran had formed one of those groups that seem to emerge from time to time in all ages and among all classes, who are violently opposed to all with whose views they do not agree. They did not agree with Madame Guyon's suggestions as to how to pray. Within hours of her arrival in Marseilles they had created such a disturbance, demanding that the Bishop should drive her away, that she found herself laughing. She remembered how, shortly before she left Grenoble, one of the girls she had helped had come to her in great distress. She had had a nightmare, in which she had seen the Devil. 'Madame Guyon is going away,' he had told the girl, 'But I'll catch her yet. I'll be ahead of her everywhere she goes, and stir things up against her.' He certainly had lost no time in Marseilles, Madame Guyon reflected wryly as she set off to see the Bishop, in response to his summons.

However, the Devil was evidently not so successful with the Bishop as with the disciples of Monsieur de St. Cyran. He proved to be quite cordial, said he had read her book and found it very good, that the disciples of Monsieur de St. Cyran were a perfect nuisance, upsetting everybody, and that by insulting her they had insulted him. He urged her to remain in his diocese, assuring her that he would protect her.

But he could not prevent anonymous letters being written to her, nor malicious rumours from Grenoble being circulated, and after a week of it she decided she could not stay on in Marseilles either. She seemed to have no alternative now but to go to the Marquise de Prunai, and hearing that she could get to Turin via Nice, she decided to go that way.

So she set off on what proved to be the worst journey she ever took in her life. It was uneventful and pleasant enough along the coast road from Marseilles to Nice, but on arrival there she learned to her dismay that she could not travel by litter north to Turin as she had expected. No muleteer was prepared to take her up through those mountains, she was told. Putting up in an inn with her two maids and the ecclesiastic who was accompanying her, she simply did not know what to do.

'I saw myself without refuge or retreat, wandering and vagabond. All the workers I saw in their little shops appeared to me happy in having a dwelling place and a refuge, and I found nothing in the world so hard for a person

like me, who naturally loved honour, as this wandering life.'
She remembered the words with which she had been
impressed, spoken by Jesus Christ, about foxes having their
holes, birds their nests, but the Son of Man being without a
home, and she felt that she was partaking very acutely of
those sufferings. She had been prepared for ignominy, but
that did not save her from the sense of shame that accompanied it. As she walked through the streets and markets of
Nice, by the sparkling blue waters of the Mediterranean, she
thought she knew the depth of the bitterness of homelessness.
But worse was to follow.

She was told, unexpectedly, of a way whereby she could
reach the Marquise. 'A small sloop is going to Genoa
tomorrow. It will only take a day to get there,' she was told,
'and as it passes by Savona you can be landed there if you
like. It will be easy for you to get a litter in Savona to take you
to Turin.'

The little party boarded the sloop with their baggage, and
as they sailed away Madame Guyon found herself longing
for: 'A little hole in a rock, to place myself there and to live
separated from all creatures. I pictured to myself that a
desert island would have ended all my disgraces . . .' When a
storm arose, and the others were crying out with fear, she was
quite calm and intrepid. They could not understand it, and
perhaps gave her credit for a faith she could not, in all
honesty, have claimed at that time. It was her longing to be
done with life, to be engulfed by the sea, that made her so
indifferent to the danger they were in.

Instead of the voyage taking a day, as had been claimed,
they were on that sloop for eleven days, battered by the wind
and waves. They could not disembark at Savona, and had to
go on to Genoa, and here they encountered storms of a
different nature. The Genonese, being Italian, did not like
the French, who had bombarded their city a few months
previously. The arrival of a Frenchwoman who looked like
an aristocrat, accompanied by a couple of maids and an
ecclesiastic, all of them pretty bedraggled, and none of them

speaking much Italian, aroused contempt and cupidity, but
no mercy. They were jeered at, insulted, and the innkeeper
who agreed to take them in charged as much per person as it
would have cost for the whole party in a good hotel in Paris.
Madame Guyon saw such inroads being made on her
finances, that she would soon be without money – and in a
country which if not actually at war with her own, was at
least in a state of cold hostility.

And it was the beginning of Holy Week. Unless she could
reach the haven of the Marquise's home before Good Friday,
she would be stranded in Genoa for several days. The Doge
had departed, and seemed to have taken all the available
litters in the city with him, and she was at her wits' end when
she was told of a muleteer who would convey her in his litter
(at a price) as far as Verceil.

Could he go no farther? Could he not take her to the estate
of the Marquise de Prunai? No! He did not know where the
Marquise de Prunai lived, so that was that. He could take her
to Verceil but no farther. Take it or leave it!

She had no alternative but to accept, though when she
saw the evil-faced muleteer and his two lame mules, her
heart sank. As for what Father La Combe's reaction
would be to her unheralded arrival, right in the middle of
Holy Week, with all its extra ceremonies and services, its
festivals and fasts, she scarcely dared to speculate. In fact,
that worried her almost more than anything now, and
concern that he should be warned of her arrival made her
decide to take the risk of travelling without the protection
and help of the ecclesiastic. She would send him on
ahead, so that he could arrive a day or two before her, and
notify the Bishop who, after all, had originally invited her,
that her plans had been changed, and that she was coming.
The ecclesiastic, conscious of his unpopularity as a
Frenchman in Italy, set off alone, while Madame Guyon and
the two maids, seated in the litter, rumbled out of Genoa
unescorted.

It was unconventional, to say the least. Three woman

travelling without the presence of an ecclesiastic to add respectability to their entourage, were laying themselves open to insult – and worse. Their muleteer made no attempt to disguise his scorn, and when nightfall came, instead of taking them to an inn, brought the litter to a halt outside a mill, opened the door on to a room where some men were already settling down for the night, and told them they could stay there.

'Here! In a room with those men! Certainly not!' Madame Guyon, the two maids cowering behind her, rose to her full height and indignantly refused to enter. 'Take us to an inn at once!' But the muleteer refused. He knew he had the upper hand, and intended to use it. He was going on no further, he said, and if the three women didn't want to spend the night in the mill, they could make their own way to the inn. At ten o'clock at night, therefore, the three of them, carrying their hand-baggage, stumbled out into the darkness, the muleteer shouting and jeering after them.

'I bore my humiliation with pleasure,' she wrote, adding candidly, 'but not without seeing or feeling it. But Your will, my God, and my abandonment to it, made everything easy to me.' It was in these extremities of fortune that the deep inner peace sustained her.

Mercifully, they were well received at the inn. 'Those good people did their best to refresh us from our fatigue, assuring us that the place where we had been taken was very dangerous. The next day we had again to return on foot to find the litter, the man refusing to bring it to us.' To crown it all, he refused to go on any further, and forced her to go on by post chaise, instead of in a private vehicle.

The arrival of the post chaise with its three female passengers at a frontier town was the occasion for further humiliation. The postillion drew up, as usual, at the inn, but when the mistress of the house heard he had three women as passengers, she stoutly refused to admit them. The argument that ensued between them drew a crowd, including some officers from the garrison, who heard the innkeeper assert that she would have no prostitutes in her establishment.

'She's not a prostitute,' argued the postillion. 'She's a very good woman – very religious. Her maids are respectable girls, too. You've got no reason not to take them in. Come and see them for yourself.' At last she was persuaded to do so, and as happened not infrequently, one look at Madame Guyon was sufficient to make her change her mind. She saw a demurely-clad middle-aged woman with a black hood shielding a face from which the pockmarks had subsided, still beautiful in contour, but completely devoid of make-up, and with such an expression of evident goodness that the mistress of the inn was won over.

'Come in,' she said. 'But lock yourselves in this room. If my son knows you are here he'll kill you. We had a lot of trouble here a few days ago. A bad woman murdered a very respectable man in this house, and it has cost us a lot of money. My son vowed he'd kill any other woman who lodged here, he was so angry about it. Lock yourselves in and don't make a sound. You must get away tomorrow without him seeing you.'

Thus ignominiously did they depart, and not much more dignified was their arrival at an inn at Verceil. On the eve of Good Friday unannounced guests were not very welcome, especially when they proved to be three travel-stained Frenchwomen who could speak very little Italian. The innkeeper's attitude changed when he learned that Madame Guyon was acquainted with Father La Combe, who was well known and greatly respected in the neighbourhood, but Father La Combe himself, when he met her, could not conceal his dismay. The unfortunate ecclesiastic whom she had sent on ahead had only just arrived, having had a very bad time of it on the road, so La Combe, during the busiest week in the year, suddenly found himself saddled with an added problem, and an embarrassment.

'People will say you've come here after me!' he said irritably. It was just what Madame Guyon herself feared, and she offered to leave immediately and go she knew not where, but he waved the foolish suggestion aside, and continued, 'I don't know how to tell the Bishop you've arrived. He's invited you to come three times, and you've refused, and he's stopped enquiring about you. What he'll think about your turning up like this, I don't know!' Father La Combe was obviously fed up with her, and that was the worst blow of all, as her autobiography revealed.

'It was then, it seemed to me, that I was cast out from the surface of the earth, and that all creatures were combined together to crush me. I spent the rest of the night in this inn, without being able to sleep, and without knowing what course I should be compelled to take, persecuted as I was by my enemies, and a subject of shame to my friends.'

She reached rock bottom that night. She had believed she could bear shame and ignominy when, in her ardour, she had asked for it, longing for the opportunity to prove her devotion to her God. When it came in this form, she found she had nothing to say, expect that it was the outcome of her own decision. Her eagerness to save herself from the accusation that she was running after Father La Combe, which was at the back of her decision to go to Marseilles rather than to the Marquise, had landed her in a worse situation than if she had accepted the providential opening in the first place.

However, she was not left in that state. The following day the Bishop, on learning that she had arrived, sent his niece to bring her into her own home and there, although she became seriously ill for a time, she was treated with respect and appreciation. The Bishop proved himself a true friend, and one who genuinely supported her.

'One could not be under greater obligation than I was to this good prelate. He conceived as much friendship for me as if I had been his sister, and in the midst of his continual occupation, his sole diversion was to spend a half-hour with me, speaking about God.' He wanted her to remain in his diocese, hoping she might help him to form a community there, but her ill health made that obviously impossible, and eventually, on the advice of her doctors, she decided to return to Paris.

But not before paying a visit to the Marquise de Prunai. It is worthy of note that during the short time she spent with her, she inspired and helped her hostess to found a little hospital, similar to those started in Thonon and Grenoble, passing on her recipes for simple remedies, and teaching her how to compound ointments.

In the welter of her experiences in the realms of the spirit, that brought her eventually on to the stage of world history, Madame Guyon's practical achievements were usually overlooked, not only by others, but also by herself. She referred to them almost as an afterthought in her auto-biography. 'I nearly forgot to mention that we started a little hospital . . .'

Two other occurrences of those last few weeks in Italy affected her far more deeply. One was the arrival of an affectionate letter from the Duchess of Charost, with whom she had almost completely lost touch. This renewed contact with her old friend, now living in Versailles, was a comfort as she prepared to proceed, with many misgivings, to Paris. She had little idea of how much she was to owe to that renewed contact in the years that lay ahead.

The other occurrence was of a different nature, and was to have a different outcome. It was an order to Father La Combe from the Superior of the Barnabites to proceed to Paris. The order went further. He was instructed to escort Madame Guyon to that city.

At the instigation of Father de la Mothe this arrangement was made. The reason he gave was that there was a great need in the capital for preachers of Father La Combe's calibre. It was not right that such a man should be left in Italy, where his eloquence would be wasted. Father de la Mothe further suggested that as his sister, who was in poor health, had to come to Paris, Father La Combe should be the ecclesiastic to accompany her, and so the Barnabite House in Paris, already poor, would be saved the expense of bringing him there. Once again the very thing they both wanted to avoid was thrust upon them. They were to travel together.

They arrived in Paris on the eve of St. Magdalene's Day, exactly five years after Madame Guyon had set off for Geneva.

About the same time, away in Rome, a Spanish priest named Molinos was being brought before the Inquisition.

The Joy of the Cross

Self-love no grace in sorrow sees,
Consults her own peculiar ease;
   'Tis all the bliss she knows:
But nobler aims pure Love employ;
In self-denial is her joy,
   In suffering her repose.

Jesus, Avenger of our fall . . .
Oh tell me – life is in Thy voice –
How much afflictions were Thy choice,
   And sloth and ease Thy scorn!

Thy choice and mine shall be the same;
Inspirer of that holy flame
   Which must for ever blaze!
To take the Cross and follow Thee,
Where love and duty lead, shall be
   My portion and my praise.

Jeanne de la Mothe Guyon

8

Imprisoned in Paris

The ecclesiastical climate in France, which had been electric for years, had broken in a storm at last. With the revocation of the Edict of Nantes, which had ensured religious liberty for the Huguenots, who were Protestants, these now found themselves at the mercy of the dragoons. Their churches were destroyed. Soldiers could be billeted in their homes and make free with anything – and anyone – they found in them. Unless their officers put restrictions on them, no one else dared to do so. Tens of thousands of Huguenots had already fled the country, and more of them were on the move, while those who remained were under constant pressure to be converted to the Roman Catholic faith. Only so could their civil rights be assured. Anyone suspected of having Protestant sympathies was liable to be branded as a heretic, and there was tension in all the religious groups that were not strictly orthodox. The Quietists, similar in many ways to the Puritans in England, were in particular viewed with suspicion. Although Madame Guyon had never joined them, her views, and her emphasis on the development of the inner life of the soul, were in many ways similar to theirs, and she was considered to be one of them.

The political climate in France was electric, too. With Protestant Europe up in arms at the treatment being meted out to the Huguenots, Louis was all the more eager to maintain good relations with Rome, though determined to assert the right of the Gallican Church as outlined in 'The Declaration of the Clergy of France' in 1682. In such an atmosphere it was not difficult for astute persons to bring about the downfall of those against whom they had a grudge, as Madame Guyon and Father La Combe were soon to find.

Even as they travelled towards Paris their spirits were oppressed by a sense of impending tragedy.

'All along the road something within said to me the same words as St. Paul: "I go up to Jerusalem and the Spirit tells me everywhere that crosses and chains await me." I could not prevent myself expressing it to my most familar friends, who used their efforts to stop me on the road,' Madame Guyon reported.

'What do you want to go there for?' she was asked in Grenoble, where she had gone to collect her daughter and the maid. 'To be crucified? Don't go to Paris! Don't go!' But go on she must, impelled by the same inner conviction as sent the apostle Paul to Jerusalem.

With Father La Combe it was the same. 'Would it not be a fine thing, and very glorious to God, if he desired to make us in that great city serve as a spectacle to men and angels!' he said. Theirs was the true spirit of martyrdom.

Actually, things went very well for La Combe at first. He was given important preaching assignments, and his eloquence and evident sincerity had people flocking to hear him. His star was in the ascendant, and had it not been for Father de la Mothe it might well have continued so.

Father de la Mothe, however, had different plans for his junior colleague, whose success as a preacher stirred his jealousy, and whose close friendship with his half-sister stirred his avarice. She still had an income on which he would have liked to lay hands, and Father La Combe, as her spiritual director, could have instructed her to hand it over. This he had refused to do. Furthermore, he was handling a financial matter for her of which Father de la Mothe disapproved. It had to do with the girl Madame Guyon had saved from sexual involvement with the little Bishop in Gex. She felt herself responsible for the girl, as it was due to her influence that she had now left the new Catholic convent in Gex and was seeking admittance into another Order. Madame Guyon knew the value of a dowry in such circumstances. 'As she is beautiful, although extremely discreet, there is always ground for fear when one is exposed without a fixed settlement.' So she had deposited a sum of money for that purpose with Father La Combe, and Father de la Mothe let him know that if he did not persuade Madame Guyon to give it instead for a wall he himself wanted built in his own monastery, there would be trouble.

'But Father La Combe, always upright, said that he could not conscientiously advise me to do anything else than what he knew I had resolved to do in favour of the girl.'

On such a trivial matter (the sum of money was not great) Father La Combe's fate was apparently sealed. Father de la Mothe, already prejudiced against him, got to work to bring about his downfall.

Father La Combe, he told his fellow Barnabites, was a disgrace to their Order. It was a scandal that he had actually stayed in inns with Madame Guyon on their journey to Paris, instead of going to spend the night at the Barnabite monasteries en route. (He did not mention that there were no Barnabite monasteries en route). Furthermore, Father La Combe was a Savoyard, and the yoke of the Savoyards in their Order should be shaken off. It was an insult to the French nation that every six years a Savoyard should be made Provincial of the Barnabites, he said.

Then rumours were circulated that Father La Combe's theology was wrong, that he was connected with the Spanish priest Molinos, the leader of the Quietists, who had just been tried and found guilty of heresy, and charged with immorality into the bargain.

Father La Combe's theology had already been passed as correct when he was called to Rome, and he had Attestations to that effect, which would have exonerated him from the charge of heresy. The suave Father de la Mothe, on the pretext that he wanted to show them to the Archbishop of Paris, and thereby prove La Combe's orthodoxy, obtained possession of the precious documents. They were never seen again.

The next step was to make representations to the King

himself. Father La Combe was suspected of heresy. A *lettre de cachet* was issued ordering Father La Combe not to go outside the Barnabite House until he had been questioned by the ecclesiastical chancellor. But Father de la Mothe saw to it that Father La Combe was not told of the royal order. He therefore went about his duties in the usual way, and when news reached him that one of his penitents had been knocked down by a cart, he went, as requested, to her to receive her confession.

That was sufficient. His absence was reported. He had disobeyed the King's order! He was arrested, and sent to the Bastille.

Although he had known nothing about the *lettre de cachet* and its orders, he was not taken by surprise. For weeks he had been conscious of Father de la Mothe's suppressed antagonism, and knew what it might lead to. 'The weather is very lowering,' he wrote significantly in a letter to Madame Guyon during that period. 'I do not know when the thunderbolts will fall, but all will be welcome from the hand of God.' and one day, when she went as usual to his confessional, he managed to tell her that he found himself longing for the 'disgrace and ignominy' that he sensed awaited him.

'I am going to say the Mass,' he said. 'Listen to it – and sacrifice me to God, as I myself am going to sacrifice myself to Him.' It was his conscious act of submission to the will of God.

The solemnity of those quiet moments in the confessional box, when the monk from the hills of Savoy murmured the familiar words of the Mass, and the woman whose spirit was knit to his knelt with her head bowed, must have been not unlike that which reigned in Gethsemane.

They never met again. Five days later came his arrest, and she knew her own hour would soon come.

It came after a period of tension and humiliation, mainly caused by Father de la Mothe. Pretending concern for her, he told her she also was under suspicion and urged her to flee from Paris, back to Montargis. This she refused to do, saying that flight would be tantamount to acknowledging her guilt, and would further implicate Father La Combe. Then he tried to incite the Archbishop of Paris against her, but she was so ably and loyally defended by the guardian of her children, a Councillor of Parliament, that that attempt to incriminate her failed too.

Meanwhile, rumours reflecting on her moral character were being spread abroad, and especially her connection with La Combe.

'Everyone cried out against me, except those who knew me personally, and knew how far removed I was from those things,' she wrote. 'But the others accused me of heresy, sacrilege, infamies of every kind, the nature of which I am even ignorant of, of hypocrisy, knavery. When I was at church I heard people behind me ridiculing me, and once I heard priests say that I ought to be thrown out of the church.' It was in circumstances like this that her spirit so often soared rather than sank. 'I cannot express how content I was inwardly, leaving myself entirely without reserve to God, quite ready to suffer the last penalty if such was His will.' But she had her periods of deep depression too, when she felt herself forsaken by God as well as by man, and despairingly abandoned herself to the eternal separation which she felt her sinful nature merited. Once again she fell ill, with headaches which nearly drove her crazy, and a violent cough.

Meanwhile Father de la Mothe, having failed to get her in his power by becoming her spiritual director (she stead-fastedly refused to accept him in this capacity) devised a plan whereby she should be put in detention. The King was informed that she was a heretic, that she had constant correspondence with Molinos – 'I, who did not know there was such a person as Molinos in the world until I learned it in the *Gazette*!' – that she had written a dangerous book and to cap it all, that she held secret assemblies. All her teaching on prayer and the cultivation of the inner life had been done on a one to one basis, but from Father de la Mothe's point of view, they were secret assemblies. On the shaky foundation of this last accusation a great many people she had never seen or even heard about were exiled, including one man whose sole crime was having been heard to remark that her little book on prayer was very good.

The holding of secret assemblies constituted a threat to public security in the tense atmosphere of those days. To reinforce this particular accusation a letter purporting to have been written by her was forged, in which she said she had great designs, but that the arrest of Father La Combe had endangered them, that she no longer held assemblies in her own house, as she was too closely watched, but that she would hold them elsewhere.

'It was on this fictitious letter, which was shown to His Majesty, that the order to imprison me was given.' On the Eve of St. Francis de Sales, in January 1688, she was sent to a convent in a suburb of Paris, where she was shut up alone in a small room with only a hard-faced nun to bring her meals and report on what she did. The worst of it, from her point of view, was the complete separation from her daughter, with whom no correspondence was to be allowed, and of whom no news would reach her. In this state of isolation she was kept until the time of her first interrogation.

*　　　*　　　*

Madame Guyon usually acquitted herself very well when she was brought before interrogators and judges. The latent ability which had revealed itself when, as a young married woman, she had dealt successfully with the demand from Monsieur for the payment of a debt she had never incurred, when as a widow she had straightened out her husband's tangled affairs, was brought into play when she had to defend her faith and her activities. The only times when she failed were when, through anxiety to do and say the right things, she became taut and watchful of her own reactions. She blamed herself for this, and learned to commit herself, her words and her reactions to God as she went to answer the questions that would be fired at her. Time and time again she was to prove the reliability of the promise Christ made to his disciples when he warned them they would be arrested and brought to trial, and then said, 'Settle it therefore in your minds not to meditate beforehand how to answer, for I will give you a mouth and wisdom which none of your adversaries will be able to withstand or contradict.'

She was in a good position to stand on that assurance, for she had nothing to hide, and a carelessness of what happened to her freed her from tension. She went to the first interrogation calmly, to face a Doctor of the Sorbonne and an official. Polite preliminaries over, they started their questioning.

Her association with Father La Combe was the first subject to be raised.

'Did not Father La Combe take you with him from France to Savoy?'

'No. He could not possibly have accompanied me when I went to Savoy. He had not been in France for ten years when I went there.'

'But he has taught you the practice of prayer, has he not?'

'It is not Father La Combe who has taught me to pray. I have practised prayer from my youth, long before I knew him. Actually, I never even met him until he came to my husband's home bringing a letter to me from my half-brother, Father de la Mothe. I did not see him again for ten years, when I left France and went to Savoy.'

The Doctor of the Sorbonne, who was merely performing his official duty in interrogating her, put an end to that part of the discussion. There was no point in pursuing it when the facts could be so easily verified.

'There is no ground here for a serious enquiry,' he said firmly. 'Let us pass on to the next question. Madame, this book entitled *Short and Easy Method of Prayer* written under your name. Is it not true that Father La Combe really wrote it?'

'No, he did not. I wrote it myself. He was not even in the neighbourhood when I wrote it. He was in Verceil, in Italy.

I was in Grenoble in France. I had no thought of its being published,' she continued. 'That happened when a friend of mine, a Counsellor of Grenoble, saw the manuscript on my table one day when he came to visit me, and asked if he might read it. As he found it helpful, he asked me to allow it to be printed. He asked me to write a preface and divide it into chapters, which I did one afternoon. Father La Combe had nothing to do with it.'

Father La Combe's name was dropped from the interrogations after that. The contents of the book itself would now be examined, she was told.

Her reaction was prompt and disarming. She was glad that it should be examined. She had never intentionally departed from the faith of the Holy Church, she declared. She would, indeed, give her life for it. She had already submitted the little book to the theologians, and was prepared to do so again. She had had no theological training, and could readily understand if some of the expressions she had used needed correction. All she had wanted to do was to help people who did not know how to pray.

'But do you not want to do away with the vocal prayers said in church?' her interrogators asked, and pointed to a place in which she had advocated the quiet, slow recital of the Lord's Prayer in private as being worth more than repeating it automatically many times aloud.

'But to teach a prayer with attention and application to one's own condition is not to do away with prayer. On the contrary, it establishes prayer, and makes it sincere.'

The Doctor of the Sorbonne nodded. He had no fault to find with that. 'If you had explained yourself like this in the book itself, you would not be here,' he said, after raising several other points, all of which she answered to his satisfaction.

'But the explanations *are* there,' she protested. 'You will find them at the end of each chapter. If there is anything wrong with them, you should not hold me responsible, but the doctors who approved and passed them!'

She had won another round, and the interrogations took

another line. The men arrived for the fourth time, this time with a letter which the official read aloud to her. It was the forged letter, of which she knew nothing until she listened to what she was supposed to have written to a Father Francis, of whom she had never heard.

'My Father, do not come to see me at the Cloister of Notre Dame. I am being watched, and can no longer hold assemblies at the usual place.' The letter went on to refer to plans against the State, and ended with the significant words, 'I do not sign because of the evil times.'

'There!' said the official with an air of finality. 'You can see, Madame, that after a letter like this there was good reason to put you in prison.'

'Yes, sir,' she answered. Then she added drily, 'If I had written it!'

'But you did write it.'

'No, I did not. Anyone who knows me would tell you it is not in my style, nor in my handwriting. It is a forgery.'

'Then we must find out who the forger is!' said the official contemptuously.

'It is the scribe Gautier,' replied Madame Guyon. She had heard about that man's secret profession from his own wife, and from the official's start of surprise she perceived that she had hit the nail on the head. She perceived something else, too. The guilty way in which he folded up the letter and said they would say no more about it convinced her that what she had already suspected was a fact. But the official was in league with Father de la Mothe, and with the affair in his hands there was little hope that she would be exonerated. The Doctor of the Sorbonne, his duty in taking part in the interrogations fulfilled, put in a good word for her, but it had no effect. She remained imprisoned in the convent, and occupied her time in writing poetry, letters to friends, and what was to prove of even greater interest to posterity, her autobiography.

The thought of La Combe was persistent as she wrote it. He had urged her years ago to do it, and she had been reluctant to obey at the time. Now it seemed to be the one practical thing she could do to demonstrate her submission to him as her spiritual director, and also to vindicate him by relating the truth about their association. From the confinement of the little convent cell where she spent months alone, came the strange medley of incidents and experiences, dreams and visions, homilies and prayers which were to bewilder and mystify, challenge and inspire her readers for centuries to come. While others were busying themselves with her affairs outside, she was producing something which would go on speaking long after the strident voices of her enemies had been silenced and forgotten.

When the official interrogations were over her long periods of solitary confinement were interspersed with interviews of another character. She had feared for her daughter, and when writing to one friend ended her letter with the touching words, 'When I came here my daughter was taken from me. Those who took her from me do not allow me to know where she is. You will permit me, if you can obtain a knowledge of her situation, to ask your friendly interest on her behalf.' Her fears were not without foundation, for she was approached with suggestions that she should consent to the girl being married to a nephew of the Archbishop of Paris. If she would agree to the marriage, she was told, she would be set free within a week.

Madame Guyon knew enough about the man proposed as her son-in-law to refuse the suggestion out of hand.

'I said I would not purchase my liberty at the price of sacrificing my daughter; that I was content to remain in prison as long as it should please our Lord.' They tried more than once to wrest her consent from her, but she adamantly resisted. On other occasions she was urged to write a confession that she had been wrong in some of her views, and that she had been unduly influenced in them by Father La Combe.

'I would rather die than tell such a falsehood!' was her reply. She had heard that Father La Combe had been very kindly treated in the Bastille, and that when he had been transferred elsewhere the commandant in charge of him had recognised his godliness.

'Consequently the commandant, full of love for the truth, wrote that this Father was a man of God, and that he begged some alleviation of his imprisonment might be granted.' That letter reached the Archbishop of Paris, who showed it to Father de la Mothe – and La Combe was taken off to a desert isle, out of reach of the commandant who favoured him. 'O God, nothing is concealed from you. Will you for long leave your servant in ignominy and grief?' she wrote feelingly. The last thing she was likely to do was betray the trust of one with whom she was so one in spirit as La Combe. On the face of it, his lot was harder than hers. Although she sometimes felt that all her friends had deserted her, and that she would be incarcerated in the convent for life, she had evidence from time to time that there were those in influential positions who were loyal to her, and working for her release. La Combe had no such assurance. The Barnabite from Savoy had no friends in court in Paris, and the evidence that should have told in his favour, those Attestations from Rome, had been suppressed. For him was reserved the honour accorded to those referred to in the book of Hebrews, as being those of whom the world was not worthy. As Madame Guyon wrote, 'only eternity will show who have been the true friends of God.'

Meanwhile, a series of events in no way related to her was taking place in the court of France itself, which were to lead to her deliverance from an entirely unexpected quarter. Madame de Maintenon, by now the morganatic wife of King Louis XIV, and the most powerful woman in the kingdom, took up the cudgels on her behalf. This is how it came about.

Madame de Maintenon, having made a moral man of the King, and setting the example of piety in a court that had been renowned for its corruption, took little interest in its social activities, and showed herself there but seldom. She provided the King with a comfortable domestic life, and when he was not performing his kingly duties he was usually to be found in her apartment, whence he retreated, like any other happily married man, when it was time to go home. Her own personal preoccupation, however, was not to be found in the palace of Versailles, which held out little attraction for her. The darling project of her heart was in the establishment of what amounted to a sort of boarding school for girls of noble birth whose fathers were in what might be termed reduced circumstances. At St. Cyr they would receive a good education and practise a devout life. It was something new, and she was responsible for bringing it into being. She appointed the staff, was consulted on all matters concerning it, and took a personal interest in the pupils.

One of them was a pretty little girl who was likely to be rather homesick, so Madame de Maintenon suggested that her older sister, a canoness, should join the staff in order to be near the child. Now it so happened that the canoness was a first cousin of Madame Guyon's, knew of the injustice of her imprisonment, and seized an opportunity to speak to Madame de Maintenon about her. Nothing came of it at the time, but her name was introduced.

Then Madame de Maintenon heard it again, this time from a personal friend who had gone to visit the prioress of the very convent where Madame Guyon was imprisoned, and came back with a surprisingly good report of her. The prioress and her nuns, who had been filled with righteous indignation at what they had heard of the heresies and the immoral behaviour of their prisoner, had all changed their minds. They could not speak highly enough of her piety, her sincerity, her humility, her love for God. They simply did not believe the tales that had been told about her.

Finally, a relative of Madame de Maintenon herself, an abbess, had come to Paris on business matters, one of which concerned the young nun from the New Catholics in Gex. The abbess was very annoyed with the Archbishop of Paris, and said so. The girl was to enter her Order, Madame Guyon was prepared to pay her dowry, but Madame Guyon was imprisoned in a convent, and the abbess could not get at her.

The Archbishop of Paris refused to allow anyone to see her. 'It is a business of charity Madame Guyon is doing in favour of a poor girl, whom I want to make a nun in my House, and the Archbishop is hindering it. I can't get that dowry. It is very unjust,' said the abbess.

This got things moving at last. Madame de Maintenon compiled the facts of the case, then brought them before the king. The accusations brought against this woman had never been proved, and yet she was still being held a prisoner. The king shrugged his shoulders, and ordered the Archbishop to set her at liberty. The Archbishop hummed and hawed a bit, saying certain formalities must be observed first, but though he managed to delay things for a few days, he had to yield to the command of His Majesty. When the day came for her release, the guardian of her children came to take her to the home of Madame de Maintenon's personal friend, where she was re-united with her family. To crown it all, a thoroughly suitable marriage was arranged for her daughter. She was betrothed to the Count of Vaux, a relative of her old friend, the Duchess of Charost.

The tide had turned for Madame Guyon, and she would not have been human if she had not been thankful for it. All the same, her friends and well-wishers exhibited greater relief and excitement than she herself, and in her auto-biography she wrote a strangely revealing little sentence, 'I had more perceptible joy on entering my prison than on leaving it.' Inner peace and joy, she had proved, are not dependent on circumstances. But there was something about the whole affair which kindled her amazement as she looked back to those early days in Gex, remembering her anxiety over the young nun, and then the steps she took on her behalf to ensure her security.

'I marvelled, O my God, at Your divine providence, and the special evidences of Your control. This same money, which has been the first source of all my troubles, through Father de la Mothe's desire to have it, You have made, O my God, the means of my liberty!'

I think we should be careful, in stating the doctrine of faith, not to place it in opposition to reason. On the contrary, we only say what is sustained both by St. Paul and St. Augustine, when we assert that it is a very reasonable thing to believe. Faith is different from mere physical and emotive impulse; and it would be no small mistake to confound those who walk by faith, with thoughtless and impulsive persons and enthusiasts.

Faith is necessarily based upon antecedent acts of intelligence. By the use of these powers of perception and reasoning, which God has given us, we have the knowledge of the existence of God. It is by their use, also, that we know that God has spoken to us in His revealed word . . . And it is our duty, in the exercise of faith in the goodness and wisdom of Him who issues the command, to yield obedience, and to go wherever it may lead us, however dark and mysterious the path may now appear.

Francis S. Fenelon, Paris, August 11th, 1689,
in a letter written to Madame Guyon

9

Enter Fenelon

The Abbé de Fenelon, tall, courteous, immaculately dressed, every inch an aristocrat, was on his way to Paris from Poitou, whither he had been sent to convert the Protestants in the neighbourhood to the Roman Catholic faith. He had gone willingly enough, but on one condition – that the militia were to be withdrawn. He would have in his area no dragoons invading Huguenot homes, roasting the men before the fire, rifling their coffers, raping the women-folk, all in the name of religion. The gentle Abbé was horrified at such tactics, and would have none of them. If people could not be convinced inwardly, their conversion would be utterly false and worth nothing. He had set about convincing them by his quietly persuasive arguments, his eloquent preaching; more than anything, perhaps, by his own unselfconscious goodness. If his task had been made the easier by the undeniable fact that converts to the faith would regain the civil rights they had lost with the revocation of the Edict of Nantes, that was through no conniving on his part. Nor did he hold it out as a reason for accepting the primacy of the Pope along with the Holy Scriptures. His success in Poitou was due to no outward violence or inward subversion, and the ecclesiastical world in France and beyond knew it, and approved. The Abbé de Fenelon was recognised as an up and coming ecclesiastic in that year of grace, 1688, destined for a high position in the Catholic hierarchy.

If similar ideas concerning his career had presented themselves to him, he would have thrust them from him in shame. His aim was to follow His Master, share His ignominy, suffer with Him, not to gain earthly promotion, even in the Church. The mystical streak in his nature drew him towards the fathomless depths and heights of a spiritual relationship of oneness with the eternal. This was the goal towards which he strove, and he refused to be diverted towards anything else. He was familiar with the writings of the mystics, St. John of the Cross and St. Francis de Sales among them. But he was on his guard against the heresies that could so easily insinuate themselves into the teachings of the uninstructed and viewed with reservation the Quietists, whose leader, Molinos, was still in the news, on trial before the Inquisition. For this reason his interest in a woman of whom he had heard, a Madame Guyon who was reputedly secretly one of them, and whose influence on many of the people he knew had surprised him, was tempered with a fear lest both her theology and her moral character were faulty.

As his way back to Paris led through her home town, Montargis, he made some discreet enquiries about her, and found her reputation there was beyond reproach. She was known to be very devout, extremely generous to the poor, and her gentleness and patience under great provocation had gained for her the name of a saint. He went on to Paris with his interest in her quickened, though he was cautious enough to keep quiet about it when he met his fellow-clerics, especially those like Bossuet whom he had loved and admired from his youth. Bossuet, he had reason to know, had little sympathy with the Quietists. In fact, he realised that he was more likely to hear about her from members of the laity, like the Dukes of Beauvilliers and Chevreuse, or the Duchess of Charost, all friends of his.

Eventually it was through the Duchess that he first met her personally. The Duchess invited him to her home to meet Madame Guyon, an old friend of hers, with whom she believed he would find he had much in common. And so came about a meeting which was to fall into the category known as historic, when a woman suspected of heresy met a scion of the established Catholic Church of Rome, and they found themselves to be one.

Not that it happened immediately. When the aristocratic Fenelon, his inherent reserve clothed in the cultured urbanity of the age, first met the demurely dressed widow of whom he had heard, he did not take to her, and she realised it. 'I felt within me that this first interview did not satisfy him,' she wrote in her autobiography, and she was sorry about it. She had had one of her intuitive flashes about him, and had expected an immediate affinity, a recognition of spiritual unity. 'He did not relish me.' However, she met him again the next day, and this time as they talked together he understood her better. As they were both to return to Paris that evening (he was Superior of the New Catholic Establishment near to where she lived), they travelled in the same carriage, her maid accompanying them. During that quiet journey he learned enough about her to realise that she was not the neurotic religious charlatan that some had represented her as being, but the genuine article, a woman of God, with a depth of spiritual experience and perception that matched, perhaps even surpassed, his own.

This was her opportunity to disclose what was in her heart, to talk to one whom she felt instinctively to be a kindred spirit, to share and compare experiences in prayer, and the knowledge of God. She believed all could pray, have direct access to God, she said. 'All who are willing to pray can easily do it with the assistance of the Holy Spirit, Who is given to all Christians.' She knew this from her own experience, and that there is a swift, silent, inward prayer that can be made at all times, without distracting from the business on hand. 'It is not the prayer of the head, but the prayer of the heart.'

For what did she ask when she prayed? From her point of

view, prayer was not so much to receive anything from God as to please Him, place herself at His disposal, do His will. Fenelon agreed. But she taught others to pray – how did she do this?

'I tell them that one way to place themselves in His presence is by meditation. Meditation by reading. I tell them to take some mighty truth which provides food for thought, and also for practice. I warn them not to rush from truth to truth, but to ponder on one – to read just a little, say two or three lines, then stop and think about it. Bees cannot draw out the juice of flowers by flying over them. They must settle and suck if they are to draw out the nourishment. So with us.'

Faith was essential, too. They must believe that God had come to dwell within them. Jesus Christ Himself had said that if any man loved Him and kept His commandments, He and His Father would come and make their abode with him. But for God to have complete control there – ah, that was something deeper. Conversion was not complete as long as it only turned from sin to grace. Rectifying outward bad habits and behaviour was an indispensable step, but it was only the first one. The inner life must be purified, too, and only God could do that. 'He had a drawing power which attracts the soul always more and more strongly to Himself, and in drawing it He purifies it.'

God purifies it? Then what about the value of self-imposed mortification and austerities?

God's salvation is given, not earned, she declared. All virtue which is not given from within is only a mask, like a garment, merely covering what is really there. Man-made virtue becomes self-righteousness. Take the Lord's parable of the publican and the Pharisee. 'The publican seeing in himself only sinfulness, hates himself. The Pharisee, on the other hand, supported by the great number of works of righteousness he feels he has performed, seems to hold his salvation in his own hands, and regards heaven as the recompense due to his merits. . . God apparently preferred the sinner!'

'All true virtue comes hand in hand with the possession of God.' The knowledge of God, union with God, – Fenelon realised that this was what absorbed her, this was the goal to which she had been urged. And the greatest obstacle in achieving it, she declared, was the subtle, tenacious enemy within – SELF. It had to die.

'Whatever is of man, and of his own doing, must die. However noble and exalted it be, it must die. All our self-sufficiency must be destroyed. And God alone can do it. We can never do it ourselves. We love our ego, our SELF, too much. We don't want it to be destroyed! If God did not do it Himself, we would never consent to it.'

But that brought up the matter of the freedom of the will. Has not God given to man free will, the right to choose?

'Yes, indeed. I cannot endure people saying we are not free to resist grace. We *are* free to resist grace.'

Then this destruction of SELF, to which we cannot consent, how explain God's action in doing it, if it is contrary to our own will? Where is the freedom of the will?

Madame Guyon had a very simple answer to that.

'The freedom of the will implies the right to surrender it. A person who has given himself to God at the beginning of his Christian course, has given an active consent to whatever God should do.'

Again, she could speak from experience, and made no effort to disguise what had been involved. There had never been any doubt but that it would include suffering. Had not Jesus Christ clearly said that those who would be His disciples must be prepared to deny themselves, take up the cross and follow Him? But what form the cross would take was not usually divulged. God warned that it would be painful, without specifying what form the suffering would take. 'If we knew and understood beforehand, we would shrink back. But God only asks of us our free will. It is the only thing we have that we can sacrifice to Him. So we surrender our own will that He may make of us what He pleases – for time and for eternity.'

Fenelon had nothing to quarrel with in that. It was no new theology. Jesus Christ Himself had said, 'Not as I will, but as Thou wilt.' The surrender of the will was a voluntary act. Only through death could the new life come. The seed must die to bring fruit. But life, abundant life, truly followed death, and fruit was brought from the seed that died. No one seeing and listening to her could have doubted that.

But what about those seasons of spiritual dryness, which all the saints seemed to have experienced? Sometimes God hides Himself, she said, to rouse us from our lethargy and laziness, and make us seek Him earnestly. But there is something else. There is a pathway to be trodden from relying on feelings of peace and joy and zeal, to naked faith.

Naked faith. It was a phrase she often used. Faith that is not dependent on feelings.

'It is very important to prevent people from dwelling on visions and ecstasies, because this arrests them all their life.' She had had her share of visions and ecstasies, but they had not prevented that long, long period of spiritual darkness while still in Montargis. 'Besides,' she continued, 'these graces are very subject to illusions, for what has form, image and distinctness, together with the delight of the senses, can very well be imitated by the devil. . .'

One can only speculate on the subjects that were touched on in that quiet drive to Paris, during which the gracious, intelligent Fenelon found himself completely at one with the widow who, if she expressed herself rather incoherently, quite obviously knew what she was talking about. It was the beginning of a life-long fellowship which stood the test of acute trials, particularly in the case of Fenelon, whose loyalty to her cost him very dear.

The relationship was completely free of the sexual element without which the twentieth century finds it almost impossible to recognise a spiritual unity between a man and a woman, although it is in line with mystics of the past – St. Francis of Assisi and Clare, St. John of the Cross and Teresa of Avila, St. Francis de Sales and Madame Chantal. However, the wildest imaginations of rumour-mongers could find no grounds on which to suggest that there was anything of that sort between Madame Guyon and Fenelon. But of the spiritual affinity there can be no doubt. As Madame Guyon wrote, in her usual ardent style, 'It seems to me that my soul has perfect rapport with his, and those words of David regarding Jonathan, that "his soul cleaved to that of David" appeared to me suitable for this union.'

During the two years following that conversation, a voluminous correspondence was maintained between them (over one hundred letters from Madame Guyon, thirty-odd from Fenelon) and occasional meetings in the homes of mutual friends. One of those was the Duke of Beauvilliers. When he was appointed as Governor of the household of the Dauphin's eldest son, second heir to the throne, he immediately appointed Fenelon as the child's tutor. The little Duc de Bourgogne was known to have an abominable temper, so Fenelon would have his work cut out to mould him into a wise and self-controlled prince, one who would be fit to mount the throne of Europe's greatest kingdom. But Madame Guyon had no doubt about his ability to do so – so far, that is, as he acted in complete dependence on God, and by dying to himself, as she did not fail to remind him. As for his royal pupil, she was convinced that God would make a saint of him. The gradual transformation of the boy's character during his years under Fenelon's tutelage proved her to be correct.

As for Madame Guyon herself, she had reached the peak, humanly speaking, of her varied and dramatic career. She was now the intimate friend of some of the noblest in the land, including the powerful Madame de Maintenon herself, who invited her to visit St. Cyr and instruct the young ladies there in the path of simple faith and prayer, and the acceptance of the will of God in their personal lives. Her days were often filled, as in Grenoble, with private interviews, and she maintained a wide correspondence with the individuals she had been brought in touch with over the course of the years.

One of these was Father La Combe. She devised means of communicating with him by letter from time to time, and on one occasion wrote advising him to employ his time in imprisonment in the way she herself had done when confined to the convent. Writing had been her outlet then – her autobiography, her poems, and letters to friends. Writing had, in fact, always been an outlet for her, a means of giving expression to her thoughts and aspirations, her feelings and the spiritual revelations that had been given to her. Now he was shut off from the active ministry that had filled his life previously, might not his letters from prison, like those of St. Paul, eventually have an even wider influence on generations to come?

But Father La Combe was not made that way.

'Alas!' he wrote in reply. 'Can the dry rock send forth flowing fountains? I never had much power or inclination for such efforts; and this seclusion from the world, this imprisonment, these cold and insensible walls, seem to have taken from me the power which I once had. The head, not the heart, seems to have become withered and hard, like rock. Like the Jews of old. I sit down by the waters of my place of exile and hang my harp upon the willows.

'It is true there has been some mitigation of my state. I am now permitted to go beyond the walls of my prison into the neighbouring gardens and fields, but it is only on the condition of my labouring there without cessation from morning till evening. What then can I do? How can I meditate? What can I think? – except upon the manner of subduing earth and of cultivating plants. I will add, however, that I have no choice for myself. All my desires are summed up in one – that God may be glorified in me.'

Prisons Do Not Exclude God

Strong are the walls around me
   That hold me all the day;
But they who thus have bound me
   Cannot keep God away;
My very dungeon walls are dear
Because the God I love is here.

They know, who thus oppress me,
   'Tis hard to be alone;
But know not, One can bless me
   Who comes through bars and stone
He makes my dungeon's darkness bright
And fills my bosom with delight

Thy love, O God, restores me
   From sighs and tears to praise;
And deep my soul adores Thee
   Nor thinks of time or place.
I ask no more, in good or ill,
But union with Thy holy will.

Jeanne de la Mothe Guyon

10

Pilloried

Outwardly things appeared to be going very well for Madame Guyon. She was accepted as a spiritual leader by some of the highest in the land, including Madame de Maintenon herself; her books were circulating widely, her daughter had married a most suitable man, her younger son had gained a commission in the army. Although she was rarely free from the nervous disorder or physical pain that dogged her (the smallpox had left her with an eye that frequently became agonizingly inflamed) she managed to get through an incredible amount of writing, in addition to the many interviews and talks she gave at St. Cyr.

This period, however, was darkened by a continual fog of rumours about her, and suggestions that she was secretly disseminating the teaching of the heretic, Molinos.

'When I was in the country staying with my daughter, they said I instructed the peasants, though I saw none of them. If I was in the town, according to their story, they made me receive persons, or else I went to see them; and yet I neither saw them or knew them.' She longed to get away from it all. The desire that had been born in her when a child revived – the desire to retire into the seclusion of a convent, to live out her earthly existence quietly in prayer, meditation, worship, free from the publicity and the harassments that beset her everywhere she went. At one stage she got in touch with the prioress of the Benedictine Convent in Montargis, and arrangements were even being made for her to slip away there secretly, to be virtually incarcerated in a little cell for the rest of her life. She went so far as having the small amount of furniture necessary sent on ahead, when news got out of what was happening, and a stop was put to it.

'My friends and my enemies, if so one may call persons to whom one wishes no ill, opposed my project from different views; the former, not to lose me altogether; and the latter, in order to ruin me, and not allow their prey to escape. They considered that such a life as I wished to lead would give the lie to all the calumnies they had hitherto invented, and take from them all means of persecuting me more. I saw myself, then, obliged by both, who prayed the Archbishop to forbid my being received, to live in the world, in spite of my aversion to the world.'

Then, after three years of being in favour with Madame de Maintenon, she sensed a subtle change in that lady's attitude towards her. What lay behind it was not entirely clear. It may have been Madame de Maintenon's fear that the King would be angry with her for so close an association with the Quietist movement, of which he was becoming increasingly suspicious. It may have been her jealousy of the unique relationship between Madame Guyon and the Abbé de Fenelon. Madame de Maintenon tended to see herself as the spiritual mother of a renewed and pious court, yet here was Fenelon, the most heavenly-minded ecclesiastic in Paris, intimate friend of the devout and aristocratic Beauvilliers group, acknowledging the pockmarked widow, not herself, as the one from whom he derived the greatest spiritual inspiration. Indeed, on one occasion, he had written to her, Madame de Maintenon, frankly pointing out that her ego, her SELF, was still her unbroken idol. That she wanted to love God with all her heart, but not through the death of that SELF. That if she would yield herself wholly to the Spirit of God, to have all the roots of her egoism cut away, her faults would gradually disappear. Madame de Maintenon took it very well at the time, but assuming Fenelon's assessment to be accurate, it is not likely to have predisposed her towards the woman whose ego he deemed to have been completely dealt with.

If secret, unacknowledged jealousy was at the root of the change of manner of France's most powerful woman towards her, Madame Guyon allowed no such suspicion to creep into her autobiography. She wrote with uncharacteristic brevity of the tranquil period when she enjoyed her favour, summing it up in one paragraph:

'Since my release I had continued to go to St. Cyr, and some of the girls of that House having declared to Madame de Maintenon that in the conversations I had with them they found something which led them to God, she permitted them to put confidence in me; and on many occasions she testified, owing to the change in some with whom hitherto she had not been satisfied, that she had no cause for repenting it. She then showed me much kindness and, during three of four years that this lasted, I received from her every mark of esteem and confidence. But it is this very thing in the sequel which has drawn down upon me the greatest persecution. The *entrée* Madame de Maintenon gave me at St. Cyr, and the confidence shown me by some young ladies of the court, distinguished by their rank and by their piety, began to cause uneasiness to the persons who had persecuted me. They stirred up the directors to take offence, and under the pretence of the troubles I had had some years before, and of the great progress, as they said, of Quietism, they engaged the Superior of St. Cyr to represent to Madame de Mainte-non that I disturbed the order of her House by a private direction; and that the girls whom I saw were so strongly attached to what I said to them, that they no longer listened to their Superior. Madame de Maintenon caused me to be told in a kindly way. I ceased to go to St. Cyr. I no longer answered the girls who wrote to me, except by open letters, which passed through the hands of Madame de Maintenon.'

Her virtual expulsion from St. Cyr caused quite a stir. Once more her little book on prayer came under review. Having been almost compulsory reading in pious circles, it was now put discreetly out of sight except among the friends who remained loyal to her and her teaching – the influential Dukes of Beauvilliers and Chevreuse and their Duchesses with them. And the Abbé Fenelon.

Rumours about her multiplied. Questioners abounded. In order to escape from the publicity she disappeared from Paris for a while, living quietly in the country, then returned secretly to her little house in the capital. As far as she was concerned, she would have been thankful to subside into obscurity, and tried to do so. She told no one where she was living except Monsieur Fouquet, the uncle of her son-in-law, a man she could trust completely to look after her financial affairs and provide her with money as she needed it.

Her disappearance from public life only seemed to provide further opportunities for the spread of rumours, especially as it coincided with the arrival in Paris of a Sister Rose who asserted that she knew Madame Guyon to be a very wicked person who would do great harm to the Church. Sister Rose had appeared out of the blue, and as no one seemed to feel it necessary to enquire into her past, and as a good many people were quite prepared to believe what she said, the efforts of Madame Guyon's few influential friends to clear her reputation were unavailing. Sister Rose evidently had amazing powers of persuasion.

'This woman, about whom there was in fact something very extraordinary (she prided herself on knowing the most secret thoughts and having the most detailed knowledge, not only of things at a distance from her, but even of the future) persuaded Monsieur Boileau and persons of virtue and probity with whom he was in relation that the greatest service they could render to God was to decry me, and even to imprison me owing to the ills I was capable of causing.'

Subtle attacks were being made on her from other sources, too. A group of women known as the Daughters of Father Vautier went around various confessionals relating gross sins they had committed owing, they said, to following Madame Guyon's teaching. This infiltration, which cast reflections on her morals as well as her theology, eventually aroused the Dukes of Beauvilliers and Chevreuse to take action on her behalf. They and their wives knew her intimately, and were ready to stand by her. They prepared a

memorandum outlining her life and activities which they
intended presenting to King Louis himself. Coming from
such a source, from aristocrats in high positions of responsibility, known for their integrity, it could scarcely have failed
to have its effect, especially as Madame de Maintenon had
agreed to be associated with it.

The fact that it never reached the King was entirely due to
Madame Guyon herself. She wrote years later: 'I owe them
the justice to make it known that it was no fault of theirs that
the authority of the King was not employed to shield me from
so much injustice. They drew up a memoir likely to influence
him in my favour, giving him an account of the conduct I
had observed, and was still observing in my retirement.
Madame de Maintenon was to have supported it by her
testimony.'

Then she added the significant words, 'But having had the
kindness to communicate it to me, I believed God did not
wish me to be justified by that channel, and I required of
them that they should leave me to the rigours of His justice,
whatever they might be. They consented to defer to my
request. The memoir already presented was withdrawn, and
they adopted the course of silence, which they have since
continued, being no longer able to do anything in my favour,
owing to the outburst and prejudice.'

And so she closed the door on what could have been her
way of escape. Beyond the cryptic sentence 'I believed God
did not wish me to be justified by that channel' she gave no
indication of what may have been the reasons for her refusal.
It is possible that she was already beginning to realise that
something was going on which was aimed to bring about the
downfall of people of far greater distinction than herself. In
her secluded life she knew little of the wider issues that were
at stake, or of the budding intrigue in which she would be
little more than a cat's paw. Even with her prophetic
intuitions she could not foresee that two of the leading
prelates of France would be in open conflict over her
teaching, and that the conflict would widen until it involved

the King and the Pope. But she was wise enough to recognise that she, a widow from the provinces, was of insufficient importance to make it worthwhile to build up such a case against her, and that her little book on prayer would probably have been swept away unnoticed in the current flood of literature had it not received so much publicity in high quarters.

She had little doubt as to who would be embroiled. The friends who were planning to come out openly in her support were none other than those who had been entrusted with the upbringing of the second heir to the throne, the little Duc de Bourgogne. If her enemies succeeded in bringing her down, those who would suffer through having their names associated with hers were the Duke of Beauvilliers – and the Abbé Fenelon.

If this consideration is what weighed with her, bringing her to the point of refusing, in the name of God, the proffered help, it was one of the noblest decisions of her life. However, Madame Guyon rarely seemed to consider she had done anything worthy of mention. Giving away her fortune, renouncing her rights, founding little hospitals, setting poor people up in business – she passed them off in a few words, almost forgetting to mention them. It was a different matter when it came to what she suffered, although here again, the physical sufferings endured in difficult confinements, frequent eye inflammations and similar ills, were referred to as being of secondary consideration. The sufferings which she felt most acutely were the mental, emotional, and spiritual ones. These were the crosses to which she referred again and again in her autobiography. She accepted them (not always without a struggle) as from the hand of God for her own discipline and purification until she reached the stage when she no longer felt them as a personal affront, when the SELF within her no longer reacted in pride or anger or self-pity. She had learned, in the words of St. Paul, to reckon herself dead, as no longer existing, having no will apart from God's will. Fenelon, in one of his early letters to her, summarised her teaching better than she did herself, when he outlined the progressive stages in reaching that state.

1.   The first step taken by the soul that had deliberately given itself to God is to put right the things that are wrong in the life, and to correct evil habits. 'But it does not act alone; it follows and cooperates with the grace that is given it.'

2.   The next step is to stop depending on the feelings of joy and well-being that God often gives in the early experiences of spiritual life. 'When we lose our inward happiness, we are very apt to think that we lose God; not considering that the moral life of the soul does not consist in pleasure, but in union with God's will, whatever that may be.' We live by faith, not feelings.

3.   'Another step is the crucifixion of any reliance upon our virtues, either outward or inward . . . in our truth, temperance, faith, benevolence.' Dependence on one's personal virtues is one of the most subtle forms of SELF.

4.   The fourth step consists in ceasing to rebel against the reverses of life, but rather to receive them as from the hand of God, as necessary for the inward crucifixion of SELF. 'So clear is the soul's perception of God's presence in everything; so strong is its faith, that those apparently adverse dealings, once exceeding trying, are now received not merely with acquiesence, but with cheerfulness.'

5.   Now comes, as a fifth step, the new life, for when we have proceeded so far, the natural man is crucified, on the cross, and leads on to a life in union with God. 'It is then that there is such a harmony between the human and Divine will, that they may properly be regarded as having become one. This, I suppose, was the state of St. Paul, when he says, 'I live; yet not I, but Christ liveth in me.'

His summary did not stop there. He went on to speak of the will which is not merely passive under God's dealings, but what she called 'flexible', completely cooperative. And that the transformed soul continues to advance in holiness, with its capacity for love increasing. It was a long letter, and concluded as follows:

'Those who walk by faith walk in obscurity; but they know that there is a light above them, which will make all clear and bright in its appropriate time. We trust; but, as St. Paul says, we know in whom we have trusted.

'I illustrate the subject, Madame, in this way. I suppose myself to be in a strange country. There is a wide forest before me, with which I am totally unacquainted, although I must pass through it. I accordingly select a guide, whom I suppose to be able to conduct me through these ways never before trodden by me. In the following this guide, I obviously go by faith; but as I know the character of my guide, and as my intelligence or reason tells me that I ought to exercise such faith, it is clear that my faith in Him is not in opposition to reason, but is in accordance with it. On the contrary, if I refuse to have faith in my guide, and undertake to make my way through the forest by my own sagacity and reason, I may properly be described as a person without reason, or as unreasonable; and should probably suffer for my want of reason by losing my way. Faith and reason, therefore, if not identical, are not at variance.

'Fully subscribing, with these explanations, to the doctrine of faith as the life and guide of the soul, I remain, Madame, yours in our common Lord, Francis S. Fenelon.'

He had understood her perfectly, had expressed better than she could have expressed it herself, just what she believed.

She had found her way through these various stages, slowly and painfully, but now she had reached a point where the mental and spiritual sufferings had a new significance. They were as acute as ever, but they were borne for others rather than herself. There were souls for which she travailed, like St. Paul, until Christ was formed in them, until they could claim that the world was crucified to them, and they to the world. Although she undoubtedly led many to a first knowledge of Christ, her primary ministry was to those who already believed in Him.

'He made me understand that He did not call me, as had been thought, to a propagation of the external of the Church, which consists in winning heretics, but to the propagation of His Spirit, which is no other than the interior Spirit, and that it would be for this Spirit I would suffer. He does not even destine me for the first conversion of sinners, but to introduce those who are already touched with the desire of being converted into the perfect conversion, which is no other than this interior Spirit.'

There was also suffering of another type, as when she was confronted with evil in human form. One of these occasion was when Monsieur Fouquet brought to her a girl who admitted that she had sold herself to the devil in order to gain the affection of a valet of Monsieur Fouquet's. The poor valet, when he knew of it, went to his master in deep distress, and the girl was dismissed. However, Monsieur Fouquet was concerned for her welfare and brought her to Madame Guyon, believing that she could help her.

The moment she saw the girl, knowing nothing about her, Madame Guyon was conscious of an indescribable horror, and the girl was visibly alarmed as she faced her.

'This girl, while with me, often said, "You have something strong that I cannot endure." . . . I saw that God operated through me, without me, with His divine power. At last this power obliged her to tell me her frightful life, which makes me tremble as I think of it. She related to me the false pleasures that the Spirit of Darkness had procured for her; that he made her pass for a saint, perform visible austerities, but that he did not allow her to pray; that, as soon as she wished to do so, he appeared to her in a hideous form ready to devour her; that otherwise he appeared to her in a form as amiable as possible, and that he gave her all the money she wished.'

But he gave her no peace, the girl cried out in a terrible

voice, in reply to Madame Guyon's question, only hellish trouble.

'How different it is for me!' said Madame Guyon, and went on to assert that she had great inner happiness in serving Jesus Christ, even when she was ill and suffering incessant pain. 'And in order that you may know what that happiness is, I pray that you taste this peace of heart, if only for a moment.'

That prayer was answered with dramatic suddenness. The expression on the girl's face changed, and turning to Monsieur Fouquet, who was present, she exclaimed, 'Oh, sir! I feel so different. I was in hell, but now I'm in paradise!' Monsieur Fouquet promptly took her to the Grand Penitentiary in order that she might make her confession and promise amendment of life. The girl went on well for some months, but strange forces seemed to be abroad that were related to her. Two of those who were trying to help her were smitten unexpectedly with physical ills. The Grand Penintentiary died suddenly. A Jacobin Father who had several times tried to save her from her depraved life also died. Then Madame Guyon was taken ill, and the girl came to see her.

'I knew you were very ill,' she said. 'The devil told me. He said he tried to kill you, but he was not permitted to. All the same, he said he would raise up so much trouble and persecution about you, that you'll die.'

The girl was being enmeshed again, lured back into the darkness. What was this about Satan having talked to her, having revealed his plans to her? Madame Guyon looked at her with dismay, realising that there was something different about her, and said sternly, 'You should not listen to the devil, not for a moment. Far less should you ever talk to him. I have told you that before. On no account enter into conversation with him. Tell him to go! Tell him you renounced him at your baptism, that you belong to Jesus Christ!'

But the damage had been done. The girl admitted that the

devil had persuaded her to go back on those vows of her baptism.

'Gone back on your vows!' Madame Guyon caught her breath, then urged the girl to renew the vows while there was yet time. 'It is not too late. Oh, give yourself anew to Jesus Christ! As for me, I don't mind what I have to suffer, if only you are truly converted.'

Her evident concern touched the girl, who said, 'You must love me very much to be willing to do so much for me.' But sinister spiritual forces had been unleashed that were too strong and subtle for her, and as though under a spell she went on, 'The devil told me he would do you so much harm, and stir up so many people against you, that you would die,' and as she spoke Madame Guyon again saw in imagination what she had seen years ago, in the New Catholic House in Gex – a bluish-coloured flame which turned into a hideous, horrifying face.

'But I had no fear of it, any more than of the threats he sent me. God for many years keeps me in the frame of mind that I would cheerfully give my life, even my peace which I value much more, for the salvation of a single soul.' And she meant it. But in the case of the girl who had sold herself to the devil, her efforts and willingness for sacrifice were in vain. One day a priest went to Monsieur Fouquet enquiring about her, and Monsieur Fouquet, unsuspecting, told him they had great hopes for her complete conversion, and at his request told him where she lived.

'When Monsieur Fouquet came to see me a little while after, and spoke to me of the priest, it occurred to me that it was that wicked priest of whom she had told me, with whom she had committed so many abominations. This proved only too true. She came no more.'

But Monsieur Fouquet, who was in practical matters Madame Guyon's closest friend, began to show signs of physical weakness, and grew steadily worse, until a few months later he died.

Meanwhile, the case against the Quietist movement, of

which Madame Guyon was erroneously supposed to be the representative, was continuing. There were plenty of people who were eager enough to prove her teaching to be wrong. Purity of life springing from the inner control of a holy God had no appeal to the sensual, pleasure-loving courtiers and ladies of Versailles. Their activities had already been greatly curtailed by the changed life of the King, who no longer indulged in illicit love affairs, but confined his attentions to Madame de Maintenon, now his secret though lawful wife. As he went tap-tap-tapping in his high-heeled shoes along the sumptuous, frescoed corridors of the palace to attend Mass, the members of his court followed him dutifully, but their carefully assumed expression of piety covered considerable irritation at his altered views on outward morality. If he got caught up in this new craze for spirituality as well, with its emphasis on the crucifixion of SELF and the enthronement of the Holy Spirit, life in Versailles simply would not be worth living. They had attended the ceremony, some years previously, when one of the King's mistresses, Louise de la Vallière, had taken the veil and disappeared for good into a convent, and the affair had provided an unusual and therefore welcome occasion for a court outing. It would be an entirely different matter if they were all expected to strive after a similar level of piety and self-control, even though not to the extent of entering monasteries and convents. They rebelled at the thought of having to exchange the gaiety of balls and theatres for religious meetings and prayer, flirtations and the festive cup for quiet studies of the Bible and the writings of the mystics, the thrill of the hunt for visits to the poor to improve their lot. In short, there was no lack of advocates at court for the suppression of 'Guyon-ism'. The ecclesiastics who were also against it had plenty of support from the high-born penitents who visited them for confession periodically, and duly obtained absolution. If between them it could be proved that Madame Guyon's teaching was false, it would be to their mutual satisfaction, though for different reasons.

Things came to such a pass that the Dukes of Beauvilliers and Chevreuse and the Abbé Fenelon again decided some action must be taken to clear her and vindicate her teaching. Their loyal plan to present her case to the King having been rejected, they came up with a different suggestion. Since it was her teaching that was being condemned, let her apply to the man whose opinion in these matters would be most highly respected, and ask him to examine her writings.

To this she agreed. It seemed to be a good idea. If anything she had written was contrary to the accepted doctrines of the Church, she would willingly alter it, although she had gone through it all before, with other theologians.

And so the day came when a new figure entered the scene, one who was to play a decisive role in the drama of her life. The Duke of Chevreuse brought to meet her Bossuet, the Bishop of Meaux.

A Little Bird I Am

A little bird I am,
  Shut from the fields of air:
And in my cage I sit and sing
  To Him who placed me there;
Well-pleased a prisoner to be,
Because, my God, it pleases Thee.

Nought have I else to do;
  I sing the whole day long;
And He, whom most I love to please,
  Doth listen to my song.
He caught and bound my wandering wing,
But still He bends to hear me sing.

Thou hast an ear to hear,
  A heart to love and bless;
And though my notes were e'er so rude,
  Thou shouldst not hear the less;
Because Thou knowest, as they fall,
That Love, sweet Love, inspires them all.

My cage confines me round,
  Abroad I cannot fly;
But though my wing is closely bound,
  My heart's at liberty.
My prison walls cannot control
The flight, the freedom of the soul.

O! It is good to soar
  These bolts and bars above,
To Him whose purpose I adore,
  Whose providence I love;
And in Thy mighty will to find
The joy, the freedom of the mind.

Jeanne de la Mothe Guyon,
written in the Prison of Vincennes.

11

To the Bastille

If Madame Guyon had any natural apprehensions about an interview with the most prominent churchman of the day, the preacher who could hold his listeners spellbound, the controversialist who could prove his point in the fiercest theological debates, those apprehensions were speedily dispelled. The Bishop was genial and reassuring. Some years ago he had read her little book on prayer and also her commentary on the Song of Solomon, he told her, and thought them very good. He was not at all opposed to inward religion – quite the reverse.

'This prelate said to us such strong things on the interior way and the authority of God over the soul, that I was surprised. He gave us even examples of persons he had known, whom he deemed saints, that had killed themselves. I confess I was startled by all this talk of the Bishop of Meaux. I knew that in the primitive Church some virgins had caused their own deaths in order to keep themselves pure; but I did not believe, in this age, where there is neither violence nor tyrants, a man could be approved for such an action.' She knew, at any rate, that nothing she had written contained such strange sentiments, and had no hesitation in letting him see all the books she had written, whether printed or still in manuscript form. She wanted to conceal nothing. She wanted him to know the reasons for her faith and convictions, and in order that he might the better understand her and the experience through which she had passed, she went further, giving him something she had never intended for publication.

She gave him her autobiography. All she asked was that it should be treated with the secrecy of the confessional.

It is difficult to understand what prompted her to give

such an intimate and uninhibited revelation of her experiences, practical and mystical, into the hands of a man she had never before met. The trustfulness of the action is evidence of her naiveté, and of her complete confidence in Bossuet himself. Her best friends had introduced him as being the one most likely to give her a fair hearing, and his kindly attitude towards her was disarming. Humanly speaking, she saw no reason for withholding it.

'At that time I flattered myself (though I accused myself of my faithlessness) that he would support me against those who were attacking me. But how far was I from knowing him! And how subject to error is that which one does not see in God's light, and which He does not Himself disclose!'

Bossuet took the enormous bundle of writings off with him, and some days later intimated to the Duke of Chevreuse that he had found in what he read 'an unction he had found nowhere else'. It was all very encouraging. They were not to know that he declared elsewhere that his stomach was turned again and again as he read her books. The intuitions, the visions and the interpretations put on them in her younger days which he now read were too much for him. To a literal-minded man with no bent for mysticism, they made no appeal.

Several months passed before he did anything more about them, but early in 1690 he made an arrangement to meet her and discuss what she had written.

The interview was a disaster from her point of view. Bossuet arrived at it with twenty carefully planned objections, and brought them out so vehemently that she was taken aback. She managed to answer some of his criticisms correctly. 'God assisted me, so that I satisfied him on everything that had relation to the dogma of the Church and the purity of doctrine,' she recorded, but continued, 'But there were some passages on which I could not satisfy him. As he spoke with extreme vigour, and hardly gave me time to explain my thoughts, it was not possible for me to make him change upon some of those articles, as I had done on others. We separated very late, and I left that conference with a head so exhausted, and in such a state of prostration, I was ill from it for several days.'

Some of the passages that the Bishop of Meaux objected to were not in her published writings, but in the autobiography she had so trustingly handed to him. According to him, she saw herself as the Woman in the Apocalypse, and made all sorts of claims beyond what the greatest saints would claim, regarding her relationship to God.

'The Bishop of Meaux raised great objections to what I said in my *Life*, of the Apostolic state. What I have meant to say is that persons who, by their state and condition (as, for instance, laymen and women) are not called upon to aid souls, ought not to intrude into it of themselves; but when God wished to make use of them by His authority, it was necessary they should be put into the state of which I have spoken. . . That this state is possible we have only to open the histories of all times to show that God has made use of laymen and women to instruct, edify, conduct and bring souls to a very high perfection. . . . "He has chosen weak things to confound the strong." '

There can be little doubt that those few hours of mental battering had a profound effect on Madame Guyon – perhaps rather a salutary one. Until that time it had seemed to her unnecessary to define the meaning of what she had written on the spur of the moment. Now that she had to explain what she meant, she was hard put to it to do so.

'I have a defect, which is that I say things as they occur to me, without knowing whether I speak well or ill; while I am saying or writing them they appear to me clear as day; after that I see them as things I have not known, far from having written them. Nothing remains in my mind but a void. . .'

If the Bishop of Meaux had been prepared to discuss things quietly, and had given her time to explain herself, the interview would have been much more to her satisfaction. As it was, all she could do was to pursue him with letters, endeavouring to clarify the points he had raised, which she had been too bewildered to answer at the time. Although he eventually responded kindly enough, assuring her that he found nothing in her that was not Catholic, he also intimated that there were certain views she held with which he could not agree.

'I am ready to believe that my imaginations are mixed up as shadows with the divine truth, which may indeed conceal it, but cannot injure it. I pray God with all my heart to crush me by the most terrible means, rather than I should rob Him of the least of His glory,' she wrote.

This whole episode shook her badly. It raised questions in her own mind as to whether she had inadvertently misled others. She could not guarantee that she had never been deceived, she wrote to the Duke of Beauvilliers, but she called him to witness that she had never done so intentionally. As for being proud, as the Bishop had implied – well, maybe she was, since she knew she was capable of anything bad! 'But the fire will purify all. I can very well believe I may have been mistaken, but I cannot complain nor be afflicted at all.' She took comfort, she said, in the fact that God was not less great, less perfect, or less happy for all her errors. As for herself, 'It appears to me I am below all creatures, a veritable nothing.'

During this period she lived a very secluded life in a small house in Paris, knowing little of what was going on outside except what Monsieur Fouquet told her. It was through him that she learned of the fantastic stories being circulated about her by Sister Rose and others. Her first reaction seems to have been to creep away altogether. She was obviously feeling very depressed when she wrote to the Duke of Chevreuse that she must 'once more become a wanderer, without hearth or home, ill and abandoned by all the world', but that since God evidently intended it, she consented to it with all her heart. She would disappear into a village where no one knew her, and live like a peasant!

Her little group of influential friends evidently protested against this idea, and, in fact, she gave it up herself. To run away now would be tantamount to admitting that the rumours had some truth in them, and she realised that if her morals were brought into question, it would reflect on her teaching. Instead of following her natural inclination to be done with it all, therefore, she did exactly the opposite. She wrote to Madame de Maintenon, explaining that as long as she was only accused of praying and teaching others to do so, she had remained in obscurity. 'But learning I am accused of things which touch honour, and that they speak of crimes, I thought it due to the Church, to my family, and to myself, that the truth should be known.' Then she went on to ask to have her case investigated by men of recognised integrity, half of them to be ecclesiastics, half laymen, in order that her morals as well as her theology should be brought to the light of day. This, she felt, was a justice refused to no one, and she added that while her case was under review she would go with the maid who had served her for fourteen years to any prison the King should indicate.

The reply she received from Madame de Maintenon really upset her, although on the face of it it appeared reasonable enough. It was given through the Duke de Beauvilliers, who had acted as go-between.

'Madame de Maintenon answered him that she had never believed any of the rumours that were circulated as to my morals; that she believed them very good. But it was my doctrine that was bad – that in justifying my morals, it was to be feared currency might be given to my sentiments, that it might be in some way to authorise them. And it was better, once and for all, to search out what related to doctrine, after which the rest would of itself drop.'

So once again there was to be an examination of her writings and teaching, but this time in the full glare of publicity, and with the scurrilous rumours about her allowed to persist unchallenged!

'They tried to tarnish my morals to tarnish my faith. I wished to justify the morals to justify the faith. They will not have it. What more can I do?' she wrote rather desperately. 'If they condemn me they cannot for that remove me from the bosom of the Church, my mother, since I condemn all she could condemn in my writings. I cannot admit having had thoughts I never had, nor having committed crimes I have not even known, far from committing them; because this would be to lie to the Holy Ghost. And like as I am ready to die for the faith and the decisions of the Church, I am ready to die to maintain that I have not thought what they insist I thought when writing, and that I have not committed the crimes they impute to me.' She was prepared to submit to the authority of the Church if she was ordered to refrain from teaching and writing. This prohibition she accepted, but beyond that she could not go.

It was at this time that she made a serious mistake, which was to cost her very dear. The Archbishop of Paris himself sent her a message that he had received a number of false memoirs about her, and asked her to come and see him. He would extricate her from her troubles, he said.

'He would have fully justified me, according to what I have since learned on good authority,' she wrote. 'I owe this justice to the fidelity of my God, that He did not fail me on this occasion, and that He put it into my heart to go to him. I even believed myself obliged to obey the voice of my Shepherd; but my friends . . . did not allow me to go, nor follow the inclination I had.'

Now her friends had their reasons. The Archbishop's offer of help was prompted by no concern for Madame Guyon, nor any particular approval of her teaching, but mainly because he cordially disliked the Bishop of Meaux, that upstart who was gaining altogether too much influence at Court and in ecclesiastical matters! If he, as Archbishop, intervened in this affair, he would be proving his superior ecclesiastical authority.

But behind the Bishop of Meaux, in the shadows, was the powerful figure of Madame de Maintenon, who had secretly authorised the commission. Political as well as ecclesiastical forces were at work, and Madame Guyon's friends, with the best intentions, persuaded her not to accept the Archbishop's invitation. Not surprisingly he was extremely annoyed, and forthwith banned her writings.

So the investigation went ahead in what came to be known as the Issy Conferences. For months Bossuet, Bishop of

Meaux, took time off from his full and busy life to meet de
Noailles, Bishop of Chalons, and the highly respected old
Monsieur Tronson, and for hours at a time the three of them
discussed what Madame Guyon meant by what she said.
This led them on to examine such obscure theological
subjects as whether or not it was possible for a devout soul to
love God so selflessly as to be prepared to spend eternity in
the torments of hell, if He so willed it. A hypothetical
question based on an impossibility, some might have called
it, but at any rate it revealed the diligence with which they
applied themselves to the task in hand. Pure love had to be
accurately defined, and since Madame Guyon had raised the
matter by something she had ecstatically written, it should
be gone into.

If the Bishop of Meaux had had his way, she would have
been condemned outright as a heretic and a dangerous
woman, but she had an unexpected advocate in the aged
Monsieur Tronson, who had taken the trouble to make
enquiries on his own account about her conduct and
character. From the Bishops of Geneva, Grenoble and Turin
came the same report in varying degrees of enthusiasm. Her
moral character was beyond reproach, her generosity to the
poor was outstanding, and the influence she had had on a
large number of people had been for good, and drawn them
nearer to God. In the face of such testimonies it was difficult
to designate her as a dangerous woman, and since she had
made it quite clear she renounced anything that was
contrary to the doctrines of the Church, she could scarcely be
branded as a heretic. When it came to the crunch, they could
find nothing in her doctrine that was contrary to what was
already accepted in the Church. So the Issy Conferences
eventually came to a conclusion with the production of some
thirty articles of elementary faith, all of which she believed
and subscribed to without difficulty. What disturbed her was
that their production had ever seemed necessary, implying,
as she thought, that 'those given to prayer believed neither in
God nor in Jesus Christ'. She saw them as an indirect
indictment of her teaching. However, they were seen in a

different light by one who might have been as hurt as she by their publication. Somehow Father La Combe, in his imprisonment in Lourdes, got wind of the affair, and managed to send a reassuring letter to her in which he emphasised the importance of such orthodox truths as the articles contained being absolutely safeguarded. There was nothing for her to be worried about. She had done quite right to sign them. As a woman she was not expected to solve theological debates. Whatever may have happened to Father La Combe a few years later, he was evidently in his right mind when he wrote that letter.

By this time Madame Guyon was no longer living in Paris, but in a convent in the diocese of the Bishop of Meaux. The censure of her books by the Archbishop of Paris after her refusal to see him had made the place too hot for her, and trustingly she had agreed to Bossuet's suggestion that she should make her temporary home with the nuns of St. Mary.

In all but one way it proved a good move for her, and not so good for him. The nuns may have been prejudiced against her before they met her, but she won them over completely. Her arrival one night in mid-winter, having spent some hours in a snow drift, alone with her maid in a carriage abandoned by the driver, was dramatic, but half-frozen as they were the two women made no complaint. During the six months she remained with them there was perfect harmony between the devout, orthodox nuns of St. Mary and their visitor who was suspected of heresy.

The nuns saw another side of their usually benign and urbane Bishop, too, for he came one day when Madame Guyon was recovering from an illness, and really bullied her. He wanted her to sign a document in which it was implied she had fallen into some of the religious errors that the Church condemned. He was quite genial about it at first, but when she explained mildly that she could not do that, he spoke more vehemently, but to no effect. The quieter her voice as she answered him, the louder his voice became, and the Prioress, standing by, was dismayed to observe that the Bishop was in danger of losing his temper.

It was a disturbing scene, one that was enacted several times during Madame Guyon's stay in the convent, and one day, the Bishop having gone again without getting his way, the Prioress said to Madame Guyon, 'You ought not to have answered him so gently. If people stand up to him he calms down, but if they don't he raves on. It's his nature.' But it was not Madame Guyon's nature to be otherwise than gentle, whether verbally attacked by a bad-tempered mother-in-law or an angry Bishop. The Prioress was cast in a different mould, and on at least one occasion protested strongly to the Bishop at the way he was treating this resident in her convent. He admitted then that, having thoroughly examined the writings of Madame Guyon, he had found nothing wrong except some terminology not completely orthodox, 'but a woman is not expected to be a theologian.' With which sentiment, of course, everyone agreed. He further intimated that he was being egged on to extract a confession of heresy from her by people in a very powerful position.

No names were mentioned, but when Madame Guyon heard of it she had little difficulty in identifying one of them. It was Madame de Maintenon. Bossuet was making no empty boast when, discussing the affair with the Prioress, he said, in an unguarded moment, 'This business will gain for me the Archbishopric of Paris or a Cardinal's hat!' He was working for promotion, and aiming high. 'But God won't allow him to have the one or the other,' said Madame Guyon confidently, when the Prioress told her what he had said. And in that prophecy she proved to be right.

Interestingly enough, it was the man who was unobtrusively supporting her, Fenelon himself, who obtained an archbishopric. The See of Cambrai, on France's northeastern border, fell vacant about this time, and Fenelon was nominated as successor to the Spanish archbishop who had just died. This did not mean he would spend much time there. The appointment was not to be allowed to interfere with his duties as tutor to the young Duc de Bourgogne. He would remain at court for part of the year, only visiting

Cambrai when convenient. Viewed from a worldly and financial point of view, this was definitely preferment. Fenelon, though an aristocrat, was a poor man, with only one small benefice, but he immediately surrendered that on his appointment – to the surprise of some of his fellow-clerics who saw no harm in the quiet retention of such wealth as came their way. One archbishop, on hearing of it, remarked drily that Fenelon, thinking as he did, had acted well in surrendering his benefice, and that he himself, thinking as he did, had also acted well in keeping all of his. Let each man act according to his convictions!

This appointment, which put Fenelon on an equal footing with Bossuet, did nothing to improve relations between the two men. All the same, it may have influenced Bossuet to modify his attitude towards Madame Guyon, since Fenelon was known to approve of her teaching. Whatever may have been the reason, having failed to extract from her a confession that she did not believe in the virgin birth, and that she and Father La Combe had both taught heresy, he eventually gave up trying to force it from her. (The Madame Guyon who confronted him with such firmness was a very different Madame Guyon from the browbeaten young bride who had tried to win over an insolent servant with meekly-proffered presents.) Instead, after she had been in the convent about six months, he presented her with a testimonial which was of such importance that she sent it to her family for safe keeping. It read as follows:

'We, Bishop of Meaux, certify to all whom it may concern that, by means of the declarations and submission of Madame Guyon which we have before us subscribed with her hand, and the prohibitions accepted by her with submission, of writing, teaching, dogmatising in the Church, or of spreading her books printed or manuscript, or of conducting souls in the ways of prayer, or otherwise: together with the good testimony that has been furnished us during six months that she is in our diocese and in the convent of St. Mary, we are satisfied with her conduct, and have continued to her the participation of the Holy Sacraments in which we have found her; we declare, besides, we have not found her implicated in any way in the abominations of Molinos or others elsewhere condemned, and we have not intended to comprehend her in the mention which has been made by us of them in our Ordinance of April 6th, 1695: given at Meaux, July 1st, 1695.'

A few days later she was given another testimonial, hand-written, a copy of which had been given to Bossuet. It must have touched her as it must touch the thoughtful reader in the twentieth century, coming down the corridors of time as a sort of memorial to three unknown but courageous and loyal women who did what they could to stand for the truth. This is what she read:

'We, the undersigned, Superior and nuns of the Visitation of St. Mary of Meaux, certify that Madame Guyon, having lived in our House by the order and permission of the Bishop of Meaux, our illustrious Prelate and Superior, for the space of six months, she has not given us any cause for trouble or annoyance, but much of edification; having never spoken to a person within or without except with special permission; having, besides, neither received nor written anything except as the Bishop has permitted her; having observed in all her conduct and all her words a great regularity, simplicity, sincerity, humility, mortification, sweetness, and Christian patience, and a true devotion and esteem of all that is of the faith, especially in the mystery of the Incarnation and Holy Childhood of our Lord Jesus Christ. That if the said lady wished to choose our House to live there the rest of her days in retirement, our Community would deem it a favour and gratification. This protest is simple and sincere, without other view or thought than to bear witness to the truth. Signed. Sister Françoise Elizabeth le Picard, Superior, Sister Magdalen Amy Gueton, Sister Claude Marie Amouri, July 7th, 1695.'

There were times when, in her distress, Madame Guyon wrote of being 'abandoned by all the world', when, like Elijah, she saw herself as the only one left who was faithful to the revelation of the God whose Kingdom is in the human heart. And, like Elijah, she was wrong. In the France of the seventeenth century, as in Israel hundreds of years before Christ, God had His hidden ones who would not bow the knee to any Baal.

As there was now no reason for Madame Guyon to remain in the convent, she asked and obtained permission from the Bishop to leave, and departed with two friends who came to escort her to their home. The testimonial he had given her would answer any further accusations about her doctrine, it seemed, though the rumours about her moral character continued to circulate. She had in her possession letters from Cardinal Camus and a Benedictine Prior, both of Grenoble, both testifying to her purity of conduct, but there was no way in which she could use them to vindicate herself. She read them over sometimes, those reassuring words, written by the indignant Prior denying that he had ever supported foul accusations against her.

'. . . fabricate a calumny against you! and they made me the instrument of it! I never thought what they put in my mouth, nor of making the complaints of which they pretend I am the author. I declare, on the contrary, and I have already many times declared, that I have never heard of you anything but what is very Christian and very honourable. I should have taken good care not to see you, Madame, if I had believed you capable of saying what I would not dare to write, and what the Apostle forbids us to name. If it is, however, necessary to your justification I should name it, I will do it on the first notion, and I will distinctly say there is nothing of the kind, that I have never heard you say anything similar, nor anything which has the least resemblance to it . . . They have already written to me on the subject, and I have already given the same answer. I would do it a thousand times more if I were asked a thousand times.' Let her apply to him again, if necessary, and he would bear testimony to the truth. He would not wound his conscience by a cowardly silence!

If she had been allowed to defend herself in a court of law, she knew she had sufficient evidence and convincing witnesses to prove her innocence. As it was, she was denied that privilege. Hers was deemed a case for the ecclesiastical authorities only. The testimonials she had received, which in a free country in the twentieth century would have made headline news in the media, could not be made public, and in a matter of days the most important one, that given her by Bossuet, had to be secreted to preserve it, for he sent to demand its return. And through the Prioress he ordered, not only the return of the testimonial, but the return of Madame Guyon to the convent.

With that demand, sent on by the Prioress, came a private letter from the courageous woman herself. 'Don't obey the command,' was the gist of what she said in it. 'Things will be even worse for you if you fall into the Bishop's hands again. Much as we want to have you with us here, we'd rather you stayed away for your own sake.' Madame Guyon understood. The Bishop had offended Madame de Maintenon, in whose eyes he had slipped up badly in giving her that testimonial, and agreeing to her leaving the convent. Now he was trying to retrieve the mistake. The one way in which her move to the convent did not prove good for her was that by doing so she had placed herself under his jurisdiction. When she did not obey the order to return, he gave out that she had left without his permission, by escaping over the convent wall.

Madame Guyon had escaped from the convent of St. Mary in Meaux over the garden wall! So the rumour got around, and she knew the net was closing about her. Unwilling to involve her family and friends in her disgrace, she declined invitations from two or three of them to retreat quietly into their homes in the country, and set off secretly with her maid for Paris. Once there, she went into hiding.

'As I was informed my enemies were about to push things with the utmost violence, I believed I should leave to God all that should happen, and yet take all prudent steps to avoid the effect of the menaces that reached me from all sides.' She rented a cheap apartment in a secluded tenement, staying indoors the whole time while her maid went quietly out of a side door for the necessary shopping, and to bring back what news she could.

Rumours abounded about the notorious Madame Guyon who had so mysteriously disappeared.

Lieutenant le Gres had orders to find her.

The police were searching for her everywhere!

She was to be arrested and tried – then she would have her head chopped off!

No – she was to be burned at the stake, and her ashes scattered to the four winds!

She managed to get letters out to her friends occasionally, and in one to the Duke of Beauvilliers she referred quite humorously to the threats of execution, asserting that they had delighted her for a whole day, and that she couldn't wait for her ashes to be flying. The very thought of it just suited her, she said. It is probable that her friends were having a worse time of it in some ways than she herself, for they knew what was going on.

Worst of all, they knew what was being said, and the way in which Madame Guyon was being ridiculed. Bossuet, unable to find ways of convicting her of heresy, had made her the butt for vulgar jokes instead, and he had used her own autobiography to do it.

That autobiography, written when she was younger, and with the extravagance of thought and expression which came naturally to her, had been given to him on the one condition that he treated it with the secrecy of the confessional. She had been assailed by doubts as to the wisdom of letting him see it after she had done so, and sent a message asking for its return, but he retained it for months before letting her have it back, and by that time he had assimilated its contents. Some of the things she had written were quite intimate, for she had never intended it for publication, but had obeyed the instructions of Father La Combe, her spiritual director, to write exactly what she had experienced. One little incident in particular the Bishop of Meaux remembered, and now made full use of. She had been present on an occasion when a group of people were discussing some passage in the Bible, and she realised they were putting the wrong interpretation on its meaning. This distressed her. Too reticent to dispute the point, she kept quiet, but was so overcome with suppressed emotion that she started panting and it seemed she was likely to faint. Then it was, as she wrote quite frankly in her autobiography, her tight-fitting bodice and stays had to be loosened, and on this trivial intimate detail the Bishop of Meaux fastened. 'She was so overcome she had to loosen her stays . . .' One can imagine how the corridors of Versailles would ring with laughter as the phrase was taken up in suggestive conversation, and in whatever context it was used, Madame Guyon was the name attached to it. The Bishop of Meaux may have failed to produce evidence to prove her a heretic, but he succeeded in making her an object of ribaldry. The little group of those at court who were known to be loyal to her had to endure that shame. It is sometimes harder to stand by someone who is being laughed at than someone who is being opposed.

If Madame Guyon was conscious that the net was being drawn around her, the Duke of Beauvilliers, in charge of the household of the Dauphin's children, and Fenelon as their tutor, had good cause to suspect that it was also being spread for them. Their names were so closely associated with hers that any action taken against her would inevitably affect them.

There was a sort of lull during the months in which she was successfully evading the unjust arrest awaiting her. No less an impartial witness to the whole affair than the aged Monsieur Tronson got a message to her confirming her in remaining out of sight, assuring her that she had good reason for doing so. But the period of quietness and comparative comfort in her own little home came to an end when her place of hiding was discovered. This happened two days after Christmas, 1695. Her maid, out on an errand, was recognised and followed home. The police entered the house, arrested Madame Guyon, and with her maid she was taken to the castle in the forest of Vincennes, near Paris, and there imprisoned.

Simple Trust

Still, still, without ceasing,
I feel it increasing,
This fervour of holy desire;
And often exclaim,
Let me die in the flame
Of a love that can never expire!

Had I words to explain
What she must sustain
Who dies to the world and its ways;
How joy and affright,
Distress and delight,
Alternately chequer her days.

Thou, sweetly severe;
I would make Thee appear
In all Thou art pleased to award,
Not more in the sweet,
Than the bitter I meet,
My tender and merciful Lord.

Thus Faith, in the dark
Pursuing its mark
Through many sharp trials of Love;
Is the sorrowful waste
That is to be passed
In the way to the Canaan above.

Jeanne de la Mothe Guyon

12

It does not end here

Fenelon, Archbishop of Cambrai, was in a predicament, and Bossuet, Bishop of Meaux, intended to keep him in it. It had been at the instigation of the Bishop that Madame Guyon was incarcerated in Vincennes, and he was determined that the Archbishop should agree that he had done right. The woman must be branded as a heretic, thus vindicating him in the eyes of all for the action he had taken against her, and, incidentally satisfying Madame de Maintenon on whose approval so much depended. The difficulty was that the Archbishop did not see eye to eye with him, and the Archbishop was very highly esteemed in some influential quarters. It was a complicated situation, needing tactful handling, but it had to be done, so the Bishop set about it in an oblique manner.

He did not demand of the Archbishop public support of his action, open agreement that Madame Guyon's teaching was contrary to that of the Church. Instead, he wrote a book.

His ostensible purpose in writing the book was an admirable one, and the subject he chose was thoroughly relevant to the current ecclesiastical preoccupation. In other words, it was topical. It dealt with the whole matter of mystical prayer and the inner life as practised and recommended by such recently canonised saints as St. Francis de Sales, Saint Teresa, and St. John of the Cross, not to mention those of earlier vintage. And Bossuet, Bishop of Meaux, wrote as an ardent advocate of the subject. If it had not been a topic of major concern to him before, it evidently was now. He wrote of it in all its varied stages and aspects. Certainly he was in favour of prayer, and an inner life in union with God! What he feared, what he deplored, what he was opposed to, was the introduction of dangerous errors and heresies like those of Molinos and the Quietists. These were what should be guarded against. Having written the book he sent it to Fenelon, his old pupil and erstwhile friend, for his approval. If that could be obtained the breach between them would be seen to be healed and he, the Bishop, would be seen to have been in the right.

But Fenelon, after glancing at the manuscript, politely refused to read it. His reason? He had detected in the margins quotations from Madame Guyon's writings which were produced as examples of the Quietist heresies. As he explained to the Duke of Chevreuse, his friend, he saw immediately that the book was a covert attack on her own little publication *A Short Method of Prayer*, and he was quite unwilling to add his name to what amounted to a condemnation of her. The least he could do for one of his friends in adversity, in whose integrity he had complete confidence, was to keep silent while others condemned, he said. It would be simpler to return the book unread than to read it and refuse to approve it, so would the Duke kindly act on his behalf by returning the manuscript promptly to the Bishop, and explaining his reason for doing so?

The Duke, who understood the situation completely, accepted the charge, and no doubt came in for a display of the Bishop's displeasure as he expressed himself amazed, shocked, indeed scandalised at the Archbishop's attitude, creating as it did an open breach between them. The leading ecclesiastics in France seen to be at variance! What damage it would do to the Church! And all over a pockmarked widow who fancied herself as a prophetess! If the Bishop did not put it in exactly those words, that is no doubt what he meant.

But the Archbishop was adamant. He did not deny that Madame Guyon was given to exaggeration, and that she expressed herself imperfectly, but he knew her personally, and her basic faith as well as her practice was entirely conformable to Catholic doctrine. In any case, her writings had already been passed by one lot of theologians and then by another, she had accepted with the utmost docility all the corrections they had suggested, so what was there to complain about?

That is as far as he went in open defence of her, but like the Benedictine Prior of Grenoble, he refused to wound his own conscience by a cowardly silence. He used the same method as the Bishop.

He, too, wrote a book.

He called it *The Maxims of the Saints*, and although he did not mention her name, it included and expressed more clearly than Madame Guyon herself had done her teaching on the inner life. And as he was a rapid writer, and his book was shorter, the Duke of Chevreuse rushed it through the press and got it into the hands of readers six weeks ahead of the publication of the Bishop's more ponderous work.

It all caused as great a flare-up as the proverbial fat when it gets into the fire. Those who were not intimately involved were outwardly appalled and inwardly delighted at the prospect of a row between leading prelates in the Church. Those who knew what lay behind it were alarmed, and as for the Bishop himself, he was furious. Madame de Maintenon, knowing he had the sympathetic ear of King Louis himself, made one or two ineffectual attempts to calm the situation that she herself had been largely responsible for bringing about, for she still had a deep respect and affection for Fenelon, but her efforts were in vain. The King had his own reason for disliking Fenelon (Fenelon had rebuked him strongly on one occasion for his indifference to the sufferings of his own people brought on by his ambitious wars) and was willing enough to listen to Bossuet's accusation against him.

The Bishop, of course, went about it in the correct manner. He approached His Most Christian Majesty in a penitent attitude, asking for his forgiveness, and then explained that there was something he ought to have revealed before. It was about the Archbishop of Cambrai. The Bishop feared that his fellow-prelate was becoming very fanatical. The fact was, he had serious leanings towards the heresies of the Quietists, having come under the influence of Madame Guyon. He was thus a danger to the Church and also to the Crown, for was he not the tutor to His Majesty's grandson, the Duc de Bourgogne, second heir to the throne? What insidious heresies might not be spread throughout the court and then the realm through the influence of the Archbishop of Cambrai! Could His Majesty forgive him, the Bishop, for not having revealed this earlier?

His Most Christian Majesty expressed himself horrified at what he heard, and was thoroughly worked up about it. He graciously forgave the Bishop, as Bossuet of course knew he would, but made it plain that something must be done about Fenelon, as Bossuet, of course, intended that it should.

And so the gathering storm broke. Fenelon appealed to Rome, requesting that his book should be scrutinised there, to receive from the Pope's ultimate authority either the Papal approval or condemnation. He wanted to go to Rome in person, to present his case himself, but for that he needed the King's permission to leave France, and this was summarily refused. He must not cross the French border. The seventeenth-century equivalent of the twentieth-century exit visa was as difficult to obtain, in certain cases, as it often is now. On the contrary, he was ordered to leave the capital and return to his remote diocese of Cambrai *and remain there*. This was tantamount to telling him he could no longer hold the position of tutor to the second heir to the throne. He was virtually dismissed. Not even the heartfelt plea of the King's own grandson, the young Duc de Bourgogne, on behalf of his beloved teacher, could move the King to alter his decision. The purity of the Catholic Faith was at stake, he told the boy piously, and therefore he could not grant personal favours. He must defend the Faith at all costs.

Bent on rooting out 'Guyonism' as he called it, he turned his attention to St. Cyr, where it had flourished for a time. He went personally to the place, got the local Bishop to condemn all Madame Guyon's writings found there, and had three of the staff members known to be loyal to Madame Guyon turned out. At the same time her younger son was stripped of his commission in the army.

The King did not stop there, either. Bossuet saw to that. His activity was now directed towards Rome. The Pope must be persuaded to condemn in the strongest measure *The Maxims of the Saints*, and thereby finally crush the Archbishop of Cambrai. So started the series of intrigues and consultations, the urgent messages and the covert threats, the flood of literature that made headline news in court and Church circles in France and Italy, which threatened to bring the King of France and the Pope into open conflict.

Meanwhile, the innocent cause of all the trouble was locked up in prison, writing poetry.

*   *   *

What would have been a shattering experience for most women of her upbringing had no apparent adverse effect on the spirits of Madame Guyon. She had long ago learned to endure physical hardship and natural privations, had a mind armed with a willingness to suffer, and entered prison with all the poise of the martyr prepared to die for her cause. So far from being appalled by the conditions into which she entered, she appeared thoroughly to enjoy the first few months in Vincennes. She had longed for isolation from the world, and the freedom to devote herself to quiet meditation, prayer, adoration and worship – now she had got it. If the room in which she was incarcerated was cold and damp, it was rendered as comfortable as her devoted maid-servant, who shared it with her, could make it. Her rank was respected to the extent of being allowed to have a few pieces of her own furniture in it, and she was not deprived of pen and paper. She wrote of her time in Vincennes quite glowingly:

'During the time I was at Vincennes and Monsieur de la Reinie interrogated me, I continued in great peace, very content to pass my life there, if such was the will of God. I used to compose hymns, which the maid who served me learned by heart as fast as I composed them; and we used to sing Your praise, O my God! I regarded myself as a little bird You were keeping in a cage for Your pleasure, and who ought to sing to fulfil her condition of life. The stones of my tower seemed to me rubies; that is to say, I esteemed them more than all worldly magnificence. My joy was based on Your Love, O my God, and on the pleasure of being Your captive; although I made these reflections only when composing hymns. The depth of my heart was full of that joy which You give to those who love You, in the midst of the greatest crosses.'

There was one occasion, however, when that peace was spoiled, and she blamed her own faithlessness for it.

'I was considering beforehand one day, the answers that I should make to an interrogation that I was to be subjected to the next day. I answered it all astray. And God, so faithful, who had made me answer difficult and perplexed matters with much facility and presence of mind . . . permitted that on this occasion I could with difficulty answer the most simple things, and that I remained almost without knowing what to say. This infidelity of mine spoiled my peace for some days; but it soon returned, and I believe, my Lord, that You permitted this fault only to make me see the uselessness of our arrangements on such occasions, and the security of trusting ourselves to You. Those who still depend upon human reasoning will say, we must look beforehand and arrange; and that it is to tempt God and to expect miracles, to act otherwise. I let others think what they please; for myself, I find security only in abandoning myself to the Lord. All Scripture is full of testimonies which demand this abandonment. "Make over your trouble to the hand of the Lord; He will act Himself. Abandon yourself to His conduct; and He will Himself conduct your steps." God has not meant to set snares for us in telling us this, and in teaching us not to premeditate our answers.'

However, after a few months she was removed from Vincennes to a convent in Vaugirard, a village near Paris, and here she was not so happy. She preferred the gaolers to the nuns, she told the Duke of Chevreuse in a letter. Her maid-servant was left behind in Vincennes, and the convent regime proved harsher than that of the prison. It was here, too, that the final attempt was made to discredit her in the eyes of the world.

Her relationship with Father La Combe, who had been a prisoner for ten years by this time, again came under review, and with 'fresh evidence' which she was called upon to answer. She had become accustomed to interrogations by this time, but the one she had to face in Vaugirard was the worst of them all. The local Curé, who had hitherto conducted them, was accompanied this time by an Archbishop Noailles, and confronted her with a letter purporting to have been written by Father La Combe from the prison in Vincennes, where he had now been taken. It was addressed to her – but it had first got into the hands of Bossuet, who had had copies made of it and circulated them. La Combe's letter called upon her to confess, as he was now doing, the misdemeanours and sins of their relationship, to repent of them, and henceforth to live a penitent and blameless life . . . The implication that they had indulged in immoral practices was unmistakable.

'Let me see the letter,' Madame Guyon said. 'It is probably a forgery.' She had had to defend herself against forgeries before. After scrutinising the letter she handed it back saying, 'If he wrote this it must have been under the torture.' Then she added slowly, 'Or else he has lost his reason.'

And that indeed was what had happened, though his insanity was not divulged at the time. He died some years later in a lunatic asylum. What had turned his brain, poisoned his sensitive imagination, must remain a secret until the Day when everything will be revealed.

It is doubtful whether even those most eager to do so really believed there was anything in Father La Combe's 'confessions'. Certainly Madame Guyon steadfastly refused to acknowledge there had ever been anything wrong in their relationship. She recollected that there had been one action which might have been misconstrued. She had once embraced him on his return from a long journey. There had never been anything beyond that. But it was her word against his – and against the array of powerful people, from the King down, who readily seized on the 'confessions' of a man who had been imprisoned for ten years before making them. They reflected on the morals of the friend whom Fenelon persisted in defending, the notable Madame Guyon, and therefore added further weight to the case being built up against him. Madame Guyon and what happened to her were now matters of secondary importance, although the scandal created through the 'confessions' was sufficient to land her eventually in the Bastille. But Fenelon was the central protagonist in the case now. Supported in the background by the Dukes of Beauvilliers and Chevreuse and their Duchesses, his most powerful antagonist was not now merely Bossuet, Bishop of Meaux, but the King himself, while the judge was the Pope. On his pronouncement Fenelon depended for the vindication of his teaching on what constituted pure love of God, and whether it is possible for man to attain it.

If the Pope, a man of over eighty, had been left to make the decision, the indications are that the final decision regarding *The Maxims of the Saints* would have been quite different from what it was. The political overtones of the situation, with the threat of a rupture between France and the Holy See if the King's demands were not met, evidently weighted the scales against Fenelon's book. In the event, the King's demands and Bossuet's deep desires were not met, for from their point of view the Brief of Condemnation that was eventually issued in March 1699, was not nearly strong enough. There was no mention in it of heresy, which was what they had hoped for – the book was merely condemned because it contained 'evil-sounding propositions' and the reading of it 'might lead the faithful insensibly into errors'. Privately the Pope served with a sigh that if Fenelon loved his God too much, Bossuet certainly loved his neighbour too little.

Nevertheless, the book was condemned, however mildly, and in the eyes of the world Fenelon had lost his battle.

It has well been said that crises do not make the man – they merely reveal him. The Papal verdict on his book, for which he had waited three years, reached Fenelon in his cathedral in Cambrai just as he was about to mount the pulpit and deliver a sermon. He stood still as he received the news, quietly absorbed it, then put aside the notes of the sermon he had prepared and quickly jotted down something else. Then he went up into the pulpit and preached, simply but eloquently, on the subject of submission. The text he chose was 'Thy will be done'. With complete self-possession and quiet dignity he made known the long-awaited result of the investigations into his book at Rome, accepted it meekly and with no evidence of bitterness, and went cheerfully about his business in the confines of his diocese for the rest of his life.

The curtain of history goes down at that point. The conflict was over. Bossuet was the victor, Fenelon, though still Archbishop of Cambrai, was 'disgraced', and as for Madame Guyon, she was reported to have died recently in the Bastille.

That finished it. Other matters occupied public attention, such as what would happen to the widespread empire of the weakly, childless Charles II of Spain when he died. And as he died the following year, and a few months later what went down in history as the war of the Spanish Succession broke out, the influence of the mysterious Madame Guyon was considered to be at an end.

But it was not.

In the first place, it was not she, but the maid-servant who had been imprisoned with her, who had died. In some ways this loyal woman had probably had a worse time of it than her mistress in prison, for not being of the same social rank she would have been treated with even less consideration. But she managed to get at least one letter smuggled out to her brother, which she wrote with a stick dipped in moist soot on paper that unexpectedly came her way, and it gave evidence that she had imbibed her mistress' spirit.

'Not a day passes that I do not thank God that He has imprisoned me here. I cannot forget the time when I laid myself upon His altar to be His in joy or in sorrow.' She regarded her imprisonment as the evidence that He had accepted her sacrifice. Then she went on to write of Madame Guyon:

'Having known her for twelve years, I think I know her thoroughly. It is an honour to share in her sufferings. It seems to me I have seen the divine nature manifested in her in a remarkable manner.

'We are now separated from each other. I am in this prison, she is in another, but we are still united in spirit. The walls of a prison may confine the body, but they cannot hinder the union of souls. It is the love of Christ that unites us . . .

'My dear brother, I do not go into details. I just say that she was an instrument in the hands of God to bring me to a knowledge of Himself – that God whom I now love and shall love for ever. She taught me the great lesson of self-denial, of dying to the life of nature, and of living only to the will of God. So do not wonder that I love her, because she and I love the same God.

'This love has the power of uniting our hearts in a way I cannot express; but it seems to me that it is the beginning of that union which we shall have in Heaven, where the love of God will unite us all in Him.'

She and Madame Guyon had lived and travelled together for so long that it is not surprising that a rumour of the death of one of them in prison should have led to the conclusion that it was the mistress, not the maid, who had gone. The fact that Madame Guyon was still alive became known when it was reported that she had again been interrogated by the Chief of Police, and that she had defended herself with great ability and firmness. Nothing could force from her a confession that she had done or deliberately taught anything contrary to the accepted doctrines of the Church of Rome. Eventually all efforts to do so were given up. Her health was failing, and it seemed likely that before long she would die in the Bastille, that notorious habitation of cruelty, to which she had been condemned. But in 1703 a strange turn of events took place. What induced His Most Christian Majesty to change his mind about the prisoner who had caused him so much disturbance in the court and the State is not quite clear, but the fact remains that he granted permission for her to be released from the Bastille and taken to Blois for a period of six months to recover her health – but only on the condition that she was kept under the strictest surveillance of her daughter and son-in-law who had an estate there, that she was to be allowed no communication with anyone else, and that if she was found doing so she would be returned to the Bastille immediately.

And so she emerged alive, one of the very few to do so, but silent as to what had happened to her within those thick, impregnable walls. Like everyone else who was taken there, she had had to promise on oath that she would never divulge what she saw or heard or endured there. All she ever revealed were a few sentences in her autobiography, written years later.

'When things were carried to the greatest extremity (I was then in the Bastille), and I learned of the defaming and horrible outcry against me, I said to You, O my God, "If You desire to make me a spectacle to men and angels, Your holy will be done. All that I ask of You is that You save those who are Yours, and do not permit them to separate themselves. Let not the powers, principalities, sword, etc., ever separate us from the love of God which is in Jesus Christ. For my own case, what matters it to me what men think of me? What matters it what they make me suffer, since they cannot separate me from Jesus Christ, who is implanted in the depth of my heart. If I displease Jesus Christ, though I should please all men, it would be less to me than the dirt." Let all

men, therefore, despise me, hate me, provided I am agree-
able to Him. Their blows will polish what is defective in me,
in order that I may be presented to Him for whom I die every
day until He comes to consume that death. And I prayed
You, O my God, to make me an offering pure and clean in
Your blood, soon to be offered to You.'

The worst times of all were when she felt that even God
was against her. 'Sometimes it seemed God placed Himself
on the side of men to make me suffer the more. I was then
more exercised within than from outside. Everything was
against me. I saw all men united to torment me and surprise
me – every artifice and every subtlety of the intellect of men
who have much of it, and who studied to that end; and I
alone without help, feeling upon me the heavy hand of God,
Who seemed to abandon me to myself and my own obscurity;
and entire abandonment within, without being able to help
myself with my natural intellect, whose entire vivacity was
deadened this long time since I had ceased to make use of it,
in order to allow myself to be led by a superior intellect;
having laboured all my life to submit my mind to Jesus
Christ and my reason to His guidance.'

Had that strong metaphysical tendency in her nature
carried her away too far, depriving her of the ability to
exercise the 'naked faith' of which she so often spoke when
feelings were deadened? Or had she been brought to the last
extremity, tasting the agony of Jesus Christ when he cried,
'My God, my God, why hast Thou forsaken me?' She did not
analyse herself now, she merely recorded what she experienced in her soul during some of those dark, dark days in the
Bastille.

'During this time I could not help myself, either with my
reason or any interior support; for I was like those who have
never experienced that admirable guidance from the goodness of God, and who have not natural intellect. When I
prayed I had only answers of death. At this time that passage
of David occurred to me; "When they persecuted me, I
afflicted my soul by fasting".'

So she reverted to some of the old practices, fasting rigorously and inflicting penances, but all to no avail. 'All seemed to me like burned straw.' Then she added a simple, illuminating sentence, 'One moment of God's conducting is a thousand times more helpful.'

In one moment He could calm the agitated mind and revive drooping spirits, and He did not delay that liberating moment for any longer than was needful for the purifying fire of affliction to do its work. One afternoon in March 1703, she emerged from the Bastille to be taken to Blois, one hundred miles to the south-west of Paris, and there she remained for the rest of her life. The six month's leave was extended indefinitely, and although she suffered incessant physical infirmities and illnesses, she lived peacefully for another fourteen years without encountering any further opposition from the ecclesiastical authorities, though they evidently kept an eye on her.

'Take care what you say to so-and-so,' she was reminded from time to time, and when, after a friendly conversation, the visitor or visitors departed, she was told, 'You shouldn't have said that in front of those people! It could be miscon-strued, and get you into trouble again. You really should be more careful! You are too naive.' She agreed she was too simple, but she could not help it, she replied. She couldn't be on her guard against anybody, and everything seemed to go off all right. 'O carnal prudence, how opposed I find you to the simplicity of Jesus Christ!' she wrote privately in her autobiography. 'I leave you to your partisans; as for me, my prudence, my wisdom, is Jesus, simple and little. Though I should be Queen by changing my conduct, I could not do it.' She was surprised to find that people liked to come and see her, and that whoever they were she seemed able to talk to them on their own level. 'God gives me a free air and makes me converse with people according to what they are, giving me even a natural cleverness with those who have it; and that, with an air so free, they go away pleased.' It must have been not unlike her early days in Grenoble, when people who had heard about her came to find out for themselves what was the secret of her piety and her prayerfulness and her quiet power.

They came from quite a distance, some of them – from England and Germany, the Protestant countries, as well as from her native France, and she received them all alike, speaking to them of Jesus Christ, the Divine Word. 'He alone is the truth. He said, *"Sanctify them in your truth. Your word is truth."* He also said, "I sanctify Myself for them." Oh, how well these two things agree! To be sanctified in the truth is to have no other sanctity than that of Jesus Christ. May He alone be holy in us and for us. He will be holy in us when we shall be sanctified in His truth by that experimental knowledge that to Him alone belongs all sanctity, all justice, all strength, all greatness, all power, all glory; and to us, all poverty, weakness, etc. . . .

'Jesus Christ will be holy for us, and will be to us everything. We shall find in Him all that is deficient in us. If we seek anything for ourselves out of Him, if we seek anything in us as *ours*, however holy it may appear to us, we are liars, and the truth is not in us. We seduce ourselves . . .'

It was the same message with which she herself had commenced her spiritual pilgrimage. 'The kingdom of God is within you.' Christ must reign supreme in the heart, and the SELF must die. Experimental knowledge had convinced her of the reality of it.

Among those who came to see her there arrived one day a Chevalier de Ramsay, reputed to be of Scottish stock, but a Chevalier for all that. Little enough is known about him, except that he had been in Cambrai, had met Fenelon the Archbishop, observed his manner of life, seen him giving away his considerable income with a free hand to those in need, opening his palace to refugees and wounded from both sides in the War of the Spanish Succession. He had seen a tall, thin, dignified figure moving with infinite compassion and humanity throughout his diocese, listening once a week with sympathy and deep understanding to those who came to make their confessions. The Archbishop of Cambrai had become a legendary figure in his own day, and through him the Chevalier had become a Christian. Now he went to see the lady whose influence on the Archbishop had been so great.

The Chevalier remained with Madame Guyon for quite a time, and during the course of their conversations the matter of her autobiography came up. Yes, it was still in her possession, though she had not added to it since she was taken to the prison in Vincennes. She had not really wanted to write her own story, had only done it out of obedience to her spiritual director, Father La Combe. It was the earlier part of that autobiography that had made so much trouble for her with the Bishop of Meaux, who had kept it for months before returning it to her. The latter part she had written because she felt it a duty to record the true facts of the case that involved others besides herself.

Would she be willing to have it published now, he asked? No, she would not. But after she was dead, it could be published. And so for the second time in her life she gave her autobiography into the hands of a man she scarcely knew, again with a proviso – not that its contents should be kept secret, but that they should not be revealed until after her death.

Before she handed it to him she read it through again, and as she did so felt a little uneasiness. What would be the reaction of those who read it against the persons who had treated her so badly? So she added a few more sentences at the end.

'I pray those who shall read this not to be angry against the persons who, through a zeal perhaps too bitter, have pushed things so far against a woman, and a woman so submissive.' They had been blind, had not known what they were doing. As she saw things now, the suffering they had inflicted had been necessary for her purification. And on that note she ended the story of her life. It was dated December 1709.

Chevalier de Ramsay kept his word, so he had the manuscript in his possession for ten years. She lived until 1717, two years longer than Fenelon. Her biography was eventually published in Cologne, in 1720.

Living Water

The fountain in its source
　No drought of summer fears;
The farther it pursues its course
　The nobler it appears.

But shallow cisterns yield
　A scanty, short supply;
The morning sees them amply filled,
　At evening they are dry.

Jeanne de la Mothe Guyon

Epilogue

A book, once distributed, is a lot heavier than thistledown, but it has a similar characteristic. One never knows where it will find its way, in what unlikely and remote place it will reveal its presence. It passes unnoticed over man-made boundaries, remains undetected for years, then takes root and flourishes. It may be discovered and stamped out in one place, allowed to blossom in another.

Several of Madame Guyon's books were published and distributed during her lifetime. Though they were eventually banned in France, nothing could prevent them being published elsewhere. Papal disapproval proved no deterrent to Protestant printers in Protestant countries. On the contrary, it provided welcome additional publicity. Her first little book on prayer, published almost casually in Grenoble, was being printed and distributed over the borders. The name of the woman the Roman Catholics would not own and the Protestants could not claim was known in many circles, and once her own story, written by herself, was released, there was no difficulty in getting it published. The slender thread on which it had been preserved through the years of her imprisonments and internal exile had held, and once it was released there was no stopping it.

There was no stopping the translators, either. An abridged translation into English was published in Bristol in 1772. In 1776 John Wesley produced *An Extract of the Life of Madame Guyon*, for although he disapproved of some of what she wrote, he handsomely admitted, 'I believe Madame Guyon was in several mistakes, speculative and practical too. Yet I would no more dare to call her, than her friend Archbishop Fenelon "a distracted enthusiast". She was undoubtedly a woman of very uncommon understanding, and of excellent piety. Nor was she any more a "lunatic" than she was a heretic'. He warned against the dangers of introspective mysticism, but he could not justly accuse her of being so preoccupied with herself that she forgot to do good to her neighbour.

About the same time William Cowper was lent three volumes of her poems, and was so impressed that he set about translating them. Some of them have been appearing in hymnals ever since.

Her books crossed the Atlantic, and early in the nineteenth century a Congregational theologian in the U.S.A. named Thomas Cogswell Upham was introduced to them. Her emphasis on the inner life of holiness found a deep response in his own heart. He believed it was no new doctrine that she taught, but that which reached back through the Reformation, through the traditional Catholic views on piety, right to the apostolic age when Paul wrote, 'I live – yet not I, but Christ lives in me.'

Having immersed himself in her autobiography and other published works, he wrote the book that was to be reprinted time and time again, right into the second half of the twentieth century – *Life, Religious Opinions and Experience of Madame Guyon*.

The fact that Thomas Taylor Allen of the Bengal Civil Service did not approve of the way T. C. Upham had interpreted his subject was all to the good in the long run, since it spurred him to the action of translating for the English-speaking family the *Autobiography of Madame Guyon* from the French.

And so the story of the woman who learned by experience that the Spirit of Jesus Christ can reign supreme in the human heart has come down through the centuries, reiterating the unchanging demand of a holy God: 'Be ye holy, for I am holy.' As for the suffering involved in the accomplishment of it, she herself might have written the words that came from the pen of a Chinese Christian imprisoned for his faith three hundred years after she was imprisoned for hers. They came out written on a flimsy piece of toilet paper, sent as a message of encouragement to his family, using a poetic form to conserve space.

Suffering often brings joy;
Daniel was tried in the den of lions,
Since days of old there has been order in suffering and joy;
After you have emptied the cup of suffering,
Then comes the cup of blessing.
How can a son not receive chastening from his father?
A gardener's pruning has no ill intent;
Only to ensure that the tree bears good fruit.
Without fire, how can impurities be separated from gold?
Without striking the iron, how can it become a tool?
Without chiselling, how can jade become a work of art?
Without pressing, how can grapes become wine?

A LONDON SPARROW

Phyllis Thompson went to China as a member of the China Island Mission in 1936 and wrote her first book, *They Seek A City*, three years later, shortly before the Japanese attacked Pearl Harbor. She escaped from Honan Province to Free China and lived in Chungking, China's wartime capital, until the end of 1943.

After her first leave in England she returned to China, travelling widely on the Tibetan and Mongolian borders. She lived under the Communist régime until 1951, when she left China. Since then she has been engaged in literary work and has written a number of books including *Within a Yard of Hell, Proving God, God's Venturer, Faith by Hearing, Firebrand of Flanders, Dawn Beyond the Andes* and *Climbing on Track*.

PHYLLIS THOMPSON

A London Sparrow

Contents

1 THE PARLOURMAID 13

2 THE PERSISTENT CALL 23

3 JOURNEY TO CHINA 31

4 THE INN IN YANGCHENG 43

5 INSPECTOR OF FEET 49

6 WAR IN THE MOUNTAINS 59

7 DAVID'S DILEMMA 67

8 TREK WITH THE CHILDREN 78

9 THE STUB OF A SWORD 91

10 A SPARROW FROM LONDON 105

11 LAST YEARS IN CHINA 119

12 IN THE ASCENDANT 131

13 THE SMALL WOMAN 145

14 IN ORBIT 152

15 THE FALLING STAR 166

16 GLADYS MAKES A COME-BACK 178

Foreword

This book will give pleasure and encouragement all over the world. The author has herself what she claims for her subject – 'the skill of the true story-teller' – and makes you feel it all happening as you read.

One high value is that before the close of Chapter Eight we are in the *sequel* to the story that is so well known and taken beyond the Edinburgh House BBC 'Undefeated' booklet, Alan Burgess' classic *The Small Woman* and that very popular film, *The Inn of the Sixth Happiness*. Now we have the full picture. Now we know what happened in the last thirty years of Gladys Aylward's adventurous life, including the *This is Your Life* television episode.

The *beginnings* are also filled in for us. How good to know that following her upbringing in a Christian home, it all really came to life when the Rev F. W. Pitt (known years ago to great monthly audiences at Kingsway Hall) and his wife were used of God in her conversion. There are other details, too, that are in neither of the two books nor the film, filling out the portrait and telling the whole epic tale.

You will be disturbed at some of the things you read in this book. Her Chinese attitude to things, for one. You will be challenged. Her utterly selfless compassion for others, for example, and you will be intrigued. Her premonition over the rape of Tibet, her simple creed, insight into her romance and how God compensated her – all are here for you. You will revel in tributes paid to her by Dr Hoyte of the Borden Memorial

Hospital on the banks of the Yellow River, by the public schoolboy ('It was the way she talked about God, as though she knew Him'), and by the celebrated Chinese author, Hsu Soo.

But read it for yourself, the life story of Ai Weh Teh, 'The Virtuous One', and gird up your loins! As she herself translated a verse in 1 Chronicles 22 from her Chinese Bible: *'Do not be afraid and do not wobble. Is not your God with you?'*

GEOFFREY R. KING

Acknowledgements

To obtain accurate information about Gladys Aylward, of whom so much has been written and reported, has been a task full of surprises. Some of the things I expected to find I could not – other things that I had not looked for emerged! My personal acquaintance with her commenced in China, in the early 1940s, but I met her only infrequently after that, and I am deeply indebted to many people who knew her personally, some of whom were even able to produce letters she had written to them – very welcome grist for the biographers mill! Many have provided information based on personal knowledge of her, and when it comes to acknowledging them all it is easier to know where to begin than where to end. Those who were her relatives, friends, colleagues and acquaintances have, in almost every case, willingly shared with me their reminiscences of her when asked to do so. The amassed evidence of many people has been invaluable to me in presenting, to the best of my ability, an accurate picture of her life and character. If at any point, through lack of information, I have conveyed a wrong impression, I am sorry.

Her life falls naturally into four periods of time, when she made her home in different countries. I would like to thank all those whose names are listed below, at the stages in which they came into her life, for the help they have given me.

1902–32 ENGLAND. Mrs Violet Braithwaite, Mr L. Aylward, Mrs Queenie Cocup, Mr and Mrs J. Jago, Miss Ada Warin, Mrs L. Gaussen.

1932–49 CHINA. The Rev and Mrs David Davies, Dr Stanley Hoyte, Mr and Mrs H. Fisher, Dr Handley Stockley, Miss Annie Skau, Mr and Mrs S. Jeffery, Mr and Mrs D. Woodward, Dr Olin Stockwell, Major Jarvis Tien, Mrs R. Butler, Mr Julius Bergstrom, Dr Francis Chu, Mr and Mrs A. Saunders, Mrs N. Douty, Miss J. Woodward, Mrs D. McCammon, Miss Grace Jephson, Mr N. Blake, Mr and Mrs G. Vinden.

1949–57 ENGLAND. Miss Ruby Rook, Miss Violet Bralant, Mrs R. Tyndale-Biscoe, Mrs H. Gordon-Dean, the Rev S. Wang, Miss Esme Wilson, Sister D. Gemmell, Mr L. T. Lyall, the Rev Geoffrey R. King, the Rev the Hon Roland Lamb, the Rev F. Harding, Mr and Mrs P. Parry, Mr Alan Burgess, Miss Nada Cholerton, Mr J. Erskine Tuck.

1957–70 TAIWAN. Dr D. Dale, Mrs Esther Huang, Mr Reuben Wang, the Rev Clifford Liu, Mr Leslie Huang, Miss K. Langton-Smith, Mrs E. W. Carlburg, Mrs Lilian Dickson, Mrs Twinem, Mrs Lilian Martin, Miss M. Sells, the Rev Samuel Wu, Dr Abraham Mok, Mr Chester Cheong, the Rev Bernard Barron, Mr E. E. Cooke.

I am especially grateful to Mrs Roland Lamb for lending me Miss Aylward's Chinese Bible, her school report, and personal letters written to a friend during her early years in China; to the Advent Testimony and Preparation Movement for permission to quote from the leaflet 'An Air Raid in China'; to Mr Yang of the Christian Witness Press for obtaining permission to quote from an article in the Chinese magazine, *Good Tidings Monthly*; to Mrs Gladys Donnithorne, Mrs I. Teasdale and the Rev J. McNicol for exceptional help given in collecting material; to the Overseas Missionary Fellowship for help and hospitality generously given in Hong Kong and Taiwan, and also for providing extracts from their Candidates Committee Minutes; to Chaplain Malliett of the US Navy for a tape-recording of an address given by Miss Aylward; to Mr Alan Burgess and the Rev Bernard Barron for sharing their reminiscences so willingly; and to Mrs Violet Braithwaite, for intimate and colourful glimpses into the Aylward home life, and her encouragement in the writing of her sister's biography.

Three people read the MS through critically – Miss Violet Bralant from the point of view of a personal friend, Mr Arthur Saunders as one with many years' experience in China and among the Chinese, and Mr E. E. Cooke as a Trustee of the Gladys Aylward Trust from 1966, and as one of her Executors. I am extremely grateful to them for their conscientious scrutiny, and have been glad to act on their corrections and suggestions.

Lastly, I thank the publishers for entrusting me with the task of writing this biography of an ordinary little woman who became famous in a materialistic age because, as far as she was concerned, God was not dead, but very much alive.

PHYLLIS THOMPSON
London, 1971

CHAPTER ONE

The Parlourmaid

The telephone was ringing insistently, like an alarm clock, and the diminutive housemaid in her neat uniform and crisp white apron eyed it rather uneasily. A heavy aggressive-looking thing it was, standing there with the receiver hanging on a hook, trembling slightly now from the vibration of that continuous raucous clangour. She knew there was no one else in the house but herself to lift the receiver, so she advanced determinedly towards it, held it to her ear, and shouted down the protruding nozzle,

'Hullo.'

A faint female voice at the other end of the line asked to speak to her mistress.

'She's out,' said Gladys shortly.

'Oh. Well, will you tell her that I shan't be able to come and see her after all,' said the voice, adding in explanation, 'I've got scarlet fever.'

That was the end of the conversation, for Gladys slammed the receiver back on its hook and retreated rapidly. As she explained when relating the incident later,

'I didn't want her germs!'

There were plenty of family jokes in the Aylward home in Edmonton, and this was typical of them. It was just like 'our Glad' to see an army of germs travelling at the same speed as sound along the telegraph wires and then leaping at her through the mouthpiece of the telephone! Dad and Mum had long since recognized that their eldest child was not what might be called the brainy type. That report card covering her last four years at school had been revealing. Conduct and personal neatness were excellent from first to last, she 'attacked her difficulties vigorously', and was very much in earnest about her work. When it came to native talent however, her position in class told its own story. The nearest she ever got to the top was seventh and the farthest from it fifty-third, and that could not all be accounted for by absences due to bad health. Composition was good though writing poor, and there was an ever recurring reference to the weakness of her arithmetic.

What she lacked in intellectual attainments she made up for in doggedness and high spirits, and when she came home on her day off the place hummed, for Mum had plenty to say, too. They'd talk and they'd laugh, and they'd mimic the people they'd met, Violet joining in, and then one of them would get irritable, and there would be a snappy retort, and laughter would turn to angry tears, and the sparks would fly until they all subsided in sulky silence, and Dad, who was used to these scenes, would say quietly from his corner,

'Well, have you finished now?' and they'd smile sheepishly and everything would be all right again.

'All we Whiskins are a bit mad,' Mum used to say sometimes. She was a Whiskin before she married Dad, a thorough-going little Cockney with her ready wit and her love for bright colours and plenty of feathers in her hat, when hats had feathers in them. It was no wonder she had caught Dad's eye in the Post

Office where she worked and where, being a postman, he had to go and collect the registered letters. It was another of the family jokes, the way he'd been too shy to speak to her, so slipped a letter across the counter to her instead, asking if he could take her out for a walk. Two or three letters were slipped back and forth across the counter before she agreed to meet him, and then when she turned up, dressed as smart as you please, he wasn't there – he was walking up and down on the pavement on the other side of the road, unable to pluck up the courage to cross over and speak to her! Well, he'd had to face the music next morning! Mum had fairly hissed at him, like an angry cat with all its fur on end, demanding that he should give an account of his ungentlemanly behaviour, and then going on to tell him, in fluent and colourful language, the utter contempt with which she regarded him, until the sight of his woebegone face suddenly made her stop. They looked across the counter at each other in silence, then she giggled and he laughed, and in the inexplicable way these things happen, the whole course of their lives was settled in that moment.

Everything was conducted in the accepted manner, of course. They started walking out, then became engaged, she cramming things into her bottom drawer while he saved for all he was worth, until on April 8th, 1900, they were married, and after a year or so in Bermondsey went to live in Edmonton, in the north of London.

It was here, on February 24th, 1902, that their first child was born. She was christened Gladys May, and when she was old enough they took her to church with them, sent her to Sunday School, and when she was fourteen found a job for her as assistant in the Penny

Bazaar. This was a highly exciting place, which had nothing on sale that cost more than a penny, but which nevertheless was able to display a great variety of articles, suitable for all sorts of uses, and Gladys announced triumphantly that she now saw how she could buy all her Christmas presents for sixpence. After a time she left the Penny Bazaar and went to serve in a grocer's shop. But then the men started returning from the First World War, wanting their jobs back, so although it meant leaving home Gladys had to go into service.

She did not stay anywhere for long. 'Can't settle down,' said Dad. 'Never know when she'll be on the doorstep, come home again till she gets another job!' Eventually she found herself as a parlourmaid in the West End of London.

Domestic servants had a hard time of it in those days after the First World War, with long hours and small pay. But as far as Gladys was concerned she enjoyed life, especially in London where there were compensations which balanced the disadvantages. Wasn't she in the heart of the great city, with its lights and its theatres, its glimpses of gentlemen in long tails escorting bejewelled ladies in gleaming silks and satins, its gay sounds of music from the orchestras in the hotels and restaurants? There was the darker side of life, too, to stir the imagination with its pathos and its passion – little ragged children, tramps on the embankment sleeping under sheets of newspapers as the trams went clanging by, women with scarlet lips and faces heavy with powder standing at street corners when twilight descended. And there were the ordinary people thronging the streets, the good-natured, grumbling Londoners whom she knew and understood so well. She loved it all, the policemen on beat, the red pillar-boxes, the newsvendors, the mothers pushing prams and the buses rumbling by.

And she liked being so near to the theatres. You could get in for a few pence if you queued up for the cheap seats.

'I'll take you to Drury Lane on Saturday,' she would say to Queenie. Queenie was her cousin, and lived in Fulham, not far from where she was working, and as the little schoolgirl's mother had died Gladys felt sorry for her, and often took her out. Breathlessly, heads pushed forward, they followed the anguished but musical adventures of beautiful, innocent blondes whose torments usually had a happy ending as they minced shyly towards the strong, silent men whose hearts had been nearly broken (but not quite) by all that had gone before.

'Wish I could be an actress,' breathed Gladys, blinking as the glaring electric lights brought her back to stark reality from the dim world of romance. Rosy dreams of holding audiences spell-bound with the limelight playing on her had to be suspended, however, for she must get indoors before the mistress started hovering round in the hall, ready to enquire suspiciously why she was late. Back in the Twenties the fear that girls might 'get into trouble' haunted the minds of those responsible for them, and young housemaids were expected to be in not a minute after ten when they had an evening off.

Once safely indoors the dreams would return, and if Gladys did not have much opportunity to indulge in the smoking, dancing, gambling and nights out at the theatre to which she sometimes referred in later years, it was not for lack of thinking about these delights. For the most part they had to be enjoyed in imagination, not in fact, and she was going nowhere in particular one Tuesday evening when a group of young people standing outside a church spotted her, smilingly invited her to come inside, then linked arms through hers and led her half-laughing, half-protesting, into the building.

She was rather annoyed. She sat through the service inwardly resentful, yet unwillingly compelled by the preacher's eloquence to pay attention to what he said. There was nothing in it that she had not heard before. All that about God being alive, and knowing what was going on in people's hearts as well as in their lives, and there being a time when everybody would have to stand before Him and give account of themselves. Of course she had heard things like that before, and about God loving people and being willing to forgive them when they'd done wrong, too. She'd heard about God from the time she could remember, but never before with this alarming sense of reality. She was hurrying to get away when it was all over when someone at the door grasped her hand, enquired her name, and then said,

'Miss Aylward, I believe God is wanting you.'

Gladys was alarmed.

'No fear!' she said quickly. 'I don't want any of that!' and scurried off, out of reach of that firm hand, but not out of earshot of the voice that called out something to the effect that she might not want God, but God wanted her.

It was a disturbing experience because, unlike the exciting impressions left by a visit to the theatre, it made her feel uneasy, as though she had done something wrong but she didn't know what it was. And instead of fading away, this sense of uneasiness increased until she was thoroughly miserable.

Eventually she decided to go and see the clergyman in charge of the church where the meeting had been held. The Rev F. W. Pitt was his name and when she got to his house and rang the bell, it was to be told that he was out. Would she like to come in and have a talk with her instead the clergyman's wife asked? So in Gladys went and told her all about it.

The clergyman's wife was sympathetic, but not particularly surprised. She seemed to understand what was going on inside Gladys better than Gladys did herself. The gist of what she told her was that she was out of touch with God. It was God she needed, and it was Jesus Christ who could put her in touch with Him.

There was really nothing new in this, either. Gladys had heard it time and time again.

> He died that we might be forgiven,
> He died to make us good,
> That we might go at last to Heaven
> Saved by His precious blood.

She'd sung hymns like that times without number, often had a nice religious feeling as she'd sung them, too, a noble and exalted feeling that was very pleasant while it lasted. The trouble was, it didn't last long. The clergyman's wife, however, made little of feelings, brushing them aside as though they were draperies in front of a window, shutting out the light. Facts were what she was concerned with, and one fact in particular. Jesus Christ was alive today, and He was willing, right here and now, to come into the life of Gladys

Aylward, bring her in touch with God, and keep her there. The clergyman's wife seemed very certain about this.

It was all rather stark and unemotional, with no music, no religious atmosphere, no dim lighting, only a draughty room with shabby furniture and the clergyman's wife talking in a matter-of-fact voice about what the Bible said. Gladys, feeling rather upset, sniffed and wiped her nose, her lips tight together, brows furrowed in concentration. She began to realize that she had to make up her mind. It was like standing at the bottom of an escalator, and deciding to get on it, and then getting on it. She had to make up her mind, and then do it.

Eventually she nodded her head, determined and unsmiling. Yes, if God was willing to take her on, she was willing to let Him. So with the clergyman's wife beside her, she knelt down, closed her eyes, and prayed that God would take her on – and as far as she was concerned, she had committed herself for life.

Nothing very dramatic happened. Visits to the theatre fell off, and attendance at gatherings called Young Life Campaigns took their place, with much hymn-singing and extempore prayer and people going up onto the platform and haltingly telling the others what a difference it had made to them since Jesus Christ came into their lives. Queenie was taken along on Sunday afternoons to a hall behind the church, where Gladys rattled away on the piano, and various housemaids of various ages ate bread and butter and cakes after the Bible Class. The lasting impression left on the schoolgirl's mind was that it was a tea-party for old ladies and that Gladys was in charge. If the entertainment value was not, in her estimation, quite up to that provided by a visit to a music hall, or 'a seat in the gods at Drury Lane,' she made no complaint, for the presence of her cousin was what mattered most to her.

Then Gladys started talking about China.

No one paid any attention to it at first. Apparently she had read a news item in a paper while travelling on a bus, which told of an aeroplane being flown from Shanghai to Lanchow, a city far up the Yellow River in the north-west of China. It was the first time it had happened, and the writer of the article commented on the fact that though this great nation was opening its doors at last to Western civilization, and hospitals, schools, railways, and now even aeroplanes, were appearing, there were still millions of people there who had never heard the Gospel. Something, the writer implied, ought to be done about it.

What all this had to do with Gladys neither Queenie nor her other friends and acquaintances knew. They could not understand why she was continually talking about it, and saying more people ought to go to China as missionaries.

When eventually Dad heard about it he was rather alarmed. He was a quiet man with strong convictions, and Gladys thought the world of him. From time to time young men paid respectful visits to the home and cast a hopeful eye at her, but the affairs always came to nothing. 'He's not like Dad,' Gladys would say, and that was the end of it. So when he suddenly flared up one day, and scolded her for talking such nonsense about going to China, she was forced to pay attention.

'All this talk about going to China!' he said. 'What do you think you're going to do when you get there? Tell me – are you a nurse?'

'No.' There was nothing to add to that.

'Are you a teacher?'

'No.'

'Then what good do you think you'd do in China?'

Dad picked up the newspaper and opened it. He had made his point. He had only one more thing to say, and he said it.

'Go on with you!' he said. 'Talk about going to China – talk, talk! That's all you can do – just talk!'

Gladys crept out into the narrow little passage that led to the front door, and stood snivelling at the foot of the stairs. Her father's words were going over and over in her mind, stinging her. 'Talk – talk – that's all you can do – just talk!' And then, as she stood there, she stopped crying and found herself whispering, 'Talk – talk – *but that's it!*'

CHAPTER TWO

The Persistent Call

Gladys had asked for time off. She wanted to keep a very important appointment. It necessitated a forty-minute bus journey from Marble Arch, which took her past King's Cross Station, alóng Pentonville Road, through a rather down-town shopping centre called the Angel, and landed her eventually at a tree-fringed square around which was built a miscellaneous assortment of shops and houses. At one corner of the square, lying back from the road in a well-kept garden of lawns and shrubberies, was a very large, four-storeyed building over the doorway of which appeared the words, China Inland Mission and Have Faith in God.

This was just what she wanted – a Mission to go to the inside of China, and faith in God with which to do it. As far as she had been able to ascertain, it was the only missionary society that would be likely to send to China someone like her – someone who was not a nurse, not a teacher, and who had left school at the age of fourteen. She had written to ask if they would take her on, and they had sent her some forms to fill in. She had answered their questions more or less accurately, and now she was coming to meet the Ladies' Council who would then pass on their recommendation to the masculine Candidates' Committee. Ladies having a voice but no vote, that was the way it was done.

It was in the Minutes of the Candidates' Committee, therefore, that the following item was included on December 12th, 1929:

MISS G. M. AYLWARD – aged 27.10 years of Edmonton, London, was interviewed. Gladys Aylward had been brought up in a Christian home and was converted at eighteen by being brought face to face with her own need as she went from home into business life. She has borne a consistent witness in her place of employment and has worked in the open air and at young people's meetings. In view of the manifest strength of character in this candidate the Ladies' Council recommended one term's testing to see if she is able to settle down to regular study. The Candidates' Committee, after very careful consideration of the case, decided to agree to this recommendation.

So it came about that early in 1930 she entered a tall house known as the Women's Training Home in a cul-de-sac in Highbury, discreetly removed by several blocks from the predominantly masculine headquarters. There were about a couple of dozen trainees that term, most of them younger than she, and they were all on probation. A bell rung at six o'clock each morning had them all out of bed, another bell had them all in the drawing-room, Bibles in hand, for morning devotions. They were divided up in shifts for various household chores, and spent hours teaching in local Sunday Schools, preaching in the open air, visiting in the back streets of Hackney.

The highlight of the week was the Wednesday meeting, held in a large, heavily furnished hall with high windows, and a square platform on which the speakers sat. On the wall beside it hung a huge map of China, sprinkled all over with little red dots, indicating the places where CIM missionaries were located. Reports about their work, information about China generally, talks by people who had actually been there, punctuated by hymn-singing and short prayers, occupied the best part of an hour and a half and when it was all over the young women returned to their Training Home more deeply impressed than ever that their duty and their destiny lay in China.

The warnings that it took over a month to get there, that they would be expected to remain for at least seven years before coming home for their first leave, that they might often be short of money, without medical help in time of sickness or police protection in times of danger, only served to nerve their endeavour. Even the knowledge that there were two women to every man in the Mission did not deter them. They were prepared to be spinsters to the end of their days if God wanted them in China.

As far as Gladys was concerned, after getting over the initial surprise of finding herself 'above stairs' instead of below them with the domestics, she fitted in quite well. She did her household chores with practised efficiency, jumped to the demands of the bells without effort, sang hymns and prayed with the rest of them, and did better than most when it came to visiting dreary homes in back streets, and keeping slum kids in order during Sunday services.

It was the studying and the lectures that baffled her. While the others sat at their desks, listening eagerly, busily taking notes, Gladys sat trying to understand, not knowing what to write in that exercise book in front of her. One of the probationers was a shorthand typist, and after transcribing her notes into long-hand each evening, let Gladys copy them into her own book. This made a good show in the exercise book, but when it came to taking the weekly exam it didn't help at all. The keen eye of the Senior Student, a qualified teacher, soon detected the deficiency, and she put Gladys through her paces, introducing her to the right reference books, asking her questions, explaining the line of reasoning in this, the conclusions to be drawn from that, but all to no avail.

'It just won't go in,' said Gladys.

The warden of the Women's Training Home looked apprehensively at those examination papers as they went off to the Candidates' Committee. She was very drawn to Gladys, spoke warmly of her zeal, her ability to get alongside people, especially those who were poor, her promptness in lending a hand when there was a job to be done. She could not deny, however, that when it came to imbibing knowledge by normally accepted methods, Gladys' powers of mental digestion seemed automatically to go into neutral, and occasionally into reverse.

No one was surprised, with the possible exception of Gladys herself, that at the end of the probationary term she was one of those who was not invited to return for further training. The Chairman of the Committee, a kind-hearted Irishman, pointed out to her gently that unfortunately the Chinese people all spoke Chinese, one of the most difficult languages to learn unless you happened to have been born to it. Months, even years, of painstaking study were required to master it, and her gifts did not appear to lie along the line of study. Her age would make it even more difficult to start now. God had a plan for her life, of that he was sure – possibly here in England. If there was anything he could do to help her ... Had she any plans as to what she would do when she left the Training Home?

No. No plans. Not now.

The shock of the disappointment was going deep, deeper than she could ever tell. They weren't going to send her to China. She had been so sure she was going to China, so sure God wanted her there, and now she wasn't going.

There was nothing in front of her now, nothing. She had no plans.

'While you're looking round for something suitable, would you like to help two missionaries who are back in this country now? They need some help ...'

So she went to Bristol to the missionary couple, and with calm simplicity they told her about their experiences through life, and how God had helped them.

'God never lets you down – never. He'll guide you. He'll provide for you, too. Trust him. He'll show you what He wants you to do.' They gave her a little card with 'Be not afraid, remember the Lord' on it. She kept it in her Bible.

In the months that followed she tried to find out what it was God wanted her to do. She went as helper for a few weeks in a hostel for working women, then she stayed with people she had known in London who were working among down-and-outs in Swansea, then she took a job as Assistant Matron in what was known as the Sunshine Hostel, where girls were taken in who needed a night's lodging. In some cases they needed it more than they wanted it, as Gladys discovered when she went looking for them down on the streets near

the docks where the sailors came swaggering along
from their ships, money jingling in their pockets. One
way and another she saw life in the raw those months
in Swansea, when the trade slump was bringing unem-
ployment, dole queues, desperate poverty in its train.
Families were living by their dozens in derelict rat-
infested houses, children half naked, women filthy,
men degraded – she had never seen anything like it
before.

'We can't let them be like this!' she exclaimed, and
recklessly giving away all the clothes she could lay her
hands on, wrote to her family demanding some of
theirs, too. When she got people cleaned up and
clothed, she insisted on them coming with her to the
Gospel Mission to hear about God. They'd got souls as
well as bodies to be saved, she pointed out with passionate insistence. She'd done what she could about
their bodies, now let God have a chance to do what He
could with their souls.

'You're doing a grand work here,' people assured
her. 'This is the right place for you!' But in spite of
everything they said, Glady knew that it wasn't.

'I can't explain why,' she had told Queenie. 'But
somehow I know it's got to be China.'

She knew it as surely as Abraham knew he had to
get out of Ur of the Chaldees, or Moses that he had to
go to Egypt to fetch those Israelites. China it had to be.
If no one would send her she'd pay her own fare and
she'd buy a ticket and go to China. She'd go back to
parlourmaiding therefore, and she'd save her money
and she'd buy a ticket and go to China. So the day
came when she found herself back in London sitting
on the edge of a narrow bed in a little room with a
china jug and basin on a wash-stand and not much

else, once more in domestic service. Beside her was her Bible, and her Daily Light and a few coppers – all the money she possessed in the world. She put them together, placed her hand on them, and closed her eyes tightly.   .

A quarter of a century later when Gladys Aylward's story was being glamourized in the film *The Inn of The Sixth Happiness*, this incident was retained almost as it must have happened. There was a reality and a simplicity about it that defied the touch of the most skilful artist to improve it, and Ingrid Bergman, the actress who took the part of Gladys, admitted that this was the scene which moved her more deeply than any other. For the London parlourmaid, almost in tears, at the end of her resources and nearly thirty years of age now, prayed with passionate earnestness.

'Oh, God! Here's me. Here's my Bible, here's my money! Use us, God! Use us!'

She heard a voice calling her name. It was only one of the other maids, with a message that the mistress wanted to see her. She wiped her nose, hastily adjusted her cap, and sped downstairs. The mistress had merely summoned her because, as she explained, it was her practice to pay the fares of her maids when she engaged them. How much had it cost Gladys to come to Belgrave Square from Edmonton?

When Gladys remounted the stairs she held 3s in her hand, ten times the amount she had placed on her Bible and as far as she was concerned it had come straight from God towards her fare to China. And if He could multiply what she gave Him as quickly as that, she'd be there sooner than she had expected!

From that time things went smoothly. She worked on her half-days and sometimes through the night, helping at parties in other houses, and saved every penny she earned. She went to shipping offices to find out how to get to China, and learned that the cheapest and quickest way, though by no means the most comfortable or safest, was to go by railway through Europe, Russia and Siberia.

She did not know what she would do when she got to Tientsin, or where she would go from there, but after a time that problem was solved, too. She went one evening to a meeting, and someone said to her,

'I've got a friend who's got a friend who has just gone to China. Her name is Mrs Lawson. She is seventy-three and has been a missionary in China for years. She came home, but she couldn't settle, so she's gone out again. She's praying for some young person to go out and join her . . .'

'That's me,' said Gladys.

She went to a travel agent and ordered a single, one-way ticket, third class to Tientsin, and persuaded him to receive the money for it in advance in small instalments until the necessary sum of £47 10s had been paid, so that she wouldn't be tempted to give it away.

On Saturday, October 15th, 1932, she set off from Liverpool Street Station to go to China – to fulfil her destiny.

CHAPTER THREE

Journey to China

She set off on that journey in a reefer coat, an orange frock that had belonged to Mum, a cap-like hat made by Vi, carrying a couple of suitcases, one filled with food, a roll of bedding, and a brown bag containing a spirit stove, kettle and saucepan tied together with a piece of string. In her corset, which was obviously the safest place, Mum had made neat little pockets to contain her passport, fountain pen, some travellers' cheques and a small Bible. If some emergency separated her from her luggage, only a catastrophe of the most unspeakable type could separate her from these essentials.

A group of friends and Mum and Vi were there at Liverpool Street Station to see her off. Dad had travelled with them part of the way from Edmonton, but left them at Bethnal Green, because he couldn't be late for work, he said.

They all understood. They knew he could not bear to stand on the platform waiting for the whistle to blow, waiting for Gladys to get on the train and sit looking out at them with those big dark eyes of hers, seeing her trying not to cry as she set out to go, alone, to China. A day's trip to the Isle of Wight was the farthest she had ever been from England's shores, and now she was embarking on an expedition that would take three weeks by train, always assuming that everything went well when she got to the border of Manchuria, where there was a war on. Dad could not face that last half-hour. He got off the train, his eyes sharp with pain, and Gladys looked at him and just said, 'Goodbye, Dad,' and stood at the carriage door watching him as the train pulled out, on towards Liverpool Street.

There was the usual hustle and bustle at the main line station where the Cross Channel train was drawn up, with porters trundling trunks and suitcases along the platform, sophisticated-looking, elegant passengers sweeping into the First Class compartments, and shabbier ones carrying their own boxes and bundles into those marked Third. Little groups of people stood talking and laughing, here and there women whose eyes were red with weeping tried to force a smile, the whistle blew, passengers hurried into the train, doors slammed, the guard waved his flag.

'Goodbye, Gladys!'

'Goodbye, Glad – God bless you.'

'Goodbye, Vi – Goodbye, Mum – Goodbye ...' She stood at the window, waving to them until they were out of sight ...

Everything went well at first. She wrote her impressions on a big writing pad, so that she could tear out the pages and send them home whenever she got to a place where she could post them. With characteristic disregard for the hampering rules of grammar and punctuation, she wrote as she talked, relating all that happened.

'The Dutch boys are wonderful they were all lined up on the landing stage, and each passenger who needs a porter is given a number, and when they get to the Custom House they just look for their number, mine

32

was thirty-one, so when I came off the boat. I just looked for thirty-one, who had all my bags on the counter.

'They did not open them, they just signed the paper, and away I went to the train, I gave him a shilling in English money, and he was very pleased. The police in Holland are very smart, but the porters here are smarter in their way, they have a strap round them, and just hook all the bags, etc, round, and you can hardly see some of them for bags.'

When she got on the train for Berlin, two of the other passengers got in after her, well-dressed, obviously husband and wife. The woman glanced at Gladys, then a look of recognition came into her eyes, and she smiled.

'Why, here is the little girl who had all the people to see her off from London,' she said.

'Did you come from London?' responded Gladys. The lady sat beside her and continued talking.

'And where are you going?' she enquired kindly.

'I'm going to China,' Gladys replied.

'You're going – *where*?'

'I'm going to China.'

'Oh! What a long way. Is your young man there?'

'No.'

'Oh! Aren't you going to China to get married?'

'No.'

'What are you going there for, then?' asked the lady, rather surprised.

'I'm going to China to preach the Gospel,' Gladys said definitely, and the lady was even more surprised. She had met missionaries before, but none like this one, and as Gladys chatted away, her interest deepened. They talked together until the train drew up at the station where the couple were to get off. 'We shall meet again,' said the lady with significant earnestness as she kissed Gladys goodbye. Gladys knew what she meant, of course. They would meet again in Heaven if not before, and she nodded emphatically. Gladys reported on her writing pad,

'... they were lovely, and we had Prayer before they got out, and I was left with a Schofield Testament, and £1 in English money.'

After they had gone Gladys had a little difficulty with the ticket collector who came along the train. He could not speak English, and she could speak nothing else, and the conversation that ensued attracted the attention of a German girl in the next compartment.

'She came in to settle him, well again we talked, and here I am in her home. She would not hear of me staying on the station, and when I have finished writing this we are going to see a little of Berlin. Hasn't God been good to me, I have had no bother with my luggage which is now in the cloakroom at the station ... The trains here run *overhead* not *underground*, and the police just stand like statues they wear long capes, and are armed with a little bayonet arrangement. Everything here is very clean and orderly, but not a bit like England.'

She boards a train bound for Moscow, and her only companion in the compartment is a Polish man. Efforts at conversation include much wagging of heads, waving of hands, and laughter, and as far as officials are concerned 'I have had no bother yet because I cannot understand what they say to me so I just shake my head.' As they leave Warsaw, and speed on towards Russia, however, she notices that everywhere are soldiers on guard. 'It seems so strange to us who are used to freedom, they get into the train, and look under the seats, and behind the curtains. They are very polite to me, and bow and diddle diddle Madame, they wear Russian boots, and look very smart in Air Force Blue with red tops to their hats ... My Polish companion is at this moment snoring very loudly and the train is rocking a little so my thoughts are a little disconnected, we have had one more talk with hands and heads, and he gave me an apple, so I have lent him my grey rug.' It was he who gave her the stamp for her letter, and went with her to post it before they eventually parted company and she was left alone in her compartment.

The train rattles on, and so does Gladys. Dad was right, they do run these trains on wood. She smelt it burning and went in the corridor to see, and the engine driver showed her all over the engine. They arrive at the Russian border, and she is very happy 'since China is now nearly in sight', although what she sees of Russia makes her thankful to God she was born English! She has just had her dinner, boiled egg, Ryvita and a cup of tea. 'I had an Oxo at 11 o'clock my little stove is wonderful and my saucepan is better than my kettle for boiling although I use the kettle for fetching my water in ... I have not yet started on Auntie Bessie's cake but am going to start it for my tea today.'

As the journey continues and water is more difficult to obtain, she sprints along the platform when the train stops, to the tap where the other passengers rush to fill their pots and their buckets. Her orange frock attracts much interest!

She arrives at Moscow, where she must change trains, and notices many soldiers, untidy-looking, down-at-heel dirty men who carry bread under their arms and pull off lumps and walk along eating it. There is something rather ominous about the atmosphere of Moscow that obviously affects her, but she cheers up again once she is on a train heading towards China. She has to share a compartment with three men, but they are very polite.

'I was not a bit nervous I curled my hair put on my smart cap said my prayers and went off sound to sleep we all got up about seven-thirty because we stopped for water, a nice young man went and filled my kettle for me.' The train chugs on, across the silent and lonely steppes, and on the fourth day she wakes feeling sad and weeps a little, until she opens her Bible at one of the Psalms, and after reading it feels better. The scenery stirs her deeply, and she describes the deep red glow in the sky which stretches right over the black clouds and makes it all look like a golden sea. She observes the animals, too, big black dogs with shaggy coats and long tails, and at night little wild things that 'look like cats but go into the ground like rabbits'.

She feels happy, so sings 'I walk with the King, Hallelujah!' and the people in the carriage smile. They seem to like it very much, though they cannot understand what it is all about. It is Sunday, as it happens, and a man gets in who can speak a little English, and at last there is someone to talk to! The carriage fairly buzzes with conversation, for everybody wants to know about her, and he acts as interpreter.

Before he gets out, however, he passes on to her a disturbing message. It is from the conductor. He wants her to know that there are now no trains running to Harbin, because of the fighting, and therefore she may be held up at the border.

'This of course worried me very much,' wrote

Gladys the following day, 'and I went to bed quite forgetting to have any supper and I lay for some time hardly knowing what to do. Then I thought, I am failing God, so I found my little Bible, and I thought, I will read my favourite part in the Old Testament the deliverance of the Children of Israel how God brought all those millions of people out of bondage. Well when I opened my Bible out dropped a piece of paper and on it were these words, "Be not afraid, remember the Lord," which was given to me when in Bristol. It was too much for me, I just cried, here was I worrying, when in Heaven was God helping me all along ... I would not if I could turn back now because I believe that God is going to reveal Himself in a wonderful way.'

After that she did not write anything on her writing pad for a week. It was the most terrifying week she had ever lived through, and from the comparative comfort and apparent security of the Intourist Hotel in the port of Vladivostok she continued her Pepys-like record to send to the family in Edmonton. She explained how a man had been sent to warn her it was dangerous to go on, but she had not understood, so when all the other passengers except soldiers descended onto the platform, she sat tight in the train.

'On we went but the fighting was right on the line so the train went back and at the first stop they made me get out.' She did not tell them she had to carry all her things, trudging alone along the railway track thick with snow, back to Chita. She did not want to worry them ... 'Well, I humped my baggage along to the middle of the platform and sat on it feeling very dazed, I had two cases, the bed done up in the grey blanket, my two rugs, my handbag and brown bag with saucepan, stove and kettle inside, my shoes tied together to the handle also two coats on. You see I had no time to pack properly, my kettle had water in it so it had to be kept upright. So there I sat, it was very cold I was hungry and very uncomfortable just hanging on to my things because all the people crowded round me trying to steal them' she wrote, and then she added, 'But they did not manage it!'

As she sat there like a lonely little sparrow among the crows, cold and frightened, she found herself saying 'Oh God, was it worth this?'

'. . . and to my mind like a flash came "Be not afraid, remember the Lord," so I prayed that God would remember me and deliver me. I believe He did but in quite a different way to what I imagined.'

No spectacular deliverance occurred during the nightmare-ish days and nights that followed, but they were punctuated by apparently irrelevant inspirations which led her through the maze. The first one came right there on the platform.

'It came to me that if I made a commotion and got *arrested* something would have to be done for me (you can imagine me making it!) well I did, and along came a soldier to move me on, but there I sat. Well three came in turn and then along came a very tall official one with a red hat on and with three others. Off I was marched, I went very quietly with my baggage without which I would not move, and put into a place so filthy oh dear I have never seen anything like it. The smell was horrible, I thought I should faint, so I brought out my passport to show that I was British so they railed me off from the others, and there I was . . .'

As the others were mainly men, several hundred of

them, of various nationalities and very rough-looking, that separation under guard was a God-send, though Gladys wrote that she nearly died with fright.

'Then all at once I saw Auntie Bessie and she had in her hand a green card and said, "Remember the Lord, He is with thee." That vision was very clear and I was at peace for I knew that my God was guarding me even in that horrible place.'

Meanwhile, the officials themselves were not without their problems. Here was a fiery-eyed little creature in an orange frock with a strange assortment of possessions from which she refused to be separated, who talked to them in staccato sentences which they could not understand, whose official papers indicated she was on a one-way journey to China, but who had got off a train which was clearly travelling in the opposite direction. If they mistook her for a fugitive from justice, it would not have been surprising. Her profession, according to the passport, was 'missionary', and what they made of that was that she was in some way connected with machinery. They were in the process of trying to explain to her that there was plenty of scope for people with a knowledge of machinery in Russia, when she had another of her inspirations.

'. . . the interpreter said evidently I was something to do with machines and they were trying to persuade me to stop in Russia as I was useful to them. When this dawned on me I did not know what to do. How I prayed and how near God seemed, so with boldness I fetched out my Bible and with a little picture Helene sent me from Germany I explained what I was. That did it, things moved then. Before I knew where I was I had a new visa, another ticket had been made out for me, then I was taken all round Chita to see it and impress me with Russia, then I was put in a train.' Instructions were given her where to change for Harbin, but when she got off the train it was to learn that the Japanese had closed in, and the line was blocked. 'Go to Vladivostok!' she was told. The first train was so crowded she could not struggle on, but she fought her way onto the next, and eventually landed at the great port in north-east Asia, on the Sea of Japan.

Again no one could understand her, and she had to spend the night on the station platform, shivering with cold.

'But in the morning I went to the Government Office having put my luggage into the cloakroom without paying for it, there I thought somebody will speak English, but no.'

Then it was that she had another of those irrelevant inspirations. She was nearly in tears by this time, and perhaps it was partly for her own comfort that she produced a picture of her soldier brother. When the officials saw it the tide turned immediately in her favour. 'They at once thought he was an officer in the British Army, (he is so smart and well dressed compared to their soldiers) I don't know what they said but they got my luggage from the station and sent me with an escort to this hotel. Can you imagine my joy to hear English again and to be able to rest. I have slept in a bed, the first time since I left home also I have been able to have a proper wash, oh the joy to be clean, this is the first time I have had my clothes off since I left home.'

That letter was written on Monday, October 31st, and ended with the words,

'I thought I knew the value of prayer before but never as now. When everything seemed against me He was there ready to help me over the difficult places and now here I am safe and happy just waiting to go on and would willingly go through it all again for the joy of knowing my Saviour as I know Him now.'

What happened shortly after writing that, she did not commit to paper. The next entry in her diary-letters was five days later, from Kobe in Japan, and commenced simply,

'God has been good to me, but I could not get a connexion from Russia to Harbin so had to come by steamer from Vladivostok to Tsuruga and thence here.' She did not mention the sinister way the official looked at her as he tried to persuade her to stay and work in Russian territory. Nor did she tell of the young woman who had sidled up beside her when no one was looking, and whispered urgently in broken English that she must get away that night or she would never get away at all. She didn't want to get Mum worried by relating the terrifying experience of the man who appeared at her bedroom door, his one intention all too evident, and who had so perplexedly backed away as she spat out defiantly, 'You can't touch me! God won't let you!' And even if she had escaped from the Intourist hotel at midnight, with the help of that unknown woman who had warned her of her danger, and had been taken on to a Japanese boat after signing some papers, and thus landed in Japan instead of China, it was all over now! Being British had ensured the help of the Consul, and now here she was at the Japan Evangelistic Band Mission Home, where everybody was very kind, and ready to help her in any way possible to get to her destination.

She was charmed with Japan, with its snow-covered mountains, pretty houses with quaint roofs, colourful fruit and flowers – 'it seems like Heaven after the desolateness of Russia'. She had a bath in a large wooden tub 'in which you boil, but was very refreshing,' and slept in a little white bed with a blue cover, and a red and blue lantern hanging from the ceiling.

Altogether, everything was lovely. The only little worry she had was that her orange dress was now very, very dirty, and when her shoes had been removed, Japanese fashion, everyone could see that one of her stockings had a hole in it.

CHAPTER FOUR

The Inn in Yangcheng

North of the Yellow River, in the province of Shansi, West of the Mountains, lay the city of Tsechow. For centuries strings of camels had come padding through it on the old trade route leading towards central China, along with mules and donkeys, and coolies swinging slowly along with their loads on carrying-poles. Now, in 1932, an occasional four-wheeled mechanical monster roared and snorted its way along the main street, to come to a halt in the pot-holed road surrounded by swarms of men and children who stood and gazed with expressionless faces at the passengers as they alighted.

On November 16th, Gladys was one of these.

She was still wearing her orange frock and her blue reefer coat, and was accompanied by a young man named Mr Lu, who had been sent to Tientsin to escort her to her destination. The boat journey from Japan to China had been without incident, the welcome in the London Missionary Society home in Tientsin warm and friendly, but she had been five days on the road since then, travelling deeper and deeper into the mountains, the object of that expressionless gaze of Chinese who seemed to appear from nowhere as soon as she arrived. It had been a relief to discover that there were missionaries in two of the towns on the way, and to go into their clean secluded homes for a few hours to enjoy the *camaraderie* that exists between exiles. Now she had arrived at the headquarters of the tiny Mission to which Mrs Lawson was loosely attached, a place she was to visit many times in the years that lay ahead.

The first missionary to live in Tsechow was a Cambridge undergraduate named Stanley Smith, who had come to China towards the end of the nineteenth century, along with six other young men from the higher strata of English society. They were known as the Cambridge Seven, and scattered far and wide in the Imperial Chinese Empire, wearing Chinese clothes, eating Chinese food, living in Chinese houses, and proclaiming the news of eternal salvation through Jesus Christ the Lord in the best Chinese they could muster.

Stanley Smith had settled in Tsechow, and travelled out from it steadily and patiently, establishing four other centres over an area about half the size of Wales, and even more mountainous, before he died. In Tsechow itself was a church and a boarding school for the children of Christians. In the other centres there was little more than a compound with some dwelling places for missionaries (if there were missionaries to live in them) and Chinese helpers.

The Mission compound in Tsechow, therefore, was quite a hub, presided over by Stanley Smith's widow, a charming old lady who after nearly half a century among the illiterate peasants of West of the Mountains had never quite shaken off the culture of the society into which she had been born. She could no more help being a niece of an Archbishop to the end of her days than Gladys could help being a London parlourmaid to the end of hers! But although she was the sort of person Gladys was accustomed to taking orders from and calling 'Madam', there was no consciousness of social distinction at that first meeting. Gladys wrote enthusiastically,

'... oh, what a welcome I had! It was lovely ... I feel that Mrs Smith is going to be my mother out here, I love her already ...'

She was quite sorry to leave Tsechow, but Mr Lu was all for pressing on, so after a couple of days they set off on the last lap of the journey. Gladys was no longer wearing her orange frock. Mrs Smith had supplied her with the attire of a Chinese country woman, wadded trousers and jacket, explaining,

'We missionaries all wear Chinese clothes. We want to be as like the Chinese as possible – and their clothes are much more sensible than ours, anyway!'

She travelled by mule litter over the mountain ranges until, in the distance, she saw a walled city set on the side of a hill. It was Yangcheng, Mr Lu told her. She looked at it with relief. She was very tired, and very sore from the continual rub of the net seat that was strung between the mules, in which she was being jerked up and down, so it was difficult to produce any very lofty reactions.

'Our journey took us two days and I thought I should be all broken in little pieces before I arrived, but when we reached Yangcheng and found my arms and legs were still where they should be I thanked God for all his goodness to me. Mrs Lawson also was very pleased to see me and many of the Mission people called to tell me how very glad they were that I had arrived safely.'

She did not mention that the Mission compound at Yangcheng was utterly different from any of the others she had seen, with its dilapidated buildings, its heaps of rubble, its buckets and its brooms left around in the courtyard and general air of neglect and untidiness. She drew a veil over the coolness of the reception she got from Jeannie Lawson, with her mop of white hair crowning five feet of Scottish skin and bones, who snapped when she saw her,

'Well, and who are you?' as though she were a gipsy who had turned up at the back door. The old lady was seventy-three and somewhat bewildered, and had probably forgotten she had sent her evangelist to Tientsin to escort a young woman she had never met to come and live with her for the rest of her life! When Gladys explained that she had written to her from London, the other just nodded and said,

'Well, do you want to come in?'

Jeannie Lawson was wonderful – once you got used to her. She had come back to China to die there, and she was determined to die 'in harness'. She took Gladys out, introducing her to the people of Yangcheng, and taught her a few sentences which Gladys reproduced fairly accurately, to bring out when she was spoken to, laughing and cheerful. And since Gladys must have a name, and the Chinese could not be expected to pronounce Aylward, she was called Ai Weh Teh instead, as the nearest that could be got to it. She translated it for the folk at home as best she could. It meant The Virtuous One.

It was Mrs Lawson who conceived the fantastic idea of turning their courtyard into an inn, so that some of the muleteers who travelled across the mountains could turn in there, and thus give her the opportunity of telling them of Jesus Christ. To Gladys fell the task of persuading them that it was a good place to come to, and very apprehensively she stood at the double-leaved gates of the compound, ready to grab the bridle of the first mule in the train and lead him in, while she called out to the muleteers,

'We have no fleas! We have no bugs!' She learned this from the cook, who assured her it was the correct approach. Had she paused for reflection, she might have questioned the validity of the claim, but Gladys was not given to reflection.

'No fleas! No bugs! Good! Good! Come! Come!' she called in Chinese with a strong Cockney accent, and leapt into the fray. It was a hazardous undertaking, especially for a Londoner who had never ridden anything more lively than a donkey on the sands at Margate, for the mules were big and could be very nasty. She decided not to mention it in her letters home. Mum might worry. And that bit about the fleas and the bugs ... No, better say nothing about it.

In any case, it was only part of the day's work, and it didn't happen every day. It was learning Chinese that had to happen every day, and she had to do it alone. Other young missionaries started with their books and trained teachers, in a well-equipped language school, and only after several months' organized instruction were they sent out to live among the Chinese. It was a method that would have been intolerable for Gladys, with her restless active nature and dislike of study. As it was, she applied herself to books for short periods, but when she was tired dropped them and went out to see what was happening in the streets of Yangcheng.

'... Even if I just go down the road I have a crowd of children. If I go to a shop I have to go to the best room and take tea, and then they serve me. I take a small boy with me, and never go alone,' she wrote, and

47

went on, 'The language is very difficult, but I am a good mimic and so am picking up little bits without study.'

So commenced her missionary career, and so she picked up, with remarkable accuracy, the language she could probably never have learned in any other way. So, also, she started to develop the independent spirit that was to carry her far beyond the spheres in which the average missionary moves. There were times when the dour determined old Scot, and the quick determined young Londoner clashed, and on at least one such occasion Gladys was told to get out!

Tearful but defiant she did so.

For a few weeks she lived with missionaries in a city represented by one of those red dots on that big map in the China Inland Mission headquarters in London. She stayed with Dr and Mrs Stanley Hoyte, who had several children, and as Mrs Hoyte had to go to Peking for an operation it was arranged that Gladys should act as nanny to them in her absence. However, while she was away news came through that Mrs Lawson was ill, and Gladys was off like a shot, back to Yangcheng. Dr Hoyte took it philosophically,

'She believed that God had told her to leave the Hoyte children and go to Mrs Lawson, so she left them, although I had to be away two days to bring my wife home,' he wrote, and added that as for the children, 'They came to no harm. The servants looked after them.'

But Mrs Lawson died. And with her, the income that had supported the Mission in Yangcheng.

CHAPTER FIVE

Inspector of Feet

It was mainly a matter of feet, where marriages were concerned. A pretty face, fair skin, a strong healthy body were all very well in their way, but it was the feet that could make or break it when it came to finding a suitable husband for your daughter. There was something exclusive about feet, something that set them apart from the rest of the body as being a sort of status symbol; the smaller a girl's feet, the more delicately she tottered on little stumps that resembled goats' hoofs, the clearer the evidence that she had been properly brought up in a genteel family, and was fit to be the first wife of an eligible son in an equally genteel family. For centuries mothers in China had looked anxiously at the feet of their daughters, bound tight from babyhood, toes crushed under, and hardened their hearts against cries and whimpers as they pulled the bandages more firmly, muttering,

'It's no use crying. How shall we ever find a husband for you, with these great feet?' And the little girls, as they grew older, looked down at their own feet, comparing them with the feet of their companions, and submitting to any treatment that would prevent them from getting bigger. Men wanted wives with small feet, and that was that!

The reason for this lay far back in history when, so it was said, one of the wives of the Emperor had escaped from the palace and run away. This, of course, reflected badly on His Imperial Majesty, and set a very bad example to all women in the Empire. If wives and concubines were free to take to their heels and make a dash for it whenever there was a slight domestic upset, where would the thing end? Women being what they were, and nature having so disposed matters that the sexes were equally divided, in no time at all half the population of the country might be running away from the other half! Even if it did not come to that, the dignity and authority of the male was in danger of toppling, and something must be done to set him firmly on his base again. Women must be permanently prevented from running away, and the simple solution to the whole problem lay in their feet.

And so, for several centuries the feet of baby girls in China were so dealt with that never in their lives could they run.

With the overthrow of the Ch'ing Dynasty in 1912 and the establishment of the Republic of China things began to change. The queues of the men, ancient symbol of servitude to the Manchu Emperors, must go. So must the custom of foot-binding. Twenty years later it was hard to find any men, other than old Taoist priests, who sported queues. However reluctant they had been at first to part with those long plaits of glossy hair hanging from their crowns they had soon got used to being without them.

It was a different matter when it came to the women's feet. The new law might have been successfully enforced in the cities and towns on the coast and on the main lines of communication, but away from them, back in the mountains and the vast agricultural plains, in the little walled villages where women rarely went beyond the confines of their own courtyards, small feet were still a status symbol. But now the Government was determined that they must go. The decree had gone forth, and it had reached, among other places, the city of Yangcheng. Foot-binding must be abolished, completely and utterly, and the magistrates of areas where it was still practised were put on their mettle. It was up to them to see that it was done away with.

This was easier said than done, for it involved *seeing* that it was done, and here the female foot presented another problem. As everybody knew, the female foot must not be seen unclothed, not even when it was being washed. How then could a man be submitted to the indignity of having to demand to see the naked foot of a woman to ensure that it was free of the evidences of foot-binding? Only a woman could be told to do that, and the magistrate of Yangcheng, after much thought and consultation came to the conclusion that the most suitable woman in the whole city to take on the job of official Inspector of Feet was Ai Weh Teh.

Once she got over the shock of it, Gladys reacted to the suggestion with enthusiasm. Here was something to write home about! The family in Edmonton might not have seen the funny side of the mules, the fleas and the bugs, and now that Mrs Lawson had died and the inn was no longer functioning she had forgotten all about it. But they would be tickled to death at the idea of her being official Inspector of Feet! What an opening for the preaching of the Gospel, and all at the expense of the Government! She was to be the recipient of a daily ration of grain, would be provided with a bodyguard of two soldiers who would be at hand to enforce her commands, and a mule on which to ride when she sallied forth to the villages. Armed with the authority of the magistrates, she could go into any home, demand to see the women and girls, sit down and talk to them, say what she liked so long as she made them finish with foot-binding.

Generations of missionaries, all over China, had waged a wordy war against the evils of foot-binding, but it is doubtful whether any of them had a better opportunity of wiping it out than had Gladys as a young missionary alone in Yangcheng. And by the time she relinquished her position, and Ru Mai a young Chinese widow with three children took it on instead, she was a familiar figure throughout the countryside, whither she went off from village to village for weeks at a time, her bedding and boxes of Gospels and tracts piled on a cart.

'We put up for nights where we can. Sometimes it is clean sometimes not. All depends! but we talk, sing and pray all the time.' And when she was in Yangcheng it was the same. She was up and down the streets, into the courtyards where women sat spinning thread or winnowing grain, quick, cheerful, interested in what they were doing, learning to do it herself, and then squatting down beside them to talk. To talk.

It was there among the peasants of Shansi that she learned by experience the art that was to bring her into the limelight on a very different stage from that at which she looked so longingly from her seat 'in the gods at Drury Lane'. It was in those lonely years that she developed, quite unconsciously, the skill of the true story-teller. With her own limited Chinese vocabulary and her listeners' limited knowledge of the outside world she had to convey messages from the Living God in a way they could understand. Away with cluttering details and accurate, deadly facts! Like a lightning artist, in vivid, bald, intimate sentences she depicted the children of Israel pouring out of Egypt, and they were all Chinese, with their carrying poles, and their babies bobbing up and down in baskets, their wadded quilts and their bags of grain, their shallow cooking pans and their bowls and chopsticks.

It was outside the wall of Yangcheng that they saw a patient young Peasant nailed to a cross, hanging there in the blazing heat of the north China sun, the flies buzzing about his head, two criminals shrieking on crosses beside him. It was in the guttering light from an oil lamp in one of their own rooms that they saw Him alive again, holding out His hands to show them the scars left by the nails in proof that it was He.

And let it be known to the people of Yangcheng that He was alive today! She knew, for He had spoken to her. Yes, it was to her, Ai Weh Teh, she who sat before them now, that He had spoken when she was in her own country, telling her to get out and come and live among them. And as she told them of the way that call had come, the drama of it gripped her afresh, and as she related the story of that terrible journey and the way God was with her through it all, her own eyes glowed and her listeners held their breath. An awesome awareness of a Presence stole over them, and they knew that what she was telling them was real.

She did not confine herself to the streets, either. There was a prison in Yangcheng, and she found her way in there.

'The prison work is going on. The change in that

place is remarkable and I am full of praise ... I don't know whether I told you of the girl in the prison. She is only twenty and has already been in two years. Her sentence is fifteen years for killing her husband, but she has come right out for God and is giving a real bright witness in there. Everybody says there is a difference ... Then four men have also really believed ...'

Ai Weh Teh became a person to be reckoned with, both in Yangcheng and Tsechow. When David and Jean Davies arrived as new missionaries in Tsechow, the first person to welcome them was Gladys, her black hair combed straight back to form a bun at the back of her head, wearing a simple cotton Chinese gown. She had come along with a deputation of the church elders, and was waiting for them at the city gate. It was she who had all the children in the school lined up, ready to sing a welcome. She knew how to organize those children, did Gladys! The Davieses were filled with admiration for this small but forceful young woman who seemed to understand everything the Chinese said and who, sometimes to their amused alarm, did everything the Chinese did. She could spit with the best of them, and when she bit on a piece of gristle at a feast it shot out of her mouth with the utmost precision to where the dog under the table was waiting to snap it up.

The Chinese adored her, David Davies noticed. 'She's one with us,' they told him, although the church elders wagged their heads sometimes over her generosity, and David went farther and wagged his tongue, telling her that people were taking advantage of her. The elders had told him that she was encouraging the wrong sort of people to come round the church by giving things away so freely. She listened, pursing her lips and nodding her head, and said she'd make inquiries about people before helping them. But her good intentions never lasted long. The false as well as the true knew where they could get free board and lodging, although they soon discovered she was as sharp as a needle over some things. 'They needn't think they can pinch my things!' she said as she glanced round to ensure that her wadded quilt, her comb, her towel and her face basin were where she had left them. And she knew just how little she could get it for when it came to driving a bargain in the market.

Those were sunlit years in Shansi, the model province West of the Mountains, as many a time she rode off on a mule to the villages, or to stay for a while with the Davieses in Tsechow. The Eighth Route Army with Chu Teh and Mao Tse-tung in its ranks was marching to settle in the Yenan, like a lion crouching in its lair waiting for the moment to spring, and the Japanese were massing their troops on the Manchurian borders, but she gave not a thought to them, if, indeed, she knew of their existence. She was solely concerned with the present. Travelling was primitive and tedious but comparatively safe, for the bandits were of the gentlemanly variety, for whom highway robbery was merely a productive little side line to be pursued when things were slack on the farm. Living was cheap, and she subsisted without difficulty on money gifts that came to her from time to time, some from England, some from missionaries who knew her circumstances.

She was lonely, it is true. The self-revelations which endeared her to thousands in later years told of her prayers for a husband, and how she looked for the answer, expecting to see a Prince Charming walking towards her over the mountains – 'But he never came.' The she hoped for a woman companion, and excitement rose when she received a letter from 'Evelyn' who wanted to join her. Gladys could not remember who she was but,

'... that does not make any difference when we are about the Lord's business, so I will try to answer your questions,' wrote she, and proceeded to fill both sides of five sheets of paper.

'Before I begin to tell you of actual things may I just say first, that if God has called you to China or any other place and you are sure in your own heart, let nothing deter you ... remember it is God who has called you and it is the same as when He called Moses or Samuel.'

She tells of her own experiences, of people trying to discourage her from going forward, and of her own effort to escape that inward conviction, but 'the urge was still there and I found nothing would do but go. I have lived in China now for over three years, and I have never asked anyone for a penny and yet God has supplied my every need.'

She eagerly goes through all her belongings, discovers she has sheets, pillow cases and towels enough for two, and goes out and buys a bed and a mosquito net in anticipation of Evelyn's coming,

'So make haste and come. Don't be too long for the time is short. And one thing more, I do not want you to think I am an old fussy creature and will want to boss you, you will be quite free only I must mother you a bit. You will let me won't you? How I have dreamt of getting you some pretty Chinese clothes ...'

But the next letter from Evelyn reveals she is still

in her teens, and even Gladys realizes that this is too young, so she does not come, either.

The longing for someone to mother does not remain unsatisfied however, for right on her doorstep are little unwanted children needing just what she has to give. She sees a hard-faced woman by the roadside, and discovers with hot indignation that the pitiable, wizened, wild-looking creature with her is a small girl up for sale. Furious, Gladys goes to the magistrate to report, but he shrugs his shoulders. There has always been a quiet traffic in women-children, and it is better not to interfere. It might prove dangerous, for the people behind the traffic are very powerful. Ai Weh Teh is instructed to pass by on the other side.

But this she cannot do. In the end, since there is no other way of saving the child, she buys it herself – for ninepence. After all, it is only one more little mouth to feed, along with the gatekeeper, and the woman servant, and Ru Mai's two children who are always in and out. So Ninepence, as she was nicknamed, came to stay, and after that Gladys had no cause to feel lonely, for she was only the first of a long stream of little children who needed to be mothered.

Meanwhile, although the people of Yangcheng had accepted her and she moved in and out freely among them, she knew there was something different about herself. She was still not really one of them. 'Why is it?' she asked herself, searching for the reason. As she faced her own question she realized that at heart she was still British. She had not renounced her national pride, and determined that this also must go. So she took a step which was ultimately to sever for ever any legal claim she had on the country of her birth. It was one that was to have far-reaching consequences that she could not have foreseen, although it would not have made any difference to the action she took. It was something she felt God wanted her to do, so she did it.

She destroyed her British passport, and applied to become a naturalized Chinese.

CHAPTER SIX

War in the Mountains

It was in July, 1937, that a shot fired across a river triggered off the Japanese undeclared war against China, unleashing a stream of misery and suffering that was to affect millions of people, sweeping Gladys along with it. In the early months, however, it disturbed her not at all except that the weeks and then the months passed by, and still no letters reached her from home, so when at last one came through and she recognized her mother's handwriting, 'I could not open it the tears came and my hands trembled, for the joy seemed more than I could bear.' Even when rumours ran through the city like an electric shock, telling of Japanese advancing towards Luan in the north, she was too busy with her visiting and her journeys to the villages, her classes in the prison and the children on the compound to give much thought to them. Life was full and happy until one morning in the spring of 1938, she and the evangelist and Ru Mai had gathered for prayer together before the work of the day began when a faint unusual hum in the distance drew steadily nearer and she recognized it as the sound of aeroplanes. An ominous sense of impending calamity deepened as the roar increased, and she found herself praying aloud, 'Lord, protect us, you are over and above those planes.'

Then came the sounds of explosions and crashing

masonry as again and again the planes swooped down nearly touching the roofs of buildings as they released their bombs, until at last they swept away, droning off into the distance, leaving Yangcheng a shambles.

Gladys emerged from the rubble and broken furniture that had turned the tidy room into a rubbish heap, and looked round. The others were scrambling slowly to their feet too, and they stood and looked at each other, faces bruised and blackened, thankful to be alive. The whole pattern of life had changed in that one terrifying hour, but life and limb had been preserved.

'My room was lop-sided and everything smashed in it. No way of getting out, only climbing through a hole in the wall, and oh, the mess! No roof left, piles of debris. But I soon realized if we had been hit so had others,' so burrowing for her little first-aid box under the rubbish, she went out into the street, Ru Mai following.

The sight that met her eyes would have been too much for her had it not been for an indefinable calm that possessed her. The people of Yangcheng, completely unaccustomed to the sound of aeroplanes, had emerged with excited interest from their homes to look at the two silver birds flying above them. When the bombs fell they were defenceless. They lay now, many of them dead, others wounded, and those who were unhurt panic-stricken and bewildered. They had never known anything like this before, and those who were not stunned by the shock of it were distraught.

If Gladys had never actually been in a Zeppelin raid over London in the First World War, at least she knew what had happened in them, and although this onslaught was much more fierce and concentrated she was not in any doubt as to what had taken place. The Japanese had bombed Yangcheng, and they might do it again. She moved straight into the situation as she found it, and wherever she went she brought a semblance of order and reassurance into the confusion, for she seemed to know what to do. Where she saw bodies trapped under masonry she started to get them out, snapping out sharp orders to the dazed onlookers.

'Here you! Come and get this man out. Careful, careful! Move that stone first ... Hot water! I want hot water! Quick woman, haven't you got any hot water in your kitchen? Ru Mai, you can bathe that child's leg and get the dirt out! Oh!' There was a body, lifeless, and after a moment's pause she said, 'Cover it over. There's nothing we can do for him now. We must help those who are still alive.'

She moved slowly along the streets that day, her face set, Chinese gown dirty and smeared with blood, yet with an authority which even the local soldiers recognized as she rapped out commands which they instantly obeyed. She seemed the one person who knew what to do, and they responded with relief that someone was in control. Not for hours did a tear come to her eyes, and then what brought it was the sight of an old man hugging a little girl of about three years old. He brought the child to her, begging her to save her, but one look, and Gladys saw that she was dead. She shook her head sadly, and as others crowded round for help the old man went wailing away, still hugging the precious little body. Gladys felt something come up in her own throat, a sob forcing its way out at last.

It was a day long to be remembered, for when eventually she reached the *Yamen* she was so dirty and dishevelled, and in tears by this time, that they did not recognise her at first. Not so did she usually enter the Mandarin's official residence! But when a basin of hot water was brought for her to wash, she was told comfortingly,

'Never mind, Teacher, we have caught the spy who gave warning to the planes.'

She merely nodded. The word 'spy' meant nothing to her then. Her mind was filled with the devastation and tragedy she had seen, and when she had pulled herself together she went back into the streets of the city to help whom she might. Then it was that she heard the name of the 'spy' who had been arrested. It was one of the men she knew, a member of her little Christian community.

Back to the *Yamen* she sped, oblivious now to the sights and sounds around her. He couldn't have done this thing! She knew he couldn't! She must save him! She pleaded to be allowed to see him, to find out the truth, the explanation. But it was in vain. 'You go and find a Chinese gentleman to stand with you,' she was told, and she went off, her head in a whirl, her heart like a tight, tense knot, to try and find someone to go with her to speak for the prisoner. She could find no one. Everyone was afraid, and anyhow, what did they really know about the man? What did she herself really know about him?

In the end she crept back to her own shattered home, shook the glass and bricks and rubbish off her bed and lay down, weeping and praying for strength. Ru Mai came to her, made her eat some food, and then together the two women lay on the bed, shivering, and somehow she slept.

'I rose early next morning,' she wrote home later, 'and, as I know China, I set off, but again I could find no one to come with me, and I started for the *Yamen* with leaden feet, when I heard shouting and yelling. I put my fingers in my ears and ran, but oh, my darlings, I was too late; his poor body lay headless and bleeding at my feet. It seemed as if my heart would break. Oh China, poor China! Pray, dears, for his dear mother and his sweet little wife and little ones and another one soon to come; how could I tell them?

'I started back home, to find a load of wounded from the previous day's awful raids waiting for my help, so set to work with a sore and heavy heart, not daring to tell anyone, for to be even thought a spy is serious. Even though he was innocent, I had no proof but my knowledge of him as a Christian co-worker. Oh God, how long? Keep me faithful and give me strength till He comes!'

The city was in a panic, for during the night Chinese soldiers had entered, evidence that they were in the fighting zone now. People were pouring out of the gates, possessions piled high on their carts and their wheelbarrows, fleeing to the country. A group of Christian men came into the city to urge her to leave. 'You must get out,' they said. 'You must all get out.' They did not say why. They did not so much as give voice to the rumour that the Japanese were advancing. One did not say these things openly – not yet. But Gladys understood.

'All right,' she said. 'I'll do what you say. But I can't be bothered to pack my things. I must go first and see those people who were hit,' and off she went, to do what she could for those whom she knew to be lying wounded in their homes. When she got back her things had been packed and taken off, the children with them, and only Ru Mai and two of the men remained, to escort her to the little village of Peh Chia Chuang.

As she looked round on her ruined home, the place where she had built her hopes, had her dreams, held her meetings, the place that had become more dear to her than anywhere else on earth, she wept weakly. This was the hardest moment for her, she admitted later, leaving it, as she thought, for ever. Rather solemnly she knelt amidst the ruins, bowing before her God. When she rose to her feet again, she was quite calm.

For the next six days she went into the city each morning, to tend the wounded until the sound of the guns came so near the city that the order was given that it must be evacuated. Then she set up a 'hospital' for wounded soldiers in a stable in the village, and those who had nowhere else to go, went there.

But there was something else on her mind beside the wounded. The little family of the executed 'spy' was suspect, and Gladys *must* do something.

She hid them for three days then decided to take them to a safer place and finally after four days hiding and walking reach Tsechow with them.

The Japanese had gained control of Tsechow, which had put up little resistance, and on that first invasion they were behaving reasonably well. Gladys marched through the streets to the Mission compound, and remained there until the Japanese retreated, for it was filled with refugees and there was plenty to be done. As soon as the way was clear, however, she was back again in Yangcheng, and from there set off to see how the little group of Christians in Chinsui had fared. It was two days' journey away, in a very scattered mountain district, and when she arrived in a nearby village she had a great reception. News that Ai Weh Teh had come reached the Chinese general in Chinsui City and he sent an escort with a horse for her, so she rode in in great style. She was, as she expressed it in a letter to Evelyn, enjoying herself A1. when a man came breathlessly with a message from David Davies. The Japanese were advancing again and he urged her to come back to Tsechow immediately.

So again she was on the run. Too late to get to Tsechow she found refuge in a Christian home in a village, and remained there for two months, sometimes not daring to go outside the front door, for it was right in the line of attack, and the guns were roaring and bullets whizzing along the streets. When the wave of fighting ebbed she made her way to Yangcheng again, through burnt out villages where the dead lay still unburied, back to the city itself, up the street that led to her compound, and into the shattered shell of a house that was her home.

It was still her home, and she intended to remain there. God had brought her to Yangcheng, of that she was sure, and the people of Yangcheng were her people. She would die with them, but she would never desert them. She clambered over the rubble into her room and looked round. Everything of value had been taken to Peh Chia Chuang and what had been left after that had been looted. But on one of the walls, where she had hung it months before, was a little motto card for the year 1938, clean and unharmed, and on it was the explanation of why she, a London parlourmaid who had never passed an examination in her life, was there. She read the words again, as she had read them many times before,

'God hath chosen the weak things.'

And underneath that announcement of the selection of Omnipotence was what she claimed as her own response,

'I can do all things through Christ who strengtheneth me.'

That was it. That was why she could speak these dialects of the Shansi mountains like a native now, why she could bring order out of chaos to distracted people, and tackle the nursing of wounded men. It was her first experience of such work, but 'as we go on, so does God', and the success of her amateur efforts was proof of it. 'It's not me, it's my God!' she protested when the wide-eyed peasants marvelled at how much she knew.

Letters from Yangcheng to London got through slowly and uncertainly in those days, but one reached the Aylward home in Edmonton containing a paragraph which was immortalized as the little parlour-maid became an almost legendary figure. She wrote in her usual artless style, about the things she was doing, the sort of food she was eating, about Ninepence, who had referred to her as a nice old lady – 'so now you know what I am in the eyes of a child of eight.' Then she continued more sombrely,

'Life is pitiful, death so familiar, suffering and pain so common, yet I would not be anywhere else. Do not wish me out of this or in any way seek to get me out, for I will not be got out while his trial is on. These are my people, God has given them to me, and I will live or die with them for Him and His glory.'

CHAPTER SEVEN

David's Dilemma

David Davis had several things weighing on his mind as he trudged northwards from Kaifeng over the mountains back to Tsechow at the turn of the year 1939–40. In the first place, he had not got his passport. It had been taken from him by the Japanese at Kaifeng. His permit did not allow him to go any farther, so the only way to get back was to leave the passport with them and give them the slip, which he did by keeping clear of the main roads and railways. The dykes of the Yellow River had been opened in an effort to hold back the advancing Japanese armies, and off the beaten track the going was hard, travelling across vast stretches of flooded territory where deserted villages crumbled into the water. Sometimes there was no road at all, only a ramshackle ferry boat or a ricketty bridge of planks hastily contrived by such peasants as still clung tenaciously to what was left of their farms and their homes.

At any rate Tsechow wouldn't be flooded, he consoled himself as he waded where he could not walk. Then he sighed. It might not be flooded by water, but it would be flooded by refugees, fleeing the flood and fleeing the famine, like human ants scattering in all directions as disaster on disaster struck their lives. The scorched earth policy might hamper the Japanese but it was a calamity of the first order for those whose homes were on the earth that was scorched ... He could see little but more sorrow, more suffering, more terror for the peasants of Shansi in the months ahead. The Japanese hold on the main lines of communication was strengthening, and the Chinese were finding it harder and harder to break those lines in sporadic attacks from their village hide-outs.

What was even worse – the seeds of civil war were already being sown. Skilfully the Chinese Communists from their stronghold in Yenan were deploying their dedicated forces among the lawless and discontented. The gentlemanly highwaymen of the past were easily persuaded to become the 'Red Bandits' of the present. There was a mysterious guerrilla army on the field now with supplies of smuggled opium passing through their hands and ways of extracting money that made people cold and silent with fear.

Oh for the old times when Tsechow and Yangcheng lived under the easy-going rule of their magistrates and their local militia! It was bad enough when a battalion of Nationalist soldiers entered, expecting free billets and food. It was much worse when the Japanese clattered in after their thunderous bombardments, passions aflame for rape and revenge. But worst of all was the fear of the 'Red Bandit' guerrillas.

Altogether, David Davies realized that he was engaged on a risky business, returning to that Mission compound in Tsechow, where over one hundred schoolchildren and a score of women had taken refuge from the varying perils that lurked in the no-man's-land of the fighting zone. So far it had been more or less inviolate as the property of an English Mission, Chinese and Japanese alike refraining from giving offence to a neutral power. Whether England would remain a neutral power was open to question, now that war had broken out in Europe. Already there were ominous signs that the Japanese sympathies were with the Nazis. One thing was off his mind, at any rate! His wife and children were safely settled at the famous seaside resort at Chefoo, with Murray in the China Inland Mission school there and American warships ready to whisk them off to safety in the event of trouble.

So thought David, ploughing on, in merciful ignorance of all that lay ahead – including the Japanese attack on Pearl Harbor. At any rate his own family, though in his heart, were not on his mind, and he was thankful. He had plenty of other matters to weigh on him, and amongst them was Gladys.

He was fond of Gladys, although he did not always approve of her actions. She had been a good friend to Jean and himself. How their hearts had warmed at the welcome she prepared for them when they first arrived, and how young Murray had gone to put his little hand in hers, right from the start! How touched they had been when she returned from a holiday at Tientsin bringing an enormous toy boat for him which must have cost far more than she could afford! She had always been ready to come to Tsechow at a moment's notice to keep Jean company while he was away somewhere, or to look after the children when Jean had to go to hospital. When there had been wounded men to tend after a wave of fighting she had come alongside with all the calm efficiency of a trained nurse, gritting her teeth as she helped him saw off shattered, hanging limbs.

'Gladys is trumps,' he and Jean agreed, 'ask her to do anything, and she'll do it.'

The difficulty was, that she was the same with all her friends, as David discovered on his return to Tsechow. To his dismay and indignation he learned that while she had been there in charge she had allowed some Nationalist officers to come onto the compound to hold a feast.

'But Gladys, you know perfectly well I won't allow men on the compound!' Had she forgotten that the first time the Japs ever came to Tsechow they had found some able-bodied men on the compound, and lined them all up and shot them dead? Hadn't that been the bitter lesson that made him, David, realize he would never be able to protect men, and that his only hope of protecting women and children against invading armies was to have a compound where no men were suspected of lurking? What would happen if the Japanese returned and learned that Nationalist soldiers had been carousing there? How to convince them that at the Christian Mission strict neutrality was observed?

Silence. It was to Gladys' credit that when she had nothing to say she did not try to say it.

Furthermore, so David had heard, the Nationalist officers had drunk wine at their feast. David was a Welshman, and with the fluency of his race demanded to know what sort of reputation the Christian Mission would get with wine flowing with who knows what results! What sort of example was that to the young?

'How was I to know they'd have wine?' retorted Gladys.

How indeed? David realized that what could have been merely a parrying question with most people was, in her case, a genuine one. She was really too naïve for words was Gladys, taking everyone at their face value! It would not have occurred to her that the courteous, charming young men who approached her about that little matter of the feast would be anything else but courteous and charming throughout, conducting themselves with quiet decorum and washing down their food with weak tea. For all her courage and her compassion, her faith and her dedication, when it came to matters that required sound judgment, Gladys was – well to put it politely, she was unwise. She admitted it herself sometimes, though the word she used was 'silly'! Just silly! Well, if that was what she said about herself, David would not argue with her. Not for a moment would he argue as to whether silly was the right word! He sighed impatiently, shrugged his shoulders and then gave a little grin. It was no use being angry with her. She couldn't help it. She was made that way!

Nevertheless, the incident served to increase one of the weights on David's mind. Gladys was a member of the tiny Mission of which he and Jean were now the only other two left in China, and he felt responsible for her. If the Japanese attitude towards Britishers hardened, and he had to cut and run for it, what would happen to her? He thought almost with envy of those other men missionaries he knew who, armed with the indisputable authority 'the Mission says ...' were chasing around the province rounding up women fellow workers and bringing them in to the central stations, ready for a quick get-away if necessity arose.

It wouldn't be any use trying that on Gladys.

In the first place, he could not quote that conveniently impersonal body 'the Mission', because as they both knew, he *was* the Mission.

In the second place, she would have resigned on the spot if he threatened to move her from Yangcheng to a place of safety. She was prepared to die for Yangcheng, but not to desert it. All this David knew, so he wisely did not broach the subject at all. Nor did he give voice to his deepest fear for her. He was not so much afraid that if she fell into Japanese hands she would be beaten up, or even killed. She was prepared for that, just as he was. No, he was afraid of something else. Tsechow had been occupied more often, and for longer periods, than Yangcheng, and he knew what had happened to some of the women the Japanese soldiers had taken off to their barracks . . .

He did not want that to happen to Gladys.

It was bad enough to know it was happening to little Chinese teenagers, squealing and sobbing in their agony of pain and shame. It would be worse to know it was happening to a fellow countrywoman and a fellow worker, and David wished with all his heart that he could persuade Gladys to get out of the danger zone. So what with anxiety provoking earnest desire, and desire turning to ardent prayer, an idea had formed in his mind which was to prove the solution of several problems.

Meanwhile Gladys was becoming more and more deeply involved with the Chinese Nationalists. Most of the peasants of the mountains were thankful if they could keep clear of soldiers, no matter which of the three fighting forces they represented. All they wanted was to be allowed to farm their land, go to market with their wares, live their lives as their fathers had lived, and die as their fathers had died. A few were dedicated to their country and ready to die for it. Some saw the chance of a little personal gain from helping this side or that side, which they did at the risk of their lives, departing as speedily as they could into the anonymous countryside when there was a change-over.

At every changeover there were bound to be a few who came under suspicion and were executed as 'spies', and as far as Gladys was concerned by the time 1940 dawned a spy she was. When she went off, basket over her arm, to visit remote villages where Christians were living, she came back and gave information about the movement of Japanese troops she saw in the neighbourhood. She had no compunction about doing this – wasn't she a Chinese citizen now, and weren't the Japanese invading her country?

She was becoming a well-known figure in that turbulent countryside. She helped train country women to do Red Cross work, she was on terms of personal friendship with the Nationalist General in the district and there was a young Colonel Lin in the Intelligence Service with whom she held conversations in David's office of a longer duration than was usual for the energetic Ai Weh Teh. Linnan she called him, and she told him all she knew.

All over the province of Shansi missionaries from Britain were objects of suspicion to the Japanese, and Ai Weh Teh was not the only one who eventually had a price on her head. It is doubtful whether any of them had given the invading Japanese greater cause to put it there!

One day, when the Davieses were away and Gladys was in charge of Tsechow and Yangcheng, a young American press correspondent, with the adventurous courage of his kind, turned up. Theodore White was his name, and he was gathering material about the conditions in war-torn China for the publication to which he contributed.

Gladys supplied him with it. In bald, vivid language she depicted the things she had seen and heard, running out every now and then to answer some call, issue some instruction, or listen for enemy planes. The young man was amazed. He had met plenty of missionaries on his travels, for missionaries were about the only westerners to be found in those rugged regions, but this one was exceptional. How she could talk, how graphically and intimately she could describe the chaos and the suffering! He stayed on an extra day to take in all he could, and then went on to the city where he was to stay with members of the Scandinavian Alliance.* When he arrived he could talk of nothing else but that little stick of an Englishwoman with her dark hair dragged back in a bun who was living alone there right on the firing line who knew everything that was going on and was evidently determined to stick it out whatever happened.

It was as well for the peace of mind of all concerned that they did not know the article he wrote for *Time* Magazine would be produced as further evidence against the prisoner when David Davies stood before a tribunal of Japanese officers, accused of being a spy ...

'It's these youngsters I'm worried about,' said David to Gladys. She nodded. One hundred and more schoolboys and girls were apparently housed on the Tsechow compound now. So far they had escaped personal harm, but the Japanese always made a strong attack in the spring, and it was likely to be an even

* Now known as The Evangelical Alliance Mission of the USA.

74

stronger one this year. If they came and stayed, those
youngsters would be 'recruited' for Japanese purposes.
If they came and did not stay, it was more than likely
that it would be the Communist guerrillas, the
'Red Bandits' who would take their place – and the
youngsters would be 'recruited' for Communist
purposes.

'We must get them out. We must get them to the
western provinces.' David and Gladys were agreed it
must be so.

It was happening all over China, that trek inland
to the cities of the west – Sian, Chengtu, Chungking.
Among the millions of distracted refugees were hundreds of groups of schoolchildren and college students,
travelling with teachers to set up school and college
again in more primitive but more peaceful surround-
ings. Sitting there in David's office in Tsechow, it was
agreed that those youngsters must be got across the
mountains, across the Yellow River to Sian, capital of
Shensi, one-time capital of the Chinese Empire, to
which place, it seemed, the Japanese could not possibly reach.

'Someone will have to go with them,' said David.

'Yes,' said Gladys.

'It can't be me,' went on David, 'I've been away too
long already. Didn't expect that hold up in Kaifeng –
then having to come the slow way because of having
no pass. Besides, if for some reason I couldn't get back
I'd be cut off from Jean and the children ...'

Gladys agreed it could not be David who took the
children to Sian. She pursed her lips, reckoned it
would not take anyone more than a month to escort
them there and then get back – probably less.

'Please God, you won't get back!' thought David

fervently. But he didn't say so. He just said they'd have to let the parents of the children know what was being planned, and find out if they wanted them to go. As the Japanese offensive was already beginning, decisions were made swiftly. One batch of about one hundred children was dispatched almost immediately to Sian, and rather to David's dismay it was a local man, not Gladys, who agreed to be in charge of that party. But news of what was happening had got around and more parents arrived with their children, begging that they might be taken too—

'He's fifteen already – he'll be conscripted . . .'

'Please take her – how can we protect a girl of thirteen?'

Some children were just quietly brought to the compound and left there. The same thing was happening in Yangcheng. And the Japanese offensive was speeding up. The main routes were already closing, and another batch of children must be got to Sian.

David and Gladys looked into each other's eyes, thoughtfully. There was no need to discuss who should escort the party, to David's relief. There was nothing more they could do to help each other, either. They were both under Authority, and they knew it.

'I say to this man, Go, and he goeth; and to another, Come, and he cometh; and to my servant, Do this, and he doeth it.'

The parting of the ways had come, and as things worked out they did not meet again for ten years. David remained in Tsechow to be arrested by the Japanese, endure months of torture and years of imprisonment, one of the many unrecorded heroes of World War Two. Gladys set off on the epic trek with the children over the mountains to Free China that was to capture the imagination of millions of people and bring her to fame.

To neither did the outcome of their decision really matter. All that mattered was that they were obeying orders to the best of their ability.

And since the future, as usual, was completely veiled, and the present was just like it had been for the years they had been fellow workers, they discussed things quite prosaically, prayed that God would continue to guide and help them, and left it at that. The compound was swarming with refugees, the Japanese were advancing and the sooner the children could be got away to Yangcheng the better. The trek to Sian must start from there.

CHAPTER EIGHT

Trek with the Children

If Gladys Aylward had not got away with those children when she did, she would probably never have been heard of again. The Japanese were in control of the main routes, the Chinese Nationalists were retreating, and in the hamlets and villages of the vast mountain area the 'Red Bandits' were pillaging and harrying. She had a price on her head by this time. The Japanese were prepared to pay one hundred dollars for information leading to her capture.

One hundred dollars was a lot of money there West of the Mountains and there would be plenty of people ready to betray her to obtain it, as she very well knew. There would be no one to ask any awkward questions, either. She was no longer a British citizen, about whom the British Government would institute official inquiries if she disappeared. She was just a naturalized Chinese woman now, and a poor one at that. When she stopped to think about it she was downright scared, until with lips pursed she reminded herself that God was with her, and that whatever happened He would never let her down.

Her mind was in a turmoil nevertheless, and she could not bring herself to leave until an urgent message from God Himself, as she firmly believed, convinced her that she must go. 'Flee ye, flee ye into the mountains; dwell deeply in hidden places, because the

King of Babylon has conceived a purpose against you,'
she read when she opened her Chinese Bible after a
desperate prayer that she would be shown what to do.
That verse settled it. God had spoken, and flee she
must.

So, one spring morning in 1940 she set off with that
heterogeneous company of children – some from the
school at Tsechow, some from families around Yangcheng, others little waifs who had been left over from
the pitiful treks of the refugees fleeing from the fighting and the floods and the famine. Every child had a
bowl and chopsticks, a face towel and a little quilt for
bedding. The teenage boys manfully shouldered
further supplies. The local magistrate sent a couple of
men with supplies of food swinging from their carrying
poles, to accompany the party for the first two or three
days. They surged out through the broken-down gates
of battered Yangcheng, the children at any rate merry
enough, and Gladys never saw the city again.

Ninepence was in the company of course, and Ru
Mai's daughter, along with some other teenage girls.
Gladys had a special plan for them. She and Ru Mai
had seen an advertisement urging people to get their
girls away from the Japanese to an organization called
'Good News', in a place called Fufeng in Shensi. After
delivering the younger children to Madame Chiang's
relief orphanage, therefore, they would take the teenage girls to Fufeng. Since 'Good News' was the term
used for the Gospel, Gladys jumped to the conclusion
that it was a Christian Church affair. The conclusion
proved to be very wrong indeed, and yet it had an important bearing on what happened later.

It was all fairly easy going the first day out, with
plenty of food, and everyone in high spirits, and in

familiar country. They all slept the first night in the shelter of a Buddhist temple. The next night, after trudging all day, they had to sleep out, huddling together at the foot of some rocks. They were moving out into unknown territory now, and the following day the two men left them to return to Yangcheng. All the food had been eaten, and from that time on they would have to fend for themselves.

There has never been any available record of that journey other than that which Gladys Aylward herself supplied. As far as can be ascertained, the astute Ru Mai was with her, but there is no evidence of any other adult being in the party. They straggled on, score upon score of refugee children trailing across that rugged, mountainous no-man's-land, a sharp-eyed, wiry little woman who still spoke her fluent Chinese with the hint of a Cockney accent overseeing the whole fantastic exodus. Sometimes they got to a small town and she went and begged food from the magistrate, sometimes villagers took pity on them, sometimes they had help from Chinese soldiers who were stationed in little bands here and there, the rear-guard of the retreating army. They warned her the Japanese were advancing. She would have to hurry if she were to get her crowd of children across the Yellow River before the Japanese got there.

The children got weary. The rollicking enthusiasm of the first day or two gradually wore away, and the little ones were fretful, wanting to be carried, wanting to stop, wanting to go back home. Gladys cuffed them and pushed them and carried them and cheered them forward, calling out,

'Come now, let's sing! All together! Ready?' and they would pipe up,

'Count your blessings, name them one by one,
Count your blessings, see what God has done,
   Count your blessings,
   Name them one by one,
And it will surprise you what the Lord has done!'

On they went, the older boys going ahead to plot out the way, the teenage girls hobbling rather painfully, the more adventurous children hiving off here and there, all of them getting more dishevelled, urged on by Gladys,

'Hi, what are you doing, you kids? Stop larking about there, you two boys, and move up to the front. Do you hear me? Up to the front where I can see you ...

'Hello, girlie, are your feet hurting? Here, I'll carry that basket for you for a little while ... What's that, sonny? Tired? We'll soon be at the Yellow River. Look, I'll give you a pick-a-back – how about that? Up you get!

'Oh dear, you're tired too, Little Sister? I can't give you both a pick-a-back at once. Liang! Liang!' calling to one of the older boys, 'There's a little girl who needs carrying for a while – can you take her? Good! On we go now, let's sing again,

'The Lord's my shepherd, I'll not want ...'

At last after days of struggling along, they got to the Yellow River. There it was, so wide, so deep, and the opposite bank so far away. There was not the sign of a boat to take them across, and the little town where they had expected to get food and shelter was deserted. Only a few soldiers were there, who provided them with some thin porridge, and after they had swallowed it hungrily they went back to the bank of the river, waiting for a ferry to take them across.

But no ferry came. The ferry was closed. Rumour had it that the short, sturdy little men from Japan, well-trained, well-equipped, fierce and dedicated were marching towards the river, and should they find boats handy to carry them across? No indeed! All the boats were on the other side, and there they would stay.

Many and many a time had Gladys told the story of how the children of Israel escaped out of Egypt and came to the banks of the Red Sea, the Egyptians in hot pursuit. Many and many a time had she related how that vast company stood helplessly looking at the expanse of water in front of them, the enemy coming up behind, and no way of escape. Many and many a time had she depicted the scene with such dramatic imagination that she might have been there herself – but she was experiencing reality now.

She looked around the dusty bank, where the children were sitting or sprawling, some playing, some whimpering a little, all hungry, all grubby. And all her responsibility. Her responsibility – the thought weighed on her, and she felt resentful. Why must she look after all those kids? If it were not for them she could have been here days before, safely over that river, safe from the advancing Japanese.

That second night by the Yellow River was the worst Gladys had ever known. They had waited all day for a boat to appear, but the river had remained empty, flowing, flowing, flowing down towards the south.

'When are we going to cross the river?' the children had asked, and she could not answer them. The older teenagers had glanced at her from time to time, but said nothing. They knew what the younger ones did not realize. They were stranded there, cut off, too late for the ferries that had taken over the other parties of refugees. They had arrived too late. They could not go on, they could not go back, and the Japanese were coming.

Gladys lay all that night trying not to think about what happened to women when the Japanese took them ...

The next morning was just like the other two. There was no sign of life on the river. But that morning one of the teenage girls came and asked Gladys a question. If God, in the time of Moses, had opened the Red Sea to let the children of Israel through, why didn't he open the Yellow River to let them, the refugee children from West of the Mountains, go through also?

Gladys was irritated by the question. That was in the time of Moses, she retorted tartly, and she was not Moses!

'You are not Moses, but God is still God,' replied the girl. 'Isn't He?'

Yes. Of course. God is still God.

Gladys, grim-faced, stared unseeing before her. Yes. God is still God. That's it. That's our only hope – God.

It's over to you now, God. I'm finished. Oh God, do something for us now. Don't let us down. Help us, God. Get us to the other side of the river. Oh Lord, get us over the river ...

After they had prayed Gladys lay down, exhausted. She did not know how long she had been there when the excited cries of the children, tugging at her jacket, roused her. A tall young officer of the Chinese Nationalists was approaching. She had not seen him before. He asked her a few questions, and then went to the edge of the water and whistled.

'I'll get a boat for you,' he said. 'You must get over as soon as possible.'

Away on the other side of the river a boat drew out from a little creek and was rowed steadily across the waters. The children lined up, chattering eagerly, and batch after batch were rowed over.

The Yellow River didn't open for them, but they got to the other side just the same. She wasn't Moses, and the Yellow River wasn't the Red Sea, Gladys reflected – but God was still God.

She felt safer once they were all across. The villages weren't so deserted, there were more people about, and the river flowed between them and the enemy. But Sian was still a long, long way.

They walked, then they boarded a refugee train, crowded with people and bundles, and with some people clinging on outside. Then they walked again, over another mountain range. Then they all clambered onto a coal train, crouching on the laden trucks that rumbled slowly through the night, close to where the Japanese might snipe at it. They were covered with coal dust when they slithered off the train. She tried to make the kids wash their faces, but she was getting too tired to bother much. Just as long as they had something to eat, and kept going, she thought. There were refugee centres along the way, so that made it easier. She was very tired. She'd be glad when they got to Sian.

But when at last they got there, she could not get in. The great walled city was already full of refugees – men, women, children, old grannies, with their boxes and their bundles and their baskets, bewildered, looking for lodgings, the streets were swarming with them.

The gates were closed to refugees, and they must go somewhere else.

Gladys wept weakly. She was seriously ill by this time, though she did not know it. Something was burning within her, urging her on. Where to go now? Sian had been the promised land, Sian was where the children were to find their refuge, and now Sian was closed. There was no other plan in her mind except – what was that place where the teenage girls were to go? Fufeng. Fufeng. They would go to Fufeng.

All the trains were carrying refugees, free of charge, and they got on a train to Fufeng, swept along with the human tide. It was when they reached Fufeng that she collapsed, like a gallant little sparrow battered by the gales that falls to the ground at last.

She might have fallen anywhere along the way she had come, over those desolate mountains, on the banks of the Yellow River, on the crowded trains, in the towns and villages through which they had passed, or just by the side of a country track. In all those places she was a complete stranger, a tiny woman looking like one of the hundreds of thousands of Chinese women among whom she had mingled on that incredible journey. Only the cast of her features, sharp and narrow compared with their broad, flat faces revealed that she was not Chinese. She had no identification papers. No one was on the look-out for her. The only westerner who even knew she was making for Sian was David Davies, and by this time he was a captive of the Japanese.

In Fufeng also she was a stranger. The 'Good News' organization for the teenage girls proved to be a sort of second-hand bureau for supplying healthy young females to families in the north-west, where women were in short supply. It was housed in a Buddhist temple. When she discovered the truth about it, months later, she was very angry, but she was at the point of delirium now, and conscious of nothing but a feverish urge to get out and preach. That was what she had come to China to do, to preach the Gospel! With feverish zeal she set out to do it. And while doing it she collapsed.

Now it so happened that in Fufeng there was a little Christian church. In that vast, thickly populated area round Sian there were scores of towns and hundreds of villages where there was no such thing, but in Fufeng there was. It was only a small affair, an obscure little compound to which missionaries went on a visit from time to time, though none were resident there. However, the handful of people in the town of Fufeng who were connected with it, in a dilemma with this wild but zealous woman, now unconscious, on their hands, knew where to take her. They did not know who she was, but they knew she was a Christian and they saw she was a westerner, so without hesitation they took her to the nearest missionary, an American in a city called Hsing Ping, some distance away.

He did not know who she was either, but that did not matter. Away there on the Sian plain Protestant missionaries were few and far between. They were all strangers in a strange land, they had come to it from vastly different backgrounds, but they had all come for the same purpose. God had called them. Most of them were quite sure about that. Irrespective of mission, nation or denomination they were bound together by their discipleship to Jesus Christ. They could be relied on to help when called on, without explanation or apology, so the American missionary immediately took Gladys in, and the alert was sounded.

'Unknown British woman seriously ill doctor please come Gustafsen' he wired to the Baptist Missionary Society in Sian, then sent a message to an American nurse on another mission station to come at once. Dr Handley Stockley beat the nurse to it. Sian and Hsing Ping were connected by the one and only railway line in that part of China, so he caught the next train, complete with blood film slides, medicines, needles, syringes, distilled water and intravenous saline of glucose.

Gladys was delirious, with a temperature of 105, and reacted violently against the doctor, who she was convinced was a Japanese officer up to no good. He managed to make some blood films and sent them off post haste to Sian for a report, which arrived the next day, confirming his fears that the patient had relapsing fever.

Gladys, of course, was unconscious of all this. Most of the time she was far away. She was back in World War I, in the little terrace house in Edmonton, singing for all her worth the rattling songs that kept up the spirits of the boys in the Flanders trenches, the long way to Tipperary getting mixed up with dear old Blighty, and Mademoiselle from Armentières popping in and out. Then, suddenly, she was in the villages around Yangcheng, talking, talking, talking to the peasants there about the Living God Who had sent his Son to save them from death and the devil . . .

No! She was with Queenie in the gallery of a theatre, peering down eagerly at the graceful couple spotlighted on the stage, humming as they crooned . . .

She was screaming, yelling to the children in Tsechow, 'Quick! Get under cover! The planes are coming!' Then she was talking to Mum and Vi, confiding an amusing incident involving her mistress, mimicking her . . .

She prayed . . . In the middle of it she shouted to the gatekeeper in Yangcheng to bring her mule. She started to sing a hymn.

The doctor kept careful watch over her, checking her temperature, trying to quieten her, listening, trying to discover who she was. She was worn out with fatigue and malnutrition, it was a marvel she was still alive. The nurse had arrived by this time, and after he had given Gladys an injection he said,

'The fever will fall now. Her temperature will go below normal, and she'll perspire profusely. She'll be very weak after that. But I think you'll be all right with her now. Don't hesitate to let me know if you are worried . . .' and he returned to Sian.

He was back again five days later, in response to an anxious message from the nurse. The patient's temperature had fallen, then shot back to 105, and she was delirious again. As he was examining her he saw that a typhus fever rash was breaking out. She had also developed pneumonia.

There was no specific treatment for typhus fever in those days, but Gustafsen, who had just returned from his leave in the USA, had brought back with him some new drugs – Sulphapyridine, Sulphur 693. Any use to you? he asked the doctor. From the doctor's point of view they were providential, for he knew they were potent especially against pneumonia, and where else could he have laid hands on them, there in the middle of war-torn China? They were invaluable, and if Gustafsen could spare them . . .

'Take them!' said Gustafsen. They were one more link in the long chain that drew her back from death.

'We must get her to hospital as soon as we possibly can,' said the doctor. 'Everything depends on careful, constant nursing now, day and night. And I want to keep an eye on her ...'

He returned to Sian, interviewing the official in charge of the railway line to ask for a special van to be attached to the evening train from Hsing Ping (they both belonged to the Rotary Club, and that made it easier to ask a favour) and hurried back to the hospital to make arrangements for receiving the mysterious, shrivelled little slip of a woman who raved in an uncouth Chinese dialect, interspersed with Cockney English.

There had been some alarming air-raids over Sian, so the hospital had been housed in a boys' school in the suburbs, and accommodation was limited. One of the lady doctors vacated her bedroom for her unknown fellow countrywoman. Gradually the fever abated, and after many days they learned her name at last, Gladys Aylward. Her family lived at 67 Cheddington Road, Edmonton. Mum would be worried. Yes, please, if someone would write to her ...

One Sunday, about ten days after Gladys' temperature had returned to normal, the air-raid alarm which had been silent for several weeks sounded again. The missionary doctors and nurses on the hospital compound were in the habit of going to an English service held in Sian city every Sunday evening, and decided that, air raid or no air raid, they weren't going to be done out of it, and set off as usual. Dr Stockley, however, remained behind. He was not sure how the sound of bombs exploding would react on his patient, whose recovery so far was something of a miracle.

It was well that he did. When the roar of the planes

was heard, and the bombs started exploding in the city, he witnessed the severest case of delayed shock he had ever seen. Gladys' thin little body twitched and trembled to such an extent that the bedstead on which she was lying shook and rattled, and he knew she must not go through that again.

'The planes will come again the same time to-morrow and the day after,' he said. Three days bombing in succession was the usual pattern. 'Must get her away somewhere before tomorrow evening!'

But get her where? That was the unsolved question until the arrival of a dog with an ingrowing toenail – or, to be strictly accurate, an ingrowing claw – led to the solution.

The dog's name was Alfie, and his master was Postal Director Smith. Postal Director Smith had moved all the GHQ staff out of Sian on account of the heavy bombing, and all were now fairly comfortably accommodated in the Great Goose Pagoda, some six miles from the city. There it had become apparent that Alfie had something wrong with one of his paws. There being no veterinary surgeon to whom Postal Director Smith could entrust his pet, he brought him to the Baptist Mission hospital instead. After all, the Baptists were British as well as he, and the British are a nation of dog-lovers!

It was while Dr Stockley was attending to Alfie's ingrowing claw that the problem of where to get Gladys Aylward away from the bombing was discussed in the hearing of Postal Director Smith. 'Bring her out to the Great Goose Pagoda,' he said immediately. So to the Great Goose Pagoda they took her.

'Omnipotence,' it has been truly said, 'hath servants everywhere.'

CHAPTER NINE

The Stub of a Sword

The Fishers were a popular couple. Their friends' faces relaxed into a grin when they were referred to, and they chuckled, 'Dear old Hubert! Good thing he's got Mary to look after him!' Theirs was a comfortable sort of home to stay in, however busy they might be with their Bible classes and their prayer meetings, their visits to the out-stations and their preaching in the streets. Hubert's zeal had nothing of the fanatical about it, leaving plenty of room for humour, and Mary had sufficient of the Martha in her temperament to ensure that meals were tasty as well as nourishing, even when funds were low, as they often were in those war years.

Perhaps that is why the Baptist missionaries in Sian, looking round for a quiet home for Gladys, decided that Meihsien, with the Fishers, would be just the place for her.

As things turned out, they discovered that the Fishers had met her two or three years previously, when they were living West of the Mountains, Shansi. She had passed through their mission station to attend a conference, arriving unannounced one evening. She was accompanied by two Chinese women and a Chinese teenage lad, and the Fishers had scurried round to prepare a room for them, and give them a good meal before going to bed.

Next morning Gladys and her company had a very early prayer meeting. Prayer was mingled with singing, and the Fishers were awakened rather earlier than usual by the words of a hymn wafting across the courtyard at five AM.

'When your fears rise mountain high . . .'

The quartet was singing fervently, and the sympathetic Fishers wondered what fears were alarming their guests. Judicious inquiries elicited the information that they had run out of money, so could not go on to the conference after all. The Fishers saw to it that the quartet got to the conference all right! The impression they gained of Gladys was 'not that she was spongeing on us, but simply had not calculated well enough, and probably was not in the habit of doing so.'

When they heard that she had brought some girls out from the no-man's-land West of the Mountains to Fufeng, been stricken down there suddenly with relapsing fever, and was now in Sian recovering from an illness that had threatened her life, they set off to see Dr Stockley about her. They were actually at the railway station, waiting to board the train for Sian, when a tall westerner appeared before them, barring their way. They recognized him immediately.

'Well! Reuben Gustafsen! Glad to see you! What are you doing here?'

'Come to stop you going any farther,' was the reply. 'You'd better go back home. Gladys Aylward is there.'

'Gladys Aylward in our home?'

'Yes. We'd brought her from the Great Goose Pagoda to Hsing Ping, intending to bring her to you in a few day's time, but there was an air raid warning, and she simply couldn't stand the sirens. Mildred Nelson and I have brought her here. We got into your place through a window when we found you weren't in,' he cautioned. 'Glad I got you in time. She's quite ill still – her mind's affected. Mildred's looking after her till you can take over.'

So Gladys stayed with the Fishers, out of the sight and sound of the war, for six months. Her temperature was normal, but not her mind. There were times when she wandered around not knowing where she was or who she was. Occasionally she suffered from hallucinations. It was the result of the sustained high temperature, and Dr Stockley had warned them that at times she would be deranged. She would need patient and careful handling.

She needed plenty of good food, too, the practical Mary Fisher decided, and set about giving it to her. Then it became evident that Gladys had dysentery, resulting in restrictions on diet that made things almost as hard for the nurse trying to tempt the patient to eat as for the patient who didn't really want to.

Gladys took that part of it cheerfully enough, and did not complain. She was never very interested in food. What she did want was someone to talk to, and as long as Mary Fisher would sit and listen to her stories about the old life in England or in Yangcheng, Gladys was happy and contented. When she was left alone for a while, however, Mary would come back and find her sitting and quietly weeping.

A year or two previously she had pasted into the fly-leaf of her Chinese Bible a slip of paper on which were printed the words,

> Many crowd the Saviour's Kingdom
> Few receive His Cross
> Many seek His consolation

Few will suffer loss
For the sake of the dear Master,
Counting all but dross.

Many sit at Jesus' table
Few will fast with Him
When the sorrow-cup of anguish
Trembles to the brim ...

Perhaps in those months when she was struggling
back to health she tasted something of that anguish.
There were times when she felt very near to death,
and reading in the book of Psalms one day she came
to the words, 'I shall not die.' She marked them and
wrote in the margin beside them, 'Sian, Meihsien,
1940.' It was another of the messages that came to her
direct from God, as she believed. But perhaps the
verses that meant most to her then, and which she was
to repeat innumerable times in the years to come, were
those found in I Chronicles, chapter 22, which she
translated from her Chinese Bible as, 'Be strong and
courageous. Do not be afraid, and do not wobble ...
Is not your God with you?' She marked them in red,
and in the margin above them wrote, 'Meihsien, June
1940.'

Although the periods of mental confusion recurred
from time to time for several years, her physical
strength gradually returned, and with it the old
familiar urge to be out and about. Mary Fisher noticed
with satisfaction that she was talking to the Chinese
now, telling them her experiences, especially about
how she had come to China, and the terrible things
that had happened on that journey, and how God had
delivered her out of them all.

The Chinese lapped it up. She started speaking at little meetings, always to a spellbound audience, and news about her spread abroad. After she had been with the Fishers for about six months it was decided that she was well enough to try living alone in one of the outstations.

And so she came back to Fufeng, where she had collapsed at the end of that trek over the mountains, and where the teenage girls were still housed in the temple. How glad she was to see them! She lived in the little three-roomed dirt-floored house on the church compound, Ru Mai joined her, and she reverted to the old familiar way of life. Chinese food, no set times for meals, toddling off, Bible under her arm and a roll of pictures to preach from, her days were spent wandering into courtyards where women sat stitching shoes, or spinning thread, ready to stop and talk — and listen!

She soon got tired, however, and had to lie often on the warm k'ang.* Without realizing it she missed those nourishing meals Mary Fisher had produced. It was only after she had been in Fufeng for several weeks that it dawned on her what the 'Good News' organization really was. It was no altruistic movement, but a profitable enterprise whereby a family with an un-marriageable dolt of a son could obtain a daughter-in-law, or a man with an ageing spouse a healthy young second wife all for the price of a mule.

Gladys was galvanized into indignant life. She had been deceived! Her girls were in danger of being sold off into a life of misery when she had believed they were being cared for by a Christian organization. If

---

* A k'ang is a raised brick platform used for sleeping built in houses in North China, which are kept heated during the winter.

those temple people thought they were going to dispose of her girls the way they liked, they were very much mistaken! She secretly organized a rescue operation, and the temple people awoke one morning to discover that half a dozen or so of the girls were missing. Ai Weh Teh had gone off with them, to Sian.

The temple people were furious. In the light of the customs of old China the organization was acting very reasonably, finding suitable homes for refugee girls who had fled from the invader. Ai Weh Teh had voluntarily arranged for them to be taken in, housed and fed, and if they had more than earned their keep by the work they did while there, what more would be expected? Had they taken action against her she would probably have had a bad time of it, for her Chinese citizenship did nothing to improve her status with the authorities. That the temple people eventually decided to let the matter drop is one of the deliverances in her life only explained by her own assertion that God was with her.

Back in Sian, thin and still prone to periods of confusion when she wandered around the streets vacantly, the Baptist missionaries were worried about her. They consulted together and decided to approach the British Consul and ask if he could get her home to England. The war was raging in Europe, the coasts of China were all blockaded now, but there was still a way out over the Burma Road into India, and this penniless little Englishwoman, alone in China, was surely the responsibility of the British Government? It was then that they learned she was not an Englishwoman any more. She had taken out Chinese citizenship.

They looked at each other in dismay. What could they do for her now? She had been delivered at their gates, so to speak, at the brink of death, they had seen her slowly brought back to life, their admiration had been stirred by that dogged, cheerful spirit of hers, their loyalty and affection quickened by her Cockney wit and her Cockney courage. 'London can take it!' the Londoners were writing defiantly on their pavements as they emerged from their air-raid shelters after another Blitz. Gladys could take it too.

> 'More than half-beaten, but fearless,
>   Facing the storm and the night,
> Reeling and breathless, but fearless,
>   Here in the lull of the fight.
> I who bow not but before Thee,
>   God of the fighting clan,
> Lifting my fists I implore Thee,
>   Give me the heart of a man!'

The stirring verses were stuck in the flyleaf of her Bible, and ended with the words, 'But spare me the stub of a sword.' If the Baptist missionaries had noticed those verses, they would have agreed that a stub was all she seemed to have left now, as far as physical and mental equipment went . . .

She would always be one of them in a way – and yet in a way she would never be. That almost ruthless independence of hers set her apart. She had strong convictions at which she arrived without other people's advice, and could never be one of a team. 'Me – and God' was the way she always saw it, and no other person really came into it.

'Look here, Gladys,' said the Baptist missionaries. 'Stay here as long as you need to. Come along any time you like – there'll always be a bed for you. If there's anything we can do for you, just let us know.'

'All right,' said Gladys. All through her life it was like that. There were always people who said to her, 'Come along any time you like – anything we can do to help you, let us know.' She took them at their word, too, turning up from time to time, unannounced, with a simple 'It's me!', rather like a child sure of a welcome, staying for a while, then disappearing again, back among the Chinese.

It was with the Chinese she lived there in Sian, in a tiny room that opened onto a little square courtyard where a few hens pecked about, belonging to the other refugees who had settled there. The courtyard was rented by two men, Christians, who had fled from the eastern provinces to Sian to escape the invading Japanese, and one of the rooms was turned into a chapel. Rough, backless benches, brightly coloured Scripture posters on the wall, a brick platform at one end provided all that was necessary, and this place, known as the Independent Church, became a centre to which refugees who were Christians found their way. They came with their bundles and their babies, some with a few hens tied together by the legs and carried upside down, bewildered, frightened. Gladys, who knew just what they felt like, hurried forward to meet them, found places for them to sleep, got the fire going to make some food. When it rained the courtyard was a quagmire, and her tiny room, with its old chest of drawers and table and a couple of chairs and a wooden bedstead ranged against the walls, often sheltered others beside herself.

It was the young people who specially drew out her sympathy, and as the schools in Sian were now bulging with refugee children, many of them got into the habit of going along to the courtyard where Ai Weh Teh lived. Her knowledge of English was an attraction, and, in fact, she earned some money by giving lessons to a few officials who wanted to learn the language. The schoolchildren listened enthralled to her stories of life at home, where her father was a postmaster and her brother one of the guards at Buckingham Palace! She found it easier to promote Dad and Laurie in this way than to go into laborious explanations about the different standards of living in the country she came from, where postmen were not in the least like the ragged, illiterate runners from the *Yamen*, nor soldiers like the undisciplined little groups of militia who roamed over the mountains. How else could she convey to them that her father was always spruce and tidy, and knew how to read all sorts of books? How else bring the picture before their minds of Laurie stepping it out smartly to the music of the regimental band? Her vivid imagination ran away with her as well as her hearers at times, in those gay recitals that whirled them all away from the drabness and the poverty that surrounded them.

But as she was talking her quick eyes were noting when some child had a rent in his clothes that required a patch, or that indispensible item, a face towel, that had worn to a rag, and in her practical, businesslike way she rummaged through her own scanty possessions to find what was required. She talked to them about God, and how He had sent her to China, just as surely as He had sent Moses to Egypt to bring out the Children of Israel. He was the same God now as He was then, and she urged them to trust in Him.

All the time, refugees were coming into Sian as the

Japanese advanced in the provinces south of the Yellow River. They came on the crowded trains, clinging to the doors and windows, sprawling on the roofs. They came on loaded merchandise lorries, bouncing about on top. They came on bicycles, handle bars and carriers laden with bundles. Every now and then, among the thousands of Chinese, travel-stained missionaries would straggle in, bringing with them what possessions they could, thankfully making their way to the hospital compound of the Baptist Missionary Society or the Scandinavian Alliance Mission.

Jumble sales were the order of the day then, for they had to turn their possessions into cash if they were to proceed farther west, and jumble sales were right in Gladys' line! She knew better than most what prices could be fetched for the garments and household linen and teapots and cutlery and old tin cans that were heaped in glorious confusion in the class room turned second-hand shop.

'You ought to get six dollars for that towel,' she said, 'and someone might be very proud of that teapot – might pay twenty dollars for it. Not easy to get anything for that cutlery – but this tin box! Why, it's got a lid! You'll sell that all right – ten dollars at least. I suppose you haven't got any empty kerosene tins? They're priceless! The water carriers will pay any amount for them – so much lighter than their old wooden buckets ...'

She was helping at the sale one day when a refugee missionary from one of the provinces south of the river came up to her and said eagerly.

'I say, I've just heard that you're Gladys Aylward! I'm awfully glad to meet you. I read about your coming to China all alone in a little magazine some years ago, and I've been praying for you ever since. I didn't know you were here.'

'Would you like to come and see where I live?' enquired Gladys. 'We could go along when the sale's over if you like.' So they set off together, along the broad muddy streets until they turned into a side road, and then into the little square courtyard, over to one of the doors with a padlock on the outside, which Gladys unlocked.

'Here it is,' she said, as she opened the door onto her tiny room. 'I've got a widow woman and a baby staying here with me just now. They'll be back soon.'

The other looked round silently. She had come from a very small mission station herself, where she and her fellow worker had been the only westerners in the whole area. They had lived very simply, in a little three-roomed Chinese house behind the big barn that had been converted into a chapel. From there they made their trips into the villages around, returning after a few days to drag out the big tin bath tub and thankfully to wash themselves all over in the bucket full of hot water that had been heated by their serving woman on the kitchen fire. If they were smart enough they could get rid of most of the fleas by throwing all their clothes outside as they undressed, so that when they donned a fresh lot of clothes they were more or less free of them. Their little courtyard was very small, boasting only an acacia tree and a couple of rose bushes, but it was secluded, and their kitchen, smothered in smuts from the fire of coal dust, was at least their own.

But this was different. This was a communal compound, with a shed in the corner for a kitchen, open to the weather and used by all, and a latrine that was just a hole in the ground behind a wall. There was no privacy in that tiny room, for when the occupant was at home the door would be, of course, left open. Whoever heard of anyone going into their home and closing the door in the daytime? When Gladys wanted a bath she would have to do the best she could late at night, discreetly, in her face basin. The little room was meticulously tidy, with a few tiny photographs in tin frames on the chest of drawers, and an enormous thermos flask to be filled up once a day with boiling water, so that she could always have a drink of hot weak Chinese tea to wash down a meal composed of coarse bread and a little pickled vegetable.

'It's not easy to get a meal here,' said Gladys. 'I know a little restaurant not far away, where we can buy something.' So they went along to an open-fronted shop with a few rough benches and trestle tables, where coolies came in for their bowls of hot noodles, and there, as they ate, Gladys talked. She spoke as though she were in a trance, her dark eyes brooding, glowing.

'All those kids! A long line of them stretching right over the mountain. I couldn't think how I'd been so silly as to take the job on. I started crying once and all the kids saw me and started crying too. So there we were, howling as we went on, trailing along over the mountain ... Oh God, why have you landed me with all these kids? I said.

'I was awfully ill, for months. They thought I was going to die. I guess I'd have been glad to, sometimes. Even after I was able to get around again, I was confused. Wandered around. Still do, sometimes. Sometimes one of the kids sees me, and brings me back!

'I was restless, too. Unsatisfied. There was a young man once.' She was silent for a moment, brooding, and her companion waited, asking no questions, just listening.

'There was a young man once ...' She did not say who he was. She did not say his name was Linnan. 'I don't know what he must have thought,' she said. So whatever it was, it had come to an end, thought her companion.

'It was a Chinese bishop who helped me,' went on Gladys. 'I told him how I was feeling – restless, unhappy. I was lonely – terribly lonely. It is lonely, you know, not belonging to any group. It's different for the other missionaries. They've all got their own missions. They all belong. It's lonely being one on your own ...

'That Chinese bishop helped me. He said, "Gladys, it's marriage you're wanting. You can't go on like this. You'll either have to get married or – you'll have to trust the Lord to satisfy your desires in His own way. He knows you. He made you. He can satisfy your emotional needs – if you trust Him."

'So that's it,' said Gladys.

They looked at each other across the rough table, and nodded. There were some things they understood without speech. They were not Roman Catholic nuns, they had taken no vows, they led no cloistered existence, and yet,

'He said unto them, all men cannot receive this saying save they to whom it is given ... There be eunuchs which have made themselves eunuchs for the kingdom of heaven's sake. He that is able to receive it, let him receive it.'

'Sing, O barren, thou that didst not bear; break

forth into singing and cry aloud, thou that didst not travail with child: for more are the children of the desolate than the children of the married wife, saith the Lord ... for thou shalt forget the shame of thy youth and shalt not remember the reproach of thy widowhood any more ... For thy Maker is thy husband; the Lord of hosts is his name ...'

'So that's it,' said Gladys.

CHAPTER TEN

A Sparrow from London

'Tongkuan has fallen! The Japanese have entered the city . . .'

'If it is true, we must get out, and quickly . . .'

'Perhaps it isn't true. You know how these rumours get about.'

'It seems true enough this time. We must get ready to leave – you know that was the arrangement. If Tongkuan fell, we must evacuate here immediately.'

'Well, we can't do anything tonight. Let's sleep on it, and in the morning we'll know for sure whether Tongkuan has fallen or not.'

That seemed wise enough counsel, so that is what they decided to do – the Fishers and the little group of missionaries who were staying with them, including Gladys and her old friend, the Senior Student. It was in 1943, and after another period of comparative inactivity the Japanese were on the march again, drawing nearer and nearer, bombing more and more fiercely.

If they were on the march, then Britishers and Americans were quite sure they must be on the run, away from the invader. There was no question any more about neutrality. The Second World War was at its height, and Japan was the enemy of the USA and Britain, as well as of China. She was the enemy of Norway as well, if it came to that, as Annie Skau was well aware.

Annie was the youngest of the whole group there on the Fishers' mission station, and she was the largest. A regular giantess of a Norwegian was Annie, making even Hubert Fisher look like a slim sapling. She positively towered over Gladys and the Senior Student, chuckling and laughing as the two of them related some of the things that had happened to them since those days in the China Inland Mission's Women's Training Home when the Senior Student had tried unsuccessfully to coach Gladys for the weekly exams.

Annie was very junior to them all, having only been in China a mere five years, and she was nearly always prepared to do what she was told by her elders and betters. But on this occasion, when morning broke and the Japanese were firmly asserted to be now entrenched in Tongkuan, she was not prepared to pack and make a run for it.

'I do not tink de Lord wants us to go,' she confided to Gladys and the Senior Student. 'He has spoken to me. He has given me His Word. Look, see what I have been reading ...' and solemnly she read the words from the little book *Daily Light*, which she held in her hands,

'Behold, I will send a blast upon him, and he shall hear a rumour and return to his own land ...'

'De Lord spoke dis to me dis morning, very early,' continued Annie. 'I was not looking for it – it was in de place where I was reading. I do not tink we should run.'

The Senior Student and Gladys looked at each other, and they looked at the text, and they looked at Annie, and slowly they nodded. They knew Annie. She was not given to hasty conclusions arrived at on the spur of the moment. There had been times in their own lives when something they read in the Bible became personal, with a significance that could not be ignored.

'Let's leave the others to get on with their packing,' they said. 'And let us pray about it.' So pray they did, kneeling together the three of them, and as they prayed the conviction deepened that it was going to be all right. This message sent to an Israelitish king thousands of years before somehow became relevant to them in the middle of China in 1943. So relevant, in fact, that they packed nothing at all. 'He shall hear a rumour and return . . .'

That is just what happened. The tide of war was already beginning to turn in the Pacific, and the Japanese heard that Americans had landed on one of their islands, so instead of advancing they retreated. That very autumn, instead of being on the run, Annie was back in her old station in the mountains of Shensi, and the Senior Student was continuing her Bible teaching.

Gladys, however, was on the move again. She was still liable to those periods of mental confusion, and the children she had brought out from West of the Mountains were scattered into new homes, into jobs, into the armed forces. There was nothing to hold her in Sian now – perhaps she was restless as a result. When she received an invitation from Dr and Mrs Hoyte to stay with them in their home in Lanchow, up in the north-west, the gateway to the long, long routes that led into Central Asia, she accepted.

The clear blue skies of north China spread like a dome over the city whose name she had first heard when she was sitting on a bus in London, reading that little news item about the first aeroplane to fly from Shanghai to Lanchow that awakened within her the urge that was to remain for the rest of her life – the urge towards the Chinese. Now she was actually here, seeing the place for herself. Perhaps this would be the place where God wanted her to serve Him?

The Hoytes lived at the Borden Memorial Hospital on a barren hillside on the banks of the Yellow River, opposite the great walled city. The hospital was a centre of healing to which people travelled sometimes for hundreds of miles. It sprawled along the hillside above the road that led to Central Asia, along which strings of camels and heavily laden lorries headed for the deserts. Picturesque Tibetans, Turki men with embroidered skull caps and leather knee boots, long-bearded Muslims whose women dressed like nuns mingled with the blue-clad Chinese who moved along that road, and passing in and out through the hospital gates were men and women whose faces bore the unmistakable marks of leprosy. There was plenty to be done, there in the hospital and in the leprosarium, and everybody on the big compound was busy. For Gladys there was a home and security.

'Stay with us as long as you like – stay here until you have really recovered,' the Hoytes said to her. But she was restless still. News reached her of a little town hid in the mountains where there was a tiny handful of people who believed in Jesus. They needed someone to teach them, and there was no one to go.

'I'll go,' said Gladys. Her visit to Lanchow lasted about a fortnight!

'I did not think she was sufficiently recovered, and urged her to stay longer,' wrote Dr Hoyte, 'but she insisted on leaving at once . . .

'Whilst she was with us I do not recall any noteworthy incidents or sayings,' he continued. 'It was what she *did* that made the great impact. She was transparently honest, utterly sincere, her life was completely in harmony with what she said. She was cheerful, never spent time talking about her feelings, her likes or dislikes, and never sought sympathy for her sufferings, was only occupied with how wonderfully God had brought her through, and what kind, good people she had met on her journey through life.

'She was entirely single-minded. She was out to serve God and the Chinese and never thought of herself or her own comfort.' Or, as the Senior Student put it once,

'The thing about Gladys is that when she sees a need she plunges straight in,' and then she added quietly, 'without any thought of the consequences to herself.'

So she went south again to a lonely little group in a remote town in the mountains, and spent a hard, cold winter there. The local people were bigoted and resentful, very different from those in her beloved Yangcheng. Women rarely appeared in the streets, and when they did were likely to be cursed by the men, and Gladys had to bear her share of this. She wrote in the margin of that Chinese Bible of hers,

Tsingsui 1944

> Lonely! The very word can start the tears …
>   Who walk with Christ can never walk alone.
> Alone, but not alone. He is here. G.A.

There were some things she wrote in the margin of her

Bible to which she put her initials and this was one of them.

She was very poor. The members of the little church provided her with some grain and occasionally a little money, but there were many days when her room was without heat. As always when she was ill at ease, she had little to say and appeared almost unfriendly, and somehow she was not at ease in Tsingsui. She confided to someone later that she was oppressed by the spirit worship that went on in the place, for some of the women were mediums, and there was a sinister atmosphere that disturbed her.

The brightest part of that stay in Tsingsui was the friendship of some of the teenage boys who were there in a refugee school. If the local peasants regarded Ai Weh Teh with suspicion, the young students regarded her with active interest. She was a foreigner, she came from England, she spoke English, and she was prepared to teach them to speak it, too. They crowded into her little room, and when they discovered she had no fire clubbed together to buy some charcoal, huddling together round the pan of glowing coals, listening eagerly to her descriptions of life in her own country. Those mental excursions carried Gladys as well as the boys into realms where facts were lavishly embellished by imagination, and probably did as much to enliven her as her hearers!

She taught them some English sentences, too, and always turned eventually to the Bible, speaking in that compelling way of hers about the Living God Who was calling them to be followers of His Son.

When the boys left, she gave them a little photograph of herself.

To Chu Fu Li,

May you ever be a true soldier of Jesus Christ, and therefore a good citizen of China. G. Aylward

she wrote on the back of one and gave it to the lad with a letter of introduction to the Senior Student, for he was going near to Sian. And she made a note of his name and address, that she might keep in touch with him, just as she tried to keep in touch with those other 'children' of hers, the refugee youngsters from West of the Mountains.

But she could not settle in Tsingsui. This was not the place for her. She went to a neighbouring CIM Mission station, and stayed with the resident missionaries for several weeks. It was there that she started talking about Szechwan.

'I'm going to Szechwan,' she said. 'I feel God wants me in Szechwan.'

'It's very different from north China,' she was told. 'The climate's hotter, and humid. Always cloudy. Dogs bark at the sun down there, the Chinese say! The people of Szechwan are difficult to understand, too – they don't speak our northern Mandarin.' But still she talked about going there, although she appeared to do nothing about it. It was only to God she explained that she could not go unless He got her there, since she did not have the money for the ticket.

'If you feel you must go to Szechwan, you'd better go to Chengtu first,' the missionaries told her. 'There's a CIM Mission Home in the city, and you can go there first until you know what you're going to do.' So they bought her a ticket, sent a telegram, saw her off on a ramshackle bus, and she set off for the city, hundreds of miles to the south, for what proved to be her last four years in China.

Sam Jeffery in Chengtu was accustomed to receiving telegrams announcing the imminent arrival of missionaries, known and unknown, so when one was delivered to him with the cryptic message that Gladys Aylward was coming he merely observed, 'I've never heard of her before,' and passed the message on to his wife so that she would have a bed ready. Gladys arrived in the middle of the night, but that was not unusual, either. That was the time when visitors often turned up. The Jefferys took it philosophically, showed her to her room, told her not to worry about the breakfast bell, she could stay in bed as long as she liked and have something when she had had her sleep out, and left her.

Late the next morning she found her way into the dining-room, and as she was eating her breakfast a friendly Englishwoman who was hovering round inquired casually,

'Where do you come from?' It was a common question in those days, when so many refugees were on the move.

'Yangcheng in Shansi,' replied Gladys. Four years had elapsed since she left there, but Yangcheng was still home.

'I was in Honan, south of the river till the Japs came,' said the other. 'Village work. Very different from this great city ...'

'Yangcheng was a country place, too,' said Gladys. 'I don't know what people are talking about here. I heard them talking last night about a jeep and a GI. What *is* a jeep? What *is* a GI?'

'Oh, a jeep is an American all-purpose vehicle that goes over all sorts of rough roads, and a GI is an American soldier. Like our British Tommy, you know, only American. Are you planning to stay here in Chengtu, or are you going on somewhere else?' she continued conversationally.

'Don't know,' said Gladys shortly. She had no plans to discuss, so what was the use of trying to discuss them? As usual, she had no money, and she did not want to impose on the good nature of complete strangers for longer than necessary. A few days later she announced that she had met a Chinese doctor who was a Christian, and he had offered her a tiny room in the courtyard of his little hospital. There were ways she could help him there, he said. He was needing someone to talk to the patients and preach at his little meetings, so she departed with her few boxes and bundles to revert to an entirely Chinese manner of life.

'How did she get to know people in such a short time here, a complete stranger?' the missionaries asked each other. They met her from time to time, in the street or at church, and noticed that sometimes she behaved strangely, as though her mind were confused. Then the Fishers arrived, with another batch of refugees from Sian, and heard her name mentioned.

'What she needs is plenty of good food,' said Mary Fisher briskly. 'She'll be all right then. Doesn't look after herself properly. I'll invite her here for a day, shall I?' So it became a regular thing for Gladys to go along to the CIM Mission Home once a week, to have a bath and wash her hair, and have a couple of good meals. And to talk, in English.

Perhaps it was having someone to talk to in her own

tongue that meant more to her than anything. 'When Mrs Jeffery knows Gladys Aylward's coming she just puts everything aside and gets out her knitting!' chuckled the young missionaries who were living there while they did their language study. 'Mrs Jeffery knits and smiles, and Gladys talks and talks! It's a life-saver for her.'

One day she went along with a large birthday card. 'I want you all to sign it,' she said. 'My mum thinks I'm here all alone, without any friends, and this will cheer her up no end.' But after a few hours she disappeared again, back among the Chinese, back to the tiny room with a bed and a table and a chest of drawers and a chair or two – and that huge Thermos flask in which to keep hot water to provide her and her guests with drinks for the day.

It was while she was living in the Chinese doctor's courtyard that Jarvis Tien first met her. Jarvis was twenty-two, and had just passed his entrance exam for the Chinese Air Force. He hailed from the province of Yunnan, South of the Clouds, so he was far from home, very poor and very lonely. He went to church more for something to do and somewhere to go than anything else. He had heard the Christian Gospel in Yunnan, though it had made no impression whatever upon him. But a church was a place where you could sit with other people, free of charge, and out of the rain.

It rained a lot in Chengtu. His own mountainous province was bright and sunny, but here in the thickly populated city of Chengtu the air was heavy, the sky seemed always overcast, and it drizzled and drizzled and drizzled.

So Jarvis went to church, and before long his whole

attitude towards the Christian Gospel had undergone a complete change, and for the most unlikely reason. It was not through hearing a stirring sermon, or through some devastating mystical experience, but through a simple statement made 2,000 years before by Jesus Christ about birds.

'Behold the fowls of the air,' He had said, 'for they sow not, neither do they reap, nor gather into barns; yet your Heavenly Father feedeth them.'

It is difficult to explain why this made so great an impression on Jarvis. He would have been hard put to it to explain it himself. Like everyone else, he was accustomed to the sight of birds, and took it for granted that they lived in the way they did, without any of the prudence displayed by some of the other creatures, who laid in secret stores for the winter. There was something about the words, 'your Heavenly Father feedeth them' that touched him deeply. They seemed to bring God suddenly very near, seeing those perky, twittering little sparrows descending on the ground, pecking around for a moment or two, then sweeping upwards again, obviously without a care in the world. This awareness of God brought about so unexpectedly by the ubiquitous sparrow brought faith to the hitherto unbelieving heart of Jarvis. He became a Christian and was baptized.

Very shortly after that he met Gladys, a sort of little human sparrow with her slightly beak-like nose that took a somewhat wayward course as it travelled down her face, her eyes like black beads, her trim little head thrust eagerly forward and, as he soon discovered, no visible means of support. She spoke to him after one of the services in church, asking his name, where he came from, how long he had been in Chengtu. The lonely young cadet responded shyly, told her about himself, how he had been a teacher in Yunnan, but was now in the Air Force and, furthermore, had become a Christian.

'I've got a book you ought to read,' she said. 'It'll help you,' and she started giving him books, *Pilgrim's Progress* and others. 'Jarvis,' she said, 'you must learn to pray. Prayer is most important in the Christian life. Come along to the prayer meeting.'

Christmas drew on. The war in Europe was over now, but the claws of Japan were still dug firmly into China. The economy was in a state of inflation, and money, as soon as it was received, was turned into stores, people buying rice, oil, fuel, cloth, in a frantic effort to invest their money before it lost its value still further. No one had money in hand for anything other than necessities, but Christmas was Christmas, and could not be allowed to pass without those little exchanges of gifts and greetings that characterize the season of good-will among men.

Jarvis, who, like several other young refugee students, was in the habit of going to Gladys' home when he was at a loose end, happened to be there one day when the Chinese pastor, Christian Chang, arrived on his bicycle, jovial and smiling. He had designed some Christmas cards on very cheap paper, and was now making the rounds of his friends, to bring his personal greetings at the Christian festival of the Holy Birth. He gave one to Gladys, which she received with enthusiasm, and after chatting for a while left his bicycle by her door while he went off to find the doctor and give him a Christmas greeting, too.

When he had gone Jarvis noticed Gladys go to the saddle-bag hanging on the pastor's bicycle, quickly open it, and slip some money inside. Then she fastened it again, and turned away. It was all over in a flash. He knew *that* money was probably nearly all she possessed.

It was strange, the things that made an impression on Jarvis. The flimsy cheap little Christmas card, the warmth and simplicity of the conversation, the swift, secret act of charity were burned indelibly on his memory. 'I saw what Christianity really meant,' he said many years afterwards, 'and Christian giving. I learned this from Ai Weh Teh.'

From that time he always went to see her when he had a holiday, and she did what she could to give him a good time, taking him to visit her friends, talking to him about his plans, or just wandering along the streets with him, looking at the things on sale on the stalls or in the little open-fronted shops. When he came along one day and told her he had been selected to go to the USA for training she promptly started planning. 'We must get you in touch with people over there,' she said. 'Now let me think – the Jefferys! They're American. They'll help.' So to the Jefferys she went, demanding letters of introduction for Jarvis, that when he got to America he wouldn't be left on his own. And she gave him a letter addressed to 'To Whom It May Concern', to have ready for an unexpected opportunity.

When he was feeling a little lonely in America one day, he opened it to see what she had said about him and saw she had referred to him as her 'adopted son'.

That clinched things as far as Jarvis was concerned. He was her son to the end of her life, and that of course gave him the opportunity and the responsibility of doing what he could to help her. His finances flourished in the USA, and from time to time he sent her money.

'I used your gift to have a holiday in the mountains,' she wrote to him once, but most of the time the money just went the way money usually went when it was given to Gladys. Like the birds of the air, she did no gathering in barns, for there was always someone under her very nose who needed some food, or clothes, or money for rent; or some young student who couldn't pay his fees.

'It's no use giving her money,' her friends said. 'She only gives it away. Same with food. If you take her food you can be sure half of it will have been handed out to someone else before your back is turned!' The best way to ensure that she had a good meal was to sit by her until she had eaten it.

'And she's too trusting!' She helped one young fellow to attend a course in a Bible School, and one day received a letter from him asking for some more money. She could not write well in Chinese, so replied in English, and he had to go to a missionary to get it translated. The missionary, who happened to know him for a rather unsatisfactory student who smoked quite a lot of cigarettes on the quiet, glanced at the letter and then looked at him very straight. There was silence for a moment – a rather significant silence. Then the missionary read the letter to him.

In it Gladys urged him to get on with his studies, and explained that she could not send him any more money, as she was already going without one meal a day to provide him with what she was giving.

CHAPTER ELEVEN

Last Years in China

Christian Chang drank so much beer and liquor in his youth that he died from cirrhosis of the liver in early middle life. In the period between sowing his wild oats and reaping them in his own body, however, he experienced a transformation of soul which changed the whole course of his residue of years, into which he managed to pack as much service for Jesus Christ as many Christians do in their three score years and ten. That is why he went to a Theological Seminary in Nanking, then to Chengtu, where he was appointed pastor of the big Methodist Church.

It was there that he met Ai Weh Teh, who was a member of the congregation. In her long dark-blue Chinese gown and home-made shoes, her hair scraped back from her face, sitting among the Chinese women on their side of the church she looked just like one of them, except for her nose. It soon became evident that she was no ordinary member, though, one who went along to services on Sunday and then disappeared for the rest of the week. She had a way of spotting things that needed to be done, and doing them. She talked to people about God, and it was evident she knew Who she was talking about. And she obviously knew the Chinese manner of life and thought so well that she moved about among them like one of themselves.

She was different from most missionaries, who were

either very polite, or very jovial, or very diffident, and almost always smiling, as those who are not quite sure of their acceptance, and want to be friendly. Not so this Ai Weh Teh, who only smiled when there was something to smile about, glared when she was moved to indignation, frowned when she was puzzled (which occurred often in connection with the ramifications of arithmetic) and laughed like a child when she was happy.

She was, in fact, as transparent as water, and her theology was the same, clear and uncomplicated. There was a living God, and she was His servant. There was a loathesome Creature called Satan, and she was his enemy. There was an immortal soul in every human being proceeding to an eternity in either Heaven or Hell. Her job in life was to convince people that if they would but put their trust in Jesus Christ her Lord, who had died on the cross for them, they would get straight on the road to Heaven. And since Jesus Christ had come to life again, and had promised to be with those who trusted and obeyed Him, however beset with trials and temptations the road to Heaven might prove to be, they need fear nothing, for He would never let them down.

Theological seminaries have a way of making things rather more complicated than that, but when it boiled down to it Christian Chang's theology was really much the same as Gladys', and he was very glad to have her help with some of the things he was doing, such as visiting in prisons. The Chinese Government, the Kuo Min Tang, gave permission freely to propagate religion in their prisons, and Gladys obtained that permission in Chengtu without difficulty.

Very upset she was at times when she emerged. Ai

Weh Teh was very tender hearted, as everyone knew. 'Oh, that poor fellow in fetters! Oh, Lord, let them take the fetters off! Lord, release him from those fetters, whatever it is that he's done!' When she went again and saw that the fetters had, in fact, been removed, she was over-joyed. 'You see, there is a living God, and He answers prayer!' In and out she went, praying and preaching, and as in Yangcheng, so in Chengtu, there were criminals who became convinced to the point of committal that what she told them about Christ was the truth.

When Pastor Christian Chang, therefore, was faced with the necessity of appointing a Biblewoman in the church, he decided that Ai Weh Teh was the one to fit the bill. There were plenty of well-educated young Chinese graduates from Bible Colleges who would have accepted the invitation had it been extended to them, but his choice fell on Gladys, and she accepted. She was probably the only westerner ever to be employed in such a capacity in China. She was given a little room behind the big church building, she received the normal allowance given to a Biblewoman, and her status was that of a servant of the church – no more if no less.

One of the jobs that fell to her was cleaning the church, and when she took a look round that gallery it put her on her mettle. What a mess! The dust, and the bits of rubbish, and the general air of neglect and untidiness aroused within her the crusading spirit. This was a challenge to God Himself! Here was His House in a state of disrepair, like when her favourite Bible character, Nehemiah, went to Jerusalem and set about putting things to rights! She tied a towel round her head, and she grasped a brush, and she swept and she tidied, and as she did it she prayed to her God and defied the devil, all in one breath. There was no sitting pretty with a Bible under her arm when there was a battle to be fought, where Gladys was concerned.

'Oh, God, fill this pew on Sunday! Bring the people in to hear Your Word! Beat the devil, Lord, make him loose his clutch on people's souls. Satan, I defy you — in the Name of the Lord get out and stay out!' She sat in a pew and prayed and defied, then she went to the next pew and dusted it, sat and prayed and defied again, all round that gallery, day after day. 'Oh, God, bring the people in! Fill this pew on Sunday!'

Probably the beginning of the answer to that prayer was when she met young Hsü the leper. Hsü had been a bank clerk far up in the north-west of China, and when he discovered he had leprosy he was in such despair that he tried to commit suicide. He did not succeed. Instead, like Pastor Christian Chang, he had one of those transforming experiences which changed him from a gloomy, despairing man into one with a purpose in life. He came to Chengtu to a leprosarium connected with the West China Union University, and a dismal place he found it. The trouble was not in the building and the facilities, but with the leprosy patients themselves. They were for ever quarrelling with each other and refusing to obey the rules of the home, and Hsü didn't like the atmosphere at all.

'It's horrible,' he told Gladys. 'They're all following the devil.'

'God can change things,' she answered. 'God can beat the devil.' She pressed her lips together and looked at Hsü, and he looked at her, and they agreed that God could do it, and it was up to them to enter the conflict on His side. So they set about doing it.

Gladys went with him into the leprosarium again and again, talking to the men, preaching, telling them about the Living God who had told her to come to China, and doing what she could to help them when they needed something. Faith and good works always went hand in hand where she was concerned.

The outcome was that some of them started going to church on Sundays. They could not sit among other members of the congregation, for the fear of leprosy was too great, but there was the gallery, empty, swept and furnished with benches, and Gladys waiting to lead them up there during the singing of the first hymn. There they sat, with their maimed limbs and distorted faces, out of sight, heads bowed, quietly following the service until they slipped away as the last hymn was being sung.

Good Friday drew near, and Gladys urged that a special Communion service should be arranged for them in the leprosarium. Christian Chang was a little hesitant about taking part at first, but the missionary in charge Dr Olin Stockwell, just back from the USA, managed to convince him there was no risk of contagion.

'You lead the service and I'll help you,' he said, and so it was arranged. It was an unforgettable occasion as the lepers came slowly forward, some limping, some unable to kneel, some holding out stumps of hands to receive the bread and drink the wine. The atmosphere of the place had been transformed, as Dr Olin Stockwell observed, and it became an entirely new institution in spirit and practice.

It was while she was living in the little room behind the church that Gladys became 'mother' to a lad she named Gordon. She was in great demand among the students because she was willing to teach them English, and a rattling good time they had when she was on that job! 'Say it to music,' was one of her methods.

> Chengtu will shine tonight
> Chengtu will shine tonight
> When the moon comes up
> And the sun goes down
> Chengtu will shine tonight!

She set it to a tune, and had them all singing it, and when they begged her to do so, gave them English names. This pleased them greatly, and she usually had a group of them around her – and that pleased her!

It was one winter evening, when the room was being prepared for a meeting, that a pressure lamp which Gordon was pumping, exploded. There was a flash, a shriek, then gasps and cries as it was seen that his face and hands had been badly burned. He had to be taken into hospital, seriously injured, and even when he was discharged for convalescence he could do nothing for himself. His hands were still useless.

At this stage Gladys took over completely. She did everything for him. He had been living with an uncle who was very unkind to him, but now he was on the church compound, and Gladys was his 'mother'. Gradually he was nursed back to health, his hands completely restored, and Gordon, a gentle shy teenager, was a committed Christian. When Gladys went out to preach in some courtyard, or went off to a nearby village, Gordon went with her. She wrote to Jarvis, now in the USA, about her youngest son Gordon, his zeal, and his devotion to the Lord. The time came when she was very ill, lying in her little room, sometimes delirious, and it was Gordon then who did everything for her.

'He was the only one who could quieten me,' she told a friend. 'I'd rave, and insist on getting up, and then he'd come along and say, "Now, Mother, don't be impatient. Just lie quietly," and he'd stay beside me till I dropped off to sleep.' Word eventually got to the Stockwells that she was ill, and they carried her off to their home until she recovered. Gordon used to go along there, rather shyly, to visit her, and as he left she would go outside with him and they would pray together in the still of the night. There was tenderness in that relationship between the woman in her mid-forties and the lad who was still not twenty which touched those who saw it. Gladys had several 'adopted sons' in the course of her life, but none more dear than Gordon.

Meanwhile, China's short-lived period of peace after the war was disturbed by ominous news from the north of the country. The Communists were emerging from their lair in Yenan with a steel-like discipline and a dedication before which nothing seemed able to stand.

'It looks as though they'll take over eventually,' westerners in China said. 'But of course, it'll take them years to do it – ten years at least ...' But the news from the north began to belie this optimism, and there were rumours of wealthy Chinese families pulling out of China while the going was good. When the few missionaries who were scattered in the city of Chengtu met from time to time, they talked about it.

'We'll stay, of course,' they said, 'But it'll be difficult. If our Consuls begin badgering us to leave we'll just have to ignore them. We must stay. The Christians are going to have a hard time of it ...' And then, as they talked, they thought about Gladys Aylward.

'Wish we could get her out of it,' they said. 'It's all very well for us to stay on – after all, our Governments will ask awkward questions if anything happens to us. But she's a naturalized Chinese now. If the Communists got control here and arrested her, we couldn't do a thing ... Not a thing. Wish we could get her out of it.'

Dr Olin Stockwell cautiously broached the subject to Gladys herself. Her job in the church had been changed, and she was now appointed to visit the smaller churches that lay between Chengtu and Chungking, which took her out of the city for several weeks at a time. When she returned, it was to the Stockwells' home that she went, and she had become a personal friend.

'It was always a joy to have her,' they said. 'Her over-flowing joy and laughter and spiritual life, and her ability to adjust to every situation, made her a delightful guest.' But she was in no way their responsibility, and they knew that to suggest she should get out of China merely to save her own skin would probably have the reverse effect. So Dr Stockwell merely asked her how many years it was since she left home, and didn't she think it was about time she went on leave? She agreed that she'd been out for about seventeen years, and her parents were old and she'd like to see them again – but she had no money. However, she said, she would pray about it, and if the Lord wanted her to go, she would go.

While she prayed, therefore, Dr Stockwell got busy. He wrote first to the Orphaned Missions Committee.

This was an organization that had been set up by the major missionary societies in China during the war to find support for German missionaries and others who were cut off from their home countries. He told the Committee that he had an 'orphan missionary' who ought to return to England, and when he explained who it was, they agreed to pay her boat fare from Shanghai. Then he asked the China Inland Mission to provide her board and room at their headquarters in Shanghai while she was there, and that, too, presented no difficulty. There remained the air passage from Chengtu to Shanghai, but he had a fund for evangelistic work from which to draw, and if Gladys Aylward hadn't done her share of evangelistic work, he didn't know who had! He paid for the air ticket out of the funds and never had a qualm of conscience over it, not even during the nine months when the Communists had him 'confessing his sins'.*

Getting out of China proved even more complicated for Gladys than getting into it. She had to obtain a Chinese passport and that involved going to Nanking before she ever got to Shanghai. Arriving there, further formalities awaited attention, for an alien could not enter Great Britain on the same terms as a citizen, and sponsorship papers were required, involving the business manager at the China Inland Mission in many a journey to various officials to get everything properly arranged. Gladys herself was scarcely aware of it, however, for she had her time cut out getting in touch with some of the youngsters she had met elsewhere. Just as years before, among the swarms of refugees, groups of schoolchildren and university

* Dr Olin Stockwell was imprisoned in China for two years, from November 1950 to November 1952.

students had moved from east to west China to evade the Japanese, now they were moving to the coast, to evade the advancing Communists. The little island of Taiwan had been ceded back to China from the Japanese after the war, and it was to Taiwan that many were going now. The exodus had started. Mukden had already fallen to the Communists, and although it was not until October 1st, 1949 that General Mao Tse-tung officially proclaimed the People's Republic of China, the writing was on the wall as far as the Chinese Nationalist Government was concerned. The great port of Shanghai saw more going than coming in those days, as ship after ship drew out, laden with Chinese who were leaving the land of their fathers for ever.

Among them were some of the students Gladys had known in the western provinces, and with whom she had contrived to maintain a link by correspondence. One of these lads was amazed, one day, to see a letter addressed to himself stuck up on the notice board of the place where he was staying, written by Ai Weh Teh, asking him to come and see her at an address in Sinza Road. What was Ai Weh Teh doing in Shanghai? He went along to Sinza Road in a large compound with great, four-storeyed buildings, where she was staying at the China Inland Mission headquarters.

She greeted him eagerly. He was going to Taiwan? She was going to England. God had provided her with a ticket. Indeed, He was providing for her all the way along the line, like He always had done. Only that day she had gone along to the reception desk, and there in her pigeon-hole was an anonymous gift of US $10! When her young visitor left she gave him an electric torch, and a silver dollar, and he wasn't the only one, either. Those young people, her 'children', she might never see them again, and she must do all she could for them while she could. Little wonder if she was practically penniless as the time drew near for her to board the vessel that would take her to England when, one day, she had an unaccountable urge to go to the Hongkong and Shanghai Bank.

She did not know how to get there, but someone from the CIM offered to go with her. Thinking she was going to draw out money, her companion on arrival naturally led her to the appropriate counter, but Gladys looked dazed, and said, 'No, I have to meet someone who works here.' That was all she knew.

Her companion, somewhat perplexed, went to the lift man for help. He ushered them into the lift and let them out at the first floor, into a large room with about fifty desks, at all of which people seemed to be working.

'Can you see the person you want?' Gladys was asked. She continued to look dazed. She did not know who she wanted to see. All she could say was,

'The Lord told me to come here to see someone.'

Then suddenly, a tall young Chinese, smartly dressed, came quickly towards her, smiling broadly and holding out his hand.

'Miss Aylward! What are you doing here? Where are you going?' he asked. She looked at him blankly.

'I'm one of your "children",' he said. 'You don't recognize me, do you?' Then he told her his name, and her face lit up.

'I'd never have known you! Why, you've grown so tall! ...' They chatted together happily for a minute or two, then he asked again,

'What are you doing here in Shanghai? Where are

you going?' And when she told him he said 'Then if I may I should like to give you something for your travelling expenses,' and forthwith proceeded to do so. The Chinese are very generous on such occasions . . .

CHAPTER TWELVE

In the Ascendant

Gladys Aylward's rise to fame is one of the strangest 'success stories' of the twentieth century. When Dr Handley Stockley was once asked why she hadn't died as a result of that terrible illness in Sian following the trek with the children over the mountains, he answered rather quietly, 'I can only think it is because God has other work for her to do.' It is difficult to find any other explanation than a supernatural one for the fact that her name can be grouped with people like Dr Albert Schweitzer and Helen Keller, and known to millions who never went inside a church except to get married.

When she arrived back in England in the spring of 1949 she looked so small and insignificant that her own parents did not recognize her. They had gone to the London terminus to meet her off the boat train, and hurried up and down searching for her in vain. Not until responding to an announcement over the loudspeaker requesting those who had come to meet Miss Gladys Aylward from China to go to the station-master's office did they realize that the bewildered little Chinese woman standing there with a miscellaneous assortment of bags and bundles was their daughter. As for Gladys, she looked without recognition at the bright-eyed little elderly woman a-sparkle with diamante ornaments who hurried towards her.

'My mum had come all out in diamonds!' she said later when describing her reactions to Mum's gallant efforts to brighten the austere fashions of post-war Britain. In her confusion she talked in a mixture of Chinese and English, complained rather irritably of the cramped conditions in the little home in Cheddington Road, stared blank and unsmiling when introduced to Violet's husband. There seemed no place for her here in England, where she was now in the 'alien' category, and had to go along to the police station to report periodically. Everything was strange, and she thought longingly of the old, familiar life in China.

She soon found there was plenty for her to do, however, for Mum was an unofficial, unconscious publicity agent of the first order. A regular little gad-about in a thoroughly respectable way was Mum. She was glad to get out and leave the running of the house to Violet, for she was in great demand as a speaker at women's meetings, a prime favourite down Hoxton way, and liable to turn up at all sorts of church functions unimpeded by any denominational barriers. 'Our Gladys in China' had been her subject for many an address and many a conversation, and when, in the course of her peregrinations, she ran into the well-known journalist, Hugh Redwood, author of the bestseller *God in the Slums*, he began writing about her. So one way and another, invitations to speak at church meetings began rolling in as soon as it was known that Mrs Aylward's daughter was back from China. And Hugh Redwood inserted a little paragraph in the London daily of which he was the night editor, to the effect that a Miss Gladys Aylward had returned to England after seventeen years' missionary work in China. It took about a couple of lines of small print.

Now it so happened that about that time a BBC producer was working on a dramatized series of true stories for the BBC, called *The Undefeated*. His name was Alan Burgess, and as he was always on the lookout for copy, he made a point of glancing through the papers for any likely clues. When he saw that some woman who had been for a very long time in China was back in England he made a note of it. Might be a story there somewhere. He'd go along and see her some time.

When he eventually made his way to Cheddington Road, Edmonton, and knocked at the well-polished knocker of No 67, it was Gladys who opened the door. She was alone in the house, and when the young man on the doorstep explained that he was from the BBC, was producing real life radio plays, and wondered if she would grant him an interview, she said immediately oh no, certainly not. He pleaded a little, and although she asserted that nothing had ever happened to her worth making into a play, she relented towards him. After all, he looked a nice young man. In some ways Gladys never grew up. She was always rather susceptible to nice young men, and this one looked disappointed, and uncomfortably warm. It was a hot day.

'Come in and have a cup of tea,' she said. 'I'll show you a real Chinese tea-box – a sort of tea cosy.' And while he sat down by the table she went out into the scullery, put on the kettle, and produced the tea-box into which the teapot could be stowed and it would keep hot for hours and hours.

With the contrariness of human nature Gladys, renowned among her friends for her stories of personal experiences, with which she had been known to hold up many a meal-time, closed right down at the prospect of having them reported. She seemed determined to keep the conversation centred on the tea-box.

'You must have had many strange experiences in China,' the young man ventured. Gladys admitted she had, but doubted whether people would be interested in any of them. 'Now just look and see how this thing works! Much better than a tea-cosy ...' It took Alan Burgess at least a quarter of an hour to get anything out of her, but after persistent though cautious questioning he elicited the information that she had once taken some children across the mountains in north China.

How long did it take her?

A month or so.

How much money did she have?

Money? She didn't have any money!

How many children?

She didn't know exactly, about a hundred.

'I see,' said Burgess. What he saw was not how she had done it, but that he had struck journalistic oil, that this unassuming little woman in her queer get-up had a most remarkable story. It might take him several journeys out to Edmonton to get it, but he knew they would prove to be worth it.

The half-hour dramatization of her story was produced that autumn on the BBC, and it was a hit. The following spring a paper booklet appeared in the religious bookshops entitled *Gladys Aylward ... One of the Undefeated.** But by the time it appeared she was already widely known as a speaker.

She made people sit up – literally! The Rev the

* Told by her to R. O. Latham. Published by Edinburgh House Press.

Hon Roland Lamb noticed this when he invited her to speak, soon after her arrival at an afternoon meeting largely attended by elderly ladies. The usual preliminaries over, the cup of tea partaken of, the time came for the address to be given. The speaker stood up, a very small, rather odd-looking woman in a funny Chinese gown, and the elderly ladies settled back on their chairs, prepared to take it easy for the next twenty minutes. One or two of them closed their eyes. They were ready for a nap.

'And God said to Abraham,' started the speaker. Then she suddenly shouted,

'GET OUT!' The elderly ladies shot up in their seats, eyes wide open with alarm. For the next hour they sat, eyes glued to the speaker, time forgotten, as she related the things that had happened when the same message from God had come to her as had come to Abraham – 'Get out from your own country . . .

'At the time when I went to China I was the most unlikely person to do anything, let alone go to China. I had never passed an examination. Me go to China? Gladys Aylward, I said, why you? You've never even passed an examination . . .

'But God wasn't asking me if I could read properly. He was saying,

"Gladys Aylward, would you allow Me to open your ears and your mouth, and let me drop in Chinese? Because it's to these people I want you to prove My glory and tell of My salvation . . ."

'Friends, if God ever worked a miracle in this whole wide world, He worked one in my head. I speak Chinese! Oh, I do! But don't think I am proud. I am only humble before a great Almighty

God Who says, "When I call, I will equip." And He does. You just have to say, "Well, here I am. You just do what you like with me."'

There were those alarming duties of the early months in China, when Jeannie Lawson decided to open an inn for muleteers in order to preach to them ...

'... She was the old Scots woman who I should say was the drawing power to get me to China. We opened a new inn. Now don't think I opened the inn! No, I didn't. I would never have had anything to do with mules if Jeannie hadn't forced me. No, I certainly wasn't in love with mules! But you know, you get into corners and you just have to go forward, that's all.

'I have tried to think sometimes, I wonder what would have happened if when I was outside the door, perspiring all over, grumbling and grousing in my heart, waiting for those mules to come up the road, and I was supposed to grab them in ... Well, supposing I hadn't grabbed them in!

'Oh, the awful thought! At least one man would not be in eternity with the Lord of Glory ...'

There were so many things she had to tell about the children. One of those she had taken in at Yangcheng, for instance, who wandered out into the street and met a little beggar boy, complete with his begging bowl and stick to beat off the dogs, and asked him ...

'What have you got in your bowl?'
'Nothing.'
'Got any money?'

'No.'

'Had anything to eat today?'

'No.'

'I have! Ate to the full on porridge and bread this morning. Ate to the full on noodles for dinner.' Pause. 'Where did you sleep last night?'

'Under a wall outside the city.'

'That's where I used to sleep.' (Then, in a tone of deep satisfaction) 'I don't sleep there now, though! See those gates over there?'

'Yes. I see them.'

'That's where I live now. Eat to the full every day there ... You can come and live there if you like ...'

She had the elderly ladies laughing one minute, crying the next, and when they left the hall, fifty minutes later than usual, they were telling each other they could have gone on listening for hours.

For the next twenty years she went on telling those stories. The exploits of Gladys Aylward were her stock in trade. She ruthlessly exposed the things 'that silly little Gladys Aylward' had done, and the wonderful way the Living God had worked in spite of her stupidity. When most of the epics of the Second World War had been published and forgotten, hers continued to hold her audience like a spell. She started her career as a speaker in a small way, back in 1949, at weekday meetings in inconspicuous churches, and was quite likely to be found sitting on the kerb somewhere in the vicinity, taking a rest, a bag beside her containing a few Chinese curios and her Chinese Bible. That Bible accompanied her everywhere, held together in places with strips of sticky tape and freely marked with under-linings and notes in the margins. She was convinced

that some of them were messages from God to her —
Luke 21:15, for instance, alongside which she had
written while waiting in Shanghai her own free translation — 'I will give you eloquence' and noted under
it 'Promise for journey, March 1949.'

That promise was speedily fulfilled, and in an in-
credibly short time she was receiving invitations to
speak to larger audiences.

The first time she knew that the local mayor would
be present, complete in his regalia, she was somewhat
dismayed, and tempted to get out of the arrangement.
She didn't want to move among the nobs, she said. But
then she took herself to task.

'Gladys,' she demanded sternly, 'Hasn't *he* got a
soul?' So she went, and before long she was taking
mayors in her stride, and bishops too, for that matter.
After all, they were nothing more and nothing less
than human beings with immortal souls. If Nehemiah,
her hero, when he was butler to Artaxerxes King of
the Medes and Persians had referred to his master
merely as 'this man', she need not be abashed by
bishops. And when one or another of them shared the
platform with her, and saw her rapier-like technique
of whirling on her audience in the middle of one of
her stories with the challenge, 'Will you search your
hearts and see if you are willing to obey this wonderful
God?', sensed the awe and the Presence as people sat
breathless, and here and there tears began to flow ...

Well, the bishops who knew themselves to be but
mere men were the first to acknowledge that it was
usually the parlourmaid who stole the thunder.

As for Gladys herself, she went along to the meetings
in a very matter-of-fact way, as though she were going
to her daily work. She travelled everywhere by public

transport, and had her little grumble, 'Keep having to say the same thing over and over again – makes me feel like a gramophone record!' When money began to roll in from collections that were given to her its destination was obvious. It rolled towards China. The missionaries in Chengtu had quite a time of it trying to understand her muddled instructions, distributing the money to the best of their ability, though sometimes against their better judgement. Young Gordon Wang was acquitting himself well as an assistant pastor, but not all the recipients of her gifts were like him! She kept up a correspondence with as many of her Chinese friends as possible, and assured them that she was hoping to return soon.

They replied guardedly. Then the news began to filter through of the reign of terror under the Communists, as they gained full control, with the secret arrests and the long indoctrinations, the interrogations and the accusation meetings at which brother betrayed brother, and the mass executions in public places.

The horror of it preyed upon her mind, and on one occasion, when she happened to be sharing a room with a friend, she was unable to sleep, moaning and crying in her distress.

'It's my children,' she wept brokenly. 'Something awful is happening. They're in danger – I know it!' It was as though she was fey, enduring the mental agony of one appointed to death. Her body trembled and she was bathed in perspiration as they knelt down together, praying through the hours of the night for Ninepence and Less and Liang and Gordon, and dozens of others.

'I'm going back to China,' she said. 'I must get back to them.' But about that time a letter reached her from far inland China. It was couched in unusual language, explaining that if she came back she would not need much – only six feet of ground and a strip of cloth. And if she went back some whom she knew there would only need six feet of ground and a strip of cloth, too.

Her presence would make things even worse for the very people she wanted to help, for she was already suspected as being a spy for the Imperialists.

She knew it was the end, as far as returning to China was concerned. But it wasn't the end as far as the Chinese were concerned. There were Chinese in London, restaurant-keepers and laundry-workers, and smart young students, too, from Hong Kong and the Malaysian peninsula. She heard of a Pastor Stephen Wang, a refugee from China who was starting to hold Sunday services for Chinese people and she wrote to him saying she would like to help him. He welcomed her, and when she was in London on a Sunday she went along to the services, and in the meetings at which she spoke talked about the work among the Chinese in London.

'They want you to go along and tell them about it, Pastor Wang!' she said enthusiastically, and began making arrangements for him to travel to various parts of England in order to do it. She was rather irritated when he demurred. As he said, his job was to hunt up the lonely Chinese in London, and help them. If he spent his time going around talking about what he was doing, he would have no time left to do what he was talking about.

It was a logic with which she could not but agree, and was inclined to act upon it herself, when the need of an individual conflicted with the timing of a meeting. The individual must come first! A couple of days before one big meeting at which she was due to speak the organizing committee received a little note from her to say that she was very sorry, she would not be able to come. The committee was thrown into a state of panic. The notices were out, coach loads of people from the surrounding neighbourhood were coming to hear Miss Gladys Aylward, the famous woman missionary, and now she wasn't coming.

'Can you possibly help us – can you persuade her to come?' they pleaded with a friend of hers who happened to be in the district. So she put through a long distance phone call, and when Gladys answered it, started off,

'Look here, Gladys, about this meeting you're supposed to be coming to the day after tomorrow ...'

'Yes, I know, I'm sorry about that,' said Gladys airily. 'But there's someone I *must* see that evening.'

Some Chinese I suppose, thought her friend, though she didn't say so.

'But this meeting – they've advertised it – crowds of people are coming.'

'I'm sorry,' said Gladys firmly. 'I can't come – someone's passing through London that night, and they're going on next morning early, and I *must* see them.'

'But Gladys, you can't do this sort of thing. You *said* you'd come!' Then, with a flash of inspiration, she added, 'Let your yea *be* yea, and your nay, nay.'

There was a brief pause at the other end of the line. Gladys knew who had first said that: Jesus Christ her Lord in the Sermon on the Mount.

'All right – I'll come,' she said. Then she added quickly, 'But I must get back to London that night. I can't stay – I must get back.'

'There's a train at eight-thirty, and I'll see you catch it – if you can stop speaking at twenty past,' was the prompt reply. 'It's up to you!' It was well known that Gladys never spoke for less than one hour, but on that occasion she confined herself to forty-five minutes, and caught the train.

Many were the stories her hostesses had to tell about her. The way, for instance, she would sometimes leave little gifts of food secreted in homes where she felt her presence might have added strain to the family exchequer. One hostess found a packet of bacon under the bed a fortnight after Miss Aylward had left! In another home there was anxiety about a member of the family who was always going off to the public house, and returning the worse for drink. He was there on the evening when Gladys was to arrive, and she found her hostess nearly in tears. Gladys pursed her lips. This was a challenge, and she accepted it.

'We'll get him out!' she said. 'We'll *pray* him out!' and she forthwith proceeded to do so.

'Lord, get him out!' she prayed, her fists clenched. 'Lord – make his beer taste 'orrible. Make him hate the taste of it. Tell him to push it away from him across the counter ...

'Lord, make him get up off that stool. Bring him over to the bar door ... Make him push it open and come outside ... Bring him across the road ... Make him walk along the street, back home ...'

There was a sound at the front door. The prodigal had returned! And to Gladys as well as her hostess, that mattered a lot more than the fact that the evening meeting was packed to the doors.

Within a year of her return to England she was in constant demand, travelling far and wide, often returning to London so late at night that to get home to Edmonton involved arriving in the early hours of the morning if she missed the last train. As in China, so in England – there were always the people who said, 'There's a bed for you any time you like, Gladys.'

One of these was the assistant in Bethany. Bethany was a sort of refuge for women run by Sister Gemmel of the Church Army in a basement flat at Marble Arch, and Miss Bralant helped her. Gladys soon had a nickname for Miss Bralant. 'The Coolie' she called her once, laughing, and the name stuck. 'I've got a couple of rooms in a house not far from here,' said the Coolie. 'There are two beds in my bedroom – you're very welcome to come there any time you like. I'm out most of the time, so I'll give you a key.'

The claims of Bethany kept the Coolie from her two rooms in Westbourne Park all day and much of the night, but she returned late one evening and realized Gladys had been there. The place was very clean and very tidy, as Gladys always left it, and on the table was a little piece of paper torn from a small notebook, on which was some pencilled scribbling in Gladys' rather childish handwriting. The Coolie picked it up and read:

'Thank you dear. It needs no more than that from me, for *He* will reward you.

I have loved the quiet.

I will come some other time even when I have not a meeting.

Will let you know,

Yours, Gladys.

Isa. 53: 1–12. I love it all.'

The Coolie was touched. It was she who had shared the room with Gladys on that night when she had been almost fey, agonizing over her 'children' in China. She had heard some of the inner conflicts of those lonely years, some of the sufferings and humiliations. She had seen the little figure in the simple Chinese dress lugging a big bag through the London streets and down into the Underground setting off for a round of meetings when she was feeling too tired to bother to get herself a proper meal. She couldn't do much for Gladys, but she was glad she had two little rooms up on the third floor of a rather shabby house near central London to share with her when she needed them. She read on, and suddenly became aware that she was standing on holy ground. Gladys had finished her note of thanks with the words,

'In your quiet room I have renewed my vow to follow all the way.'

The Coolie was a tidy person, not given to hoarding, throwing out old magazines relentlessly and tearing up letters as soon as she had answered them. But she could never bring herself to throw away that scrap of paper, on which Gladys had written her 'thank you' letter.

CHAPTER THIRTEEN

The Small Woman

The half-hour dramatization of Gladys' story on the BBC in 1949 was such a hit that it was decided to reproduce it two or three years later. And since it was known that Miss Aylward was still in England, it was agreed that the programme would be strengthened if she herself would add a short epilogue in her own words and her own voice. Alan Burgess went along to see her about this, procured the recording, the programme was duly produced again, and that might have been the end of it, had it not been that a publisher happened to tune in at the time it was on, and listened right through to the end.

A few days later he put through a telephone call to Alan Burgess.

'I want you to write a book about that woman,' he said.

'Nothing doing,' was the prompt reply. 'I've written five books already, and got less than £400 for the lot! Nothing doing! No money in writing books.'

'I'll pay you £400 down if you'll take it on,' persisted the publisher. Burgess remained unenthusiastic. However, he eventually agreed to go and see Gladys and find out if she would be willing to provide him with the material. She's pretty sure to say no, he said to himself.

To his surprise, she agreed immediately. She

thought a book would be a very good idea. She happened to know that the booklet produced after the first broadcast was still selling like ice cream in summer at the religious bookshops. (It went into seventeen impressions within eight years.) What she wanted, however, was that this new book should be written for an even wider reading public than had been reached already. The more people who knew what God had done for her, the better.

'I didn't want to write that book,' Alan Burgess admitted years later. 'Don't know why I did it.' Then he added, 'I suppose I just had to . . .'

Getting the material involved him in interviews with Gladys nearly every day over a period of about four months. By this time she was sharing a little house in a mews near Marble Arch with Mrs Rosemary Tyndale Biscoe. The two of them had met after one of Gladys' meetings, and as Rosemary had come to a cross-roads in her life, Gladys said casually, 'You can come and live with me if you like. I've just got a little place in a mews.' So Rosemary went and lived with her, and soon discovered that Gladys' main concern in life was getting clothes and money sent to refugees escaping from Communist China in Hong Kong. Some of the missionaries Gladys had known in China, including Annie the young Norwegian giantess, were right there, doing what they could to help them. Gladys had a way of inspiring people to action, and many of her friends, including Queenie (married and with her own family now, but still devoted to her cousin), helped in the collecting of unwanted clothes to send out to the refugees.

Into this work of sorting, packing and posting Rosemary threw herself. She came originally from that stratum of English society where other people did the packing, but what she lacked in experience she made up for in enthusiasm. There were times when Gladys looked round in despair and fled for refuge to the Coolie in Bethany. 'Rosemary's got so many clothes and packages and bundles everywhere I can't get into the place!' she complained. The Coolie smiled soothingly and made her a cup of tea. She thought it wiser not to mention that a day or two previously Rosemary had been round, almost in tears because Gladys had got the place so filled with Chinese she couldn't get on with the packing . . .

On one occasion Gladys went to Belfast to speak, and returned with an inarticulate little Chinese widow. Wang Kwei had been brought from Hong Kong as a nanny, landed up in a mental hospital where no one could understand her, since she spoke no English, and where she might have remained till her dying day had Gladys not gone security for her and brought her back to London. She lived in the house in the mews for about a couple of years and eventually returned, hale and hearty, to her family in Hong Kong.

Into the house in the mews went Alan Burgess, picking his way over parcels and bundles of clothing to sit down with Gladys and delve into her memory for material for the book to be written for a very wide readership. She took it all quite seriously, determined to give him a true picture of her life in Yangcheng, with the consequence that day after day he was escorted on preaching trips to the villages in the wake of Gladys, complete with a roll of Gospel posters and her Bible. He did not know much about missionaries. He felt he knew enough however to conclude that a woman missionary going out to a village to preach was in the same category as a dog biting a man when it came to making news. They were simply doing what might be expected of them. Not until the man bites the dog is Fleet Street interested, and not until Gladys did something else than go off to a village to preach would there be anything for him to write about. It was extremely difficult to deflect her from this course of action, and he had to listen patiently, his experienced ear cocked for any word that might lead to a real story.

One such came when, as usual, she was preparing to go out to a village with Mr Lu, the evangelist, but was delayed for a few hours by trouble in the prison. However, they got away at last, and she had the two Ways Poster with her ...

Prison! The journalist stiffened in his chair at the magic word. Prison! A village isn't news, but a prison is!

'Hold on a minute, Gladys,' he said. 'What was that about the prison?'

'Oh, they stopped me just as we were going out to the village.'

'Who stopped you?'

'The people from the prison.'

'But why?'

'There was a riot in the prison.' Then she added scornfully, 'Silly things.'

'But what had that to do with you?'

'The Governor wanted us to go and stop it.'

'They wanted you to ... ! Well, did you?'

'Yes.'

Whew! And he might have missed it! Burgess leaned forward and said firmly,

'Now Gladys, I want you to tell me about that riot

in the prison. Never mind about preaching in the village – tell me about that riot in the prison.'

So she told him. The gist of it was that one of the prisoners had got hold of a hatchet and was rushing round with it, hacking people, and the rest of them were milling around, fighting each other. The Governor, appalled by the din, was afraid to go in himself, and had sent for her because, as he reminded her, she was always preaching about the Living God Who was with her, and if He was with her she ought to be able to quell the riot. So Gladys, put on her mettle, went in, demanded that the man with the hatchet give it to her at once, which he did, and then gave them all a scolding for being so silly. Burgess, stifling his amazement, quickly asked her questions to fill in the background for what he realised would be one of the highlights in the book. He had to get them, and he had to get them *now*, before she went off to preach in that village!

So it went on. When he got from her as much as she could remember of those first few years in China, he said,

'Well, Gladys, I'll write this up, and we'll go halves on whatever we get for it. There's £200 apiece for us now, and we'll see what else comes in.' A legal document to this effect was duly drawn up and signed by them both, he went away to sort the material and write *The Small Woman*, and Gladys to continue that everwidening circle of meetings, arranged for by an everwidening circle of friends. For Gladys made friends wherever she went. She was a popular guest, easy to please, full of humour, and always a favourite with the children. There seemed to be an instinctive mutual attraction between them, and when headmasters of schools knew she was in the neighbourhood they urged her to come and speak about China. They soon discovered, however, that they must be prepared for an alteration in the normal schedule. It was useless to expect Miss Aylward to confine herself to fifteen minutes at Assembly! Even the headmaster at Gordonstoun discovered this. An Air Commodore and his wife who knew Gladys well, and to whom they had given the key of their large West-end apartment to go in and out as she liked, introduced her at Gordonstoun when the young heir to the throne was a pupil there. A few weeks before Gladys went, His Royal Highness the Duke of Edinburgh had gone there to speak to the boys, and the Principal had respectfully warned him that no one could hold their attention for more than twenty minutes.

If he told Gladys the same thing, it made no difference. She spoke for about an hour and a quarter, and the boys listened spellbound. The headmaster said it had never happened before, in all his long experience of boys. Later, at another well-known public school after she had spoken to the boys and was having dinner in the headmaster's private quarters where no boy was ever allowed to go unless invited, the manservant approached the headmaster to announce that a group of boys was at the front door asking if they could speak with Miss Aylward. That was the end of the dinner party as far as Gladys was concerned, for the boys were nothing more and nothing less than human beings with immortal souls, whether they came from the British aristocracy, the mountains of China or the Welsh valleys.

One of those boys was asked, years later, what it was about her that impressed him, and after a moment's thought he answered, 'It was the way she talked about God – as though she knew Him ...'

In 1957 *The Small Woman** was published by Evans Brothers Ltd, and Twentieth Century-Fox Films wanted to dramatize it. Alan Burgess said to Gladys,

'What about it, Gladys? Shall we let them make a film of it?'

Yes, she thought it would be a good idea. It would be a way of reaching more people. It did not occur to her that everything would not be produced just as she liked it, that she would not be invited to choose the cast and control the script writing.

She thought it would all be just like it was with the editor of the *Sunday Companion* who was so interested in her plans to return to the Far East.

For that was what she was intending to do now. The one person who she could not have hurt by leaving England again had died. Bright-eyed, vivacious little Mum's earthly pilgrimage had ended. Mum, with her saucy, gay, defiant little home-made hats and her impish ways, her Cockney wit that had her listeners rocking with laughter till her sudden transitions to the cross where Jesus died stilled and melted them – Mum was gone.

'I promised her once that I wouldn't go back while she was alive,' Gladys told Violet. 'But I'm free to go now. I'm going back.'

She set sail for Hong Kong in April 1957, after putting her signature to the agreement whereby the film rights of *The Small Woman* were granted to Twentieth Century-Fox Films.

* Pan Books, 1959.

CHAPTER FOURTEEN

In Orbit

The next four years of Gladys' life, viewed in retrospect, are like a series of whirlwinds in which she was carried to dizzy heights, then plunged to terrifying depths as she trod the perilous path of fame and notoriety. There were occasions when her cabin on a liner looked like that of a film star as she set off on one of her tours, gay and fragrant with baskets and bouquets of flowers, and her arrival was liable to be announced over the radio as a piece of current news. She was one of the people at whom Press photographers quickly raised their cameras when she appeared in a crowd attending a function. But in those undated, unpunctuated, jumbled letters of hers to Queenie she wrote,

'You know I didn't want all this hoo-hah! I'm still the same Gladys you knew when we went together into the gallery at Drury Lane,' and on another occasion, 'I've got two photographs I don't know who will want so I'll send one to you and one to the Coolie. It's a picture of me and the Arch.' As Gladys was in Hong Kong, Queenie looked forward to seeing a picture of Gladys standing in an oriental setting under an elaborate arch, but when it arrived the 'Arch' turned out to be the Archbishop of Canterbury.

Floods of letters reached her. A suitcase of unanswered correspondence seemed part of her baggage. She became involved in the business side of running orphanages and mission halls which revealed over and over again that basic weakness in arithmetic which the best efforts of her teachers in the primary school in Edmonton had failed to rectify. Her most devoted admirers had to admit that she had no head for business, and in the course of the tumultuous years those who tried to manage her affairs were sometimes hard put to it to understand her instructions and interpret her silences.

As for her close personal friends, they held their breath many a time for quite another reason. It was not only that they did not know what Gladys would do next – they were afraid of what she would say next. It is one thing to talk freely when you are an ordinary person of no importance. It is quite another thing to talk freely when you are a public figure whose words are likely to be reported in the Press. Interesting news items appeared from time to time reporting that Miss Gladys Aylward, the tiny woman missionary of China, now had another fight on her hands. She had taken on the giants of Hollywood over the filming of *The Inn of the Sixth Happiness*. What she said about them was whittled down to a few terse but colourful sentences of an inflammatory nature. She learned to avoid press conferences, with their cross-examinations that so easily elicited from her the wrong answers, or things she would not have said except in confidence.

Some of the things she wrote would have had even greater news value if they had got into print. Fortunately, she confined most of them to letters to her friends, to whom she wrote without inhibition. Queenie used to keep those that came to her in a special box, to lend to people who helped her in collecting and dispatching clothes to Hong Kong refugees. It helped to maintain their interest, to read for themselves what Gladys was doing. There were times, however, when Queenie's face grew very alarmed as she perused the latest epistle from Gladys, and on thinking it over she decided not to add it to the pile in the box. It might get into the wrong hands! So she took it quietly out into the kitchen and consigned it to the flame instead. It seemed the safest thing to do. Better have nothing in her possession to provide evidence in the event of Gladys being sued for libel!

When she was on the platform her power to move her audiences was amazing. Her artless descriptions of her own experiences, her realistic 'conversations' with God, her direct challenge to her listeners to a life of faith and sincerity had its effect on old and young, rich and poor, simple and intellectual alike. The well-known Chinese author Hsu Soo went to hear her at a rally in Hong Kong, and attended it three successive nights to listen to her speak. True, he had heard about her years before, while still in China, when her name had come up in a debate among University students. One of them told of a little foreign woman named Ai Weh Teh who lived in his own town in Shansi, and how she had impressed him with her dedication to the cause of China and her ability to control the children in her charge. Hsu Soo had been interested then, wondering what was the motive power behind this life of sacrifice, so when he had the opportunity to see her it is not surprising that he did so. What is significant is that having heard her, he went again and then again.

Later he wrote about her, likening her to a philosopher who uses very simple illustrations to make clear a deep and difficult teaching; to a skilful writer, making her main theme significant; to a successful actress who can convey the inward feeling of the person she is representing. Then he went on to write,

'The small woman is a very outstanding philosopher, studying topics the past philosophers could never solve. The small woman is also a writer using her life to write a very dramatic history. The small woman is also an actress on the stage of life. God made her one of the greatest figures in our history,' and he finished by testifying that from this time on his attitude that Christianity was a figment of the imagination changed. He now believed there was a God in the universe.

Her friends had no cause to fear the effect of what she said when she was just herself, the witty little London parlourmaid recounting her experiences and producing her own evidence that there is a living God. The influence she could exert with her limited ability seemed limitless. It was when she went beyond her ability that she got into difficulties, like a little girl learning to swim who suddenly finds herself out of her depth. Her horror of Communism, born during that nightmare-ish journey across Siberia, fostered by what she knew about the 'Red Bandits' in Shansi and what she saw and heard among the refugees in Hong Kong, forced from her statements which were difficult to substantiate when they were challenged. And her generalizations on current affairs sprang from an emotional reaction as much as an informed mind. There were times when the promoters of her meetings had rather anxious little talks with individuals afterwards, trying to explain that Miss Aylward had not meant exactly what she said . . .

When she left England in 1957, however, she was merely a very well-known missionary whose departure was reported in some religious journals but made little stir elsewhere. *The Small Woman* was released for publication just about the time she left, so although it immediately got good reviews she was not on the spot to be affected by them. She was heading for the Far East, to live again among her people, the Chinese, and that was what interested her.

She arrived in Hong Kong and was almost delirious with excitement as she greeted those who had come to meet her – Chinese and westerners alike, many of whom she had known in China. Hong Kong was the nearest she could ever get to the beloved country, the mainland of China, and it was here that there were the greatest opportunities to help those frightened, destitute refugees from Communism who were still flooding quietly across the well-guarded border. She went among them almost immediately with Michael, a young refugee from Canton, of whom she had heard while still in England, and one of those whom she had been helping to support. She wrote home of the conditions in which the refugees were living, of the poverty.

'... hundreds of little huts of all shapes and sizes, the only homes these people now know.

'They moved me by their earnestness and keenness, and I wondered how many of you would remain happy under such conditions. Yet every morning at seven the Christians are praying in the little chapel. While I was there, we had torrential rains and many of the huts collapsed and were swept away. Everyone suffered in some way for it is impossible to keep the water out. I gave out the money which had been sent me by the Oxford Committee for Famine Relief.'

As her friends knew, that was not all she gave away.

The Air Commodore's wife in London received a phone call one day from a very irate lady who said she had just returned from Hong Kong where she had visited Miss Gladys Aylward. 'I thought you were a friend of hers!' said the very irate lady. 'And there she was, living in utter poverty in a little room about eight feet square ... I thought you were a friend of hers!'

'So I am,' said the Air Commodore's wife. She sighed as she put down the receiver. What was the good of trying to explain to anyone who didn't know Gladys, that however firmly you insisted that *this* money was intended for her and no one else, you knew as you were saying it that it wouldn't make any difference? And in a place like Hong Kong, among all those refugees, what was the good of expecting that Gladys would spend the money on herself?

But Gladys did not stay in Hong Kong. The decisive act of years ago when she relinquished her British citizenship and became naturalized as a Chinese decided things for her now. In Hong Kong as in England her status was that of an alien, and it is very difficult indeed for an alien to remain permanently in overcrowded Hong Kong. In the autumn of 1957 she went on alone to Formosa, last bastion of the Chinese Nationalists. From that time the little island was her home, the place to which she proudly referred as 'Taiwan, Free China'.

From Taiwan she sallied forth on her speaking tours to the USA, Canada, to New Zealand and Australia, to England, to Korea and Japan. In Taiwan she rescued abandoned babies as she had done long ago in Yangcheng, toddled off to preach in mountain villages with Gospel posters under her arm, welcomed lonely youngsters into her home and became their adopted mother. Taiwan was the scene of her greatest joys as well as her deepest sorrows, and in Taiwan her little body lies today.

It was at Taipei, at the extreme north of the island that Gladys settled after the first full and exciting day when she was accorded what amounted to a civic reception, with announcements over the radio that she had arrived. A number of Chinese appeared who claimed to have known her long ago in China, including an elderly gentleman who said he had been in Yangcheng when she was there, and a young woman who insisted that she was a daughter, one of the orphans who she had brought over the mountains. The validity of some of those claims was open to doubt, but of some there could be no question, from officials who had known her in Sian to students she had 'mothered' in Chengtu.

Jarvis, stocky and steadfast, was one of these. He was there at the quay to meet her when she arrived. An officer in the Air Force now, he was eager to take her to his home in the south of the island to meet his wife and children. 'They are your grandchildren, Mother,' he told her, and she took them to her heart. Jarvis was always 'my eldest son' to her.

She moved around a lot during her first weeks, staying here and there, meeting this one and that one she had known in China. But then she slipped quietly into the sort of life that suited her best. She rented a small room in a Chinese house in a lane on the outskirts of Taipei. And it was when she was walking along that lane, beside which meandered a sluggish stream, that one day she met Esther.

Esther was the wife of an officer in the Nationalist Army. A gentle, smiling, plump little person was Esther, and she loved the Lord Jesus. No one who met Esther was left long in any doubt about that. There are those who assert that religion is a personal matter and should not be talked about to all and sundry, but Esther did not take that view. Her attitude was that if you had good news the thing to do was to pass it on, and as Gladys was of the same mind the two of them were friends right from the start, when Esther approached her with a smile and said how glad she was to meet her. She had heard about Ai Weh Teh, she said, heard about her heart of love towards God and towards man. Ai Weh Teh must come and visit her, for weren't they both children of God and therefore sisters? And when Esther visited Gladys in return, and quietly observed the privations in which she was living, many were the gifts of food and money she inconspicuously passed on to 'her sister'.

She did something else, too.

'You are all alone here in Taiwan,' she said to one lonely young man who had been brought as a refugee schoolboy to Taiwan when the Communists gained control of the mainland. 'Would you like to have a mother here? I know someone who wants a son.'

Yes, indeed he would like to have a mother! He was working by day and studying by night, and there was no one to call his own, no honourable old one to give him advice, help him in his difficulties, and pay his respects to! Indeed he would like to have a mother. So Esther brought a son to Gladys. Esther didn't stop at one, either. She was a happy mother of several children herself, and saw no reason why Gladys should not have a family large enough to fill her heart which was obviously of considerable width. Esther produced several young people, all eligible in her estimation to join the adopted family of Ai Weh Teh. An unusual type of match-maker was Esther, and by no means an unsuccessful one. Over the years Gladys' animated if not very lucid letters to friends in England contained endless references to her sons, their wives and then to her grandchildren, several of whom she named after members of the Aylward family and her close friends.

Besides the sons there was Daughter, who claimed Gladys as 'mother' when first she arrived in Taiwan. Surely Ai Weh Teh remembered her! Ai Weh Teh's memory might be very bad, but she could not have forgotten! Daughter was married, and Son-in-law soon became just as dear to Gladys as any of her other 'sons'. Gradually it became evident that Daughter and her little family were closer to Gladys than anyone in Taiwan.

There was only one shadow over her life in those first years in Taiwan and that was the matter of the filming of her story. The memory of signing that fateful document scarcely crossed her mind until she began receiving letters asking if she knew what was happening. Did she realize that a Hollywood film company was making a film about her? Could she imagine what distortions of her life would be the outcome? Had she heard who was to impersonate her? What was she thinking about to allow this thing to continue? Cheap publicity! Love scenes! When she was alone in her little room the realization of what she had agreed to so naïvely when she put her signature to that contract covered her with a sense of shame, plunged her in despair, and occasionally stung her into a fury. Her letters to her friends sounded desperate. She was a broken-hearted woman, she told them. When that film came out none of them would want to have anything more to do with her, although she did not know what was in it or what it was all about. She had never had a love scene as such in her life! It would be best for everybody to forget all about her. The world could be very nasty, in fact, it was a very wicked place. She had been besieged with letters, horrid letters, and if she ever returned to England, which was very unlikely, they would find her a very different woman to the one they knew. She would consider no one, no one at all. And if anyone ever again put anything into print about her without her permission, she would sue them immediately. She would not hesitate a moment.

Everybody, or nearly everybody was against her, she asserted. The only one who had not failed her was God; but although she had made many mistakes, especially letting that film be made, she knew He had forgiven her. He was wonderful, and she did want to be the best for Him. The devil had got her down but he hadn't got her out, and she was going forward, whatever happened, film or no film. God was with her, and that was all that mattered. The little girl who 'attacked her difficulties vigorously' when at school in Edmonton lived on in Gladys. Tear-stained but determined, she continued her pilgrim's progress.

The film was produced under the title of *The Inn of the Sixth Happiness*, with many Mikado-like touches, with the tall, beautiful Ingrid Bergman playing the part of Gladys, and with a happy ending of her return into the arms of a tall Eurasian officer in the Chinese Army skilfully implied.

In vain did well-meaning friends try to console

Gladys with the assurances that in spite of the obvious distortions it was really a very moving film with quite a high moral tone; and that no intelligent person would pay any attention to the Hollywood-type love scenes, and no one who knew her would believe they had ever taken place. Gladys refused to be comforted, and she refused to see the film. It was banned from Taiwan, so she never came into direct contact with it. Yet in a remarkable way it brought her into the public eye and opened unexpected doors, largely through her own unconscious action, when she went to America in 1959.

She had decided to re-visit England. This decision was made after some babies had been virtually left on her doorstep. She often told the story of the arrival of one of them.

'I was very happy. I was going out preaching every day, as busy as I could be. Then one night, when I got home after a meeting, I found someone had broken in. But they hadn't taken anything.

They'd left something behind. They'd left a baby! There it was lying in my room, and I looked at it and I said, "Oh no, Lord. No! Definitely no! I don't want any more babies. I'm nearly sixty, and that's too old to have babies . . . No, Lord! . . ." '

Then followed one of her conversations with God which ended with her saying,

'All right, Lord. If you want me to take in babies – all right, Lord!'

So she started taking in babies as well as going out

preaching. Daughter and Son-in-law were with her continuously now, and Michael was in Hong Kong working among refugees. There was not enough money for all they wanted to do. Gladys thought of her friends in England, how sympathetic they had been when she told them of the little orphans in Yangcheng, how ready to send clothes to refugees in Hong Kong. Wouldn't they be even more willing to help if she could make them see now the pathetic plight of those little scraps of Chinese humanity that no one seemed to want, whimpering and crying so weakly in their helplessness?

She would go back to England and tell them about those abandoned babies. She would go by air, though she was a bit scared of aeroplanes, as it would be quicker. She would go to America first.

She did not really know why she felt she should go to America first. She had never been there before, and didn't know anyone, but that made no difference to the feeling that she ought to go that way. It was one of those incomprehensible urges that she got from time to time and, as usual, there was someone on hand to give her the help she never thought of seeking. An American in Taipei cabled to his brother-in-law in the USA saying a Miss Gladys Aylward would be passing through the country en route for England. She had very little money. Could he help her?

It so happened that his brother-in-law was an executive in World Vision Inc, an organization that lived up to its name by giving generous help to all sorts of people in all sorts of places. Its President, Dr Bob Pierce, brought suffering Korea into focus in Christian circles all round the world as he travelled from country to country with a picturesque, winsome, well-trained choir of Korean War orphans dressed in national costume. And Dr Bob Pierce, so it transpired, had met Gladys Aylward years before, in China. By all means help the little woman! Let her be the guest of World Vision while in the States! A great little person – deserves all the help we can give her!

Gladys was whisked off to Los Angeles, and put up in a hotel at World Vision's expense. At the end of her first week there World Vision Inc was mystified by the hotel bill. It appeared that Miss Aylward did not eat food. She just occupied a bedroom. No meals had been charged to her account, and later, when they got to know her better, they found out why.

She wasn't used to staying in hotels, she admitted, and didn't realize that all she needed to do was to write a chit for anything she had in the dining-room. The price of meals alarmed her, she was afraid she wouldn't have enough money to pay for them, so she crept round to a cheap hamburger stand when no one was about, explained to the waitress that she did not know anything about American food, and would the waitress kindly advise her what to have – not too expensive, please.

World Vision Inc saw to it that that never happened again!

Shortly after her arrival in Los Angeles she was invited to speak at the Mariner's Club. This was held in the Hollywood First Presbyterian Church, though there is no record that any of the 'film giants of Hollywood' were present. About a couple of hundred young people were, though, and they were so impressed by this amazing little woman with her story of faith and courage that they sent a deputation to the minister of the church requesting that she be asked to preach in it. She took the pulpit one Sunday morning, addressing a congregation of over 1,500 people with the same effect as at the Mariner's Club.

Then it got around that this was the very woman whose exploits in China had inspired the writing of the best-selling book *The Small Woman*, and the production of the film, just released, *The Inn of the Sixth Happiness*. She wasn't in the least like the film made her out to be – she was only about five feet high, and her hair was scraped up in two little plaits over the top of her head; she wore a gorgeous Chinese gown but apart from that you wouldn't look at her twice, not until she started to speak. But then – oh, boy! You couldn't take your eyes off her then! You could hear a pin drop while she told about the way she went to China because she knew God had called her, and how her senior missionary opened an inn for muleteers and she had to grab the mules – and then the way she whipped round and challenged everybody, were *they* willing to step out for God? Made you feel ashamed of yourself and your flabby faith ... You ought to go and hear her. A great little woman ...

Gladys did not know when she went there why she had to go, but afterwards she had no doubt that God had launched her into the USA.

CHAPTER FIFTEEN

The Falling Star

The World Vision representative was puzzled. Then he was worried. Something had gone wrong with Gladys and he didn't know what it was. They had been travelling together for weeks, going from one meeting to another all over Canada, and they had got on fine! Indeed, Gladys had told him that she felt he understood her better than any man she knew, which was very gratifying for a young man who had the responsibility of acting as a sort of business manager to a famous missionary speaker nearly twice his age. She confided all sorts of things to him, including the difficulties she had had during her first lonely weeks in the USA, and how angry she had got when people asked her frivolous questions like what food did she eat, had she seen the film, had she met Ingrid Bergman? He had noticed this himself, and had been surprised at the meek way people accepted her retorts. 'I think mainly because they realized her depth and because they felt she had suffered and felt deeply about the questions they asked,' he explained to someone later.

As far as he and she were concerned, however, they had laughed together and eaten together and prayed together, and never the suspicion of a cloud between them. Then suddenly Gladys had turned morose. He asked her what was wrong. No reply. He couldn't get a word out of her, and sitting opposite to her at meals on trains or in hotels three times a day, plunged in gloomy silence had become quite a strain. He searched his words and his actions to try and find how he might have offended her, but could find nothing.

Eventually, when Sunday came, he could stand it no longer. They were both due to preach at a morning church service, and he knew he would feel like a hypocrite if he did so.

'Gladys,' he said. 'We've got to have this out. I'm not going to that service until I know what's wrong. I'd be a complete hypocrite, standing up there preaching when there's this undercurrent between us. What have I done to upset you? If you don't tell me so that I can put it right, I refuse to go and preach.'

He was utterly unprepared for the answer.

'It's Tibet,' she said. Her gloominess had nothing whatever to do with him. She had had an awful premonition, a sort of vision of terrible Communist persecution in Tibet. She hadn't told him because she'd been afraid he would laugh at her, but she had been praying for hours in the night, for Tibet. She couldn't get it out of her mind, what she knew was happening there.

A week later, as they emerged from a restaurant in Toronto, the early noon edition of one of the newspapers was on sale, and the headlines ran '3,000 massacred in Tibet'. Gladys saw the announcement, and broke down. If only she had prayed more earnestly, she wept, if only she had entered the spiritual conflict with greater faith and sincerity, those poor people might have been saved!

The World Vision representative was silent. Her compassion for suffering humanity that was so evident in her almost reckless involvement of life and possessions was well known – but this was different. It was not often that Gladys revealed how deeply she plunged into the unseen spiritual realm. Perhaps that was the secret of her unique power to strip off shams and face people with stark reality in her preaching, and of her apparent fearlessness in facing new situations.

'The eagle that soars in the upper air does not worry itself how it is to cross rivers,' she wrote once in her Chinese Bible. It took a Gladys Aylward to visit the Chinese offshore island of Kinmen immediately following a terrible bombardment from the Communist guns, get straight down to practical work among the wounded, visit and encourage tiny Christian groups, and so acquit herself as to be officially accorded the title of honorary citizen. Most people would have thought it utterly impossible to obtain permission to visit what was virtually the front line, even if they would not have been deterred by the danger. But Gladys felt God wanted her to go, so she went. Eagles don't worry about how to cross mere rivers!

But eagles encounter storms that the earthbound avoid. When she arrived in Hong Kong after an extensive speaking tour in Australia and New Zealand she was so exhausted that the tour arranged for her in Canada had to be cancelled. Bewildered and battered she made her way up to the Haven of Hope in Junk Bay, where the large-hearted Annie Skau had now opened a sanatorium for TB patients. Here she wept and talked and talked and wept. The film. The publicity. The confusion in her mind about those years in China, so far in the past now. The things she had said on the spur of the moment that had been reported. 'I wish people wouldn't ask me about those things that happened so long ago. I sometimes wonder if what I tell is truth – or is it imagination?' she sobbed. 'I'm scared – scared that I'm not telling the truth . . .'

'Gladys,' said Annie. 'You must stay here. Stay here with me. You need rest. We can help you here.' So Gladys stayed in the Haven of Hope. And in a letter home she explained.

'I have high blood pressure, low blood count and doctor says I am on the edge of a nervous breakdown and must stop all meetings and anything that worries me. But everything does worry and I get horrible dreams. At times I am not sure whether the people or facts are real or a dream' . . . and then she added, 'I only know I am trusting *Him* and *He* will see me through.'

Weeks passed before she was ready to return to the whirl of her busy life, but as soon as she could face it she was back again. With some Chinese Christian men she had established a little Mission in Kowloon, with Michael in charge, and when she went along to preach the place was crowded. Ai Weh Teh had a reputation not only as a speaker but as a philanthropist, and there was much poverty in the neighbourhood.

But Taiwan was her country, and she was always glad to get back to Taipei city with its street vendors and open-fronted shops, its streams of bright-faced Chinese youngsters, its maze of alleys lying back from the main streets, and to her own little home. There she would return from her speaking tours abroad, and her visits to country churches and student retreats in the island itself, in through the large, double leaved gates to the little paved courtyard, across to the front door of the single storied house, and into the large entrance hall that served as sitting room as well. There were always piles of letters waiting for Gladys, and as soon as she arrived there would be visitors coming in to see her, 'sons' and their children, Esther – and, of course, Daughter and Son-in-law and their family. They lived nearer to her than any of the others. Daughter and Son-in-law were responsible for the running of the orphanage, for which support came from various sources as a result of Gladys' tours abroad.

In some ways, looking after orphans had been easier in Yangcheng than it was in Taipei. It was simple to have a free-for-all establishment on your own mission compound in a remote part of Shansi, but in Taipei, with its high standards and its modern way of life, you couldn't do it just like that. There was the problem of whether you could have boys over a certain age living in the same house as girls, and whether the servants would look after babies as well as school children, and what you did with the babies if they wouldn't. There was the business of getting a sponsor for each of the children, someone in America or Australia or England who would undertake to pay so much each month for a certain child; and there was the business of sending that person news about the child from time to time, and snapshots. To say nothing of the confusion when the landlord of the place you were renting wanted the place back, and you had to find somewhere else for the children. And even if, providentially, an organization of warm-hearted Americans was found which had just the right building, beautifully equipped and empty, into which the children could go, another set of problems presented themselves because it then had to be decided whether the children were still yours, or whether they were now the responsibility of the organization into whose building they had come, so to speak, to roost. And if they weren't yours any more, you had to explain to all the sponsors that their children were now being provided for by someone else, but there were some new ones being left on doorsteps pretty well every day, who were all being taken in and looked after, and would they like to take them on instead?

All these, and more, were the sort of problems that attended the running of an orphanage in Taipei. And if that wasn't enough, there was the unreasonable attitude of governments and organizations towards money. In Yangcheng, when a money order reached you from Mum, or some friendly missionary sent you a few dollars, you simply went and spent the money on what was needed. And as it was always needed immediately, if not by you, certainly by someone else, it was spent immediately. With governments and organizations however, if you received money you were supposed to enter it up and pass it on so that it could be entered up somewhere else and passed on, and promptly come back to you with very clearly typed instructions that as the donor gave it for such and such a purpose, for such and such a purpose it must be used, and no other. All in order to satisfy governments, fulfil obligations to donors, ensure that auditors could balance the books and secure the right amount on deeds of covenant. And, of course, there were committees . . .

It was so much simpler if you obeyed the Scriptural injunction not to let your right hand know what your left hand did! And it was more sensible. It left more time for really important things, like going out preaching. So thought Gladys. And if money was given to her for her work, why not use it without all that silly bother?

Altogether, it is not surprising that World Vision

Inc and Gladys eventually decided to run their affairs separately.

'You will know that I personally have nothing more to do with World Vision. I am sorry because they have been very good to me, and I liked to feel I belonged,' Gladys wrote early in 1963 to her World Vision friend of the Canadian tour. If she wasn't part of the organization any longer, it didn't make any difference to the people in it who were her friends. 'I do not yet understand where the misunderstanding began. But I am free, and God knows my heart. He has blessed me and the work, and I praise Him. Open doors on every hand. We only need courage and time to go in them. God has given me souls in nearly every meeting I have taken lately. In the prison at Christmas there was a real move, and we praise God it is still going on.'

In her little house as she wrote were three babies, one of her 'sons' on a short leave from the Navy, and a missionary who had come for the weekend. But Gladys was used to that sort of thing and scribbled away,

'We have eighty-six children in the orphanage.' Daughter and Son-in-law made wonderful parents, she said.

'I am well and very happy. Gordon, my baby who just one year ago was left on my step when he was five days old, was very sick for three whole months. All hope was given up, but I claimed him for God and he was wonderfully healed.'

She didn't mention that she had looked after the sickly baby herself right from the start until he was so ill he had to be taken into hospital; that it was she who sat by his little cot, night after night, ready to tend him when he needed it; that when she was presented with the hospital bill she looked at it in dismay, and then asked if she could pay it off monthly, please . . . and that the doctor had called out to her from his office, 'That's all right, Miss Aylward. No charge.' That was all involved in being a mother, and taking in babies for God!

'What a great and wonderful God we have, how small we feel when we realize how great He is. To know He saved and called us is something that I will never really understand; why He should want a person like me who does so many silly things. But I do love Him and want to do His will.

'We are all very busy getting ready for a Billy Graham Crusade. All churches joining in. We are expecting great things. Prayer meetings all over the place and tracts etc given out, visiting of all homes with invitations so we are busy.'

Then she continued,

'I am also, on top of this, trying to clear up, for on 28th I fly at invitation of BBC to London. I prayed for an open door to see my loved ones there, and here it is.' She did not say what the BBC wanted her to do when she got to London, for she did not know! Letters and cables had been speeding their way to America and Asia, as well as in England, in preparation for the *This Is Your Life* programme in which Miss Gladys Aylward was to appear, but she knew nothing of it.

She boarded the plane on March 28th, 1963, to go to London, and she had the chubby little Gordon with her. Couldn't leave him behind! She took him along to the BBC, too, although not until she arrived did she know what it was all about.

The millions of people who viewed that programme saw her just as she was – an excited, uninhibited little woman in a Chinese gown, squealing with delight, bright bead-like eyes nearly popping out of her head, as one after another people were introduced to her who had played a part in her life – Violet, her sister, Laurie, her brother, David Davies her fellow missionary in Shansi, Handley Stockley the doctor who had saved her life in Sian, and others ... and then, crowning joy of all, there was handsome young Son-in-law! She could scarcely believe it! She had left him in Taipei only four days before, and here he was, with her, in London. To everybody's delight, she leapt at him, he swept her up in his arms, and the BBC brought to a triumphant unrehearsed conclusion one of the most successful *This Is Your Life* programmes they had ever produced.

A few days later the telephone rang in a basement flat at Marble Arch, and Coolie answered it. Gladys was at the other end of the line, and after a word of greeting announced,

'I'm going to lunch with the Queen of England tomorrow.'

The Coolie gasped. 'You're going to lunch with the Queen?'

'Yes,' replied Gladys. 'I couldn't tell you before, as it all had to be very hush-hush. Don't let anyone else know until it's all over, will you.'

'What are you going to wear?'

'Oh, it depends on the weather. I may wear what I had on for *This Is Your Life*, or I may wear another nice gown I brought with me. See what the weather's like.'

'How will you get there?'

'Oh, that'll be all right. I'll just get a taxi. I need a new handbag, though. I'd better ring off now, and go round to Marks and Spencer's to get one ... Do pray the food will be what I can eat, Coolie. You know, there are some things I just can't take, and it would be awful to make a fuss . . .'

The Coolie walked away from the telephone feeling rather dazed, and perhaps just slightly uneasy. To hail a taxi and pop round to the Palace didn't seem quite the way it ought to be done.

Pastor Wang didn't think so, either. Gladys told him about the invitation, and he asked the same question as the Coolie – how are you going to get there? and when she told him he said,

'But Gladys, you can't do that! You're representing Free China! You can't just go to Buckingham Palace to lunch with the Queen in a taxi. Leave it to me. I'll see to it for you.' So the next day a dignified Pastor Wang arrived in a sumptuous car, chauffeured by its owner, a member of the flourishing Chinese Church in London, and escorted her to Buckingham Palace. She arrived in fine style, and when she emerged, there was the car and the escort waiting for her.

Pastor Wang had decided she might as well make a day of it, and had arranged to take her on to visit the Houses of Parliament. That part of his plan did not work so well. Gladys was so obviously bored after about twenty minutes in the House of Commons that he took her on to the House of Lords, and fifteen minutes of that was more than enough. 'You can take me back to Marble Arch and drop me there,' she said. She wanted to go and tell the Coolie all about it, and scuttled down the iron stairway to the basement flat called Bethany as fast as she could.

Everything had gone off very well. The food was good but simple, and she hadn't any trouble eating it. There were eight guests, and she was the only woman.

They'd been allowed to peep into the room where they were to lunch so they could see where they'd be sitting. She'd been put next to Prince Philip, and he was very nice to talk to, she didn't feel in the least bit awkward. The Queen had shown her the flamingos in the garden, and said they were very difficult to rear. She seemed very touched to receive the embroidered scroll that was presented to her from the orphans in Taiwan, and called her husband over. 'Look at this, Philip,' she said. 'Isn't it lovely?' She said she would have it made into a fire screen.

Altogether, it had been a lovely experience, and a great honour. Gladys and the Coolie agreed on that. Gladys didn't say anything about going to the Houses of Parliament afterwards. There was really nothing to tell. She had enjoyed going to lunch at Buckingham Palace, and found Royalty very easy to get on with – but as for Her Majesty's ministers of State she didn't know what they were talking about.

Gladys eventually returned to Taiwan accompanied by one of the Trustees who had been looking after her affairs in England. Gladys was delighted. It was wonderful that someone who had been supporting the work all these years could see it personally, and so be much better able to tell people in England about the orphanage. As the Trustee knew quite a lot about book-keeping, that side of things could be explained, too. Son-in-law would help.

The books were opened.

The Trustee looked perplexed.

Then the Trustee looked worried.

Then questions were asked ...

Then Son-in-law looked angry.

Something was seriously wrong. Shock followed shock. Then a petition was filed in Taipei in which the Superintendent of the Gladys Aylward Orphanage was sued for embezzlement of funds, and the Trustee returned to England. The one best able to give the necessary evidence was on the spot, and she spoke Chinese – Ai Weh Teh.

CHAPTER SIXTEEN

Gladys makes a Come-back

The allegation that Son-in-law had been embezzling funds (over one million Taiwan dollars were missing) was the bitterest blow Gladys had in her life. It cut her far more than the publicity brought about by the film. She would not even believe it at first. There must be some mistake! He would never have done it, never! She knew him, she trusted him utterly. Then, as the evidence was produced, item by item, she urged him to confess. If only he would confess some way out would be found! She wept, she threw her arms round Son-in-law and Daughter, pleading with them to repent and confess – in vain.

The next two or three years were the worst Gladys ever knew, for if ever East met West in collision they met then, in her little body. The Western viewpoint was that one who embezzled money donated for helpless orphans must face the Law! Chinese justice agreed. When the matter became known in Taipei, as of course it did, a Very High Official stepped in, saying that it was a disgrace to the Chinese nation that anyone should cheat a woman so known and respected for her self-sacrifice and good works as Ai Weh Teh. The man accused of doing this thing, therefore, since he had been a sergeant in the armed forces, must be tried as a soldier, not as a civilian. Had Gladys not gone to plead against this decision, which carried the maximum penalty, things would have gone much harder for Son-in-law than they did.

All the same, to bring the affair into the light in this way went against the Chinese grain. It shouldn't have been dealt with like that. It shouldn't have been made public. Face should have been saved, and the case settled out of court. But there was no way out now, and the British woman who had become Chinese had to go on with it.

The case became a scandal. It dragged on for two years, and during this time she was quite ostracized. She was already discredited in the eyes of westerners because of her reaction to the film, and now in the eyes of the Chinese because of the court case. Only a few of those closest to her stood by her, quietly trying to comfort her, but by and large she was avoided. There were times, too, when she was acutely aware of active secret antagonism. On one occasion she was threatened by a man who unsheathed a knife and it was probably the providential appearance of a doctor who knew her well that spared her from assault. For all her fearlessness in plunging into unknown situations she had a natural timidity which those who knew her best had often noticed, and during those years there were times when she dreaded being alone in her little house at night.

Worse than that, something seemed to have happened within her own personality. Westerners and Chinese alike observed it. 'From trusting everybody she's changed to trusting nobody,' they said. Only to her intimate friends did she write of the struggle she had in those days. She felt as though even her faith in God was failing now.

It showed itself in various ways. 'Her stock went very low,' said an American missionary who had known her long ago, in China, and had respected her. 'Her stock went very low. It went low in the eyes of the westerners, and it went low in the eyes of the Chinese.' He paused for a moment, and then he added rather deliberately,

'But she made a come-back.'

The inside story of those years she shared with only her most intimate friends. She was so confused that she did practically no preaching.

'I have not taken any meetings now for nearly a year,' she wrote to one, a nurse who was running a rehabilitation home for mental patients in the south of England. 'I have not been too busy, but too mixed up in my mind. How can I help anyone when I really need help myself? ... I feel I have not been all I should be to you. I wanted to help so much, but these two years have been so tied up. I long to be free, and be able to get out and do what I know is what God called me for. I have stagnated for two years...'

She was conscious of having very few friends. Esther came from time to time, looking at her anxiously, urging her to eat more, putting food in the refrigerator because she knew Gladys did not bother to do anything about it herself. One or another of her 'sons' came, sometimes just at the right moment when there was something to be done that needed a man's strength. But she received very few letters. She who had for years got so many that she could not cope with them all, now had days when not one came.

'This has been a most trying and heart-breaking time, and I wonder many times how I have come through. I have been going to send to you and tell you I was giving up, but it never really came to that. Every time God sent someone or something to remind me that I was His, and He was going to manage.'

She felt she knew why the little lad, Gordon, had come to her. She had looked after many of the babies herself until they were either adopted or ready to go into an orphanage, and how she had missed them when she had to part with them! But this one was her own. 'I know why God let me have him, for I do not know what I would have done without him. When things were so bad it was as if he knew, bless him.'

At one stage her nurse friend was having difficulties in her own work, and Gladys wrote,

'Now, I know exactly what you are going through, because I am going through the same thing. This has been my most terrific year, and I do not believe I could stand another one like it. It seems as though everything I do is wrong, and only my faith in a Loving and Living God keeps me going, because I get one bang after another. The latest is that we have to get out of the building we are in, where the orphanage is, and so I am busy going around looking for a house. This is something that tires me very much. It takes time and energy and I get tired so quickly, because I have had a really bad summer. I have been up and down all the time, not only with prickly heat, but with a funny head – something like I used to have, you know – blackouts. Well, I can keep going, but only as I trust the Lord.

'So, dear, I believe that God has called you and me,' she continued, 'and it is not to walk as other people have walked in a nice, rosy way, but just along the way He walked to Calvary; and one day we will be able to look back and understand why all these things have had to be. I shall pray, when I feel so tired and so head-achy and my back aches, for you as your back aches. I shall pray, when I am razzled with money, about your money and I know that as I look for a building I will think of your building. We are walking hand-in-hand along a road which He asks very few people to walk and, as I say, one day we will know and understand why.'

In 1966 she paid her last visit to England. The long-drawn-out court case was over, with Son-in-law sentenced to a term of imprisonment. Perhaps she was thankful to get away for a while from scenes that had been so painful, and sometimes frightening. Back in England there was the same welcome as before, for she was a favourite with the Press and the BBC, and had become almost a legendary figure.

'Are you Gladys Aylward?' children would come and ask her when they saw her in the street. It was like encountering Joan of Arc or Mary Slessor to be meeting in person someone they heard about in school!

'Yes, that's me,' she would answer cheerfully, 'And here's Gordon!' The sturdy, chubby little Chinese toddler, accompanied her everywhere. On one occasion some friends had arranged to meet her at a restaurant in the City, and on approaching the place noticed people pausing, bending down slightly, then passing on with a piece of paper in their hands and a smile on their faces. A Billy Graham campaign was in progress and Gordon was handing out advertising leaflets. 'People will take them more readily from a child,' said Gladys in explanation as her friends greeted her.

She was just the same as she had always been, it seemed to them. Fame hadn't really made any difference to her. She still wore her simple Chinese clothes and flat slippers, her hair was still scraped back into two little plaits and pinned over her head. The only outward evidence she gave of being 'Mum's daughter' was that she came out, not in diamante jewellery or saucy hats, but in orchids! She had been given one to wear very early in her tours abroad, and had been so taken with it that she rarely appeared in public without wearing an orchid after that – though it was usually an artificial one!

'She's just the same old Gladys,' her friends and family said. And although she knew that she could draw the crowds as no other missionary could, and was in demand in circles to which others of her ilk would have no entrance, she accepted it all with a matter-of-fact simplicity. She'd got quite used to moving among the nobs by this time and quite enjoyed it, she said – it made a nice change! It was none of her doing, though.

'You know, Helen,' she said once, as she sat with the Air Commodore's wife, having a confidential chat. 'I wasn't God's first choice for what I've done for China. There was somebody else. I don't know who it was . . .' She stared straight in front of her, her dark eyes glowing like those of a seer, and Helen waited silently. She had seen Gladys in that mood before. There was something fragile, other-worldly about it, that must not be disturbed if the revelation were to be given.

'I don't know who it was – God's first choice. It must have been a man – a wonderful man. A well-educated man. I don't know what happened. Perhaps he died. Perhaps he wasn't willing . . . And God looked down . . . and saw Gladys Aylward . . .'

Suddenly Gladys' forefinger shot out and pointed downward with dramatic suddenness, and she continued,

'And God said – "Well – she's *willing*!"'

She packed a tremendous lot into those months in England. The memory that was so inaccurate when it came to facts and figures seemed to hold an incredible number of names of people she loved. The families of her friends were her families, and she knew them all. There were visits to schools, some of which had Aylward Houses in them, and there were numerous meetings to address. She appointed new Trustees of the Charitable Trust. Always there were letters to write – to her 'sons' and their families in Taiwan, to Michael in Hong Kong, and to Kathleen.

She wrote frequently to Kathleen in those days. Kathleen Langton-Smith had arrived in Taiwan to join her just about the time when Son-in-law's dishonesty was brought to light, and that arrival was one of the most providential happenings in Gladys' life. Kathleen had been a postmistress in Nottingham for some twenty years when she saw Gladys in 1963 in the *This Is Your Life* TV programme. Until then she had never a thought of going to the Far East to work among Chinese orphans. Her arrival in Taipei a few months later, having sold up her home and uprooted herself completely from her old life was as daring, in its way, as Gladys' arrival in Yangcheng thirty years previously.

'Have you had any experience with children?' Gladys asked her.

'No,' replied Kathleen. She was unmarried, and an only child.

What could she do, then?

'I can do accounts,' remarked Kathleen. Twenty years in the Post Office had equipped her for that anyway.

'If God's brought you for nothing else, it's for that!' exclaimed Gladys. It turned out that Kathleen could do quite a lot of other things, too, including adapting herself to life in a new country among people whose language she did not understand. And if history repeated itself when two strong personalities clashed, it repeated itself also in the loyalty of the younger to the older that lasted right to the end.

'It is cold here in England and I do not like it. When the wind is so keen I find it hard to walk round the corners,' Gladys wrote to her, 'I have cried several times, for I wanted to run back to you all,' and added emphatically 'I love you, I trust you, I long for you and miss you terribly.'

Early in 1967 Gladys went back. To her disappointment, Michael and his wife decided to go to Canada, but there were Chinese Christian men connected with the Hope Mission in Hong Kong who were prepared to take responsibility, and so that work continued. Back in Taiwan there were occasional crises in connexion with the Babies' Home as when new premises had to be found in a hurry, but on the whole those last few years were peaceful ones. Chinese officials did their best to ensure that. They knew that Ai Weh Teh had no head for business, so they didn't bother her with it. Legalities required of others were by-passed in her case. If you know your man, you can trust him says the wisdom of the ancient East, and they knew her.

And Gladys made her come-back.

She made no effort to do so, of course. It would not have occurred to her to try and make herself popular. She just went on doing the same things in the same way. If there were arrangements to be made in connexion with her work, she made them herself, without trying to get help from anyone else. She was quite astute in some ways, and dealt with a Chinese businessman who would not return money he owed her, in a good old-fashioned Chinese way. When he held a large reception she gate-crashed quietly, sat down among the guests and aired her grievance to them. Consternation! The host could not refute what she said, and did not try to do so. Self-appointed middlemen scurried to and fro, but Gladys, tearful yet composed, refused to be silenced. For centuries wives (or daughters-in-law) who could stand things no longer had obtained alleviation of their lot by appealing to public opinion in an outcry in the street, and the method still worked. The affair was settled promptly, out of court, and Gladys got her money back! But those in need knew that the compassionate Ai Weh Teh was the one to go to. She was there like a flash if someone was in distress. Unwanted babies gravitated mysteriously in her direction. The longing to spend all her time at the Babies' Home was strong, for from the time when, as a little girl, she scampered home from school day after day to wheel Laurie out in his pram and help give him his bath, she had loved babies. When requests came to her to speak at meetings here and there, all over Taiwan, she sometimes went grudgingly – but she went.

'Lord, keep me strong in the sense of Thy call,' she had written in her Bible years before, and she knew what that call was. She had to tell people about God – her God, the Living God. She hated Communism. Didn't Communism deny the existence of God? Therefore she, Ai Weh Teh, hated it, and didn't hesitate to say so when occasion demanded it. There was no staying neutral on that point, where she was concerned.

But her main theme, as always, was the exploits of that silly little Gladys Aylward, and the greatness of her God.

As 1969, the last year of her life dawned, this was what she spoke about at the New Year's meeting she had been asked to address at the US Base in Taipei. She was a frequent visitor there, for although *The Inn of the Sixth Happiness* had been banned in Taiwan, it had had a good run in the USA, and many of the Americans who were stationed in Taiwan had seen it. The tiny heroine was in great demand among them, up and down the island. So at the beginning of 1969 she spoke to some of them and harked back, as she had done so many times before, to that fateful day when she boarded the train to start on her long journey to China.

'... And I looked at that little group of people on the platform. They were there to say goodbye to me. They were my friends. And as the train started to move, I said to myself, 'Well, that's the last I shall see of them.' And I wanted to cry.

'But I didn't cry, because suddenly some words flashed into my mind. "Give Me two, and I'll give you five. Give Me five and I'll give you twenty ..." something I'd read in the Bible.'

Gladys gave a little giggle. 'I didn't remember it right,' she admitted. Then she added firmly, 'But I remembered it the way I believe God wanted me to!' And she continued,

'Twentyfold – Sixtyfold – Hundredfold; And I said, "Lord I'm giving up my mother and my father – I want mothers and fathers wherever I go! There's

my sister and my brother – Lord, I want sisters and
brothers wherever I go! I'm giving you my friends,
Lord, that little group of people there on the platform. Lord, I want friends wherever I go . . ." '

And she received them, all the way along the line –
one hundredfold.

The last year of her life slipped by. It was a happy
year. She had a car, provided through legacies, and
although she could not drive, Kathleen could, and this
eased things a lot for her. Two or three times a week
she was driven the seven miles to the Babies' Home,
and spent hours playing with the toddlers there. Gordon who lived with her was a little schoolboy now, and
far too big for babies, but Saturday afternoons were
often spent by the sea, splashing about with him in a
secluded cove. He frequently went with her to meetings she addressed, and although he was no better than
any other little boy in private life, he behaved remarkably well on the platform, smiling rather solemnly
when she referred to him as the bundle of rubbish she
had picked up, a baby just five days old. But beforehand he often said warningly 'Don't talk too long,
Mummy!'

One night in the autumn there was a typhoon which
struck Taipei with such violence that roofs were
ripped off, trees crashed, and rain poured down surg-
ing through the narrow alleys, gurgling under gate-
ways and doors, right into the houses. Water poured
down from the flat roof of the Babies' Home and the
stairways became like waterfalls. Kathleen phoned in
desperation to the US Army chaplain who lived
nearby, and he went along immediately, dodging
sheets of corrugated iron that hurtled along the street

like skilfully thrown discs, and after some hours managed to stem the flood. The little house in the city did not escape either, and Gladys reported afterwards that as the water came rushing in Gordon with gleeful excitement suggested that they should pray to God to send a submarine.

Just about this time Gladys started preparing for Christmas, by buying hundreds of dainty calendars with Chinese pictures to send to her friends. She hadn't always been able to do it but this time she wrote little letters as well to personal friends, to donors, to fellow missionaries, to schools she had visited in England.

Her thoughts went back to years of long ago. London. She had two illustrated tea cloths of London scenes stuck up in a corner of her drab little bedroom – St Paul's Cathedral, a policeman on duty, a red pillar box and a newsvendor huddled with his coat collar up displaying a poster 'Evening Special! Summer late this year.' How lovely it would be if Violet could be with her! It would be like old times to have her own sister again. 'Violet is being very good to us right now. She's been wonderful since Bill died,' she wrote to Coolie. 'I wish she would come out here, and spend a bit of time. I'd love it.'

But if her own blood relations were on the other side of the world, those who were hers by adoption were very near at hand, and the house was astir because of them. Presents for everyone, right down to the latest grandchild! Gladys could not help giving presents. She was addicted to it.

1970 dawned. The weather was damp and chilly, and there were a lot of colds about. Gladys had one, and it made her feel rotten.

'You ought to stay in bed,' said Kathleen. 'You're not fit to go out.'

'Must go out,' said Gladys firmly. 'Got to speak at that New Year meeting to women at the US Base.'

'Ought not to go,' mumbled Kathleen but she knew it would be useless to try and prevent her. 'If you insist on going I won't go to the Babies' Home today. I'll take you to the meeting by car and bring you back, and see you safely tucked up in bed.'

Gladys went to the meeting, preached for over an hour, as usual, and returned very tired. Yes, she'd go to bed. She felt rotten.

Kathleen phoned the doctor. He came about 6.0 PM, said the patient had flu and a touch of pleurisy, gave her an injection. She settled down for a while after that. Gordon got into his little bed on the opposite side of the room and went fast asleep. Kathleen crept out, but she couldn't really rest. She went in and out of the room every hour or two. Gladys had thrown her blankets off – Kathleen replaced them. Gladys was very quiet. Gladys hadn't moved. Then Kathleen touched her hand and it was very cold.

Kathleen caught her breath and stood very still. Then she went quietly over to the other bed, picked up the sleeping boy, head nodding over her shoulder and backed out of the room.

The little body was left alone, dark eyes staring up at the ceiling, the two illustrated tea cloths of London on the wall.

But of course Gladys was not there. When the news flashed round the world, and her death was announced over the BBC she was not there, nor when long crowds of silent Chinese filed past the glass-topped coffin at the lying-in-state either. The funeral service in Taipei was attended by more than a thousand people, and memorial services were held for her in all sorts of places in America, Australia, England, but it all meant nothing to her. It could not affect her, not even when they buried the little body in the soft earth on a hill that faced towards the mainland of China, towards the city of Yangcheng, where they knew her heart had been all these years.

It was all in the past, and she was not there any more. She had moved on to join those who, like her, had given evidence that they knew they were only on pilgrimage, seeking a city of more lasting substance than any they could find in Time. It did not even matter that, as with the patriarch so with the parlour-maid, the promise had been fulfilled: 'I will make thy name great.' The only thing that mattered now was that on rendering her account to her Maker she could do it without shame. For, as she wrote once to a diffident teenager:

'Don't worry about your education.
'God won't ask you for certificates; He'll only ask if you've been faithful to your call.'

PILGRIM IN CHINA

Also by Phyllis Thompson
Freely Given
To the Heart of the City
The Gideons
An Unquenchable Flame
Mister Leprosy
The Rainbow or the Thunder
China: The Reluctant Exodus
Capturing Voices
Minka and Margaret
Within a Yard of Hell
The Midnight Patrol
A London Sparrow
Firebrand of Flanders
Faith by Hearing
Proving God
Matched With His Hour
Dawn Beyond the Andes
God's Adventurer
Climbing on Track
No Bronze Statue
Desert Pilgrim
Beaten Gold
Aflame for Christ
There Came a Day
They Seek a City
Our Resources
Countdown for Peter
Eight of God's Agents
Bible Convoy

Books for children
Teacher Jo Likes Little Cats
King of the Lisu

PILGRIM
IN CHINA

A MEMOIR

Phyllis Thompson

CONTENTS

Letter 1	Conversion	7
Letter 2	Burning my bridges	21
Letter 3	Spiritual struggles	29
Letter 4	Call to China	39
Letter 5	Preparation	42
Letter 6	First Mission station	55
Letter 7	Interlude	63
Letter 8	Coping with singleness	66
Letter 9	Learning and preaching	74
Letter 10	Eastern Light and Auntie Eva	81
Letter 11	Angels at the gate	93
Letter 12	A soldier and a beggar	103
Letter 13	Brief return to Hwaiyang	114
Letter 14	Shanghai	121
Letter 15	How the writing began	135
Letter 16	Three deacons	142
Letter 17	The Women's Preaching Band	157
Letter 18	Depression and the way out	166
Letter 19	Guerillas in Siangcheng	171
Letter 20	An answered prayer	186
Letter 21	Famine and an importunate boy	191
Letter 22	A new directive	198
Letter 23	Departure From Siangcheng	206
Letter 24	Postscript	214

**To Irene and Doris
my fellow missionaries
in Siangcheng**

1

Dear Edward,

As I walked out of the Charing Cross Hotel with you this afternoon, into the pouring rain, my heart was singing. And as I sat on the bus that was to take me back to Newington Green, on the border of Hackney, where I've lived for nearly a quarter of a century, I could scarcely believe it was true. I had been commissioned to do the very thing I most wanted to do, and let off doing what I did not want to do. I smiled gratefully as we separated after our talk, put up my umbrella, and set off for home.

You had wanted me to write my own story. You had mentioned it once or twice and, because I respected your judgment, I hadn't been able to say a definite 'No!' but the thought of doing it had depressed me. I'd gone to meet you this afternoon knowing you would broach the subject again and, sure enough, you did; but I could not come to terms with the idea. I simply did not want to write my own story.

Who am I, anyway, that anyone should want to read it? I'm such an ordinary sort of person, have achieved so little, started no flourishing Christian work, performed no acts of heroism. True, I went to China as a missionary in 1936, was there during the Sino-Japanese war, and eventually withdrew, along with all the other missionaries, in 1951, when Communist pressure became too strong for us to stay. True, the experiences of those years have coloured my whole life, which, without them, would have probably taken a very dull course. But there was nothing exceptional about them, nothing to justify me writing a book about myself.

Besides, it would be so boring a task for me. The best part of writing a book, from my point of view, is the research involved, and the interesting people it brings one in touch with. I'm not a creative writer, and inspiration comes to me through other people, not from within myself.

All this I tried to explain to you as we sat drinking coffee in the spacious, comfortable lounge. You looked slightly surprised when I said I'd find it boring to write about myself, and suggested, 'But it wouldn't have to be so much about yourself, as the way God has dealt with you, the way He has led you, provided for you. . .'

Even that did not stir me. After all, every Christian has a story to tell along those lines, so why me? And after about half an hour I said, 'I'm sorry, Edward. If I believed God wanted me to do it, of course I'd do it, even if I did find it boring. But I just haven't any urge in my own heart; no word from Him either.' Then I added, 'I'll tell you what I'd like to do. I'd like to have a shot at writing the story of Madame Guyon.'

A rather resigned expression passed across your face, and you said, 'All right. You go ahead. If that's how you feel I think you should go ahead and do it.'

I knew it wasn't what you wanted, wasn't what you had hoped would be the outcome of our interview. As my literary agent, you'd had quite a different idea. But you said, 'Go ahead,' and when I said, 'What? Write it first, without a contract, then see if anyone wants it?' your answer sent my spirits soaring.

'Oh, I'll be able to get a contract,' you said airily, and mentioned a couple of publishers right away. 'And if they don't want it, Highland—my own publishing firm—will do it.' So I knew it would be all right. It seemed too good to be true. To be able to do the very thing I most wanted to do, and to be assured of a publisher! Sitting on that bus I felt so grateful, so happy, that I had quite a sense of release about writing my own story.

'I'll have a go at it, just out of gratitude,' I thought. 'But I'll do it in a different sort of way— just writing letters, as memories come to me. Then, when I've finished, I'll let Edward see them. If they are any good, then he can go ahead and get them published. If not, no harm will have been done.'

One thing you had said when you were still trying to persuade me to write my own story had encouraged me. It was: 'It would start with your call to China, wouldn't it? What happened before that doesn't really matter.'

But some of what happened before matters very much. So I'll start in the year 1933.

No need to go into those first twenty-six years of my life, with their pleasure-seeking and the misfiring of love affairs: when the young men I could have liked, didn't like me and those who did, I didn't like. The only time when feelings were mutual was in the little correspondence school of journalism where I was working, in Adam Street, off the Strand. My senior colleague and I fell in love with each other and I went through all the traumas and heart-rendings of being in love with a married man.

If I'd been living then in the climate of the present day, I am sure the affair would have gone much farther than in fact it did. What a merciful deterrent to immorality was public opinion! To have been co-respondent in a divorce case would have brought shame on a respectable tradesman's family; to the credit of the man concerned, it must be said that he never tried to persuade me to take that step. The upshot of it all was that he found himself heading for a nervous breakdown, we agreed that we must separate, and I left the office.

But all that was in the past by the spring of 1933. My father was prospering in business and had bought another shop, this time in Andover in Hampshire, and we had moved there as a family of four—father, mother, sister, brother. We got on very well together and had our congenial circles of friends. My own life consisted of dances, bridge-parties, cinemas and smoking, with novel reading to fill in the empty days and hours when there was nothing else on. We played tennis, too, thought I didn't much enjoy it. I wasn't any good at the game but of course I had to play, to keep in with the right people.

It must have been hard for my father sometimes —he had stopped playing cards, drinking and smoking, and went to church regularly when he wasn't out preaching himself in some of the little country chapels around Andover. He always cycled to those little chapels. He wouldn't take the car on Sundays, for fear people got the impression that he was out joy-riding. As a Christian he didn't want to set a bad example by appearing to desecrate the Sabbath. Standards of the 1930s were very different from those of the 1980s. He had to come back to a drawing room full of smoke, where his family were playing bridge. He would look at us rather reproachfully, but make no further demur; and when he invited a preacher to lunch we always tried to behave ourselves and refrain from levity. More or less.

It was at one of these lunches that things got started for me. My father was the moving spirit in organising periodical meetings in the Town Hall on the subject of prophecy and, on this occasion, the preacher—at one time a missionary in the Far East—was our guest. Now Dad, who rarely spoke to me on religious matters, always tried to persuade me to attend those meetings on prophecy. He had given up trying to get me to church, but a meeting in the Town Hall was different. Sometimes I went, sometimes I didn't. He tried again, very guilefully, at the lunch table.

'Are you coming to the meeting this afternoon, Phyl?' he asked pleasantly. It was an awkward moment for me but, before I could reply, the preacher himself turned to me quickly and said, 'Oh, don't feel you've got to come just because it's me, will you?' He could see I was being trapped, and made the way out.

That did it. I felt he had been sporting. Very

sporting indeed. So I went to the meeting.

What he preached about—what prophecies he mentioned in the Old Testament that were being fulfilled in the present day; whether or not he pointed to the events in the Great War of 1914–18 which led up to the Balfour Declaration with its promise of a national home for the Jews in Palestine—I do not remember. I had heard a great deal about it all before: and how it was all part of the divine plan leading up to the culmination of the ages. It was not only the fulfilment of prophecies in the present that interested me, but also speculations as to how prophecies would be fulfilled in the future. Peering into the future had its attractions and was the main reason, apart from wanting to satisfy my father, for my going to those meetings at all.

There was probably nothing very different about what the preacher said that day from what I had heard already. They had all asserted that the consummation of all these prophecies, and the end of world history, would be the return of Jesus Christ to this earth. I'd heard all that before—but this time it had a slightly alarming effect on me. For the first time it dawned on me that this thing was really going to happen. The words I had repeated automatically in the Creed on the rare occasions I had attended church—'. . . and He shall come again with glory, to judge both the quick and the dead'— meant what they said. Jesus Christ was coming back.

And I knew I wasn't ready to meet Him.

I had had no intention of attending the evening meeting, for I had another engagement—one to which I had been looking forward rather eagerly. A group of us had arranged to motor over to the neighbouring town of Salisbury and go to the cinema there, then stop off on the way back for a meal in a café. It so happened that, at that particular period, two young men—one a farmer and the other a teacher—had been showing an interest in me. My natural vanity was flattered, and I had been playing them off against each other. Both were to be in the group going to Salisbury that evening, and since the one for whom I had a secret preference had shown signs of retiring from the field, I was anxious to meet him again and do what I could to revive his flagging hopes.

But the impact of that afternoon meeting was so strong that I felt I could not go off to the cinema in Salisbury.

'I'm really sorry, Charlie,' I said to the young man who had come to take me. 'I can't come after all. It's been such a wonderful meeting. I don't know how to explain it—but I just can't come to Salisbury this evening. I *must* go to the evening meeting.' So the young man, docile though disappointed, went off without me.

I've wondered sometimes what would have happened if I had crushed that new sense of awareness of God and had gone off to enjoy the pleasures of the outing. The first stirrings of life are indefinable, and easily ground down—but how much depends on them! I am very thankful that I made the right choice, and went to the evening meeting instead. Not that anything spectacular happened—I just came away with the awed realisation that I'd have to stand before Jesus Christ one day, and that I'd better try to improve myself.

My efforts along that line were rather half-hearted. Worldly pleasures would have to go, I thought, so I cut down on some of them, but not on those I liked the best, such as ball-room dancing. Dancing was my passion—the waltz, the fox-trot, the lancers, the tango. I did not stop going to dances, when I had the opportunity. Yet underneath it all was this vague awareness of God, and of coming Judgment. I started to pray, adding little personal petitions to the set forms I recited by my bedside at night as we had been brought up to do. The empty formality of 'saying my prayers' at any rate had one virtue—it provided a sort of sanctuary in which to commence a search for God.

'Oh, God, give me faith,' was one of those personal prayers, for somewhere I had heard that faith was a necessary ingredient if I was to be ready to face Jesus Christ. I had also heard something of the doctrine of predestination, and wondered whether I was not predestined to be saved; whether I was one of those for ever outside the circle of God's elect. However, that did not worry me overmuch. It seemed reasonable to pray that if I were, if He had not chosen me, He would make an exception in my case and take me in. I did not start attending church, but I did undertake to do the secretarial work for an evangelistic campaign that was being planned in Andover. I thought that was a pretty good thing to do and would weigh in my favour.

Meanwhile, the date for the next meeting in the Town Hall on the subject of prophecy and the second coming of Christ was fixed, and the time was drawing near. I was looking forward to it with a strange feeling of anticipation. I felt that would be the day when something of great portent would happen. I did not know what it would be, but it was as though I was coming up to a crisis; as though I was going to have my one chance of being saved. I'd heard the phrase used, and took it to be a dramatic experience that made one feel entirely different.

The first Wednesday of May dawned. There was no question this time as to whether I would attend the meetings. I wanted to. I went to the afternoon meeting with a keen expectancy of what would occur. Perhaps it would be a vision, a voice, a revelation given to me. I listened eagerly, waiting.

But nothing happened. The speaker—a gentle, courteous, typical Anglican clergyman of the old school—said nothing that specially enlightened me, though at one point in his talk he quoted a short sentence of Scripture with such an expression of rapture on his face that it brought tears to my eyes.

'And the King of glory shall come in,' he said, and momentarily it was as though he had been transported and was actually seeing that King of glory. I caught my breath. For the first time in my life I realised that God is a person, a Being to draw out the affection and loyalty and devotion of the heart. I wished I knew God as that man on the platform knew him.

When the meeting was over my father took the speaker and two other men back to his office over the shop, for tea. I went along too—to pour tea and act the hostess, as my mother wasn't around. I sat there in my smart little fur jacket, with my well-coiffured hair, listening to them as they talked. Then, looking at the clergyman to whom I had only just been introduced, the thought came to me: 'That man will think I'm a Christian—and I'm not!' And because I did not want to be a hypocrite, I butted into their conversation with the explanation which I thought would make clear my position, and at the same time satisfy him: 'I'm not saved— but I'm trying to be!'

There was a sudden silence in the room. My father and his two friends who knew me slightly, stopped talking, though one of them leant forward as though he wanted to speak. But something restrained him. Perhaps Someone restrained him. And the gentle, courteous clergyman looked across at me with surprise and said earnestly, 'Oh, don't try! It's all been done for you.'

It was my turn to look surprised. Don't try! But I thought that was just what I had to do. Try to improve myself, try to be religious, try to be a better person.

The clergyman saw that I was mystified, and said with a smile, 'If your father gave you a horse, or a car, what would you do?'

Well, the horse made no appeal, for I didn't ride. But to have a car of my own would be a different matter. My father had one, my mother had one, my brother had one, but when I wanted to use a car I had to borrow one of theirs. A car of my own?

'Oh, I'd make whoopee!' I said promptly. It is doubtful whether the clergyman knew the meaning of the current slang 'making whoopee', but he got the idea and continued, 'You'd take it and enjoy it, wouldn't you?'

'I certainly would!' I answered.

Then he spoke the sentence that I can only say

was the opening of the Kingdom of God for me.
I've repeated it over and over again through the
years that have passed since then, passing on the
message as it was given to me that day. Just one
simple sentence. This is what it was: 'Jesus Christ
died on the cross to give you everlasting life, and all
you have to do is accept it.'

I stared at him. Everlasting life *given*? All I had to
do was to accept it?

I am sure I must have heard the same message
before if not the same words but it had never
meant anything. This time it was different—like
suddenly hearing one's own name at the end of an
announcement over a public address system. This
time, it was addressed to me personally. I was being
told that what I had been trying to obtain by my
own efforts and sacrifices was being offered to me
for nothing . . . if I would take it.

That same evening, alone in my bedroom, I
faced the issue. If I accepted that gift of everlasting
life, whatever it might be, it would certainly mean
letting go of something. Looking back over the
years to what I realise now was the greatest crisis in
my life, I am amazed at how almost casually I regarded it, at how little I understood of what was
involved. I was just conscious that an indefinable,
other-worldly glow had appeared over the horizon
of my life, and that I was being drawn towards it;
but to reach it I had to leave something behind.
Vaguely I realised that this was my old way of life,
my ill-defined ambitions to have a good time. I
would have to relinquish what I knew for what I
did not, leaving behind the familiar for the unknown. So I thought about it for a while. I was not

at all sure I wanted to take the plunge: it seemed like diving off at the deep end, into nothingness.

In the end I decided that I'd take the risk. It was not the fear of hell that brought me to that decision, but the feeling that if I didn't take the plunge, I'd be missing the best. Whatever the consequences might be, I'd accept that gift of everlasting life. So down I went on my knees, down went my head on the bed, and I prayed.

'Oh, God, I do accept Thy gift of everlasting life,' I murmured—and waited for something to happen. Nothing did, so, thinking I might not have done it in quite the right way, I prayed again: 'Lord Jesus, come into my heart.' I'd heard that sentence somewhere, and it seemed appropriate for the occasion. Still nothing happened; so, rather mystified, I prayed a third time: 'Oh, God, I do have faith. . .' Then, since there seemed nothing else to do, I undressed, got into bed and went to sleep.

Next morning I woke up, as usual, feeling no different, but with the thought at the back of my mind: 'I must be saved! I don't feel as though I am, but I did what that man told me to do. I accepted the gift.' I went around doing the usual things, but now and then the thought would come again: 'I must be saved. I accepted the gift, like that man told me to.'

That afternoon my mother had a few of her friends in to play bridge. There were five of them altogether so they took turns in sitting out. During the course of the afternoon, I wandered into the drawing room and went and sat beside Mrs. Watson, whose turn it was to wait while the others played. She was sitting on the window seat, overlooking our terraced garden with the tennis court below. I joined her and she turned to me with a smile. After the usual preliminaries, she started talking about the state of the world, about the things that were happening in Germany (it was 1933—the year when Hitler was coming into power) and about what was worrying her most of all—the threat of another war.

'It would be terrible,' she said. 'Poison gas, and that sort of thing. We'd all have to go underground and live in cellars . . . food out of tins. . .' She enumerated a few more horrors that she had read about somewhere, then suddenly she turned to me and said, 'What do you think is going to happen, Phyllis?'

And I knew my moment had come.

So suddenly and unannounced come the opportunities of life at times. Swift and fleeting, they have to be grasped without premeditation, or they are gone and nothing can bring them back. It was so in the drawing room that warm afternoon in May. I knew I had to say something about what I believed, right there and then, and the bridge-players intent on their game could nevertheless not fail to hear what I said.

I swallowed hard, then said in a clear voice, 'I believe that Jesus Christ is coming back again.'

My mother told me weeks later that I might just as well have dropped a bomb on that game of bridge. Nobody made any comment, but they started playing wild, trumping their partner's tricks and so on. Phyllis—talking about Jesus Christ! Whatever had happened?

Well, something had happened at last. It had

happened to me. Not a light from heaven, or a breathtaking revelation, or anything spectacular or dramatic. But as I had said those words, there had come into my heart the quiet, unshakeable conviction that I was saved—saved for eternity. I'd been struggling to believe it all the morning; now there was no more struggle. I *knew*. I suppose it is what is referred to in one of the epistles as being 'sealed with the Holy Spirit of promise'. I knew that the gift of everlasting life had indeed been given to and received by me; that I possessed it; that I was born again—a child of God for ever.

Less than twenty-four hours had passed since the man had said those unforgettable words: 'Jesus Christ died on the cross to give you everlasting life, and all you've got to do is to accept it.' I sometimes refer to this as my 'overnight conversion' and no doubt there were some who thought it was too quick, that it would not last. But it has lasted for fifty-one years—that deep, unshakeable inner conviction that I have everlasting life. And fifty-one years is quite a long time.

Well, that's the story without which my call to China would never have taken place; the story of the complete turn-about in my life, which got me facing in an entirely different direction and setting out on my spiritual pilgrimage. Having got it down, I can turn to what I really want to do—research into the life of that remarkable Frenchwoman who lived nearly three hundred years ago, whose spiritual journey into the love of God has inspired so many, including me—Madame Jeanne de la Mothe Guyon.

2

Dear Edward,

A couple of weeks after my conversation with you in the Charing Cross Hotel I met a friend at the National Art Gallery for a brief get-together, not having seen her for about six months. As we sat in the restaurant over our lunch she asked me what I was doing now, and I told her I was starting on another book.

'What's it to be this time?' she asked and when I said, 'The Life of Madame Guyon,' an expression of mingled delight and amazement passed over her face. She looked at me with her eyes wide open and exclaimed, 'Oh! How wonderful. She's my favourite character!'

This was new to me—I'd wondered whether, like so many other people, she would never even have heard of Madame Guyon. But she was the second person to react similarly when I'd mentioned what I hoped to write: 'Madame Guyon! She's been a great inspiration to me. What a worthwhile assignment!' So now I asked my friend what it was about Madame Guyon's story that had so impressed her, and she answered thoughtfully, 'Well, somehow I was able to relate to her. My experiences haven't been anything like hers, of course, but it was her sufferings, and what she learned through them. . . Yes, somehow I was able to relate to her.'

And this is what I am finding as I research into her life again, starting with the book which was written over a century ago, and is still being printed —*The Life of Madame Guyon* by T.C. Upham. Although she lived three hundred years ago, I find some of my own spiritual experiences, and my reactions to them, are just like hers. I can identify, for example, with the fact that immediately after the revelation that came to her through the simple words of a hermit monk, which she always referred to as her conversion she made a clean cut with the amusements and entertainments of the world in which she lived.

'I bade farewell for ever to assemblies which I had visited, to plays and diversions, dancing, unprofitable walks, and parties of pleasure,' she wrote. 'The amusements and pleasures so much prized and esteemed by the world, now appeared to me dull and insipid—so much so, that I wondered how I ever could have enjoyed them.'

I can't honestly say that I cut out dancing, bridge-playing, cinema-going and smoking, primarily because they seemed dull and insipid, but because I saw, from the example of my own father's life, that such things weren't compatible with being a disciple of Jesus Christ. I wanted to be a disciple of Jesus Christ, so I just cut them out. I've always been glad I did it then, in the first flush of that first love—it might not have been so easy later on. As it was, I really had no special difficulty about it—the desire for those amusements seemed to have died. I do remember passing the cinema in Andover to which I had so often gone, thinking to myself, 'I shall never go in there again,' and feeling rather strange about it. As I walked on, conscious that a certain activity had been withdrawn, I found myself thinking, 'I wonder what Christians *do*?' How did they occupy themselves when they weren't at church or praying or preaching or reading the Bible?

I've never had occasion to ask myself the question again. Even at that time I found myself well occupied because, having agreed to act as secretary for the forthcoming evangelistic campaign, I was fully involved with making arrangements, writing letters, getting leaflets printed—all under my father's direction; and when the meetings commenced, I attended every one for the whole month.

Two vivid memories of those early months stand out. The first was the occasion when I took my mother and two friends to Salisbury, to attend another of those meetings on prophecy which had had so great an influence on me. The speaker that day was a friendly, animated little Jew, named Mark Kagan, who had become a Christian and who could speak with authority about the inner meaning of the Old Testament writings. At the end of his talk, he pressed home the implication of his message that Jesus Christ was coming back one day, and invited any present who had not already done so to ask Him to be their Saviour and to signify openly that they meant to do so by standing up, right where they were. In the hush that followed his words two people stood to their feet—the two friends who had come with me. Contrary to my hopes, my mother didn't join them, though she was rather quiet as she drove us back to Andover. But when we both arrived home she said without any explanation, in quite a matter of fact voice, 'I'm going to put off that bridge party tomorrow—I'll tell them I won't be coming. I'm going to give up bridge for the time being.' Then she added, 'I think we'll burn those packs of cards—we don't want to have them in the house.'

So she went to the drawer and pulled them out —all thirteen packs of playing cards, and took them out to the field adjoining our garden where we lit a bonfire and scattered the cards on it. They did not burn very easily and, while we were pushing them on to the flames, my father arrived home from business. Seeing us in the field, he walked through the gate to greet us. When his eyes fell on the bonfire, he stood there speechless, his face rather white, his eyes very blue. His wife as well as his daughter destroying their playing cards!

'I'm giving up cards for the time being,' announced my mother. It was as far as she would go then. She did not commit herself rashly. But before very long something had been added to the windscreen of her little Austin Seven. It was a text: 'Christ Jesus came into the world to save sinners.' She had taken her stand at last, and she didn't mind who knew it. She never referred to that experience as her conversion

'I came back to the Lord,' was the way she explained it later. She'd come to the Lord, she said, when she was a girl, in a small Methodist chapel in Cornwall. On the whole, there has been little

enough to show for it in the intervening years—
and soon she was deeply regretting this. Then one
day, reading her Bible, she came to the words, 'I
will make up to you the years that the locusts have
eaten.' This was to happen in a way she little expected; in a way that was to call for a greater renunciation than she had ever known. But neither
she nor I had any intimation of that the day we
burned the cards. It was just a step we felt we ought
to take, and we took it.

The other incident that stands out very vividly in
my memory concerns only me, and I remember it
because it involved me in doing one of the most
difficult things I have ever done in my life.

My mother and I had heard about a little group
of people who studied the Bible, preached the
Gospel, and held prayer meetings in a wooden hall
that they had built in a side street—built it with
money and materials that came in 'by faith' we were
told. It was not until we had been attending their
meetings for weeks that we learned that they belonged to the Brethren. That did not convey anything to us: it was the first we had heard of the
Brethren. All we knew was that the local group
were very earnest and were self-governing, with
four 'elders' to run their affairs. One was a jobbing
builder, one a road sweeper, one a shop assistant,
and one a tradesman's delivery man. From time to
time they went out into the market square in front
of the Town Hall and held open air meetings,
carrying long poles with texts painted on banners;
and it was this courageous witness that impressed
me. To go out into the open like that! However did
they feel, and however did they have the pluck to

do it? It was something I felt I could never do. But, as the weeks went by, there came a most uncomfortable feeling in my heart that I ought to make an open witness like that, too. I kept remembering one of the sermons which the evangelist in the evangelistic campaign had preached, using as his text the words, 'And they came to Kadesh Barnea'.

The text referred to the time in the history of the Israelites when they had escaped from Egypt, crossed the Red Sea and, having travelled for some time through the wilderness, had come to the very border of the Promised Land, to a place called Kadesh Barnea. It was at this point that twelve men had been sent to spy out conditions in the land, ten of whom had returned with such an adverse report of the strength and size of the inhabitants that the Israelites had taken fright and refused to go in and claim what God had promised them. The outcome had been that they were condemned to wander for forty years in the wilderness, instead of entering into the land that 'flowed with milk and honey'. The point of the sermon had been that in our spiritual pilgrimage we come to a time when we are faced with an opportunity and a challenge which, if our faith and obedience fail, may result in our remaining in a spiritual wilderness, perhaps for years, perhaps for a lifetime. It had been a solemnising warning.

One evening, praying at my bedside, I was completely convinced that I'd come to my Kadesh Barnea. I either had to carry that banner or wander in a spiritual wilderness for maybe forty years; the latter, I remember thinking, would bring me to the age of sixty-six. I had to do something about carrying that banner, and I must do it soon. The Brethren, I knew, were planning to have an open air meeting in front of the Town Hall in about ten days' time. I could have joined them and, with their moral support, carrying the banner would not have been so difficult; but I felt that I simply could not live through those ten days with the ordeal hanging over me. It had to be now, or my courage would fail and it might be never. This was my Kadesh Barnea.

So the following morning, I went to the elder who was the shop-assistant and who, I knew, kept the banners and poles at the back of the shop where he was employed, told him what I wanted to do, and asked for a pole and a text banner. What text did I want? I did not know—it didn't seem to matter—but I chose, 'Believe on the Lord Jesus Christ and thou shalt be saved.' He did not say much, but I was conscious of his sympathy as he placed the strap over my shoulders, fixed the pole with the banner into the socket at my waist and held open the side door for me to emerge with it into the High Street.

I did not know which way to turn, nor did I know where I ought to walk. To walk on the pavement would impede pedestrians; to walk in the road would impede the traffic. I ended up walking along in the gutter. Up the High Street, past our shop towards the church at the top of the hill, I went, my eyes looking straight ahead with what I hoped was a beatified expression, while feeling as though I was on the way to the stake. It so happened that my father, who often left the window-dressing to one of his assistants, was himself dressing the window that day and, glancing out, he saw his only daughter—grim-faced and carrying a banner—slowly pass by.

This gave him a horrible shock. He did not wait to see me turn round outside the church and walk back. He hurried up to his office and knelt down and tried to pray. He probably thought I was getting what was known as 'religious mania'; perhaps he was not the only one to think that.

'Oh, Phyl, did you really feel you ought to do it?' he asked me later.

'Yes,' I said firmly. 'I had to do it. I knew I'd never go on if I didn't do it.' I had no exultant feeling, none of the inward joy I had expected after making such an effort—quite the reverse. I was emotionally drained and it was some time before I recovered my equilibrium. But I have never once regretted taking that step. I had burned my bridges. There was no turning back now, even if I'd wanted to. And I'd been obedient to what I believed God had been telling me to do. There might be some horrifying battles ahead but at any rate I wouldn't have to spend forty years in the wilderness.

3

Dear Edward,

I know that the main reason why you feel my story will be of interest is because of my China experiences. As you said, there are now so few people who knew China in the days before the Communist take-over there, that reminiscences about that period will soon cease altogether. And since China and the Chinese—particularly the Chinese—seem to be written in my heart, I'm only too glad to hurry on with my story until I get there. However, there are one or two things that really must be told if the story is to reveal the deep happenings, rather than the merely superficial ones; for without those deeper happenings I'd never have got to China at all.

The first one was a convention for the deepening of the spiritual life which I attended at a conference centre near Bournemouth. It had been organised by the Japan Evangelistic Band, and I went there on my own, feeling rather strange and very lonely. The convention was over-booked, so I had to be accommodated outside, in a private home occupied by a freelance evangelist and his American wife, Mr. and Mrs. Dunne. I had meals at the conference centre and attended all the meetings there, so did not see a great deal of my host and hostess; but they were very kind to me, and I had some talks with them during which I admitted my private fear that I would not be able to stay the course as a Christian and would become what I had heard referred to as a 'backslider'. I've no doubt they explained many things to me, all of which I have forgotten, but one thing Mr. Dunne said has remained with me to this day. It was a simple sentence of seven words.

'It all depends on your prayer life.' I've found that to be true. Without the cultivation of an inner devotional life, the heart soon becomes unsatisfied and deterioration sets in.

The theme of the convention was really along similar lines, emphasising the inner rather than the outer Christian life, and it was here that I became aware of something lacking in my spiritual experience. I cannot remember any of the sermons, only the continual reference to the Holy Spirit and to what some called 'the second blessing' and others spoke of as 'sanctification by faith'.

'I don't care what you call it!' asserted one speaker vehemently. 'The thing is—have you got it?'

I was uncomfortably aware that, whatever it was, I hadn't got it.

It was encouraging to learn, from what the various speakers said, that there had been a time when they, too, had been aware that they hadn't got it. One man admitted that he had been a Christian for ten years before he realised he was lacking the inner power that he recognised in some others whom he met and started to seek it for himself.

'Ten years!' I said to myself. 'Why, I've only been converted a few months, and I'm seeking it! I must be getting on pretty well.' I could almost feel a sort of puffing up inside until the thought came, 'That's pride! Spiritual pride. And pride is sin.' So I started talking to myself.

'You've got nothing to be proud of. You may have been converted only a few months, and be getting on much quicker than other people, but you've got nothing to be proud of.' I tried to talk myself out of it. 'I will not be proud! Pride is sin.' But try as I would, that puffed up feeling remained. My mind was in a whirl, overladen already with teaching I hadn't heard before, with the emphasis on faith and obedience, victory over sin, a clean heart, power in service. I wanted it all but now there was this unexpected problem in my own heart. I was proud. I had spiritual pride. I'd heard about it and I'd got it and, argue with myself as I would, I couldn't crush it. It was there, and nothing I said would budge it. I couldn't expect this second blessing, this entire sanctification, this filling of the Holy Spirit, whatever it was that others had got and I hadn't, if I had spiritual pride.

As I have said, I was lonely, not knowing anyone at the convention; and in any case, I never found it easy to talk about my problems, though I was quick enough to tell the story of my conversion. That was all very clearcut in my mind and, without wishing to denigrate myself unduly, I realise now that I probably enjoyed the interest aroused. But it was one thing to tell how Jesus Christ had changed my manner of life, given me a new purpose for living and a consciousness of eternity, and quite another to admit that I had an uneasy feeling something wasn't right. And to tell another human being that I was feeling very proud of my spiritual progress would be too embarrassing. So there I was, walking along the pleasant residential roads of South-bourne, battling with myself until I got to the point when I could battle no more.

Then it was that a strange little memory came to my assistance. I had heard or read somewhere that the favourite Bible verse of King George the Fifth was, 'If we confess our sins, He is faithful and just to forgive us our sins, and cleanse us from all un-righteousness.'

'If we *confess*. . .' That meant coming out with it, admitting it.

I was at the end of my tether. There was nothing left but to try this last resource. If it didn't work, I was finished; I'd have to go on with that secret pride all my life. There was very little hope in my heart that it would work, but I'd try it anyway. So still walking along, I cried out inwardly: 'Oh, God, I confess. I'm proud. I've got this pride, this spirit-ual pride, and I can't do anything about it. Lord, it says that if we confess, You will forgive and cleanse. Well, Lord, I confess.'

It was almost defiant, that cry. It wasn't what I would have termed the prayer of faith at all. The prayer of faith, I thought, was a calm, confident, unemotional committal of something to God, with the absolute assurance that He now had it in hand. That cry of mine wasn't like that. I may have heard the phrase, 'Let go and let God,' but as far as I was concerned at that moment I was just letting go. I really had very little confidence that God was at the other end, so to speak. I was too mentally exhausted to care what happened then. If God wasn't able to deal with that pride of mine, there was nothing more that I could do about it.

But God *was* able. I had only walked a few steps when I came to the corner of the road. There, quite suddenly, I stood stock still. It was as though I was being bathed in a sort of warm glow, descending on me from above; and, in some mysterious way which I cannot explain, I was conscious that the pride had gone. It simply was not there. I could scarcely believe it.

I suppose it was what might be termed a mystical experience, of which I have had very few. And, of course, I don't wish to imply that pride never reared its head again—far from it. But that particular form of spiritual pride was gone and I went to bed that night tired out, but at rest. It was a very definite sort of experience, and reassuring.

But I soon realised that it was not what I was seeking—that inner empowering that gave victory over sin, and fruitfulness in service. I knew I still hadn't got it, and I kept on praying that God would give it to me. And the more I prayed, the more depressed I became.

Depressed is perhaps not the right word. It was something deeper than merely feeling low-spirited. It was as though there was something in my heart that was hiding there—some evil which I could not define. I could not understand it. Those people at the convention had been so free, so happy, so uninhibited; they had spoken so convincingly about the Holy Spirit's presence in their lives, and about the fact that He was God's free gift—'Repent and be baptised, and ye shall receive the gift of the Holy Spirit'—and so on. Well, I had repented, and I had been baptised (that had taken place in a village stream, near Andover, shortly after I had carried the banner) so I seemed to have fulfilled all the regulations. But where was the gift of the Holy Spirit? Instead of liberty, there was an awful sense of bondage; instead of joy, a feeling of guilt; instead of effectiveness in service, there was no evidence of influencing anyone. So what was wrong? I was getting more and more miserable, though I managed to put on an outward show of normality while wondering how much longer I could go on like that.

One day, weighted down with the heaviness on my spirit, I went to my room and threw myself on my knees. Then, as I knelt there in silence, the awful realisation came upon me that I did not love God at all—that, in fact, that evil thing hidden in my heart was a hatred of God.

I was horrified. I'd thought I was a good disciple of Jesus Christ, that I loved Him; but here, hidden in my heart but now revealed, was a bitter enmity against Him. This was something far, far worse than that spiritual pride. Hatred of God! I don't think I knew at that time the verse in one of Paul's epistles when he speaks about the natural heart being at enmity with God. I did not realise that that enmity is inherent in all of us—I thought I was the only one, and I was really terrified. I knew, from previous experience, that there was only one thing to do about this—to confess it. But how could I confess such a thing? How could I possibly kneel there and tell God I hated Him? I can remember it now—the feeling of deep alarm. I knew there was nothing for it! I couldn't conquer this feeling myself, it had to come out; but I really wondered if I would be blasted out of existence if I did it.

So there I knelt, and told God that I was very, very sorry, but I couldn't do anything about it myself—I simply had to confess that in my heart was a hatred of Him.

What happened then was very quiet and unsensational, for I heard no voice, I saw no vision; but the memory of it has remained until this day. It was a sort of revelation, I suppose. I don't know how else to describe it. It was as though I saw a beastly, leering old man, mincing affectedly along, but somehow dressed up to look like Christ. And I knew that that was my Self. My religious Self. Self that wanted to be admired, adulated; that beastly, leering Self; the Self that was at enmity with God.

Then I saw Christ on the cross. No, I didn't really see Him: it was no vision, just a sort of revelation. And I realised what it meant. Christ had taken that sinful Self of mine, on the cross: 'Our old man is crucified with Him. . .'

It was all very quiet and unsensational. I had no overwhelming sense of peace, or joy, or praise, or anything. All I knew was that the sense of guilt had gone.

Around that time, I heard of a doctrine called 'sinless perfection'. I realise now that I had completely misunderstood the teaching. As I understood it then, sinless perfection was a state into which one could almost leap if only one's faith were strong enough—a state in which one never said, thought or did a thing wrong. I thought it was just a matter of having a strong enough faith, and clung to the idea with tenacity, assuring myself repetitively, 'I do not sin, I cannot sin, I am free from sin.' However, I had to give up that idea after about a day and a half. Honesty compelled me to admit that however well it worked for others, it simply was not operating properly as far as I was concerned. What I did find later on, was that although Phyllis Thompson was very much alive, with her desires and her lusts, she could be put in her place by being reckoned dead. So if she was dead, it didn't matter if she was overlooked, or laughed at, or denied natural satisfaction. The effectiveness of Paul's arguments in Romans chapter six is an open secret, hinging on the words, 'Reckon ye also yourselves to be dead unto sin and but alive to God through Jesus Christ our Lord'. I found it only worked when I reckoned.

But still there remained this conscious lack of the Holy Spirit. The sense of guilt had gone, but where was this empowering of the Holy Spirit that I had heard about and longed for? I prayed, I waited in silence, I tried to exercise faith to believe that I'd received it, I did everything I knew, but still there was that deep sense of emptiness, and I was beginning to feel that I couldn't go on without some energising force within.

Then the day came when again I realised what was meant by living by faith. I was due to go to speak at a little meeting for children, and as I descended the stairs that afternoon I felt suddenly afraid. How dare I go to speak for God without the

Holy Spirit? It would surely be presumption. I wished I could call the whole thing off, but it was too late to do that. Then, as I reached the bottom of the stairs and stood in the hall trying to brace myself for what lay ahead, my eyes fell on a little book that had been left on the hall table.

I picked it up automatically, scarcely noticing what it was, and opened it at random. My eyes fell on a text which had been placed under a chapter heading. This is what I read: 'What things soever ye desire, when ye pray, believe that ye receive them, and ye shall have them.'

'Desire' was the operative word, as far as I was concerned, in that sentence. Desire! By this time my whole being seemed to be craving for that inner spring of life, for something that would satisfy a thirst which I could not describe. Desire!

I knelt down there in the hall and prayed as I'd prayed several times before, asking God to give me His Holy Spirit. Then I got up and went to the meeting.

Nothing happened. I was expecting a sort of effulgent glow, or perhaps a feeling of tremendous power as I spoke, but the meeting went off quite calmly, and I returned home reminding myself that what the verse said was that if I believed, I would receive. In the days that followed I sometimes found myself asking again for the Holy Spirit, then pulling myself up with the reminder that I had received, for I had prayed with desire. Then, gradually, I stopped worrying about the matter and the craving which I couldn't describe ceased. I couldn't have explained how or why, but I was satisfied.

It was about a month or so later that it began to dawn on me that there was a difference in the reactions of the children in those little meetings I had started. Previously they had been friendly and responsive enough to me as a person, but what I said about Jesus had apparently left them unmoved. Now there was a change. They listened eagerly, they wanted to pray, were sorry when they knew they had done wrong. Some of them stayed behind to ask Jesus into their hearts. It was all very unspectacular, but to me it was the quiet outward evidence that I had received what I had prayed for.

Not long after that, I knew I must go to China.

4

Dear Edward,

As I look back over my life, and particularly over the early days after I became a Christian, I realise to some extent how great an influence books have had on me. In fact, I think they've made a greater impact on me than sermons, of which fewer than half a dozen stand out in my memory. But books! There is one in particular which directed the whole course of my life, to a country I'd had no interest in before—China.

The book was given to me by Miss Tasker—a middle-aged spinster who lived in a large house in a little village called Anna Valley, about a couple of miles from Andover. A stream ran along at the bottom of her wide, rambling garden, and it was in that stream that I had been baptised, along with one or two others who were connected with the local Mission Hall. Miss Tasker invited me to speak at the drawing room meeting she held in her home from time to time, and generally took an interest in me—this Andover girl who had had rather a dramatic change in her life. She can have had no idea of the effect that her casual little gift of a book would have on me.

It was called *Something Happened*, and was written by three women missionaries of whom I had never heard—Mildred Cable and Eva and Francesca French. They had become rather famous in the 1930s through their exploits in the far away region of the Gobi Desert, on the borders of China and Mongolia; but I knew nothing about that. I accepted the book with due gratitude and, having nothing special to do one afternoon, settled down to read it.

I was alone in the room and read on and on, absolutely spellbound. The book took me to a realm I had scarcely known existed, and among people of whom I had never heard; and I saw, through the eyes of those three women, the people of north-west China, the dwellers in the remote oases, the Chinese, the Mongolians, the Tibetans, and the Muslims of central Asia.

I saw, too, the little beggar children, with their sticks to beat off the dogs, and their begging bowls. The story of one of them in particular touched me, for she was deaf and dumb, so didn't hear the dogs barking, and sometimes they were on her, biting her skinny legs, before she could ward them off. (The Trio, as they were called, eventually adopted her.) I thought of the happy, well-fed children who came to my little meetings, and compared their lot with hers. And she represented so many other children, away there in China, who had never heard of the Good Shepherd and never would hear, if someone didn't go and tell them.

I read on—about the people these women missionaries met and the conversations they held, as well as about the disasters that overtook them personally. Once one of them scalded her arm and leg, and there was nowhere to tend her except the cart in which they were travelling, through a dust storm that had blown up.

One incident moved me especially. They had been selling Gospels and Bibles during the day, but in the cool of the evening they went for a stroll round the little houses and caravanserai and booths in that oasis away in the desert. As they walked round, they noticed a man standing by a flare, reading aloud, with a group of other men squatting around him, listening intently. The three women quietly drew near and saw he was holding in his hand one of the Gospels they had sold earlier in the day. The story he was reading was the story of the prodigal son.

As I mentioned, the name of the book I was reading was *Something Happened*; and something happened in me that warm afternoon in a drawing room in a Hampshire market town. Compassion such as I had never felt before filled my heart; compassion for those little beggar children who knew nothing of the Good Shepherd and for those desert dwellers who would never know there was hope for the prodigal if someone did not go and tell them. I always refer to that experience as being my call to China, but actually it was not so much a call as a divine impulse. I heard no voice, I saw no vision; I just felt that deep compassion in my heart, and found myself kneeling beside my chair, praying.

It was one of the shortest prayers of my life.

'Oh, God! For Christ's sake, send me to them!' That was all I said. But I knew God had heard.

5

Dear Edward,

The London City Mission is celebrating its 150th anniversary this year, and as the author of the book *To the Heart of the City*, which briefly tells its story, I have to appear on the platform of the Central Hall, Westminster, to answer a few questions about it. I shall be glad when my part is over. I don't enjoy these public appearances. However, the thought of it has had the effect of stirring my memory.

I have been vividly reminded of the first time I ever stood on that platform, nearly fifty years ago, as one of the missionary recruits of the China Inland Mission, who were very shortly to sail for that country. There were about sixteen of us altogether, mostly women, and it was arranged that each of us should say something about ourselves, in one sentence.

In one sentence! How we girls talked about it, tried over our sentences, prayed most earnestly that we would say the right thing! The prospect of saying something loud enough for everyone to hear (there were no microphones on platforms in those days), without stumbling, and without going beyond a sentence, scared us more than the thought of going to China. Like all the others, I prayed very earnestly that I would know what words I should speak, and eventually I had those words really impressed on my mind, so that at least I was in no doubt as to what I had to say. I can remember it to this day. When my turn came, I stood up, conscious that the eyes of two or three thousand people were focused on me, and found myself saying, 'I must. . .' For a moment I stopped —overcome with stage fright, I suppose—but then I pulled myself together, and said firmly, 'I must work the works of Him that sent me, while it is day. The night cometh, when no man can work.'

That really summed up the sense of urgency which impelled me then and, in a way, still impels me today.

It was the year 1936, nearly two years after I had had the experience in the drawing room at home, when I knew I must go to China. What a different world we lived in then to the one we live in today! I was in my mid-twenties, yet still living at home with my parents, with no thought of moving into a flat and making a career for myself. I was just like the other girls in our set. We lived at home until we got married. If we didn't get married, we went on living at home. It occurred to very few of us to launch out and do something different. So when I told my parents that I thought of going to China as a missionary, it was like exposing them to an electric shock.

I'd been thinking about it for some time before actually broaching the subject, and I did it one evening when the three of us were sitting around the fire, and my mother had apparently dropped off to sleep. I don't remember what my father and I were chatting about, but I do remember saying, 'I feel that God is calling me to go to China.'

My mother sat up with a start. Suddenly she was wide awake, and without any hesitation said, 'I could never let you go!' And she meant it. It is an interesting reflection on the climate of those days that her unwillingness to let me go was an insuperable barrier to my going. It did not seriously occur to me to take a step in direct opposition to the expressed wishes of my parents (my father maintained silence on the subject, though I knew that he would not stand in my way): in any case the China Inland Mission, to which I had thought of applying, would not have accepted me: at that time it was against their policy to accept a young woman whose parents were actively opposed to her joining them and going to China. So there was nothing for me to do but to wait. Looking back I am surprised at the equanimity with which I did so—and also at the quiet conviction that I would go to China, and that I had better do what I could to prepare myself for what I'd be likely to do when I got there.

What would I be likely to do there, anyway? I wasn't a nurse, and I wasn't a teacher so, as far as I could see, the only thing I'd be able to do would be to go to remote villages and preach the Gospel from house to house. In order to get some practice in that sort of activity, I determined to go once a week to Charlton, a village about a couple of miles from Andover, and go from house to house, and preach the Gospel.

Whether it was that I was just plain scared of

doing it alone, or whether I felt it would be good to encourage others to do the same thing, I don't know. Perhaps it was a combination of both. At any rate, I enlisted the help of some of the children who came to the meetings I'd started for them and who had given evidence of coming to faith in the Lord Jesus Christ. There weren't many of them, but they would take turns to come, two at a time, with me on Saturday afternoons to Charlton, give out tracts, and stand by me when I had the opportunity to speak to the people who came to the doors and were willing to listen. So that is what we did.

How satisfactory it would be if, at this point, I could tell of souls converted as the result of this effort, or of some spiritual movement in Charlton; but, as a matter of fact, I know of no such outcome. The children and I went faithfully on Saturday afternoons; we prayed about the people we met; we certainly had a heart-warming sense of fellowship and satisfaction as we trudged back home again. But of the various conversations I had with people in Charlton, I only remember one. It was with an old man who stoutly declared that he had been a believer once, but wasn't any more, and that he had a very low opinion indeed of the people who called themselves Christians. Then he added, surprisingly, 'But I will say that I think more of you than I do of most of them.'

This was gratifying, though it took me aback for a moment. I asked him why. What was it, I wondered, that had won his grudging approval? I was waiting for him to say something about my having made a clean cut from the world, having turned my back on idle pleasures, being diligent about proclaiming God's word, not being ashamed to speak for Christ, or something like that. I was quite unprepared for his answer, and didn't know what to make of it. What he said was: 'Well, you do *care*, don't you?'

Care? Of course I cared. It really mattered to me that people should love God, have their sins forgiven, be born again. Would I go about giving out tracts, and talking about God when I met anybody willing to listen, and be ready to go to the ends of the earth to do so, if I didn't really *believe* what I believed, if I didn't *care*? At the time I took it for granted that I was doing what I was doing because I cared; it didn't occur to me that anyone would do it for any other reason. However, fifty years later I realise a little better what that old man meant. If love for God subsides, love for man subsides too, and that caring quality is lacking from the proclamation.

To return to my story, and how it was that I started in earnest on the road to China. It happened quite suddenly, at a weekend convention which my parents and I attended in the little village of Anna Valley. The speaker at the Sunday afternoon meeting was a missionary from China. In the course of his talk he told a moving story about an old Chinese woman, and her devotion to the Lord. It touched my mother's heart, and there and then she made a vow to the Lord from which she never went back. I knew nothing about it until, a short time later, we were sitting next to each other at the tea table and she said to me, 'I told the Lord this afternoon that if He wanted you in China, I was willing to let you go.'

That was all I needed to know. On my other side sat the Secretary of the China Inland Mission; without a moment's hesitation I turned to him and asked what I had to do to apply to the Mission and go to China.

Less than two months later I was in the Women's Training Home in Aberdeen Park, Highbury, London, and a thoroughly good time I had there. It was my first experience of living a communal life. There I was among a group of other young women in their twenties, also fervently hoping to go to China, and I loved it. Our training for missionary work in China included attending lectures, peeling potatoes, washing up the dishes, and obtaining permission from Miss Bond, who was in charge of us all, if we wanted to be out later than 10 p.m. on Saturday, our free half-day. Strangely enough, none of the restrictions irked me, though I found potato peeling for about twenty people tiring and rather monotonous. I remember on one occasion feeling so strung up after some domestic duty that I thought to myself, 'I'll go and have a good cry when I've finished—it will do me good.' But when I had finished, I looked at my watch and realised that I simply hadn't time for that good cry. Not if I was to be ready for the lectures the next day—there was too much preparation to be done. So I gave up the idea, and went to my desk in the study instead.

Another memory of those days has to do with money. Several of the girls were 'living by faith'—in other words, they had no money of their own, and were learning to trust God alone to supply their needs. Wonderful stories they had to tell from time

to time, too—postal orders arriving by post in the
nick of time, money being pressed into their hands
by friends who had no idea they were down to their
last penny, and so on. But I was in a different category: my father continued to give me the allowance
he had given me when at home, and that was
always sufficient for current expenses; so I really
had no opportunity to 'live by faith'. I was not at all
sure that I would ever be able to do it, and it
worried me a bit, until one day the opportunity
came. I was asked to attend a week-end convention
somewhere, and when I worked out how much it
would cost, I realised I should not have enough to
cover expenses.

This was the time to pray to God to send me the
money I needed. I must say nothing to anyone
about it, just pray. And I felt I must be specific.
Having found out what the expenses would be, and
how much I would have in hand to meet them, I
arrived at the conclusion that I needed ten shillings. So I started to pray each day that the Lord
would send me ten shillings. I tried to believe it
would happen, but in that fight of faith I felt I was
often losing the battle. Never had I received an
unexpected gift of money, and why should it come
now? And from whom?

The days went by, the week-end convention was
drawing nearer, and still the money had not come,
and I was beginning to wonder what I would do. It
was an unwritten law among us that we never told
each other if we were hard up, and although I
knew that if I wrote to my parents the money
would be forthcoming immediately, I felt it would
be a complete failure in faith to do this. I'd asked

God to send me ten shillings and I had to go on believing He would do it.

And, of course, He did it. One day I went up to the bedroom I shared with two other girls and over to my little chest of drawers to get a handkerchief. Opening the top drawer, I saw an envelope with my name on it. Raising my eyebrows in surprise I picked it up and looked at the writing. It was unfamiliar to me. Then I opened the envelope, and drew out its contents.

A bank note for ten shillings. Nothing else. No word of explanation—just the ten shillings. The exact sum I had been asking for.

The sense of awe that came over me as I looked at it comes to me now as I record the incident. It was for me one of the outstanding experiences of that whole year in the Women's Training Home. Even the simple explanation of where the money came from, which I learned later, could not diminish the awed wonder with which I received that ten shillings. A benevolent friend of the Mission had decided to give a gift of ten shillings to each of the girls in the Training Home, so all received the same sum at the same time. But to none of them did it mean what it meant to me. I was learning to live by faith not only in the spiritual but also in the practical sense.

The months passed, with their round of lectures, study, prayer meetings, household chores and practical experience in evangelism which meant going, trembling inwardly, to speak at meetings or visit with experienced people from door to door. All the time the thought of going to China loomed in the background of our minds, with the uncertainty as to whether, after all, the London Council of the Mission would accept us. We had been accepted for training, but it was understood that at the end of that period, if we were considered unsuitable, we could go no farther. As the dreaded day when we must appear, one by one, before that august body, drew nearer, most of the candidates were in a state of tension, but I was surprisingly calm. There was a reason for this. I had been reading some of the books written by Amy Carmichael of Dohnavur in India and had been so moved by them, so drawn to the work she was doing in rescuing little girls from a life of prostitution in the temples of India, that I almost hoped the London Council would turn me down. In that case, I decided, I would apply to Dohnavur. I went in to face the solemn assembly of men sitting round the boardroom table, who were to interview me, feeling almost jaunty.

However, they did not turn me down, although they accepted me on unusual terms. I could go out to China as a member of the China Inland Mission on the condition that my father paid for my support. I expect that at the age of 29, with no academic qualifications except a rather sketchy period in journalism, and with only a couple of years Christian experience, I was considered too uncertain a quantity to justify an unconditional acceptance, especially as my medical report wasn't too satisfactory. The doctor had said I was anaemic and highly strung. I might not stay the course, might need to come home before I'd finished the first term of service. Whatever the Council's reason, that was the condition of acceptance.

Looking back, I am surprised that it never occurred to me that my parents might not agree to it. They might well have decided that if the Mission was not prepared to accept me as a normal responsibility, it probably meant that I was not really equipped for a missionary career on the other side of the world. However, the thought never seemed to have occurred to them, either. As I travelled back to Andover in the train from Waterloo that day, it was with the assurance that I had been accepted for China, and my parents, who met me at the station, heard the news as though they had been expecting it. God had called me to China, they both seemed to recognise that, and of course they would provide the financial support for their only daughter! I asked that it should be paid into the General Fund of the Mission, not ear-marked for me personally, because I wanted to be just like everyone else, and if funds were low, as quite often happened, and a normal remittance could not be paid, I'd be in the same position as the others. That was arranged and to all intents and purposes I was an ordinary member of the China Inland Mission, not in the category of the few who were 'self-supporting'. (Incidentally, some years later I slipped into the ordinary membership anyway.)

Written like that it all sounds very practical and matter of fact, but emotionally it was a strange experience of exultation and grief. Looking back over half a century, one realises afresh how rapidly the world has changed, and how the missionary scene has changed, too. There were no 'short termers' in those days. When we joined the China Inland Mission we expected to spend the rest of our lives, until we were too old to work, in China. We would return to our home countries periodically, for a leave, but the terms of service between leaves would be of uncertain duration—possibly a decade or so. The first term of service was the only one with a specified time limit. It was understood that young people who had had to adapt to an entirely new style of life in a strange country with a different climate might, after seven years, get to the point where they needed a break, so then they would be granted leave. So my parents knew they would say goodbye to me for seven years, without any likelihood of seeing me during that time.

Those were the days before universal air travel, of course. The mere sound of an aeroplane was enough to have people stepping out of doors to have a look at it. The very idea of getting to China in a day or two was unthought-of. The quick overland route via Russia and the Trans-Siberian Railway took only about a fortnight, but the usual way was by liner via the Mediterranean and the Suez Canal, the Indian Ocean and round South Asia to Shanghai. It took just over a month. And since, as missionaries, we would be living in the interior, involving journeys by cart for days on end, the geographical separation of thousands of miles, measured in time, could be anything from four weeks to four months. No emergency at either end could bring us together more quickly than that. In fact, when we said goodbye we knew it would be for seven years, with no possibility of meeting before that time.

And we loved each other.

I can remember our parting. We had had lunch

and the maid had brought the coffee tray into the lounge: a daily ritual. So we sat down to drink our last cup of coffee together. But somehow we couldn't get it down.

'I must go!' I said with a sort of gasp and, simultaneously, we all got up. My father ran upstairs. My mother, without a word, helped me get my coat on and collect my bags. My father came downstairs and I saw he had been crying. His eyes were red and, as he hugged me, he half-sobbed, 'I'm sorry, darling. It's just the natural, you know.'

'Just the natural.' Therein lay the grief.

The last glimpse I had of them was walking back from the gate together, towards the house, looking straight before them, my mother's face sternly set.

'They're great, aren't they?' my brother said in a choked voice, as he drove me away to Southampton to join the members of the C.I.M. party on the P. and O. SS Ranchi. It was the greatest sacrifice my parents had ever been called upon to make, and they had made it. I've always felt that in the heavenly records the words that God spoke to Abraham were repeated to them that day. '. . .Now I know that thou fearest God, seeing thou hast not withheld thy son, thine only son, from me. . .' Only in their case it was a daughter.

Therein, in the indefinable way only those who have had the experience can understand, lay the exultation.

We did not say much about it. Feelings were too deep for words. It was costing them more than it was costing me; I knew that. The hardest part was knowing the suffering it caused them—something they tried not to show.

There was a word for me, too. 'He that loveth father or mother more than me is not worthy of me. . .' Well, I was proving I loved Him best, anyway.

At midnight the liner started steaming slowly away from the docks at Southampton. I lay in my bunk looking through the porthole as we passed the lights, one by one, along the quay until at last we were clear of them, and making for the open sea. That was nearly fifty years ago—but I remember it as though it were yesterday.

6

Dear Edward,

It's just a week since I finished writing the last
of these letters to you and during that time I've had
two quite surprising reminders of China, far away
from it as I am now, in London. The first one followed a knock on the front door three days ago. I
went to answer it, and there on the doorstep stood
a tall, slim, elderly man, smiling diffidently. He
knew that 8.30 p.m. was rather late for an unannounced call.

'Christopher!' I exclaimed. 'Come right in! I
didn't know you were over here. When did you
arrive?' He had emigrated to Australia about
twelve years ago, but something draws him back to
the old country every year, and I'm one of the
people he looks up. Our point of contact is the fact
that his parents were missionaries in China and,
when on leave, often used to stay with my parents.
That was over forty years ago, but my knowledge
of Christopher Fairclough stems from what I
heard of him then. Christopher, the only child of
Mr. and Mrs. Fairclough, was the apple of their
eyes and what it must have cost them to sail off for
China in the 1920s, leaving him behind in England

to finish his schooling, only God knows. I write that reverently. Only He saw the tears shed in the darkness of the night, only He knew the tugging at their heart-strings at the thought of that young schoolboy they had said goodbye to.

'I didn't see my parents for ten years,' Christopher had told me once, and there'd been a catch in his voice as he'd said it, but no tinge of bitterness; and when they'd eventually returned home for retirement, he'd made up for all the times of separation by providing a home for them, living with them, spending most of his spare time with them, right up to the time they'd died. No regrets!

And now, in his seventies, sitting in my lounge, he was happily recounting a trip he had recently made into China, along with about a dozen others of about his own age who had been at school with him in Chefoo: the school in China for missionaries' children. He could tell me all the places they had been to, and stories connected with them. Only one stands out but it is so picturesque I must recount it.

The party had arrived at the very compound where one of its members had lived as a child, somewhere in the vast interior of China. As this person had looked around, he'd suddenly remembered something.

'I used to play hopscotch here,' he'd said. Then he'd continued, 'And I had one special stone that was very easy to kick. I was very careful with that stone, and used to hide it away so no one else could find it. It was under the wall there. . .' and he'd walked over to the spot, put his hand in the hole and exclaimed, 'It's still there! The very stone!'

He'd picked it up and held it in his hand, reminiscently. The recording tape of memory had spun back and stopped to recall a little English boy in the middle of China, playing hopscotch then hiding away his stone

My second visit was from a young Englishman who heard God's call, 'Go for me to China,' through reading *God's Adventurer*, the life of Hudson Taylor that I wrote for teenagers years ago.

He only knew me as the author of the book, so when I told him, in answer to a question, that I had been a missionary in China myself years ago, he wanted to know where I had been. So I got out a huge map of China and pointed to a variety of places before my finger came to rest on the province of Henan.

'This is where I spent my first years in China,' I said. And the tape recorder of memory spun back for me, to the year 1937 when, having completed six months in the language school at Yangchow (where Marco Polo had once been the mandarin), I arrived at my first mission station.

I can see it now, that walled-in compound in the city of Hwaiyang, if I close my eyes and switch off from the present. The way to it led along one of the main streets, with its hard dirt surface (which turned to thick mud when it rained), its dark little open-fronted shops with their merchandise spilling over into the road along which men, women and children, walked or loitered to haggle or gossip, and the occasional, dog, pig or goat made its way. A huge, double-leafed door with the words 'Inland Mission' over it, was all there was to indicate that I had arrived at my destination, that spring of 1937.

My senior missionary, Mr. Jack Tomkinson, had escorted me from the Language School in Yang-chow. I have forgotten every detail of that journey, which took two or three days, but I remember those double-leafed doors and the room that lay immediately behind them, with its two or three rough benches and coloured posters on the wall, and the door-keeper whose job it was to chat to anyone who wandered in from the street, and en-sure that only those with legitimate business got any farther. I was briefly introduced to him, then Mr. Tomkinson led me through the room out along a narrow cobbled path, flanked by a couple of rooms with paper windows which were used for classes on Sundays, and on to the surprising sight of a large courtyard with a shrubbery before a colonial-style house, complete with verandah and balcony and—at right angles to it— a neat little three-roomed bungalow which I was told I would share with Irene Steele. Irene was two years my junior in age but two years my senior in China, which at that stage, counted for much more. We had met in England shortly before she had sailed and, having kept in touch with the occasional letter, were not strangers to one another; but I had never met the Tomkinsons before.

They were a middle-aged, childless Australian couple who could not have been kinder to the thirty-year-old Englishwoman now landed on them to be licked into shape as an 'up-country mission-ary' in agricultural Henan. They did everything they could to help me and make me feel at home. I never remember them once being critical or censorious—not even on the occasion when I and one of the servants had words, and Mrs. Tomkinson had to intervene and mediate.

That incident comes to mind as I am writing, so I'd better be honest and relate it. It provides an interesting glimpse into missionary life in China before the Second World War and, alas, of the faulty character of at least one of the members of a Mission generally esteemed for its piety.

One of the surprises of those early days in China was to find myself in the unaccustomed position of being waited on by servants. I came from a middle class home with one 'maid of all work' and a job-bing gardener but now I found myself in an estab-lishment in which were a gate-keeper, a cook, a goatherd, a water-carrier, a house-maid or two and, in addition to that, a sort of lady's-maid for Irene and me. They were all fairly necessary in the backward conditions of inland China in those days, with no drainage, no electricity or gas, no laid-on water, no milk deliveries, no tinned or packaged foods, no telephone, no motor transport, and several days' journey to the nearest railway. If we had had to do all the marketing, water-carrying, washing and ironing, cooking and vegetable grow-ing, cleaning and grain-grinding ourselves, we should have had no time for the preaching and teaching which we were there to do.

Another reason for employing servants was that it provided work for needy Christians, and this was the case with our lady's maid.

This damsel, an orphan, had been sent to Bible School by well-meaning missionaries but after graduation she had found no opening to work as a

Bible-woman employed by the church, so it had been decided that a job should be given to her with the Tomkinsons' two junior workers. She would do their housework, washing, ironing, mending and shopping, and occasionally accompany them when they sallied forth on a preaching foray if the church Bible-woman was otherwise employed. This was a bit of a let-down for a Bible School graduate who had hoped for a more exalted position; so our lady's-maid was not the easiest person to whom to issue instructions, far less to whom to point out faults. Gentleness and humility were not her outstanding characteristics; nor were they mine, as I discovered to my dismay when I drew her attention to some dust left on my desk. When she flared up angrily, I flared back, angry voices were raised, and Mrs. Tomkinson came across to our little bungalow in consternation to see what it was all about.

'Teacher Dong complains that I haven't dusted her room properly, Madam,' the lady's-maid burst out.

'I did not complain,' I retorted. 'I merely pointed out that there was still some dust on my desk.'

'Teacher Dong licked her finger and drew it across the desk,' continued the lady's-maid, addressing Mrs. Tomkinson, 'Now you know, Madam, that if you lick your finger and draw it across wood, it always looks as though there's some dust there, even if it's just been dusted.'

Indignantly I denied having licked my finger and drawn it across the desk.

'Yes, you did!'

'No, I didn't!'

Anything more childish it would be hard to imagine. Here was a missionary who had come all the way from England to proclaim Christ and His love, going at it hammer and tongs with a young Chinese woman who had graduated from Bible School for the same purpose—all over a little dust on a desk! Mrs. Tomkinson was the one who emerged from the scene with flying colours. How she did it I don't know but she managed to quieten us both down, in such a way as to maintain a primary, if unwritten law in Chinese society, which was that you should never cause someone to 'lose face'. Mrs. Tomkinson sorted things out without either of us feeling that we had lost face.

There is a lot to be said for that law. Granted, it can be abused,—as when it is used to cover up corruption—but the basic principle of showing consideration for another's feelings, of not putting anyone to open shame, makes for good working relations. The maintenance of self respect, which is lost when one loses face, was very important in Chinese life. Mrs. Tomkinson observed that law very adroitly in dealing with her junior worker and the lady's-maid. The matter was closed.

Or so I thought.

But I was wrong.

That night, as I knelt to pray, I found I could not do it. The memory of that brief scene came between me and God. My anger had burst out and, although it had all been smoothed over outwardly, it had not been put right inwardly. I prayed for forgiveness, but no peace came and I knew there was something else that had to be done. It did not need the words in the Sermon on the Mount, about

first being reconciled to one's brother before bringing anything to the altar of God, to convince me. It
was not just a matter of talking it over with the
lady's-maid, pointing out that I hadn't meant to be
critical, arguing that she flared up first. Who had
started it wasn't the point. As far as I was concerned, I had lost my temper so I had to acknowledge to her that I had been wrong in that.

And that is what I did, the very next day, as soon
as there was an opportunity when we were alone
together. It was all over in a minute.

'I ought not to have lost my temper with you
yesterday,' I said. 'I'm sorry.' She looked surprised
then hung her head a little and murmured, 'I
ought not to have lost mine, either. . .' We said no
more. But I had no difficulty about praying next
time I knelt down to do so. The cloud between me
and God had been dispersed.

> Oh, may no earthborn cloud arise,
> To hide Thee from Thy servant's eyes. . .

I've often found that the performance of a
simple action, like apologising or paying a debt or
putting something right, clears that cloud more
effectively than any amount of praying.

Incidentally, the lady's-maid and I got on a lot
better together after that.

7

Dear Edward,

Something has happened recently which has radically changed my attitude towards your idea that I should write my own story. As you know, I didn't want to do it, and started writing these letters in quite a casual manner without committing myself to anything. I had no word from the Lord, as I'd told you, so felt quite safe about dilly-dallying.

Well, the word from the Lord has come, so I'm writing straight away to tell you how.

I'd arranged to spend a few days with my friend, Flora Sarpy, who lives in South London, in order that I could get on with writing about Madame Guyon. I was looking forward to it and thought I had brought everything required when, on unpacking, I discovered to my dismay and consternation that I'd left behind the very material I needed for the next chapter. Without that material I could do nothing. I stood stock still in that bedroom, overwhelmed with irritation and disappointment, and the more so when the thought came: 'You can't write about Madame Guyon, but you can go on writing your own story.' Just what I did not

63

want to do! But suddenly there was a solemn sense of a Presence in the room, and into my mind the words seemed to flood: *Have not I commanded thee?*

There was no denying the authority behind those words. I saw nothing, heard nothing, but I could not doubt Who had spoken them. I knew what I had to do that day. Rather reluctantly, I admit, I wrote another letter. I'd got myself on the way to China by the time I went to bed that night and I knew that I'd done the right thing. The next day I went home, got the book I needed to continue with Madame Guyon's story, and settled down for another spell of wrestling with the problem of what to include, what to condense, and what to by-pass in her life. And I let the thought of my own story take second place, just writing another letter in a desultory sort of way until I felt rather guilty, and decided I must be absolutely sure about 'the word from the Lord'. I had been quite convinced about it that day a couple of months ago but, like Gideon of old, I wanted tangible confirmation. So I put out my fleece.

'Lord,' I prayed. 'Let me either hear that sentence, or see it somewhere, so that it comes from outside as well as inside. Then I'll know that it is from you, that you want me to finish writing my own story—and I'll obey.'

Well, within three days it happened. I was glancing through the notebook in which I am jotting down extracts for the Madame Guyon story when, to my amazement, I saw written in my own handwriting, 'Have not I commanded thee?' and the date, 9.7.1985, beside it.

There can be no doubt about it now. I'm getting

in touch with you to decide practical details, but from my point of view they are of no great significance. I've had the divine go-ahead, so ahead I will go. As I no longer have any of my China diaries and letters, I'll have to depend on memory—and I find myself wondering what it will come up with.

8

15 November, 1985

Dear Edward,

Thanks so much for your reply to my last letter: 'I think you should just keep writing and then do a final edit when it is all down. This book can grow as the Lord brings the memories to you. If you had asked me whether you should write a book in this way, I should have said "No." But you have chosen to do so, and it works!'

Yesterday I completed another chapter of the Madame Guyon book, so before settling down to the next one I'm letting my memory slip back again to that mission compound in Henan, China, where I arrived as a new missionary nearly fifty years ago.

Such apparently unimportant things come to mind and how little I remember of what must have been the major events of those days! It was the year 1937, when Japanese troops first invaded China, triggering off the Second World War as we can see now. But at the time, in our quiet compound in central China, we were unaffected by what was happening up in the north, where there had been a shooting-up incident somewhere on the Manchurian border.

The memories that come to mind are isolated

incidents, like the Sunday morning service in which I was sitting among the women on our side of the central aisle, while the men occupied the benches on the other side. (Sex segregation was strictly observed in those days, and we had been instructed time and time again in the Language School that we must never look a man in the eyes when speaking to him. We must address our remarks to the second button on his gown.) And a bird flew in.

On this particular Sunday the congregation was rather sparse and attention was not at all good, either, as Mr. Tomkinson preached on Psalm 84. There seems to be an ebbing and a flowing in most churches, and the ebb was much more evident than the flow in the church in Hwaiyang at that time, what with the Chinese pastor having been seen to observe idolatorous practices at heathen funerals, and Mr. Tomkinson, as missionary-in-charge, finding himself in a difficult position as a result. A complete break with idolatry was incumbent on anyone wanting to become a Christian and join the church; but what did you do when the pastor himself compromised on that point? I did not know the ins and outs of the affair, or what Mr. Tomkinson had said to the pastor and the elders, but I did know that the pastor had prevaricated and taken no steps to rectify the wrong example he had given to his flock. I also knew that he wanted to keep up appearances and had made a public gesture of going up to Mr Tomkinson in a friendly way, and that Mr Tomkinson had turned his back on him. This was a serious matter, for by that action the missionary had made the pastor 'lose face'. Some church members sided with the pastor, saying the missionary was too hard on him, while others took the view that the missionary was doing the right thing. After all, by publicly bowing to the idols, had not the pastor made his Lord lose face? So the atmosphere was thundery, to say the least.

Yet of all the services I attended in that church, the one I remember most clearly was that one when a little bird flew in. It came through the open window soaring up to perch on a rafter in the roof, and Mr. Tomkinson, lifting his arms to point to it, said with a thrill in his voice, 'The sparrow has found a house, and the swallow a nest for herself . . . even thine altars, O Lord of hosts, my King and my God!'

Whenever I read that verse, I see him again—that down-to-earth, practical harrassed Australian —looking up rapturously as though momentarily transported into the realm where he found his security: '. . . even thine altars, O Lord of hosts, my King and my God.'

It is not the only verse that always carries me back to that compound in Hwaiyang. On one occasion, feeling mentally weary from close study of Chinese, too tired to read the Bible and pray as I usually did, I went out into the courtyard and walked over to a little enclosed garden, in which a few gooseberry bushes and raspberry canes fought for survival among the vegetables. Opening the gate, I went in. It was very early in the morning and very quiet. The weather had been dry and hot but, there in the garden, I noticed that everything was drenched in dew. And as I walked round, without a thought in my head, unable to think, far less to pray, the words came quietly to my mind, 'I will be as the dew unto Israel.' As imperceptibly as the dew, falls the dew of God's refreshing peace on the soul. I always think of that little vegetable garden in the early morning when I come to that verse, written nearly three thousand years ago by the prophet Micah.

'He feedeth among the lilies'; that is the third verse which I always associate with my first mission station in China. The words came to me from the Song of Solomon, as I was lying one night in my little bedroom in our small, three-roomed bungalow, looking up at the sky. They reminded me that our relationship to Jesus Christ is not to be one-sided. The Song of Solomon makes that very clear; and the verse about Him feeding among the lilies brought with it the realisation that it brings Him satisfaction when He comes, as it were, into the garden of the soul, and finds it flowering. His first complaint in the messages to the churches in the book of Revelation was: 'Thou hast left thy first love.' And there is something very touching about those words in the second chapter of Jeremiah: 'Thus saith the Lord: I remember thee, the kindness of thy youth, the love of thine espousals, when thou wentest after me in the wilderness, in a land that was not sown.'

Perhaps this is a good point at which to try and address the matter you raised when you first suggested I should write my autobiography: how I have coped with being single. I have often been asked about this, usually by girls who are learning to cope with the condition themselves. Well, here is my story.

As a little girl, thinking vaguely about the future,

I had the feeling that I would not get married. Not that it worried me, of course: I was only a little girl; but every now and then, when saying my prayers at night, as we were taught to do in those days, I would add the private and personal plea, 'Oh, God, give me a good husband!' I mention this because it has a bearing on what will follow. The Lord did not answer the prayer to give me a good husband and, as I went through my late teens and early twenties, all my involvements with the opposite sex misfired: either I didn't like them or they didn't like me; or, as in the one case I mentioned, it was mutual but he was married and so we separated. So when I was converted, at the age of twenty-six, I was still single and my sights were set in another direction. I wanted to be a disciple of Jesus Christ, come what may, and as, fortunately for me, I was heart-free anyhow, singleness presented no problem at the time.

I don't remember how or when it dawned on me that it simply was not God's will for me to marry, but I do know that I became very very sure about this. At first the realisation was very daunting. The prospect of going through life alone, without the comfort and companionship of a husband, was not an attractive one. But the day came when I knelt down before the Lord and accepted His decision. I really *accepted* it. I made no vow, but I suppose it was the next thing to it. I did pray, very earnestly, that He would keep from me the temptation and the opportunity to marry, for I didn't think I'd be strong enough to keep myself. So that was that. On one occasion my mother mentioned that I might marry when I got to China, and I said, 'No—I think

I'm going to plough a lonely furrow.' It quite upset her. Most mothers want their daughters to marry. Fathers, too, for that matter. Mine wrote to me when I was in China and said he was praying that I would get married, and I wrote back post haste, in quite a panic: 'Don't pray for that! I'd be backsliding if I did!' He was thoroughly taken aback! But the conviction was that deep with me, and I have always been thankful for it. Not that it has kept me from the desires and even the strong temptations that come when that inexplicable, powerful attraction sparks off between a man and a woman which we term 'falling in love'. We cannot go through life always shielded from temptations.

'Satan has asked to sift you as wheat,' Jesus said to Peter on the very night in which he later denied knowing Him. 'But I have prayed for you, that your faith may fail not. And when you have turned back, strengthen your brothers.' Those siftings of Satan at least have the salutary effect of making us realise our own weakness, and therein lies our strength; for, as the apostle Paul wrote, 'To keep me from becoming conceited ... there was given me a thorn in my flesh, a messenger of Satan, to torment me. Three times I pleaded with the Lord to take it away from me. But he said to me, "My grace is sufficient for you, for my power is made perfect in weakness." Therefore I will boast all the more gladly about my weaknesses, so that Christ's power may rest on me.'

The simple secret of being happy, though single, lies I have found, in sublimating, not suppressing, natural desires. As Paul puts it in 1 Corinthians chapter seven, the married woman tries to please her husband, and the single woman tries to please the Lord. Such a positive attitude—deliberately choosing to do the things that will satisfy Him—provides a quiet joy in what might otherwise be tedious or uncongenial service. Brother Lawrence, in *The Practice of the Presence of God*, describes it perfectly when he speaks about doing everything for the love of God.

Not that the married woman doesn't have this attitude, of course. But there are times when she is faced with conflicting loves and loyalties. I remember the occurrence of one such occasion very vividly. I was living for a while on a mission station with a young married couple, and the husband, an ardent evangelist, had been away on a strenuous tour of the outstations. He arrived back early on Sunday morning, having roughed it for several days and all ready to be made a fuss of!

Now Sunday was always a special day for the country Christians, especially the women, many of whom walked in on their little bound feet from the villages around, coming early in order to study their catechisms, ask questions, and share their difficulties. It was the only opportunity they had; and, as—almost without exception—they were illiterate, the hour or two before the service commenced was a very precious time for them. We women missionaries, along with the Bible-woman, always made a point of being free for them then.

On this particular Sunday morning I was there, as usual, fully involved with one and another, answering questions, teaching new characters, listening to confidences. Then, just as the bell was beginning to ring for the service, I hurried back to the house to get something I'd forgotten. Entering the kitchen I gave a start of surprise. There was the wife taking a cake out of the oven! I had not realised till then that she had not been at the front of the compound with the women; and I shall never forget the cloud that came over her face as she looked at me.

'Yes,' she said before I could say a word. 'I know I ought to have been there with the women. . . But Dick wanted a cake. . . So I made him one. . .' I realised that this dilemma—a clash of loyalties— was something I would never have to face; and for that, at least, I could be thankful.

Well, I hope that is sufficient answer to the question, 'How have you coped with being single?' There is, however, just one more privilege connected with the state which to me is the most precious of all.

It is the way the Master went. I am thankful I have been called to follow the same path as He.

9

Dear Edward,

It is surprising how often during the last few days the memory of that secluded compound in the middle of China has come to mind. Even as I sit here writing in my terraced house in Hackney I can see it: the colonial-style house with a couple of old wicker chairs on the verandah; the balcony above looking as though it could do with a fresh coat of paint; the shrubbery in front overgrown and straggly. The place was clean and well swept but rather shabby. Our little three-roomed bungalow was somewhat more presentable, having been re-decorated for its new occupants. Previously it had been used as a store-room and, even after the careful planning of Mrs. Tomkinson, was sufficiently frugal to fit in with my idea of what a missionary's manner of life should be. Furnished with a bed, a washstand, a table and a chair and little else, it just suited my ardent desire for simplicity, even hard-ship in measure. And as my days were mainly taken up with studying Chinese, which I found very tedious, I took satisfaction in the reflection that the room in which I spent so many hours was not un-like the one provided by the Shunammite woman for the prophet Elisha.

Those Biblical personalities, along with many others, became very real to me. However restricted the body may be, the human spirit is free to wander backwards and forwards through time and to enjoy a sense of companionship with those whose experiences bear some resemblance to one's own, though one has never known them in the flesh. This was one of the deepest, though unexpressed, impressions of my years in China. The inevitable sense of isolation felt when surrounded by a people whose language and customs were strange was compensated for by a consciousness of intimacy with many of the human beings whom I met through the pages of the Bible. I wonder if that is what is meant by the assertion we make when we repeat in the Apostles' Creed the words, 'I believe in the communion of saints.'

A consciousness of intimacy developed also with some of the Chinese with whom I was brought into contact in those early, inarticulate days in Hwaiyang. One of these was my language teacher, Mrs. Fan, mother of five. She came along daily—a neat figure in a long gown, as befitted a woman who had received some education, rather than the jacket and trousers of those who had not. She walked on feet that had developed normally, too— another sign of distinction among women back in the 1930s. Foot-binding was supposed to have gone out with the Revolution in the early part of the century but custom dies hard and it was practised widely in the villages, where a girl's beauty was judged as much by the smallness of her feet as by the contour of her face. In any case, once a child's

foot had been bound long enough, the malfor-
mation was as difficult to rectify as it had been to
make. The custom had started in the dim centuries
of the past, when an emperor, one of whose wives
had run away, decreed that the women of his kingdom should henceforth be for ever prevented
from running away from their husbands by having
feet too small to run on. Later such feet came to be
regarded as an emblem of charm rather than a sign
of servitude.

The fact that Mrs. Fan's feet, though small by
western standards had been allowed to develop
normally, gave evidence that she came of an enlightened family. Apart from that, she resembled
the other women in that her dark hair was neatly
pulled back into a bun and long trousers were
glimpsed through the slits up the sides of her
straight gown which buttoned right up to the chin,
revealing no part of her person except head and
hands. The colour of her clothing, like everyone
else's, was blue and, beyond a silver pin in her hair,
no jewellery in the way of brooch, necklace or earrings, adorned her. Such things were rarely seen
on respectable women on the great plain of central
China. The tribal women on the Burmese border
might sport their silver ornaments and the bold-
eyed Tibetan women their swinging earrings, but
the women of the ever-expanding race of Han
depended on none of these things to enhance their
charm or draw attention to themselves. To my unaccustomed eyes they all looked the same, and we
women missionaries did our best to look like them.
We, too, dragged our hair back and wore long
trousers. Being accepted as belonging to the edu-

cated class we wore long gowns rather than short jackets, but the colour was inevitably some shade of blue.

Few of us looked like Chinese, in spite of our efforts. We were the wrong shape; our hair, if not curly, was probably the wrong colour as were our eyes and skin; our very deportment oozed the energy of the West rather than the tranquillity of the East. We were different and, as we were a rare species among the hundreds of millions of inland China, we attracted attention wherever we went. We could always be depended upon to draw a crowd. They came silently and stood simply staring at us, as people years ago must have stood staring at performing bears. For the Chinese woman who was willing to accompany one of us in public, especially before we could understand or speak the language, it must have been rather like leading such an animal around. For those who were instinctively shy and retiring, answering the questions asked about the white-skinned person's sex, age, married status, manner of eating and reason for being there was an ordeal. But it provided them with the opportunity to align themselves with those who had come to preach the Gospel of Jesus Christ, and thus take up the cross in witnessing.

I'm sure it was not without a struggle that Mrs. Fan took on this role. She had been coming daily to my room for several weeks, patiently correcting my pronunciation as I read aloud after her and explaining obscure passages, before I broached the subject of going out to visit and preach the Way. This process of visiting to preach the Way was the accepted method whereby women could proclaim

God's message of salvation without offending recognised standards of decent behaviour. The men could go to the public tea-houses and markets and talk to whoever assembled there, but the women must confine themselves to the domestic scene, addressing themselves to the women sitting on their doorsteps or in their secluded courtyards. The only way I could learn how to do it was by accompanying someone who knew the correct procedure—and who better than Mrs. Fan?

I broached the subject rather diffidently, realising I was asking her to do something beyond the task for which she was employed. She was a steady church member but not noted for her evangelistic zeal, and I wondered how she would react to my suggestion. She was courteous but somewhat reserved as a person, and our conversation until this time had been limited to polite enquiries as to each other's general condition ('Are you quite peaceful?' 'Yes, quite peaceful. Are you also peaceful?') and observations about the meaning of Chinese words. On this occasion, when she understood what I was asking, she hesitated a little, then volunteered for the first time a glimpse into her spiritual life.

'Some time ago I prayed to the Lord that He would give me the opportunity to serve Him,' she said. 'With five children to look after I have not time to do much and I did not know what I could do.' Then she went on, rather slowly, 'I think this is God's answer to my prayer.' It was evidently something she hadn't bargained for—accompanying a white-skinned foreign person through the streets and into compounds, to assist her in proclaiming the Jesus doctrine. With what inward dismay she had received the suggestion she did not divulge, except by the hesitation to respond which I had detected. But she agreed, solemnly. And when I intimated that I realised it would involve a sacrifice on her part she answered, 'You have come all the way from your own country to proclaim the Way. If you have done that, it is a little thing for me to go out with you once a week.'

That brief conversation put our relationship on quite a different level. From that time on we were fellow-workers, and she was as good as her word about accompanying me—clumsy-looking, tongue-tied foreigner that I was—to the homes of local people. She was wise in the way she did it, too. There was no haphazard emerging through our double-leaved front door to meander at random along the narrow street, hoping for an invitation to enter some courtyard or other. When she arrived on the first Saturday her plans were well prepared.

'We are going today to visit Mrs. Chang in the west suburb,' she said. I was rather surprised. Mrs, Chang, neat and thin, was the highly respected woman deaconess in the church in Hwaiyang and, on the face of it, to go and visit her was not my idea of evangelising the heathen. However, as things turned out, there was more to it than a polite, semi-social visit. Arrangements were being made to invite neighbours to meet the new missionary who had come to teach the Way and Mrs. Fan helped me to put into intelligible Chinese a little talk I had prepared, based on an illustrated poster. (In the event, Mrs. Fan did most of the talking, elucidating what I tried to say.)

And so, one Saturday afternoon in the summer

of 1937, I was launched by Mrs. Fan as a preacher of the Gospel in China. Armed with a roll on which was the illustrated poster and a few simple tracts, I walked with her out through the west gate of the city, along the dusty road of the suburb, lined with stalls and tea-shops, and arrived at the gate of Mrs. Chang's compound to find, to my delight, that my best friend was waiting there to receive me.

I'll have to stop there. Changes in my present manner of life are pending, for I have put my house on the market—a process which means, among other things, disposing of most of the furniture and possessions I have accumulated over the quarter of a century I've lived here on the border of Islington and Hackney. 23rd June is the deadline I've set for evacuating the house, and it will be for me a very significant milestone, opening up a new vista for what may well prove to be the last lap of my earthly pilgrimage.

10

Dear Edward,

Well, the move has been made, and I am happily settled into the spacious home of my friend, Flora Sarpy. As I walked yesterday from Wandsworth Common station across the well-wooded common with its little lakes, its clumps of gorse and blackberry bushes and its thick waving grass, it did not seem possible that only ten minutes earlier I had been on the busy, bustling London terminus of Victoria. I had commented on the surprisingly countrified atmosphere of the area to a chatty fellow-passenger on the train, and she had asked, 'Do you live there?'

'Yes,' I replied simply. I'd only moved in a couple of days earlier, but I lived there now.

'Lovely garden?'

'Yes.' I thought of the broad, cool lawn, the flower-beds surrounding it, the old apple tree and the laburnum, and the background of trees screening the gardens and houses of neighbours. Yes, it was a lovely garden. I am very content to have reached this Beulah land and ready to continue the long story of how I got here. So back to the gateway of Mrs. Chang's compound, where my best friend was waiting to receive me.

What is a friend? 'One attached to another by esteem and affection,' one of my dictionaries tells me, while an older one puts it this way: 'One joined to another in intimacy and mutual benevolence, independently of sexual or family love.' Both express very well the relationship between Eastern Light and me.

I met him very soon after my arrival in Hwai-yang, when Mrs. Tomkinson started easing me into the work by giving me a Sunday School class of little boys to teach, of whom Eastern Light was the oldest. A rather sentimental little boy he was, with a habit of putting his head on one side and looking sheepish when confronted with some problem that he could not solve or caught out in inattention during the preliminary exercises, yet with a certain sense of dignity, as befitting one who was the eldest grandson of the church deaconess, and the big brother of a brood of smaller brothers and sisters and cousins. From the outset he was a special friend to me for he seemed to recognise and happily appropriate the love I had for my Sunday School class. I really loved those children! Bound as I was by barriers of a language and customs with which I was not familiar, there was little I could do to express it but Eastern Light sensed it and responded. I came to rely on him quite a lot, for he had already heard most of the Bible stories that I told, and was therefore able to translate to the others what I was trying to say. And he had an inborn sense of responsibility for his brothers and sisters. One incident stands out vividly in my memory, for it held an inner significance which has meant a great deal to me ever since.

It occurred during the early exercises of the Sunday School, when all the children were together; the little ones at the front, the older ones at the back. Sitting on the very front row was Eastern Light's little sister—a wide-eyed damsel with two plaits which were braided so tightly that they stuck out at right angles from her head. Her legs dangled from the bench, for they were too short to reach the ground, and after a time, obviously bored with the proceedings, she straightened them out, slid off her seat, and betook herself off. As I watched her depart I wondered if I ought to go and bring her back but decided against it. She would not take the slightest notice of what I said and, short of forcibly bringing her back, arms and legs flaying about and screaming vociferously (I knew the young lady's temperament), my efforts would obviously be fruitless.

However, big brother Eastern Light, sitting some rows behind with the older boys, also saw her. Had it been one of the other little girls he would have ignored her completely, but this one was his sister. He also rose from his seat and walked out quietly but purposefully after her. For a minute or two nothing more was seen of the two children. Then a little figure reappeared in the doorway—a rebellious-looking little girl, dark eyes angry. She returned to her seat and scrambled up on it, defiant still, but obviously having met one whose authority she could not but acknowledge. A moment or two later Eastern Light walked in, too, and resumed his place with the unconscious assurance of one who, after all, has a certain standing which must be respected.

It was at about that time that I had been especially touched by something I had read in the Gospels: 'For whosoever shall do the will of my Father which is in heaven, the same is my brother, and sister, and mother.' It was the word 'sister' that had touched me. To the best of my knowledge and ability I was doing what I believed to be the will of God—and therefore Jesus Christ owned me as His sister. That little incident in the Sunday School in Hwaiyang, nearly fifty years ago, still speaks to me. If I wander off my Elder Brother will exercise His authority and bring me back. He has had to do it, more than once. . .

To return to the meeting in Mrs. Chang's courtyard. Eastern Light had risen to the occasion in a surprising manner. He had invited some of his school friends and it seemed that not for a moment did he forget his responsibility as host. He met me at the gate, bowed politely, and escorted me in. Backless benches had been arranged in the courtyard, and to these benches Eastern Light led his small friends, courteously finding places for them to sit down and afterwards, when it was time for them to go, escorting them to the gate, chatting politely. He and I did not have much opportunity to speak together, but we looked at each other and exchanged smiles occasionally: we understood each other. And how excited we both were when, the following Sunday, two of his school friends accompanied him to church! We looked at each other with the triumphant smiles of fellow-fishermen who have caught something in their net.

Meanwhile, Japan's undeclared war with China

was progressing with alarming velocity. The conquering armies of the invaders were gaining possession of more and more cities on the main railways and roads. News was reaching the Tomkinsons of their advances and it all became suddenly very acute when we heard that the neighbouring city of Taikang had been occupied. Two members of our Mission were stationed there.

'Taikang's gone! Miss Wallis and Mrs. King—I wonder how it is with them!' was Mrs. Tomkinson's immediate reaction to the news. She looked worried. 'Those two ladies alone there!' Her thoughts flew anxiously to her fellow-missionaries. Perhaps, too, she wondered if her husband would be called on to go to their aid and what danger it might lead him into. But he was quite reassuring.

'They'll be all right,' he said confidently. 'They're from a neutral country. We all are: English, American, Australian. . . The Japs are bound to respect us. Our governments are behind us and the Japs know it. They're not looking for trouble. They've got enough on their hands already.'

There seemed no need to be alarmed, although we couldn't help wondering how those two fellow-missionaries of ours were faring. No news came from them, but that was not surprising. If they were in any difficulty they would apply to headquarters in Shanghai for instructions or to the Mission's superintendent in Henan Province, living in Loho.

It was not long before news reached us from the superintendent in Loho. He wrote to say that he intended visiting the two ladies in Taikang, to find out how they were managing in the changed situation and to take them their remittances in cash as it was difficult to get money to them through the usual banking channels now. He would be coming to Hwaiyang on route. Then came the information that one of the ladies, Mrs. King, would shortly be returning to England on furlough. That information was followed by an unexpected suggestion. As Miss Wallis would be left alone it was felt she should have a companion, and that either Miss Steele or Miss Thompson should be re-designated to Taikang.

Mrs. Tomkinson bridled indignantly at that. One of her young junior workers to be exposed to the uncertainties of living in a Japanese-occupied city! Far better that Miss Wallis should come and live in Hwaiyang for a time, until things settled down a bit, she said. It would be so much safer. But, of course, that argument got no farther than the breakfast table, over which the matter was discussed. Personal safety was not a primary consideration. There was a job to do, a responsibility to fulfil, in Taikang. Quite apart from her spiritual work of teaching and preaching, Miss Wallis' presence on the church compound would ensure, as much as was humanly possible, that the place would be inviolate from the incursion of Japanese soldiers. There was no question of her leaving her post. It simply remained to decide whether Miss Steele or Miss Thompson should be appointed to keep her company.

The lot fell on me—probably because I was the older of the two. And so the day came when I emerged from the compound in Hwaiyang, stepped into a rickshaw, and was conveyed out through the city gate, accompanied by Mr. Weller, the Mission Superintendent from Loho, riding a bicycle, and a coolie, pushing a wheelbarrow containing my luggage. We were to pass through the enemy lines to go to Taikang.

Passing through the enemy lines sounds much more dramatic and dangerous than in fact it proved to be. It would have been very difficult to have defined exactly where those lines were. The countryside through which we travelled, with its wheat fields stretching away into the distance and clumps of trees dotted here and there to denote the presence of villages and hamlets, appeared as peaceful as ever. There was not a sign of a soldier, either Chinese or Japanese, nor the slightest evidence of war. The farmers and peasants we passed on the road were going about their business in their usual placid manner; life in the villages continued the same, with hens pecking in the dust, the occasional pig routing in a rubbish heap, children playing in the road, mothers suckling their babies at the doorways of their homes, food vendors sitting beside their stalls.

Yet it was all rather uncanny and there was an indefinable atmosphere of suspense. We were approaching the city that had fallen to the enemy. Enemy soldiers might appear at any moment but in what manner we did not know.

Eventually we saw them. There were three of them and they were evidently off duty, for they were lounging on rough benches at a trestle table outside a little thatched roadside inn, sipping tea. I would not have known that they were not ordinary Chinese soldiers had it not been that the colour of

their uniforms was a sort of mustard colour,
different from the khaki of the Chinese.

Mr. Weller drew alongside my rickshaw and,
cycling beside me, murmured, 'They are Japanese.
We'll go straight on.' Silently we drew alongside
giving no indication that we had noticed them, although I couldn't refrain from glancing at them
out of the corner of my eye to see how they were
reacting to the unexpected appearance of Westerners in this remote part of China. They were
staring, but made no move to stop us, and we
passed by unchallenged.

So we had passed through the lines! As we approached the gate of the walled city of Taikang I
wondered what awaited us. Once again, nothing
happened. A Japanese soldier was on sentry duty
there, but the usual string of coolies was passing
imperturbably in and out with their carrying poles
swinging across their shoulders or pushing wheelbarrows laden with goods. We, too, passed through
unmolested. I learned later that these Japanese
garrisons were strung out so thinly along the trade
routes and comprised so few men that they usually
kept a low profile. They could not afford to take
the risk of antagonising the populace un-
necessarily.

Taikang, to my unaccustomed eyes, looked much
the same as Hwaiyang, with the same dirt roads,
alleys of thatched hovels, open-fronted shops and
high walls enclosing the compounds of the well-to-
do, their large double-leafed gates opened to reveal glimpses of the courtyards within. It was into
one of these compounds that we turned, and I
found myself in what proved to be a large campus

with a church building prominently situated in the front courtyard, and a number of other buildings distributed in courtyards around what was to become the centre of my life for many months— the missionary's compound.

This was more imposing that the one at Hwai-yang and I was duly impressed by the appearance of the two-storeyed house with its wide verandah and balconies as I came on it through the entrance hall. The large courtyard was tidy and well swept, with two or three pomegranate trees in the centre, and low tiled-roofed buildings around it which served as bedrooms for guests.

I was impressed, too, and at first slightly awed, by the lady who was to be my senior missionary. Miss Eva Wallis was stockily built, with wavy grey hair and a fair complexion, and the Chinese gown she wore completely failed to disguise the fact that she was English, through and through. She moved with the calm assurance of one whose undisputed position was that of the mistress of a household. She came forward to meet us just as though we were guests who had arrived for afternoon tea, shook hands politely as Mr. Weller introduced me, and said, 'How do you do, Miss Thompson. I hope you had a good journey? Do come in and have some tea.' Her manner and accent were impeccable.

I felt that I had been suddenly transported back to a London suburb and that an English maid, neatly dressed with cap and apron, would appear at any moment carrying a tray with scones and cream. Such was the atmosphere of calm and security that 'Auntie Eva', as I called her after we'd

known each other for a few weeks, always managed
to convey. No matter what alarming situations
arose, what disturbing rumours were circulated,
Auntie Eva remained the well-educated, matter of
fact Englishwoman who never forgot her manners,
was unabashed by anyone, went about her duties
with unfailing regularity, enjoyed her food which
she ate unhurriedly, and had a robust sense of
humour which revealed itself quite unexpectedly
in seeing the funny side of simple things, rather
like a child. She was completely without guile, and
rose to quite unexpected situations fearlessly, as I
soon observed.

An unexpected situation arose the very night
after our arrival. After supper, Mr. Weller had led
family prayers and then we had all retired to our
respective rooms. Our lights were out, when the
sound of stones alighting one by one on the pavement of the courtyard broke the silence. Then a
man's voice was heard calling our in carefully
enunciated English, 'Mee-sis Wallis! Mee-sis Wallis!
How do you do, Mee-sis Wallis!?'

The patter of stones was resumed, then the voice
called again: 'How do you do, Mee-sis Wallis?'

There was little doubt as to whose voice it was. It
was a Japanese soldier, almost certainly drunk, who
had climbed up on the wall and was trying out his
English. I lay in my bed in one of the guest rooms,
rather apprehensively aware that if he jumped
down from that wall he would be within a few feet
of my bedroom door.

'How do you do, Mee-sis Wallis?'

Then a voice answered him from the balcony of
the house—the rather indignant voice of an

affronted Englishwoman.

'What are you doing, throwing stones into our courtyard in the middle of the night? You are a very rude man. It is very rude to throw stones into other people's courtyards.'

Auntie Eva had appeared on the balcony, arrayed in a dressing gown. I could see her through my window as I lay there in bed and the form of her remonstrance took me so by surprise that I started to giggle. There was something so incongruous about that English voice rebuking the soldier of an invading army as though he were a naughty, impolite schoolboy.

Then another voice was heard, this time from the doorway of the guestroom where Mr. Weller had retired to rest. Mr. Weller was a quiet man, probably rather timid by nature, but he had his wits about him. He realised that only the simplest of sentences would penetrate the understanding of the intruder, so he confined himself to three words, clearly spoken with polite firmness.

'Please go away.'

The whole episode was taking on the form of a comic opera: the deserted courtyard; the only light coming from the lamp held by the female figure on the balcony; the serenading soldier on the wall; the vigilant guardian down below; the 'characters' repeating their lines without moving from their positions.

'How – do – you – do – Mee-sis Wallis?' in broken English.

'Very rude to throw stones into other people's courtyards. . .' in the correct accent of a better-class London suburb.

'Please go away,' in a quiet, masculine voice of authority.

By this time I was under my bedclothes, convulsed with laughter, and wondering who would move first. Eventually the soldier on the wall disappeared, probably dragged down by wiser companions; the figure on the balcony retreated into the room from which it had emerged; the vigilant guardian below turned back to his bed. And no more stones were thrown into the courtyard.

So ended my first night in enemy-occupied territory.

11

Dear Edward,

Over two years have passed since I started writing these letters to you and during that time I've written two more books—*Madame Guyon*, which was published last November, and one about the Scripture Gift Mission, the manuscript of which I handed over to Hodder and Stoughton a couple of weeks ago.

I enjoyed that S.G.M. assignment. The research involved took me a number of times to their headquarters at Victoria and, as I commuted there from Wandsworth Common several times a week, it seemed quite natural for me to be 'going to the office'. That is what I had done in my teens and early twenties, and the routine was familiar. The atmosphere was congenial, too, and the journey home crowned the day, for when I alighted at the station I had to cross the common on which blackberry bushes were laden with fruit, just waiting to be picked. It is quite impossible for me to convey the pleasure I had, day after day, in walking across that picturesque common and picking blackberries. It reminded me of my childhood holidays in the heart of Kent, where we spent a fortnight each year with Auntie Bessie and Uncle Bill. They lived in a thatched cottage two or three miles from Lenham, standing all alone by a winding road among woods and fields—so different from our semi-detached house in Ealing. With what excitement did I dance up and down our compartment in the train as it slowed down at Lenham, and we saw Uncle Bill in his corduroys, waiting on the platform to greet us! Wandsworth Common station has somehow retained its rural appearance, similar to the one I remember, and in my eightieth year I savoured afresh the pleasure of those childhood holidays with their adventurous excursions into the wood, the feeding of free-range hens with handfuls of corn flung over the ground, and the picking of blackberries.

Well, the commuting to the S.G.M. offices is over now and, as I'm due to meet you in a fortnight's time to discuss my next book, I must control the tape recorder of my memory and spin it back—not to a cottage in Kent but to that missionary compound in Taikang on the vast agricultural plain of central China.

The months I spent there were unique in my experience, with one day in particular standing out as a highlight in my life—a day never to be forgotten, when the angels of God stood by me.

It happened some weeks after my arrival. During that time the Japanese invaders had retreated and the city had been re-occupied—not by Chinese Nationalist troops but by Chinese guerillas. I remember how surprised I was to learn that they were feared far more than were the Japanese.

'But they are your own people!' I exclaimed

when one of the servants was telling me in a voice low with apprehension, that the guerillas had come.

'They are worse than the Japanese,' she murmured, and I was to learn later how ruthless they could be: preying on their own people—torturing some, holding wealthy landlords for ransom, abducting young women. At the time, however, with my very limited understanding of Chinese, I knew little of what went on beyond the walls of our large campus.

I do remember one occasion, when the pastor and a church elder came to see Auntie Eva on behalf of a man they knew. In some way he had fallen foul of the guerillas and, now that they were in control of the city, he was in danger. They were looking for a place where he could hide until he could be smuggled out of the city, and the pastor explained, rather diffidently, that there was only one place they could think of where he would be safe: only one place that even the guerillas would regard as inviolable. That place was the Englishwoman's private apartment.

They had come to ask if their friend could be hidden in Miss Wallis's bedroom for the night.

Auntie Eva's reaction to that suggestion was prompt and unequivocal. Whether it was the impropriety of the idea or the wiser consideration that she should not get involved in local politics, I do not know; but there was no question as to what she felt about it. She was horrified. A man to be hidden in her bedroom? Certainly not! She wouldn't hear of such a thing!

After they had departed, and we had sat down to

supper, we had a good laugh together as we tried to picture what the Mission authorities in Shanghai would have said if they heard that Miss Wallis of Taikang had had a man under her bed all night.

She was quite firm about not giving asylum anywhere on the compound to men who were on the run, whether from the Japanese, the Chinese Nationalists or the guerillas. As the citizen of a neutral nation living in a country that was at war, she had to be careful to avoid any appearance of partiality, to give no cause for suspicion that she was working for one side or the other. When it came to giving asylum to young girls, however, it was quite another matter. With soldiers about in such troubled times, they were in special danger and parents were only too glad to bring their teenaged daughters to live in what was considered the safest place in the city of Taikang—the missionary's compound. There were about twenty of these girls accommodated somewhere on the premises and it was their presence that gave Auntie Eva an idea for providing her junior worker with a little experience in preaching.

'You know, Phyllis,' she said one morning at breakfast, 'I think it would be a good thing for you to have a meeting for those girls once a week. It's a good opportunity to teach them the Bible, and nothing is being done about it.'

'Oh, Auntie Eva, I couldn't!' I said in alarm. To be faced by some twenty giggling Chinese schoolgirls was a very diffrent matter from leading a Sunday School class for four or five little boys. 'My Chinese isn't good enough.'

'Hsiong Ling will help you,' replied Auntie Eva.

Hsiong Ling was a gentle, affectionate girl, who readily agreed to help me run a meeting for the schoolgirls.

This became a regular Tuesday afternoon occurrence on the compound. We taught the children a few choruses and the Lord's Prayer, read a passage from the Bible, repeated—over and over again—the text on which I was to speak, and then I had the ordeal of delivering the sermon.

I took that assignment very seriously. Most of Monday was taken up with praying about it and preparing it. My main concern was to obtain from the Lord the particular message He had for each occasion, and I found that certain verses would be impressed on my mind in such a way that I was assured they were from Him. Usually they were verses that contained some aspect of the message of the Gospel itself, centring on the Lord Jesus Christ, which, of course, presented no difficulty.

However, one Monday the verse that persistently came to mind was different. It came in the familiar words of the Authorised Version, from Psalm 34, verse 7, and I couldn't get away from them: 'The angel of the Lord encampeth round about them that fear Him, and delivereth them.'

Angels. I did not want to draw attention to angels. I believed there were such beings, of course —the Bible referred to them in a number of places—but I did not feel they should be the subject of a sermon to a group of girls who needed to know the way of salvation. I tried to turn my thoughts to a more suitable verse, but I could not do it.

'The angel of the Lord encampeth round about

them that fear Him, and delivereth them.' There was no escaping it. This was the verse I must speak on, so I learned it off by heart in Chinese and prepared a little sermon on it which I duly delivered the next day. As usual on the following morning, Wednesday, I awoke with a feeling of relief and satisfaction that the ordeal was over for another week.

It was while Auntie Eva and I were sitting at breakfast an hour or so later that we heard sounds like fire crackers going off. We thought they were unusually loud but assumed there must be some very special celebrations being observed. A few minutes later we were conscious of the swish-swish of cloth-soled feet running across the courtyard to our kitchen, and then our cook burst in, looking pale and anxious, to pass on the news he had just received.

'The Japanese have returned. They are attacking the city. They've entered the north gate already!'

So the sound we had heard was not crackers, as we had thought, but firing.

Auntie Eva was marvellous. I don't remember her showing the least trace of alarm. She had been through it before, anyway: and, as there was nothing she could do about it, she did not allow herself to be diverted from her programme. Whether the Japanese were invading the city or not, whether the guerillas were fighting back or sneaking out of the South gate—she would continue to hold her Wednesday Bible class for the women on the compound. She went off to her room to prepare for it.

With me it was different. I'd never been in a city under attack before, except during the First World

War when, as children, my brother and I had watched as a Zeppelin floated over London and dropped a few bombs, mainly on waste land. I had certainly never seen any fighting. With mingled feelings of apprehension and excitement I was standing around wondering what I should do, when something impelled me to hurry across our courtyard, through the guest hall, out into the large front compound with its school rooms, paved walks and tall church building and on to the front entrance. And as I hurried along, the words of the text I had spoken on the day before flooded into my mind like a powerful stream that submerged every other thought. 'The angel of the Lord encampeth round about them that fear Him, and delivereth them.'

The compound was filling up with men, women and children, who came pouring in through the open gates to the security of the Mission campus. Here and there I saw a bundle of bedding being thrown over the walls to be followed by a man or a boy scrambling down after it. By the time I reached the gates, the stream was thinning out; and when I peered along the street, I realised why. The Japanese had entered the city and, at the crossroads about a couple of hundred yards away, were jumping off their armoured cars, their rifles at the ready. Every now and then a shot was fired along the street—a spray of dust revealing where it had landed.

'Close the gates!' said someone urgently but the plucky gatekeeper was reluctant to do so. There were still people lurking in doorways, then slithering along the walls to disappear into the opened gates of the Mission. If the gates were closed they would be left outside and defenceless.

Yet if the gates were left open and Japanese soldiers came along the street, they might easily open fire if they saw a crowd of people congregated in the courtyard. Then the thought occurred to me that if I stood in that opened gateway and the Japanese came, they would see I was a Westerner from a neutral country and pass on.

So I stood there. I must have stood there for several hours and, all the time, my mind was submerged by verses of Scripture about angels: the horses and chariots of fire round about the prophet Elisha. . .; the angel delivering the apostle Peter from prison. . .; the ladder set up by the place where Jacob lay and angels of God ascending and descending on it. . .; the angel of God standing by Paul in the storm at sea. . .; 'Fear not. . .'

I stood there that day without fear, except for one occasion when, the sense of exultation at the presence of celestial beings carrying me away, I stepped out into the road almost defiantly. The Japanese couldn't touch *me*! The sharp sound of a shot, and a puff of dust only a few feet from where I stood sent me promptly back to the shelter of the doorway, and I realised then that there is only a step between faith and presumption. I was taught a spiritual lesson: not to go any further into the conflict than God indicates. Bravado, or even an excess of zeal, can place us in unnecessary range of the enemy's attack. I resumed my position inside the opened doorway, and did not move out again.

I forget most of the people who slipped in behind me to the security of the compound that day but there are a few that remain in my memory. One was an old man with a white goatee beard who emerged from the house opposite and crossed over the road carrying a little ginger kitten. Another was a young woman who walked steadily along the road with a baby in one arm and a big basket, evidently containing essentials for an overnight stay, on the other. And two little schoolboys, their faces white with fear, sidled silently past me. It did not matter who they were or in what condition they came. The door was there, and it was open, and whoever decided to do so could come in. I was reminded of the words of the Lord Jesus: 'I am the door. By me, if any man enter in, he shall be saved. . .'

It is a day that I will always remember, although I did nothing beyond standing at the gate. Japanese soldiers went down other roads but they did not come down our road at all; and at evening time they retreated from the city to re-enter it peacefully the next day for permanent occupation. But the consciousness I had of the presence of angels was so extraordinarily real that although I heard nothi#g and saw nothing, I knew they were there.

But some actually saw them, although I knew nothing of it at the time. It was two or three years later, when Irene Steele and I were working together in another part of the province, that we saw approaching us, one day on a country road, a little family whom we immediately guessed from their appearance were 'flee-the-famine-people'. The man was pushing a laden wheelbarrow with a child on top and his wife was walking beside him carrying a basket. We naturally stopped to enquire where they came from. When they answered, 'Taikang,' my interest was quickened.

'Taikang!' I exclaimed, adding, 'I lived there once.' I saw that the woman's interest had quickened, too, and said, 'I was there when the Japanese attacked the city.'

'You're teacher Dong!' she exclaimed. I nodded, and she continued, 'I heard about you.' Then she added words which somehow did not really surprise me. They merely confirmed what I had always been conscious of when I looked back to the red-letter day. The presence of angels.

'People said they saw Teacher Dong standing at the compound gate,' she said, then added rather solemnly, 'and two men with wings standing beside her.'

12

23 March, 1987

Dear Edward,

Someone told me the other day that *Madame Guyon* was the recent book choice on a Radio Monte Carlo programme. The news quite cheered me. I'm never really satisfied with what I have written, and that book is no exception; so it was comforting when I heard that it had been well received.

But to return to events in Taikang, once more occupied by the Japanese who had evidently come to stay this time. The city had to settle down to an uneasy acceptance of their presence, for the guerillas had departed and there was no indication that the Nationalists would appear. We had been in a sort of No Man's Land for months.

In those early days of their permanent occupation, the city was half empty for, as soon as the news had got around that the Japanese were entering by the north gate, there had been a hasty evacuation out of the other three gates. Everyone fled to find temporary refuge with relatives living in hamlets and villages in the countryside.

Late one afternoon Auntie Eva and I went for a walk on the city wall. I sensed the atmosphere of fear that hung like a pall over the place. The silence was eerie, for no one was to be seen, and the streets were deserted. From the wall we could see into the courtyards of the houses adjoining it, and the only person we saw during the whole of that walk was an old woman who emerged from a back door to shake out some grain in a basket. Old women were often left behind in times of trouble to look after the premises. Their presence aroused no suspicion and yet staked a claim until the owners returned.

On our large compound, life continued much as usual, except for the occasional visits of Japanese soldiers who strolled in from time to time when off duty. Their arrival sounded a silent alarm throughout the place, especially in the courtyard occupied by the schoolgirls, who disappeared as if by magic, for everyone knew what the Japanese soldiers would demand if they found them. The alarm was sounded in our courtyard, too, but in this case quite openly. Someone would come hurrying through the guest hall, calling urgently, 'Teacher Dong! Teacher Dong!' and I would know what was required. Whatever I was doing I would drop it immediately and with a silent prayer, 'Lord, help me!' would go as quickly as possible to meet the Japanese intruders. Almost invariably they would look at me with surprise, and I soon learned to take the initiative by asking, 'Do you speak English?'

It worked like a charm.

'Spe-eek Ee-english?' they would respond. They had all learned a little English at school, and were delighted at the opportunity to try it out on an English native. They could not speak intelligibly but they could write a few English sentences so, with the combination of their writing, my speaking and sign language, we would contrive to carry on quite a conversation.

However, the best means of communication was through the Gospel posters on the wall of the guest hall. Many of the Chinese and Japanese characters are the same, so I found that pointing to Chinese characters on the posters aided communication; it also gave me the opportunity to explain the Good News. I had come to China to proclaim the Gospel of Jesus Christ, no matter to whom. He had died for these young Japanese soldiers as much as for the Chinese, and I was really very glad to gain their attention for a few minutes, to explain the basic facts of heaven and hell, and that heaven had been opened for any who would accept Jesus as the only way. There was one pictorial poster in particular to which I turned again and again. Known as the Two-Way Poster it depicted a steep mountain path down which a number of little figures were walking with heavy bundles of sin and guilt on their backs, until they reached the edge of a cliff over which they pitched headlong into a lake of fire. That was the pathway to destruction.

But in the middle of the picture was a cross, before which one of the little figures was kneeling while the bundle was rolling off his back. That was not all. From the cross another pathway could be seen, going up the mountain to end in a golden haze of glory, and one or two little figures were seen ascending it, with no bundles on their backs. That was the way to life.

With posters like that to aid me, it was not difficult to get the Gospel across and, on the whole, I had an attentive audience. The young soldiers listened respectfully enough and, almost invariably, when our conversation was finished they walked quietly off the compound without giving any trouble. I only remember one incident in which a Japanese soldier, foiled in his evident intention to find a girl by my insisting on accompanying him wherever he went, suddenly drew his dagger and threatened me with it.

Somehow I knew he wouldn't use it and I simply walked straight on saying in Chinese, 'Huh! I'm not afraid of you!' Rather sheepishly he put his dagger back into its sheath and took himself off. Perhaps I ought to add that although I felt no fear at the time, I did not sleep any too well that night! These experiences have their reactions.

It was during the time that I was in Taikang that the Nationalists opened the dykes of the Yellow River in a vain attempt to stop the Japanese advance. The countryside was flooded over hundreds of miles, hamlets and villages were swept away and many, many people were drowned. All we knew of what was going on was through reports and rumours that came by word of mouth, but we were not left in doubt as to the gravity of the situation for long. I well remember the evening when we were told that the waters had reached the north gate of our own city and were still rising.

How one's imagination can run rife at such times! I alternately pictured myself drowning or floating back to Hwaiyang on a raft! In the event, the waters did not enter the city at all though they surrounded it and were deep enough and widespread enough to cut us off from outside communication for several weeks. In those days, of course, we had no radio to keep us in touch.

It was during this period that a young Japanese soldier did me a good turn. The first time he came into our campus he must have sauntered in without anyone seeing him, for there was no urgent call for 'Teacher Dong!' So I was quite surprised to see a Japanese soldier coming through the guest hall into our private compound unaccompanied by either the gatekeeper or the pastor who always hovered around on such occasions. As I stood on our verandah, having just come out of the door, I could not help smiling, for he looked so very young, peering around rather like a curious, slightly awed schoolboy who is not too sure of himself. When he looked across the courtyard and saw me, he gave a guilty start, then seeing the amused smile on my face, his own relaxed and a wide grin spread over it. So we stood looking at each other, two people of differing sex and age, from different backgrounds and cultures, yet conscious of our common humanity and of a simple, almost child-like, desire to communicate. We crossed over the courtyard to meet and I started with the usual question.

'Do you speak English?' He answered in the usual way, 'Spee-ek Eenglish?' A shake of the head, then 'Spee-ek Eenglish—not good. . .' I don't remember how the conversation developed. Not very far, but with sign language, a few words spoken slowly and a few more written down, we established a friendly relationship. He came back several times, sometimes bringing a friend, to try out his English. On one occasion, remembering what I'd heard about cherry blossom time in Japan, I tried to describe the flower, and suddenly he guessed what I meant.

'Sakara? Sakara?' he exclaimed, then said, 'Tomorrow'. Making a gesture as though handing me something, he reiterated, 'Tomorrow—sakara!' And sure enough he turned up the next day and presented me with a postcard on which was a picture of cherry blossom.

One afternoon he turned up to tell me that he was leaving to go to Kaifeng, the large city some hundreds of miles to the north. He had come to say goodbye.

How was he going to Kaifeng, I enquired, with the countryside flooded so that no vehicles could get through?

An aeroplane was coming for him.

But there was no airfield at Taikang. How could he board a plane if it did not land somewhere?

The plane would fly low, dangling a rope, and he would grasp it and be hauled up into the plane, and off he would go.

This conversation was conducted mainly by sign language and I thought I must have misunderstood what he was telling me. But when I repeated the antics of someone clutching a rope dangling from a plane and being swept up into it, he nodded emphatically. Yes, that was how he would get to Kaifeng.

Then I told him of what was on my mind. I was worried about my parents, away in England. If news reached them of the floods, and they did not hear from me, they would wonder if I was drowned. We wrote to each other every week, whatever the circumstances, but now there was no way of getting a letter to them. No mail was getting through now. The floods had cut communications.

I put my hands over my heart, bowed my head, and screwed up my face as though weeping, trying to convey the anxiety of parents bewailing the loss of their child. He watched me, puzzled, then a look of understanding flashed over his face.

'Letter!' he said. 'Your letter. I take . . . Kaifeng,' and he mimed the posting of a letter.

So he took my letter, and I never saw him again. But he was as good as his word. That letter, with a Kaifeng postmark, reached my parents in record time, though many were not getting through in those difficult days.

I knew that the Japanese perpetrated some horrifying cruelties during the Second World War, hard to understand and hard to forget, but I was spared either seeing or experiencing any of them. My lasting memory of the sturdy warriors from the land of the rising sun is of a friendly young Japanese soldier with a wide grin who, in the midst of the tensions and dangers of war, enjoyed trying out his English.

However, it is not really of Japanese soldiers that I should be writing, for the contacts I had with them were quite incidental as far as I was concerned, and had no significant bearing on my future. The person who made the deepest impression on me and who, quite unconsciously, launched me on my career as a writer was a Chinese beggar woman.

The first time I saw her was at the noon prayer meeting which Auntie Eva and I attended each day in the women's guest-hall. The few Christian women who lived on the compound were already gathering when I noticed among them a short, oldish little woman whose face was unfamiliar. Very poorly dressed, with a piece of old blue cloth tied round her head, she had—I was impressed to notice—a strangely peaceful expression on her face. Her eyes looked out from above her large, round cheeks with a calm acceptance of whatever life might bring. It had brought, as I soon learnt, a great deal of sorrow.

'This is Mrs. Peng,' I was told. 'She is one of our out-station Christians but has come to the city now, with her little grandson, to live in the workhouse. She's awfully poor and her home has gone now. She is full of praise to the Lord for making it possible for her to live in the workhouse.'

I saw her hands then. One or two of her fingers were missing, most of them were strangely shortened and practically useless. Years ago she had been poisoned, while working out in the fields. So now, her possessions all sold and the money all gone, she had no option but to leave her poor shack of a home in the country and come to live in the workhouse: a great barn of a place with brick beds covered with straw as the only furniture. But at any rate she had a roof over her head and there would be a bowl of thin porridge twice a day. She could go out begging, passing humbly from courtyard to courtyard with her begging bowl, waiting patiently until someone noticed her and went to get a piece of bread or the last scraping from the cooking pot.

One day she grazed her arm and came along to

the little dispensary to see if I could bandage it up
for her. It festered rather badly and often had to
be attended to. She never complained and was always so grateful for the little attention given—her
round, flat face and childlike, trustful eyes beaming a quiet gratitude as she thanked me for going
to so much trouble. One Saturday, however, she
came along looking rather a queer colour and,
while I bathed her arm, she told me that she was
very cold at nights. The weather was getting very
chilly at the time. She went on to assure me that it
was nothing much, and that when she got up and
moved about at nights the cold wasn't so bad.

But the following day, Sunday, she did not arrive
for the morning service and nothing was seen of
her for several days. During that time we had some
warm clothes made for her—the indispensable *kai-
tih*, the wadded coverlet in which to wrap up at
nights, as well as some wadded trousers and a
wadded jacket. The Bible-woman and another
Christian woman went to take them to her, and on
their return they told me, 'Mrs. Peng has been ill,
but she's better now. Praise the Lord!'

'And was she pleased to have the things you
took?' I asked. Yes, she was very pleased. She had
been so cold at night that she couldn't sleep, but
when she couldn't sleep, she prayed.

'Now look, Mrs. Peng,' the Bible-woman had
said, unfolding the bundle under her arm and dis-
closing those wadded garments and the *kai-tih*.
'See what your Heavenly Father has sent to you, in
answer to your prayers. He heard your prayers,
and He's sent you these.'

Mrs. Peng had been rather surprised at that.

'But I didn't pray for any warm clothes,' she said.

'But you were so cold you couldn't sleep. If you weren't praying for warm clothes, what were you praying for?'

'Oh, I prayed for the two missionary teachers, that God would bless them. And I prayed for the pastor and the pastor's wife and all the brothers and sisters in the church. That's what I prayed for.'

'That's right,' said another old inmate of the workhouse. 'I heard her. She was praying for the two missionary teachers and for the people in the church. She didn't ask for anything for herself.'

Perhaps you can understand what I felt like as I walked back to our warm, comfortable home in our private courtyard. While I was snugly tucked up in bed, fast asleep, that old, sick beggar woman, too cold to sleep, had been asking God not for the alleviation of her own sufferings and not for warm clothes but for His blessing on me. I was shamed in the face of such selflessness—a selflessness to which I knew I had certainly not attained. Mrs. Peng was illiterate, couldn't have read the Bible if she had had one, knew nothing of the finer points of theology and would never have thought of addressing a meeting, though she did not hesitate to urge others to put their trust in the Lord Jesus, in private conversations. She viewed the 'missionary teachers' with great respect, as those who understood the doctrine, preached and taught others, and had left their own homes in a faraway land to come and serve God in China. It wouldn't have occurred to her to consider herself in the same exalted category as they. They were beings on an altogether higher plane! Alas, if only she had known. . .!

But for all my shortcomings, I recognised true spiritual maturity when I saw it and, as I knelt by my bedside that night, I found myself melting into tears of joy as I remembered the words, 'There are many that are first that shall be last—and the last first.' How enthusiastically I would be cheering on the sidelines as Mrs. Peng, the beggar woman, went forward to receive her reward! I could thoroughly understand why such as she would be first and such as I, last.

Not surprisingly, when the time came for me to write my usual quarterly newsletter for distribution among my friends back in England, the only thing that really seemed worth recording was the story of Mrs. Peng and her prayer when she was too cold to sleep.

That letter was to have unexpected results.

13

Dear Edward,

It was good to see you again last Thursday—thanks for the lunch, especially the chocolate and nut sundae with that mountain of whipped cream to crown it. I'm glad we've decided on a deadline for the completion of this memoir. I'll sign the contract as soon as I receive it from you, and will make its writing a priority.

One thing I'm particularly thankful for is that, almost as an afterthought, I brought up those 'Learn to Read English' lessons for you to see. I wrote them about twenty years ago, inspired to do so by a W.E.C. missionary who said to me, 'There's a world-wide desire to learn English. If you could write a little course for beginners, based on the Gospel narrative, you'd have something that could reach millions.' Well, it hasn't reached millions yet, as far as I know, but it has reached thousands through the post and it has been published in Japan and Vietnam and used over the radio in India. A missionary working among Afghan refugees told me recently that she uses the lessons all the time in her work; I've no idea how many others may be doing the same. I put no restrictions on it: it was my personal contribution to the spread of the Gospel worldwide. I was very thrilled, a year or so ago, when a friend of mine, a teacher, decided to develop the material by producing cassettes with readers to go with it. She'd found the lessons very useful for teaching English to Vietnamese refugees. To my surprise, she has now produced what amounts to a set of teaching materials of over 100 pages, complete with alphabet, word construction, grammar, etc., all based on those twelve lessons. It's because she's run into difficulties about getting the material printed that I asked your advice, and I was surprised and encouraged at the interest you showed and the possibilities you saw in the idea.

'Those little lessons could prove to be the most important thing you've ever written,' someone said, and since they are reaching with the Gospel some who otherwise would never hear it, I think that might be so.

To return to my memories of Taikang. My time there was very significant, but it did not last long. The political situation was changing, with the attitude of the Japanese authorities towards Westerners no longer as impartial as it had been. To make a play on a famous phrase, all Westerners were neutral but some were more neutral than others. War clouds were gathering in Europe. Nazi Germany, with Hitler as its Fuhrer, was emerging as a militant power, annexing first Austria, then Bohemia and Moravia, with Poland under threat. The ill-fated Munich Agreement between Britain and France, Italy and Germany had succeeded in postponing the intervention of Great Britain and her allies, but the German invasion of Poland was the last straw, and in September 1939 the Second World War broke out in Europe. Although Japan was not yet officially involved, there was no doubt that her sympathies lay with Germany. During this time things had been getting more and more difficult for British nationals living in Japanese occupied China.

All this had its effect on us missionaries, and the outcome for Auntie Eva and me was that Mission leaders in Shanghai decided to transfer us to join the three in Hwaiyang, and to put a Swiss member of the Mission in charge in Taikang.

So the evening came when we rumbled along in a cart laden with our luggage along the busy, crowded streets of Hwaiyang, lighted by flaring torches, to come to a halt at the front gates of the China Inland Mission premises there. And among the little group waiting there to greet us was Eastern Light.

'Teacher Dong!' he said, his face beaming. 'You've come back, Teacher Dong?'

My face was beaming, too, as I replied, 'Yes, I've come back!' I did not know until later that, since I'd left, he had not ceased to pray that I would return.

'Are you peaceful, Teacher?' It was the polite, conventional greeting, and I replied in the same vein.

'Peaceful! Are you also peaceful, Eastern Light?'

'Peaceful!' Then he added impulsively, 'I'm so glad you've come back!'

'And I'm so glad to be back!' We smiled at each other, and took up just where we had left off.

But it was only three or four months later that I

had to go away again—and this time not only I, but the Tomkinsons, Auntie Eva and Irene Steele as well. The Japanese, who had occupied the city some months earlier, politely but firmly intimated that we were not welcome. We tried to stay, but they were adamant, and quietly organised an anti-British demonstration against us, with a few of the local riff-raff parading round the Mission premises shouting anti-British slogans while friendly neighbours, to show their sympathy, handed a huge jar of steaming, tasty soup over the back garden wall. There were several days of alternating hopes and disappointments before we finally left. But when soldiers were put on guard in our compound and would enter our rooms to see what we were doing, we knew we would have to go.

On the last Monday we were there Eastern Light arrived carrying a jug of milk. All our friends knew we liked to have milk in our tea, a taste they could not understand but smiled at indulgently. We had disposed of our goats in preparation for our departure, and the church deaconess and her family wanted to ensure that we were not without milk for our tea.

'Only an insignificant thought from my father,' he said politely, as he handed it to us. Then he added, 'My heart is very sorrowful because the teachers have to go.'

'My heart is sorrowful, too,' I told him, and we stood talking together for a while. It was not a conversation without hope, however. At such times there is always a bright star in the dark sky for those who know Him who has said, 'I will come back and take you to be with me that you also may be where I am.'

In the course of our short time together Eastern Light announced that he had held Sunday School in his house the previous day, with his small brothers and sisters as pupils.

'What did you teach them?' I asked. He hung his head on one side, and replied rather shyly, 'I told them to repent of their sins and believe in the Lord Jesus.'

Our departure came suddenly in the end. We had expected to remain two or three days more to wind up affairs and pack what we could get into a trunk apiece. Everything else would have to be left behind, we knew—furniture, books, ornaments, crockery and cutlery, clothes, personal belongings. It was a salutary experience for me and revolutionised my attitude towards things. I've never attached so much importance to things since that time.

By three o'clock on what proved to be our last day in Hwaiyang, we were on mule carts with what baggage we could assemble, rumbling out of the city. Only a few of the Christians had heard we were leaving suddenly and had courageously come to say goodbye. So, as our carts passed slowly through the north gate, we thought we had seen the last of the people we had come to know and to love.

But we were wrong. There in the crowded north suburb we saw a little figure standing on a bank at the busy crossroads, bowing towards us. It was Eastern Light. A few minutes later, as the carts drew in to the inn where the animals were to be fed, the little boy came alongside, and looking up at

me said, 'I do praise the Lord! He has guided me.'
The consciousness of divine guidance was evidently very real to him as he explained. 'I don't
know why, but my heart was feeling very unpeaceful when I was out feeding the goats. I felt I only
wanted to go into the city to see how you were. So I
went back and told my mother where I was going.
Usually I go by the short way across the fields into
the city, but today I thought I would go by the main
road, and I had just got to the crossroads when I
saw your carts. If the Lord had not influenced my
heart to leave home when I did and go by the main
road, I should have missed you and not have been
able to escort you a little way.' The courtesy of accompanying departing visitors is very important in
Chinese eyes. 'I did not know at all that you were
going today,' he added. He was quite calm and
composed, shyly polite as usual, but evidently
buoyed up by that sense of having had his heart
strangely moved: 'The Lord influenced my heart to
leave home when I did, and go by the main road . . .'

At last the animals were fed, and the carts
rumbled out on to the road again, Eastern Light
walking alongside. Then we made the conventional
remark; 'Please don't escort us any farther, Eastern
Light.' He walked on a little farther then halted
and said, 'I won't escort you any farther, Teacher.'

I looked back to reply, 'No, don't escort us any
farther. Please go back. I'll be seeing you.' But of
course, I knew I wouldn't. Not in this life.

'I'll be seeing you again,' I called, then added, 'In
Heaven!' He stood there, looking after us, smiling
still and bowing, and called back, 'In Heaven—I'll
see you again.'

I think of him sometimes, even now. I expect by this time he is a grandfather, the head of his family. I've wondered how he fared in the dark, dark days of the cultural revolution or even if he survived them. But when I think of him, it is always as a little Chinese boy standing on a bank, with his head on one side, bowing and calling out, 'In Heaven—I'll see you again!'

14

Dear Edward,

I am a Londoner, born in Hammersmith, a townswoman through and through. I think it's in my blood, derived from my mother for whom the capital had an irresistible attraction. She was the youngest daughter of a Cornish farmer. As a little girl, standing on the banks of the river Fal, she would look towards London and say to herself, 'I'll go there one day . . .' When her father, who was an alcoholic, reduced his family to poverty, she obtained a job in the accounts department of John Lewis in Oxford Street and, apart from two or three very brief visits, never returned to Cornwall. She preferred the city. This apparently unnecessary preamble is not so irrelevant as it may appear, for it helps to explain my reactions, after being turned out from our mission centre in a little city in agricultural Henan, at finding myself in the great, teeming port of Shanghai.

I was delighted! I had not realised how much I enjoyed the freedom of walking around paved streets, travelling on public transport in the shape of tramcars, talking to people in my own native language and, best of all, not being stared at by

121

everyone. No longer was I an object of interest and curiosity as soon as I emerged from the seclusion of our compound to be watched and commented on as I walked along the street, and to draw a little crowd of interested spectators if I stopped to look at the goods on a wayside stall. In cosmopolitan Shanghai of the 1930s, Westerners were a common sight and for us, returning there after several years inland, it was a fascinating and exciting place. Naturally, we did not patronise the famous race course, join the smart clubs, or enter into the merry-go-round social life of the professional and business men or of the armed services stationed there. The large compound of the China Inland Mission—with its two huge buildings providing office and housing for the headquarters staff and accommodation for the steady flow of missionaries en route for the interior or for furlough—was the centre of our lives. But excursions could be made to the shopping areas downtown, to the tree-lined avenues of the French concession or to the restaurant that specialised in old-fashioned English cream teas—if and when we could afford such an extravagance.

To offset these advantages there was the problem of clothes, for in Shanghai no Westerners wore Chinese garments, and up-country missionaries opening the trunks they had left behind found that the clothes they had carefully packed away in tissue paper were now embarrassingly out of date. However, no-one expected missionaries to be smartly dressed, and there was always someone to make helpful suggestions or alterations or to lend an article of clothing so that one could sally forth comparatively confidently on Sundays to attend services in the Cathedral or one of the other English-speaking churches.

There were attractions of a different and more inspiring nature in Shanghai, too, in the shape of the various Christian missions and institutions centred there. For those of us who had been living in an inland city where the small, struggling church to which we were attached was the only outward evidence of Christian activity, it was exhilarating to see and hear about what was going on in the Christian hospitals, schools and colleges as well as in the seamen's and rescue missions of the port. There was so much to interest and encourage, for if things weren't going too well in one area, they would be flourishing in another. And there were the special meetings held on two evenings a week in the large Prayer Hall, at which our own missionaries returning from the interior gave their reports of the work they had been doing. Shanghai, from my point of view, was a good place to be. I was in my element.

There was an even more intimate reason for my happiness in being there. It had to do with a woman named Elizabeth Robertson and what I saw as God's guidance in my life. Elizabeth Robertson was a Scot who had embarked on a rescue work among prostitutes that no-one else was attempting. The Door of Hope Mission had been started some decades earlier, to provide a refuge for Chinese girls who manage to escape from the brothels into which they had been sold, and was by this time well established in Shanghai. But there was a little stream of white women prostitutes, some of them pathetic refugees from the Communist Revolution in Russia, for whom nothing was done—until Elizabeth Robertson started to get in touch with them. I had heard about her while still inland and had been corresponding with her. Now, through no deliberate choice on my part, I was brought into contact with her personally and the work she was doing. I met her first at a prayer meeting at which she announced that she was praying for a fellow worker. She felt the need of a colleague, someone like-minded and with a desire to reach these women with the Gospel of Jesus Christ, someone who would be prepared to go to them where they were, risk the dangers of such encounters, and show them genuine friendship.

So the little group of us prayed about the matter and, as we did so, my spirits soared. Surely I had been brought back to Shanghai for this very purpose! 'Behold, I have set before thee an open door' came readily to my mind and by the time we had risen from our knees I was convinced that I was the one to be the answer to those prayers. I talked it over with Elizabeth and the little group of people who were giving her moral and financial support, and they agreed that if the General Director of the C.I.M. would release me, I should join her.

Obtaining permission from the General Director to move away from Chinese work to which the Mission was committed, was not so easy. He was obviously reluctant to see a young worker, only three years out, getting involved in something that might eventually lead her out of the Mission altogether. However, there was no reason for withholding help for a spiritual enterprise of which he thoroughly approved in principle and as there was no Chinese work into which I could be drafted at short notice in Shanghai, he agreed that until it was reasonably safe to send me back into inland China, I could work with Miss Robertson. And as she was looking for a flat and therefore had no accommodation to offer me at present, I would, of course, remain living in the Mission home.

Things had gone very smoothly so far. There was every evidence that the Lord was opening the door before me and that all I would have to do would be to enter it. Even if it eventually meant leaving the Mission altogether, the transition to another work would be simplified by the fact that my father was supporting me so there'd be no financial problem.

Only one thing was lacking, and that was the indefinable conviction, based on a personal commission from the Lord Himself, that this was the way for me. I wanted to be sure that He was leading me, so I decided to pray for a definite indication. I thought of the words that had come to mind in that prayer meeting—'I have set before thee an open door . . .' If only they would come to me again, not just in my mind, but either before my eyes, or in my ears! So I prayed that I should either see them or hear them during the next week, and having prayed, I started to write in my diary. 'Prayed that if it were God's will I should do this work with Elizabeth Robertson I should either see or hear, before next Saturday evening, the words . . .' But at that point something interrupted me and I did not finish the sentence. However, I knew just what the words were and, all the following week, I was alert to see or hear them. It seemed most likely I should do so. Surely at one of the daily prayer meetings or at the special meetings in the Prayer Hall they would be quoted; or in some book or magazine at which I might happen to look, they would appear!

I was full of expectation. Sunday, Monday and Tuesday passed uneventfully, then Wednesday. By Thursday evening I was beginning to get anxious. Only two more days in which to see or hear those words and know that the step I had taken was the right one. Saturday evening came, with the regular big public meeting in the Prayer Hall. The hymn books we used at these meetings all had a text at the top and, as each hymn was announced, my eye roved eagerly over the whole page, hoping the text would be somewhere there. As each person preached or gave a report I listened for that text. I listened for it as one and another led in prayer. But the words never came; no one even mentioned the book of Revelation in which they are to be found.

When the meeting was over and we dispersed from the Prayer Hall, I avoided the groups chattering together and hurried away. I wanted to be alone. I mounted the wide tiled stairs of the Mission Home to the second floor, walked along the corridor to my bedroom and entered with a sense of dismay in my heart. The time was up. I'd asked the Lord that He would let me either see or hear those words by Saturday evening and I had neither seen nor heard them.

I walked over to my desk, sat down heavily, opened the drawer and pulled out my diary. For some reason I had not written in it all the week—

there had been nothing special to report, I suppose. So when I opened it, I saw the last entry I had made, a week before. It read: 'Prayed that if it were God's will I should do this work with Elizabeth Robertson I should either see or hear, before next Saturday evening, the words . . .'

But the words were not there either. The significance of that blank, unfinished sentence was inescapable. I felt as though I had suddenly come to the edge of a cliff and a great void was before me. God had definitely *not* confirmed the step I had taken. What was I to do?

It was one of those occasions when I could only cry to the Lord to extricate me from the dilemma I had got myself into. I had committed myself to work with Miss Robertson, and the difficulty of my situation was accentuated because she had been taken ill and was in a nursing home, so the task of finding a suitable flat somewhere in Shanghai had fallen on me. I could not withdraw now and leave her in the lurch. I must continue flat hunting, and doing what I could to keep in touch with one of the women she had been trying to help. She had landed herself in jail but could at least be visited once a week by special permission of the authorities. She had a cell to herself but was exposed to the view of anyone passing up and down the corridor, for she was literally behind bars, as though in a cage, like an animal in the zoo. She was surprisingly matter of fact about her situation, and seemed by no means abashed by it.

My memories of those weeks spent in Shanghai are rather hazy. All I can say is that though nothing I did in connection with the White Russian prostitutes prospered, I was mercifully preserved from any disasters. In one case there was an eleventh hour deliverance from what would have been an impossible situation. Miss Robertson, before being taken ill, had undertaken to be responsible for the White Russian prisoner if her sentence could be shortened, fully expecting that by that time a suitable flat would have been found into which to receive her. But now Miss Robertson was laid up in a nursing home, we had no flat, the authorities were planning to hand over the prisoner on a certain day as arranged, and there was no one but myself to receive her and take her—where?

On the night before I was due to go to the prison to collect her, I was at my wits' end. I had not the slightest idea what I would do the next morning. I'd have to go to the prison, of course, as arranged, but what then? Where did I go from there with my charge?

I should like, at this stage, to be able to record that it was my faith in God, my confidence that He would see me through, that enabled me to sleep that night, but alas, I can make no such claim. As far as I remember, having prayed about the situation again, in a confused and desperate way, I seemed incapable of worrying any more. There was nothing else that I could do, and I felt beyond caring about the outcome, so I went to sleep.

If there is one verse in the Bible more than another that comforts me where faith is concerned, it is found in 2 Timothy chapter 2 verse 13, where the Authorised Version reads, '*If we believe not, yet He abideth faithful, He cannot deny himself.*' To me that simply means that however wobbly my faith may be, He won't let me down. Theologians may have a different interpretation to it, but that's mine, and I'm sticking to it.

Certainly it proved correct early the next morning. I was called to the 'phone before breakfast and told that I need not go to the prison after all. Instead, the pastor of a White Russian church in Shanghai would go there with his wife, accept responsibility for the woman and take her to their own home.

I do not know what strings had been pulled in the human realm to bring this about but, from my point of view, it was God who had extricated me from the alarming predicament.

Another incident comes to mind as I write which reveals, alas, the weakness of human nature, and that some, at any rate, of my inner struggles could have been avoided altogether if I had paid more attention to the voice of God in my own heart. This is what happened.

I had been on my knees in my room praying one morning, when I heard the gong for dinner, the midday meal. Now meals in the Mission Home were always served very punctually. The housekeeper, an efficient Scot, was a stickler for time and, although Jeannie Anderson was a warm-hearted person who would go to great lengths to help anyone in real need, she could become very irate with those who were late for meals, and even more so with those who did not turn up at all. She knew the exact number to be expected every time, even though there were often over seventy of us, and if one place were vacant, she would notice it. So when I heard the gong that day, I stifled the very strong conviction that I should remain in my room, in prayer. I knew that if I failed to appear at the table, not having signed the book to indicate that I would be absent, I should be in for a dressing-down. I hesitated long enough to be in danger of being late, for I would willingly have skipped the meal had it not been for fear of Miss Anderson's stern rebuke. As it was, I decided I didn't want to face it so hurried downstairs, across the hall, along to the dining room and slipped rather breathlessly into the only vacant seat I could see at one of the long tables. I was only just in time for grace. When I raised my eyes afterwards, I found myself sitting next to a young missionary whom I had not met before.

Like me, he was in his first term of service; like me, too, he was waiting to be re-designated to an inland mission centre in an area beyond the Japanese occupied zone. We were about the same age, both single, we found each other quite interesting, and an indefinable attraction that was very disturbing sparked off. It was all very super-ficial really, and I think we both knew it, but it was acute all the same. We saw very little of each other, for in those days easy friendships between the sexes were frowned on by those in authority. There would have been no thought of being alone together. One or two outings in a party of half-a-dozen or so were the most that he arranged and our conversations were limited to casual meetings in the public rooms of the Mission Home. But the consciousness of each other's presence was re-vealed as our eyes met, even when we were chatting in different groups. And it triggered off something in me that I had imagined I had safely put aside.

It was the thought of marriage. It was becoming evident that my desire for the work with Miss Robertson in Shanghai itself, with all its excitement, variety and the freedom to move about without being stared at, was not to be fulfilled. Already there was talk of places beyond the Japanese-occupied areas in need of missionary help, and of those of us who had been turned out of our centres being deployed among them. To go back to a remote inland city, and the loneliness of being a single woman there, seemed to me like stepping into my coffin. It wouldn't be so bad if I had the companionship of a husband. And the thought began to insinuate itself into my mind that perhaps that conviction that the Lord intended me for a single life was not to be permanent after all.

But it *was* to be permanent. The day came when I was told plans were being made for me to return with Irene Steele to the province of Henan, to a small city on the Anhwei border, where we would be the only Westerners, of course, and half a day's journey from the nearest mission station where a young married couple were living. And I knew that was the end of my hope of working in Shanghai, and the end of the alternative of going back to the interior with the prospect of marriage, too. It was not a matter of remaining single to do the work in Shanghai or going back to the interior with a husband. It was a matter of relinquishing all hope of that work in Shanghai *and* going back to be a single woman missionary in the interior.

I always look back to that period as being one of the most difficult in my whole life. I was reading, a day or two ago, in the book of Proverbs. Coming to the words, 'The fining pot for silver, and the furnace for gold: but the Lord trieth the hearts,' I thought about that time. The consuming of dross and the refining of gold is a painful business when it comes to the human heart. But during those dark, grey days, as I was preparing to sort out my belongings, decide what I would leave in trunks in Shanghai, what I would need for living inland, the Lord met me through a little booklet given to me by a bed-ridden old lady.

The old lady was the wife of D.E. Hoste, Hudson Taylor's successor as General Director of the China Inland Mission. He had only just retired from his position, and he and his wife were living in a flat over the Mission Home, to which young members of the Mission were invited, one by one, for short visits. One day I was invited to go and see Mrs. Hoste. I found her in bed, a gentle old lady who really knew very little about me. I can't remember anything she said to me in that short interview, but she had on the table beside her a box of tracts and booklets and, as I was leaving, she drew one out and handed it to me. It was only a simply-produced, eight-page booklet containing a compilation of short devotional extracts and poems but, as I read it later alone in my room, one of the extracts seemed to hold a message of comfort for me. It referred to the question sent to Jesus by John the Baptist when he was in prison: 'Art thou He that should come, or do we look for another?' The gist of the message contained in that extract focused not so much on the words Christ sent back as a personal message to John—'Blessed is he, whosoever shall not be offended in me'—but on what Christ said *about* John after the messengers had left.

'What went ye out into the wilderness to see?' he asked the bystanders. 'A prophet? Yea, I say unto you, more than a prophet . . .' and he went on, in glowing terms, to make the assertion, 'Among those born of women there has not risen a greater than John the Baptist . . .'

But John himself never heard these words of praise, did not know what Jesus had said about him in his absence. All he knew was that the One who was giving sight to the blind, healing the leper and raising the dead, had given him no promise of deliverance from imprisonment. He had to be faithful to death, and wait for his reward beyond it. He did not even hear those words of commendation, revealing the approval of the Master.

I was conscious of hearing no words of commendation from Him, either—only the challenge of going forward to obtain the blessing of the unoffended. The thought came that perhaps the Lord was approving even of me, as I set my face to that lonely path back to inland China. There was comfort in that thought.

There was something else in that little booklet, too—words that I have quoted many times since. They helped to explain the experience through which I was passing, and alleviate the sense of desolation.

> There is a peace which cometh after sorrow
> Of hope surrendered, not of hope fulfilled,
> A peace that looketh not upon tomorrow,

But calmly on a tempest that is stilled.

A peace there is, in sacrifice secluded,
A life subdued, from will and passion free,
'Tis not the peace that over Eden brooded,
But that which triumphed in Gethsemane.

And so I said goodbye to the city and the work I had hoped to do, and went back again to the province of Henan.

15

Dear Edward,

Glancing back over the last instalment of my memories of China, I realise it was written in a very minor key. Actually, I finished it in Easter week, just before Good Friday with its reminder of the principle that the seed must die if there is to be fruit. Resurrection is always preceded by death, and dying is a painful process.

Appropriately enough, today is Easter Monday, and I can write now of what happened after those devastating days when I felt as though I were stepping into my coffin as I left Shanghai for the interior of China. Though the weeks that followed were grey ones for me, the time came when I emerged quite suddenly from my cocoon of depression. And it happened in the last place I would have expected—in the Mission compound of Siangcheng—that very remote town near the Anhwei border that had seemed to lead into a featureless wilderness as far as I personally was concerned.

I had had the gloomiest expectations of it. It was a small and unimportant place, off the beaten track, and therefore we could expect nothing in the way of interesting, unexpected visitors. There was a little group of Christians in it, though not enough to have a proper church building, so they met in a converted barn on the compound rented by the Mission. There were four or five outstations connected with it—villages some distances from the city where even smaller groups of Christians met for services on Sunday. It did not sound very inspiring.

Irene Steele and I knew what was expected of us. We were to help illiterate woman who had become Christians with their reading, give them Bible teaching, visit them in their homes, organise Sunday Schools, go to the outstations for the same purpose, and to preach, if appropriate. But we were to be careful not to take any lead in church affairs. The aim of the Mission had been clearly defined at an important conference held some years previously. The aim was that the churches it had brought into being should become self-governing, self-propagating and self-supporting. To this end, financial support from the Mission for Chinese workers was being gradually withdrawn and missionaries were being instructed to relinquish, as soon as possible, the leadership role they had inevitably adopted in the earlier days and to encourage the Chinese to take responsibility for church affairs and for evangelism. Missionaries were to be available for advice when asked for it and to preach when invited to do so but were not to interfere in church matters.

The aim was right, of course, but not very easy to achieve. Some of the missionaries who had remained in the centres in which they had been in control, had a difficult time of it, like Mr. Tomkinson in Hwaiyang and the pastor compromising with idolatry.

However, no such problems were likely to arise in Siangcheng, for Deacon Liong, the chemist, Deacon Hsiao, the seller of cloth, and Deacon Fan, of independent means, were staunch in their Christian faith; and with the redoubtable Elder Dong of the village of Dong to support them and ensure that things were kept on the right lines, there was no idolatry in the church there. Inevitably there were other problems; family and marital as well as personality clashes when people with varying convictions came into conflict about church activities, discipline and the use of church funds. But I cannot remember any serious matter that was not dealt with far better by the church leaders than if it had been left to us missionaries.

So to Siangcheng Irene Steele and I went. We had spent some time in the neighbouring city of Shenkiu, where the young missionary in charge was an American. It was his responsibility to make sure that things were in order for us in Siangcheng and he took this seriously, seeing to it that the premises we were to occupy were habitable, and that a suitable cook was employed. It all took time, but the day came when we cycled the twenty miles, along narrow paths through fields and over bumpy roads, to enter the west gate of the city and push our bikes along the dusty streets till we came to a halt at what looked like just another shop with the shutters up and one door left ajar. We had arrived. The old gatekeeper, who spent most of his time dozing in a deck chair by the door, rose to welcome us, and we passed through the large bare entrance hall into a narrow compound bounded, on one side, by the blank wall of the house next door and, on the other, by two or three rooms used for small meetings. That led to the converted barn with its rows of backless benches, through to a neat little courtyard where Mrs. Han the Biblewoman lived with her schoolgirl daughter, and across to a gate which led to our own courtyard.

It was different from the other Mission compounds in which I had lived, with their paved walks and colonial-style houses, their balconies and verandahs. This was typically Chinese, with two little tile-roofed, three-roomed houses at right angles to each other, and an acacia tree in the middle. Beyond this little courtyard was a field in which to keep the goats which would provide us with our milk. The whole narrow compound, from front to back, was bounded by high walls effectively screening us from our neighbours. There was nothing about the place to make any natural appeal but it was as I entered it that the cloud of depression that had been enveloping me finally dispersed.

A day or two before, while reading in John's Gospel, a little phrase from chapter 14 had struck me with a sense of personal significance: 'I go to prepare a place for you.' I knew it referred to the future life in heaven but, somehow, as I read it, it seemed to hold a promise for the immediate future, too. The words came vividly to mind again as I walked through that narrow compound and felt a sudden upsurge of spiritual vitality; a sense of being in step with my Master such as I had not known for a long time. I was in the right place at last!

I lived in Siangcheng for nearly five years. Irene Steele was the missionary in charge (so she had to do the accounts!) for the first year. Before she left, among other things, she had organised a women's preaching band which became an integral part of church life. When she was designated to another area, I became the senior missionary with Doris Weller as my colleague. Doris and I had been in Language School together but afterwards she had been sent to teach in the school for missionaries' children in Chefoo, north China, so had had no opportunity to study or practise Chinese. Now, after several years in institutional life, she had to start all over again in a backward inland city without the advantage of qualified teachers, and with only one English companion.

Looking back, I realise how very unsatisfactory a fellow-worker I was to both of them, with my regrettable tendency to barge ahead with silent concentration and do my own thing, leaving them to do theirs. It speaks well for them that after all these years they are still my good friends, and we keep in touch with each other.

It was very early in this period in Siangcheng that I received a letter which I think was the most important I ever received in my life. It came from London, from the Editorial Secretary of the China Inland Mission's headquarters there. He had seen a copy of the letter I had written over a year earlier about Mrs. Peng, the beggar-woman who prayed for others when she was too cold to sleep, and it had given him an idea. If I could write eight or ten brief character sketches of some of the other Chinese I had met, he could make them into a little book. It would provide people at home with a glimpse of what God was doing in China and would meet a real need at this time.

That letter came to me not so much as a commission from the Editor as a commission from the Lord Himself. He was telling me to do the very thing that came most naturally to me; to use the particular talent that my parents had recognised when, as a little schoolgirl, I would spend a whole evening concentrating with frowning intensity on the essay that was required as homework for next morning's English class. I don't know whether we work hard at something because we are good at it or whether we are good at something because we work hard at it. Maybe the two go hand in hand. Certainly, the only sort of homework to which I willingly applied myself as a schoolgirl was that which involved writing.

'What is that in thine hand?' the Lord asked Moses. In his case, it was his rod. In my case, it was my pen. Now the Lord was telling me to take it up and use it as He directed and I responded with complete freedom and happiness. I felt as though waters that had been dammed up had suddenly been released to start flowing; or as though I had emerged from a tunnel out into the sunlight. A stream of satisfying activity was opened up that day that has continued right up to the present time.

I am actually sitting in an Underground train, *en route* to meet a friend, scribbling this, but that marvellous mechanism of memory is conveying me back fifty years, and I am again in the little white-washed dining-room with the door opening on to the small inner courtyard of the Mission centre in Siangcheng. My typewriter is on the table before me, the sun is shining, and my heart is singing as I write about a tranquil-faced old Bible-woman emerging with unselfconscious dignity from the church compound to 'preach the Way' to her neighbours; about a grubbily-dressed vegetable-grower who has won many people for Christ through a gift for healing which the Lord has given him; about the village inn-keeper who can't often get to church, but has taken down the Old Heavenly Grandfather idol from the place of honour in his guest room and put up a Gospel poster in its place; about the Christians in the village of Fan who insisted on entertaining a snow-bound party of missionaries for several days, brushing aside apologies for the inconvenience caused with the simple words, 'You are for the Lord. We also are for the Lord.'

Altogether, there were ten little character sketches in that—my first—book, which was published in 1940 under the title *They Seek a City*. It is long since out of print, of course, but I have a copy; and as I turn its pages I see them again, those lovable Chinese Christians, my friend Eastern Light among them, and I am so thankful that I can say of them all—'I'll see you again—in Heaven!'

And that is how I started writing books—launched on my career by a Chinese beggar-woman.

16

Dear Edward,

I've just been re-reading one of the books I wrote, years ago, about my time in Siangcheng. The book was mainly concerned with people not events; and as I have browsed through its pages, they have come to life again—those Chinese men and women with whom my life was interwoven so intimately in the quiet backwater of a remote city in China during the years when the Second World War was raging.

Not that we were without our dangers and alarms, for Siangcheng was in even more of a No-Man's-Land than Taikang had been. The nearest garrison of the Chinese Nationalists was in Shenkiu, some twenty miles away, while at about the same distance in the opposite direction the Japanese had their outposts from which, every now and then, they would make a foray towards Siangcheng. We had no telephone or radio, of course, but news travels quickly by word of mouth, and signs of activity on the streets, as the well-to-do and able-bodied moved rapidly with cart and wheelbarrow out of the city to disappear in the countryside, were sufficient to alert us to the necessity of packing a few essentials, locking up our rooms and departing on our bicycles for Shenkiu where we would wait until things settled down again.

However, this did not happen often; most of the time we were only affected indirectly by the Second World War. Funds were low and the post was uncertain, though I must pay my tribute to the International Postal Union, at any rate as I saw it operating in those unsettled days in China. In times of danger the local Post Office, along with all the other official departments, would disappear into the countryside and continue operating from some remote village until it was safe to return to the city again. Although many letters were lost, the marvel to me was how many got through. My parents and I wrote to each other once or twice a week, whatever the circumstances, and we were rarely more than two or three weeks without receiving a letter. Often I would get two at a time, one from my father, who went to a lot of trouble to find out the best route by which to send it, giving clear instructions that it was to go 'via Siberia and Mukden' or something of the sort, and one from my mother, simply marked 'Via quickest route'. They usually arrived by the same post.

On the whole, therefore, life was quiet and undisturbed in Siangcheng and, being largely isolated from the outside world, we had plenty of opportunity to get to know our Chinese fellow-believers. They had only been names to us before our arrival in Siangcheng, and there were few enough of them, but as the weeks passed those names became distinctive personalities.

Deacon Liong, the chemist, was tall, slim, dignified, looking out on life with an impersonal gaze. Whatever happened, Deacon Liong never lost his self-possession and unconscious air of superiority. Even when standing at the door of the Gospel Hall preaching to the passers-by, which he did from time to time (he was surprisingly open in his Christian witness), he somehow managed to convey the impression that he was doing them a favour. He spoke little in committee but was the dominating figure in the church and, in any matters of policy or administration, it was he who ultimately got his own way. A rather awe-inspiring person, he lacked the warm geniality of the good mixer and was feared rather than loved. But he was stalwart in his faith in the invisible but living God and resolutely opposed to anything savouring of idolatry. True, his morals had gone awry at one stage, when he'd taken another wife and stopped attending church, but he'd repented and done what he could to put things right. It had been a hard road for him, for his second wife, a coarse, rather slatternly-looking woman made things as difficult as possible, waylaying him in the street and airing her grievances in a loud voice for all to hear. This was a terrible loss of face for the proud, naturally secretive man, but there was nothing he could do except endure it, which he did with an impassive face. The genuineness of his repentance was revealed in his changed attitude towards his delicate, long-suffering little wife. He was very solicitous of her health, showing her a care and a courtesy most unusual for a husband in old China, writing to her frequently when he was away from home because, as she explained rather coyly on one occasion, 'he knows I get worried'.

Deacon Hsaio, the seller of cloth, was entirely different. No one was afraid of him, not even his wife, though at one time she had dreaded his return from a business trip—wondering whether he would be in a good mood, or whether she would be in for a beating. But that had been before the Christian convention. He had attended this, expecting to have a good time—only to discover himself to be a wolf in sheep's clothing and to learn that true religion, like charity, must begin at home. He had been quite different after that. Of a sanguine, easily influenced temperament, he had remained remarkably steadfast in his Christian faith and conduct when others, who were naturally quieter and steadier, had fluctuated and fallen. The church in Siangcheng had had its ups and downs and, at one period, when things had been at a very low ebb, he had been one of the very few who had remained loyal and had patiently borne jibing over his adherence to 'the foreigner', the missionary in charge.

He was a very practical man, and we could always turn to him for help in getting things done, although he was not so quick to respond to invitations to preach at the Sunday services. He did not consider preaching to be his line. He preferred to exhort people in private, and many were the illiterate old women who came regularly to worship on Sundays because he had first exhorted, then prayed for them. The more educated church-goers might find him rather tedious, but the common people heard him gladly as he harangued them with the homely illustrations they so readily understood. He was what we would call a personal worker, and rather prided himself on his understanding of human nature, and ability to handle men and affairs tactfully. One could discern a certain patient, conciliatory expression creep over his face when this was happening, along with a kindly smile. I was often conscious of being tactfully handled myself and of allowances being made for the evident fact that I had what was called a quick temperament, not a placid one.

I don't know how I would have managed during those years in Siangcheng, without Deacon Hsaio.

Deacon Fan was different from either of the other two. He was a man with a longish, rather melancholy face, who rarely had anything to say except on the few occasions when he got excited and said too much. His life seemed bound up in the church and he was always on hand to tidy up or sweep the chapel; but when it came to the deacons' meetings he would sit silently with his head down, eyes on the ground, and take no part in the discussions. If he was asked directly for an opinion he would say, 'I follow,' from which it was concluded that he agreed with the majority. On one occasion it was pointed out to him, with slightly amused asperity, that he couldn't follow two points of view, so in this case, who or what was he following?

'I follow the Lord,' he'd replied. This pious pronouncement, while failing to help towards a decision, proved unanswerable.

We wondered how he would manage when, according to the current system of local government, he was elected as head man over ten families. He was known to all his neighbours as a man of integrity, which is why he was elected. In fact, he did not like the office because, as everyone told me with a shake of the head, he couldn't fulfil it without telling lies and practising deception. In the circumstances, such conduct was generally recognised as being quite legitimate. The important thing was to keep everyone as happy as possible and ensure that nobody lost face. But the more Mr. Fan progressed in the Christian faith, the more unhappy he became at the lies he had to tell. His civic duties interfered with his church activities, too. So when we heard, after a time, that he was no longer headman, we felt relieved on his account.

But he was still not happy. The reason emerged one evening at the 'lamplight service', when about a dozen of us gathered round a table to read from our opened Bibles with the light from an oil lamp.

'I have sinned,' he said simply, and there was a sudden breathless hush. What had he done? Those who suspected the worst were quite relieved as he continued, 'I have got out of the position of headman, but I told lies to get out of it, and I know that was sin.'

Immediately a comforting murmur arose from those whose eyes were fixed on him, and someone said reassuringly, 'That's not sin. You had to tell lies to get out of the position and you had to get out of the position because you had to tell lies while you were in it!'

Mr. Fan was not convinced. He looked across at me, the only missionary present, and the only one who had remained silent.

'What does Teacher Dong say?' he asked. I could feel my forehead screwing up in a perplexed frown. I felt for him, wanted to comfort him, but I knew I must be faithful. It's no use glossing things over, pretending things are all right when we know they are wrong.

'We ought not to tell lies,' I said slowly and reluctantly.

'But if he didn't tell lies he'd never get out of the position,' volunteered someone. So what was there to do? The lies had been told, there was no way back, and poor Mr. Fan, burdened with a sense of guilt, still stood looking silently at me. I knew of only one way for him.

'The Bible tells us in 1 John, chapter 1 that if we confess our sins, God who is faithful and just will forgive us our sins, and cleanse us from all unrighteousness,' I said. So that is what we did together—claiming the promise. I never heard the matter referred to again. The forgiveness of God towards the penitent sinner is inherent in the Good News which we go to proclaim.

Many efforts were made to induce Mr. Fan to lead Sunday services but they all failed. On a few occasions he was persuaded to lead the prayer meeting that preceded it but, as this usually consisted of announcing a couple of hymns, reading a passage of Scripture and then inviting others to pray, it did not call for any powers of oratory. Surprisingly, however, he was always ready to take his stand at open air meetings, leading the singing, inviting passers-by to come and listen to the doctrine, handing out tracts—all without any trace of the embarrassment he felt when occasionally standing on the platform in church. On one memorable occasion, when there was an unexpected breakdown in the preaching, he surprised and delighted us all by stepping into the breach and speaking for about twenty minutes in a most convincing manner, presenting his arguments as though they had been well thought out and prepared beforehand. Such an excellent beginning promised well for the future; but Mr. Fan retired once more into his shell, declared that he could not do it again and refused to have his name put down on the list of speakers.

Deacon Liong, Deacon Hsaio, Deacon Fan—they are not the only ones who have come to life again as I've read through that little book I wrote nearly fifty years ago. But I'll have to leave out most of the others to make room for Mrs. Han, the Bible-woman. She was our nearest neighbour, whom we saw every day and who became my closest fellow-worker.

I met her first at Shenkiu, where she had come on a visit shortly after the funeral of her husband, whom she had nursed through a long illness. I remember—at a prayer meeting—being surprised, almost shocked, at her cheerful, composed manner and at the fact that she thanked God for relieving her of her heavy burden. It seemed to me that even if she were glad to be rid of an ailing husband, it would have been more seemly to keep quiet about it! However, I learned later that she had been devoted to him, and that what she'd referred to had not been the lifting of the burden of service, but the lifting of the burden of grieving widow-hood. She had discovered the reality of the verse in Isaiah that speaks of the One who bears our griefs and carries our sorrows. The crushing weight of sorrow had been lifted and she could face life standing upright.

Her husband had been employed as gate-keeper evangelist on the mission compound in Siangcheng and, as it was arranged that she should remain there as before and that her old father-in-law could 'watch the gate', no great change in her life was necessary. Like Phoebe of old, she was the servant of the church. A capable and diligent woman, she willingly undertook the mundane tasks of the church compound, putting aside her own affairs without hesitation to welcome guests who arrived unexpectedly, heating water for them to wash their faces, pouring tea, producing the wadded quilts which she kept well mended and clean so that they might sleep in comfort. On Sunday mornings her sitting room was filled with chattering women who came to see her before the service started. Often enough one or two of the poor or lonely ones came back afterwards at her invitation to help her prepare the midday meal—and, of course, remain on to help her and her schoolgirl daughter to eat it. Her good deeds were performed with such graciousness that they never seemed like merit-gaining charity.

She was a cheerful person, not given to reflective thought or introspection, and her faith was of such childlike quality that I sometimes felt it was almost immature. This was especially so in the case of her encouragement to the women in prison to pray that God would get them out. She and I used to go every Monday morning to visit them, complete with Gospel posters for me to preach from and tracts for those who could read. On the face of it, the women's prison was not too bad a place. It looked just like the inner courtyard of any Chinese home, and the prisoners were free to wander in and out of the rooms and talk to each other or sit out in the sunshine mending clothes or spinning cotton, while the elderly wardress, looking just like one of them, mixed with them in quite a friendly way. Altogether, the atmosphere was quite different from the dark prison in Shanghai where, although living conditions were less primitive, the prisoners were isolated from each other behind bars, and cut off from the fresh air, the sun, and the singing of birds.

So much for the outward appearance of things. There was one thing the women had not got that they all longed for—freedom. After I had preached, Mrs. Han chatted with them, and it soon became evident that there was just one thing they wanted God to do for them: 'If we pray to Him, will He get us out of this place?'

'Yes,' said Mrs. Han firmly. 'You pray to our Heavenly Father, and He will get you out of this place.'

I felt very uneasy about this. It seemed to me to be too tall an order to expect God to release them, since, after all, they were in prison because they had broken some law or other. One woman, we were told, was a murderess. I tried to explain the necessity for all of us to repent and to put our faith in Jesus Christ who had died on the cross for our sins; to assure them that the real result of doing this would not necessarily be early release from prison but peace of heart; to stress that we must be prepared to place ourselves in God's hands, and trust Him to do what is best for us, though it might not be just what we would choose for ourselves; and that the important thing was to be sure of our eternal destination . . . and so on. On the way home I broached the subject again, and Mrs. Han agreed with everything I said. But the next time we went to the prison and the women told her they were praying that God would get them out of that place, she by-passed all the theology I had tried to instil and assured them that God was able to get them all out of that place and that He would do so if they really prayed to Him.

And He did. The whole lot of them.

This is what happened. There was another rumour that the Japanese were going to raid Siangcheng again. There was the usual evacuation from the city of the able-bodied and well-to-do. We two missionaries got on our bicycles and went to Shenkiu, where we remained until news came that the Japanese, having entered Siangcheng, and stayed there for thirty-six hours, had retreated, so it was safe for us to return.

On the Monday morning after we were settled in again I went through the gate from our compound into Mrs. Han's, and said, 'We'd better go and visit the workhouse and prison again, hadn't we?' To which she replied that it wouldn't be any use going to the prison, as there was no-one there.

'No-one there! But there were about sixteen of them. There must be some of them there.'

'No, Teacher, there's no-one there. You see, it's like this. When the prison authorities knew the Japanese were coming, they all wanted to get away as quickly as possible, but they couldn't take the prisoners with them and they couldn't leave them behind either. So they just released them all, and told them to go home. There are none of them left in that place now. They've all gone.'

I was silent for a moment, letting the news sink in. Then I said slowly, 'So God answered their prayers. He got them out of that place . . .'

'Yes,' said Mrs. Han with a calm smile. 'God answered their prayers.'

As I walked slowly back through the gate into our compound, I wondered if the real reason behind the short and apparently purposeless invasion of the Japanese into Siangcheng on that occasion was simply that God had heard the cry and answered the prayers of a group of heathen women who believed what Mrs. Han told them about Him.

It was not the only time when prayer was answered in a dramatic and utterly unexpected way during my time in Siangcheng. On one occasion the answer came in a violent storm. I'll tell you how it came about.

We had a neighbour who was a good friend to us. Dr. Wang was a well educated woman from Manchuria, and a qualified doctor, who seemed to feel a special responsibility for us two missionaries and would hurry round to see us if she heard we were ill and make sure that we had money in hand when she suspected funds were low. She did not come to church very regularly. Perhaps the contrast between our informal meetings in the rough-and-ready atmosphere of the barn, and the digni-fied church services to which she had been ac-customed brought home to her too acutely the change in her circumstances since fleeing from her home in the north. But there was no doubt about her faith in Jesus Christ, and her allegiance to Him. Although she did not consider herself a teacher, and made no attempt to preach to her patients, she politely suggested they should go along to the Gospel Hall and hear the Christian doctrine, since, she assured them, 'It's good to believe in Jesus.'

One day she came through to our compound, pulled aside the bamboo screen which we hung in front of the door to keep out the flies, and greeted me rather urgently. Waving aside the customary invitation to sit and drink tea, she said, 'I haven't come on a social visit, Teacher Dong. I've come because we must pray. There is plague in the city.'

'Plague!'

'Yes. It has only just started, and I don't want to spread the news and cause a panic. But I've seen two patients already, and I recognised that it was plague. They died within hours. We can't do anything to stop it spreading, and if it does spread hundreds of people will die'. Then she added deliberately, 'Only God can stop it.' That was why she had come: to pray. So we knelt together in the little guest room, and prayed that God would stop the plague. Then she rose to her feet, explained that she must go off immediately to see a patient and, in quite a matter of fact way, took her departure.

Two or three nights later, I was awakened by the sounds of rushing wind and a pitiless downpour of rain, followed by the crashing of tree branches and the crumbling of masonry. Our rooms were built

strongly enough to resist the storm and I had no
cause for personal alarm but, as I lay in bed and
listened, I knew I was hearing the whipping off of
thatched roofs and the collapse of buildings made
with mud bricks. It was the worst storm I had ever
experienced, and I remember thinking, 'Oh, these
poor people! First, the plague, and now their
homes being flooded!' I wondered what news
would be brought in from the street to Mrs. Han
the next morning, but nothing disastrous seemed
to have occurred to anyone we knew. And, rather
to my surprise, as the days went by there was no
mention of plague.

Then one day, as I was in the street, going to visit
someone, I saw Dr. Wang. She was being wheeled
along on a wheelbarrow—the usual method of con-
veyance in our part of China. She was on her way
to see a patient in the country but when she saw me
she politely alighted to greet me.

'Dr. Wang!' I exclaimed. 'I've been wanting to
see you.' I remembered the urgency of our last
meeting and asked eagerly, 'What has happened
about the plague? Is it spreading?'

'Oh, that's all over,' she replied. 'That storm blew
it away.'

'The storm blew it away?' I must have looked as
incredulous as I felt, for I was really taken aback.
Dr. Wang was no superstitious peasant, yet here
she was talking about a storm blowing away the
plague! 'How could a storm blow it away?' Then
she went into an explanation about rat fleas, and
the breeding places of germs, and the wind and
rain blowing them away. Not understanding, I just
said 'Oh!' and left it at that. But there were no

more cases of plague in the city. Years later, when I told the story to a missionary doctor, he confirmed the explanation that Dr. Wang had given.

'Yes, it's scientifically correct,' he said. 'The germs would be carried by rat fleas, but a fierce storm like the one you describe would disperse their breeding places, and that would be the end of it.'

None of the people of Siangcheng knew what that storm had saved them from. Very few even knew that those two or three people who had died so suddenly had been struck by plague. I've sometimes thought that perhaps the sudden storms which sweep over our lives are breaking up secret breeding places of evil which we scarcely realise exist, and saving us from far greater disasters.

17

Dear Edward,

I mentioned in an earlier letter that before she left Siangcheng Irene Steele formed a Women's Preaching Band; and as one of the most memorable incidents in my time in China occurred when I was out with them, I'd better introduce the members of the band now. Here they are:

Mrs. Hsiao, Deacon Hsiao's wife—happy-go-lucky, rather unreliable, but very lovable, sympathetic and human. I had a specially soft spot in my heart for her, even though she was apt to fluctuate spiritually: sometimes being whole-hearted and keen; at other times, slack and indifferent. She was more gifted than any of the other women: quick to grasp a point, intelligent, and with an indefinable quality that made people confide in her. She was a most valuable member of the Preaching Band, for she spoke clearly and with an unexpected conviction which solemnised her listeners to an unusual degree. And her easy-going disposition enabled her to get on with the other members of the Band—even Li *Tai-tai*, who was socially a cut above the other women, having been the wife of an important official, which is why she was a *Tai-tai*.

Li *Tai-tai*, to be frank, was one of the church's problems. Not that there was anything wrong in her manner of life, for she had long since left behind all questionable practices. She neither smoked nor gambled, was honest in her dealings, had separated from idolatrous superstitions, and was a comparatively strict Sabbatarian. But she was touchy. Mrs. Han and Mrs. Hsaio, who tried to cover up for her, apologetically explained that she had what they termed 'a little bit of a temperament'. They spoke about it as though it were a snappy little dog that lived with her—sometimes safely asleep but liable to wake up at any time and bite whoever happened to be around.

'Li *Tai-tai* has a little bit of a temperament' they would say, 'She doesn't mean anything.' And usually she didn't mean anything, as the people in the Street of the Oilhouse, where she lived, had come to find out.

'Her heart's all right,' they agreed after she had gone to a lot of trouble to help one and another who was ill or in distress. And as she was a lover of law and order, heartily supporting any efforts that were made to correct the rather haphazard form of worship and procedure that prevailed in the church, the deacons viewed her with respect. Her powers of endurance were remarkable. Often, when out with the Preaching Band, she would suffer from a racking cough that kept her awake for hours but she never allowed it to prevent her from putting in a full day of preaching, walking from village to village sometimes in bitterly cold weather.

The third regular member of the Band was the

diminutive Widow Wang. She had lost her husband very early in life but by dint of thrift and hard work had managed to provide her only son with sufficient education for him to earn his living as a clerk in a store rather than a farm labourer. She had taught herself to read, too, and was quick to help any other woman or girl to do so. (Teaching illiterate women to read their catechisms and New Testaments was recognised as being of primary importance to the church at Siangcheng.) When out with the Preaching Band, she could always be relied on to chat to inquisitive people who wandered round to see what was going on, besides doing most of the practical work of carrying water, lighting the fire, preparing and cooking the food. However, when it came to the actual preaching, she was distinctly unconvincing, for in the middle of her exhortations she was liable to break into a self-conscious giggle as she realised she was the centre of interest then take fright and disappear as fast as her sturdy little legs would carry her.

Although from time to time others were invited to join the Band, these were the three permanent members, appointed by the elders and deacons to go with the missionary once or twice a year to one of the outstations, and preach in the nearby villages. We usually divided up two and two, with one of the outstation Christians to accompany us, and off we would go, armed with a roll of pictorial posters and a handful of tracts, on our evangelistic forays.

On the whole, we met with quite a friendly reception. People might be indifferent to our message but they found us entertaining, especially me: the first Western woman most of them had ever seen. It would take some time to satisfy their curiosity as to how old I was, what food I ate, my marital status and how much I had paid for the cloth of my gown; but when the questions had all been answered, my companions would explain that I had come to exhort them to follow The Way, which was the signal for me to unroll the pictorial poster (The Two Way Poster was the one I used most often) and start to preach.

I remember standing on a little hillock with a group of peasants silently looking and listening as I pointed to the figures in the picture who were going down, down the mountainside to the edge of a cliff, from which they fell into a lake of fire.

'A picture of mortal life, with death at the end of it', I explained, and then went on to proclaim the news I had come to give.

'But the True God did not want people to perish like that. He wanted to save them. So He sent His only Son into the world. Think of it! The True God had one Son, and He sent Him into this world to save us. He was born as a baby, like us, and He was given a name—Jesus. Jesus was like us in everything except that He never did anything wrong. He grew up, and did good to people: He made blind people see, deaf people hear, sick people well. He only did good. He healed many people but He did not want money for healing them. He healed them because He loved them.

'But His enemies hated Him. They wanted to kill Him. They made a cross of wood. Then they took nails, and nailed His hands to the cross.' As I held out my hands, first one and then the other, I saw some of the women wince, then screw up their faces at the thought of the pain caused by those nails being driven in; and I realised they were hearing of the crucifixion for the first time.

We have heard it so often that we have become inured to it, alas, but the physical sufferings of Christ really touched those Chinese country women; and when I spoke of His death, then His burial, there was a sorrowful hush. Death and burial—they had seen it so often, those old women with their lined, patient faces. They knew the emptiness, the hopeless end of those they had known and loved. I paused for a moment, for I seemed to savour it with them, but then a feeling of exultation rose in me.

'But that wasn't the end!' I cried. 'After three days He rose again. He came out of the tomb. He was alive!' I saw the amazement on their faces and continued, 'And He is alive today. He went up into Heaven and He's there now. You can't see Him but He can see you. You can't hear Him but He can hear you. If you pray to Him, He will hear you. If you believe in Him, He will forgive your sins, and take you to be with Him in Heaven.'

Well, that gives you an idea of how we set about condensing into an unannounced fifteen minute talk the basic facts of the Gospel for those who had never heard it before—and might never hear it again. Visits to homes would follow, when there would be fleeting opportunities to enlarge on the message we had come to deliver, then on to the next village. When we got back to our base, there would be a meeting after the evening meal for people living on the spot. Then at last, when all the stragglers had departed, we could spread out our bedding, take off our outer garments, and thankfully lie down and fall asleep.

On the occasion of which I write, we had got to that point after a very tiring day. Our base was the little mud-brick Gospel hall itself, which had been built in a field not far from the village, so it was all very quiet and peaceful. I had sunk into that deep, delicious sleep that follows extreme weariness when the sound of knocking on the door, and a man's voice demanding matches reached down to my consciousness.

Matches? It was midnight, the door was shut, we were in a field, not even in the village: who would be waking people up to ask for matches at such a time and in such a place?

'Have you got any matches in there?' the voice demanded, reiterating the question. By this time I was sufficiently awake to be very annoyed at having been disturbed. I shouted, 'Go away!'

'Have you got any matches in there?'

'Yes we have, but we're not giving any to you! Go away!'

'I want some matches! Open the door!'

Open the door and let someone in to get some matches? At midnight! Not likely!

'What sort of a person are you, coming at midnight to a place where there are only women, asking for matches?' I retorted indignantly. 'No, we won't open the door. Go away!'

'If you don't open the door, I'll throw it in,' said the man. And he did just that. The roughly made wooden doors fitted into sockets, and it required only a strong hand and arm to lift them out. There was a clatter and a thud, and the double-leaved door lay on the ground to reveal a tall man with a gun in one hand and a powerful torch in the other.

'Where's that man?' he demanded, shining his torch round until the light came to me, glowering at him over my quilt. He had thought it must be a man, talking to him like that. And I still went on talking: 'What sort of behaviour is this? No decent person would come in the middle of the night to a place where women were sleeping!'

By this time he was walking round the room, pocketing any oddments he noticed lying around— torches, hand towels, cash. Having made the round, he walked out.

'Oh good, he's gone,' I said. 'Can you put that door back in its sockets?' I knew the women were accustomed to that type of door. 'Then we can go back to sleep.' It was the one thing for which I craved. Sleep! Then I saw that my companions, unlike me, were all up and fully dressed. Even as I spoke, Mrs. Hsaio slipped across the room and hissed, 'Teacher! Teacher! Get up! Get up! He's coming back, and there are others outside!'

Reluctantly I slipped out from under my wadded quilt and reached for my outer gown, still so sustained by my irritation that I had no fear. Besides, I had remembered something.

The angels at Taikang!

If I had had no need to fear the well-trained, ruthless Japanese soldiers, why should I be afraid of a mere Chinese bandit? I felt quite defiant and, when he returned and started going round the room again, picking things up, I was all ready to start arguing with him again. Then, quite suddenly, God spoke to me.

And He spoke to me in Chinese.

I don't mean that I heard a voice, for I didn't.
But as I stood by my camp bed, buttoning my gown
and glaring indignantly at the man, my mind was
suddenly and powerfully flooded with a sentence
from the Sermon on the Mount. The words were in
Chinese, but I understood them, for I had read
them many times in my Chinese Bible.

'Do not resist an evil person.' They came with
such overwhelming authority that I knew without
the shadow of a doubt that God was speaking to
me, and that I had no option but to obey. With a
very bad grace I did so, standing in sulky silence as
the man swept my money off the table into his
pocket, looked round to see if there was anything
else worth taking, and departed.

We departed, too, after being sure the bandits
had really gone, and spent the rest of the night in
the security of the village, lying in a row on a heap
of straw in a barn. It was all very ignominious, quite
the reverse of the quiet triumph of the experience
in Taikang. It taught me that God does not always
deal with us in the same way.

Not very long afterwards it was brought home to
me how near I had been to death that night. A
young Swedish woman and her two-year-old child,
passing through Siangcheng, came to our compound for a brief rest. While eating the meal we
hastily provided, she told us her story. She had
been travelling with her husband in an area not so
very far away and at midnight bandits had come to
the inn where they were staying. The young husband had gone to confront them and, without hesi-

tation, they had shot him dead.

I realised then that but for that sudden authoritative command—'Do not resist an evil person'—the same thing could have happened to me.

18

Dear Edward,

As a fellow missionary once sagely reminded me, life is a pilgrimage—inward as well as outward. Especially inward. When I look back over those years in Siangcheng, there are two or three brief inner experiences that stand out vividly, while the days, weeks, even months of outward activity have faded from the memory. However, it was the days, weeks, months of outward activity that brought me to one of the spiritual crises of which I will write now.

I was jaded, dull, bored. Indeed, it was worse than boredom; it was fast becoming a depression from which I saw no way out. I felt hemmed in— there in the narrow compound with the ceaseless round of little meetings, of visits to women in small courtyards, of hours spent trying to teach some of them to read, and the lack of any mental or emotional stimulation.

If I had been back in England it would have been different. I could have refreshed myself by going for a walk, visiting a friend for a chat, listening to some music or reading a new book, perhaps, or even spending a few days by the sea or in the hills.

166

But in Siangcheng there were no such outlets. Where could I go for a walk in the narrow streets or even along the paths through the wheatfields, without meeting people who stared at me or expected me to stop and talk and answer the inevitable question, 'Where are you going, Teacher?'

In any case, where was there to walk to? Once outside the walls of the city, the flat wheatfields spread for as far as the eye could see, without even a little hill to relieve the monotony of the landscape. In times of peace, missionaries on the plain had gone for a yearly holiday to a hill station in the south of the province but the war had made that impossible. The hill station was beyond the Japanese lines and inaccessible.

One way and another, I felt as flat as the landscape. We had very few books (we had had to leave our small libraries behind when we left Hwaiyang), and no music. The narrow streets and the dark houses were devoid of beauty and there were no gardens. The only flowers we saw were those that Irene—and later Doris—managed to grow in our small back compound, and our only contact with the outside world was through the few letters that reached us. We have no idea how much these things contribute to our enjoyment of life until we are deprived of them. There was a vacuum in my mind when I was weary, and there seemed no way to fill it. There were times when my memory took me back to what years ago had been the place of my chief enjoyment—the dance hall. The shaded lights, the orchestra striking up, the couples gliding together on to the polished surface of the floor, the music, the gaiety of the foxtrot or the sensuous languor of the waltz ... I pulled myself up from lapsing into a desire for that atmosphere of merriment and light-heartedness and turned sternly to the duties of the day.

But I was inwardly dry. I maintained my habits of Bible reading and prayer morning and evening, alone and also with Doris, but I needed something more. I felt parched.

One day the barrenness of my own soul became intolerable. I knew I could not go on like this and, having half an hour to spare, I went to my bedroom, threw myself on my knees, and cried desperately, 'Lord! Lord Jesus! You said, "If any man thirst, let him come unto Me and drink." Lord, I'm taking You at Your word. I'm thirsty! And I've come! I'm parched and I want to drink.'

I waited expectantly, but nothing happened, so I cried again, with the same lack of result. I knew that only as I remained deliberately and consciously in the Lord's presence could I expect the answer I longed for, but to remain there silent, trying to concentrate on God, was beyond me. My mind would wander, I knew. I must find a way to occupy it, and decided to pray for other people. Perhaps that was what I ought to be doing, anyway. I had a list of names and addresses of friends at home, so I got it out and went down the list, praying one by one for them, for about half an hour. Then I rose from my knees, went out into the courtyard and got on with whatever it was I had to do. There was no time now to think of myself. Other matters claimed my attention; and it was not until two or three hours later that it dawned on me that I wasn't feeling bored or depressed any more.

Nothing noticeable had happened, there had been no upsurge of joy, but the dryness was gone. I was just quietly contented, back to normal, satisfied to be in the place where God had put me, doing what I believed He wanted me to do. It was as though, silently and imperceptibly, the waters had risen and the stream was flowing again.

That experience marked a new phase in my life, and illuminated for me a sentence which I came across at about the same time in the book of Job. As usual, I was reading in the Authorised Version, and in verse ten of the last chapter I saw the words, 'And the Lord turned the captivity of Job, when he prayed for his friends . . .'

I wasn't focusing on the tribulations of Job, or the resentment he might have felt towards the friends who had misjudged him; a resentment imprisoning his mind. My circumstances were quite different; none of my friends appeared to be misjudging me. But I knew what it was to have a mind in captivity to an unsatisfied desire, to the boredom of monotony, to discontent with my lot. And I knew I had been released from that captivity after I had spent time with the Lord, praying for my friends.

From that time on, I knew what to do when I found dryness and depression beginning to enfold me. Praying for others always had a liberating effect on me. It was the method I employed because I had found it worked. But it merely illustrates what those who believe have discovered for themselves down through the centuries: that 'a little talk with Jesus makes it right, all right.'

The negro slaves who sang, 'Steal away, steal

away, steal away to Jesus,' had reached the heart of the matter, too. And I remember an old Chinese woman living in the Siangcheng workhouse, to whom we had spoken of the Heavenly Lord who opens His arms and says 'Come', telling me rather shyly one day how she had done that.

'I felt I wanted to pray,' she said. 'So when everyone else was out in the courtyard, I went into the room alone and sat down and said, "I've come." But I don't know how to pray, and I didn't know what to say, so I said, "I've come because I want to have a little chat with you." That was all—I didn't know what else to say. But then—my heart became so peaceful.'

'My heart became so peaceful.' That's just how it was with me.

That verse about the captivity of Job always carries me back to that narrow compound in Siangcheng; so, even more poignantly, does a verse in the book of Jeremiah. It came to me one terrible night, after Mrs. Yen had been tortured by guerillas and faced the prospect of more to come if she did not give her youngest daughter to one of their officers as his second wife. And it had all come about because she had acted on my advice. But as that is rather a long story, I will leave it until I write my next letter.

19

Dear Edward,

The appellation 'terrorist' is frequently heard these days. Kidnappings, people being held as hostages, prisoners being tortured—these horrors appear time and time again in the media, reminding us of the perilous days in which civilisation finds itself. The story I am going to relate for you now is one of terrorism. Mrs. Yen was the victim but I, too, was involved, for if she had not acted on my advice she would have avoided it all, as I realised on that terrible night after she had been tortured.

Mrs. Yen was married to a baker and lived in the north suburb of Siangcheng, sharing a courtyard with one or two other little households whom she bossed as firmly and benevolently as she did her own family. She had been a church member for quite twenty years, and was referred to on odd occasions as 'deaconess'—a title which always embarrassed her, for neither she nor anyone else seemed to know how she got it. For years she had been in possession of a catechism which she always brought to church rolled up in a blue towel kept specially for that purpose; but—not being

171

academically minded—she had never learnt to read it and tended to shy off when I offered to teach her. She made it clear that she wished I wouldn't harp on the value of reading the Bible for oneself, which obviously wasn't possible unless one had learnt to read, and tended to avoid me. Had it not been for the little matter of the four dollars, I doubt whether the gulf between us would have been bridged. It was just this little matter that first brought us together.

I learned about the four dollars quite accidentally after a Sunday morning service, when I found Mrs. Yen preparing the noodles she had bought to give a meal to the poor. Four dollars' worth of noodles, she told me and, knowing her own circumstances, I was touched at her generosity.

'That's very good of you, Mrs. Yen,' I ejaculated.

'Oh, I didn't want the money,' said Mrs. Yen. 'What would I want with the four dollars? I said to myself, "I'll give them to the Lord, then it'll be all right." That's why I bought the noodles to give to those poor people. I said to myself, "I don't want those four dollars."'

'What four dollars?' I asked mystified.

Then it all came out. With many embellishments and observations she told me the story of what had occurred a few days before, and this is the gist of it.

Her husband had gone off to deliver orders for steamed breads, her son was in the city hawking fried dough-strings, and she was sitting, as usual, under the awning of rush mats outside the open door of the house—a basket of bread and a cardboard box containing a few coppers and grubby ten cent notes beside her. It was a hot afternoon, there were no customers and she had dropped off to sleep. When she woke up and looked at the cardboard box, there she saw a roll of dollar bills. Four of them! All along with the other change. They seemed to have dropped from heaven, right into her box. Her daughter-in-law had been reminding her that they were nearly out of oil and that Hsiang needed a new jacket. And now, there were those four dollars! Mrs. Yen looked up and down the road, saw no-one, tucked the notes inside her jacket and sat back, fanning herself.

Shortly afterwards she was conscious of a stir in the distance. A man was hurrying along, obviously disturbed, and when he saw her he stopped and asked, 'Mrs. Yen, have you seen four dollars? I've lost four dollars. I had them with me when I came along here about half an hour ago, but I've got a bit of trouble just now, and I must have put them down somewhere without thinking. When I got home the four dollars were gone.'

Mrs. Yen frowned at him.

'How should I know what you've done with your four dollars?' she asked crossly. 'I've been asleep and can't remember a thing. I didn't even see you pass. How should I know what you've done with your four dollars?' He nodded and off he went.

Off went Mrs. Yen's peace of mind, too.

'I couldn't help the four dollars getting into my box, could I?' she said, looking at me anxiously. 'I've never stolen anything since I repented and believed in the Lord. Everybody knows that. And as for Mr. Li, he's a stupid man. How am I to know whether the four dollars are his, anyway? If I can't keep what's in my own money box . . .'

With many involved explanations she told the story: the thoughtless acceptance of what was not hers; the sudden temptation to retain it; then the arguments of self-justification that failed to bring peace of mind.

'So I decided to give the money to the Lord,' she concluded, looking at me rather like a child waiting for the reassurance that that would make everything all right. I felt so sorry for her.

'But Mrs. Yen,' I said reluctantly. 'The Lord doesn't want that sort of money.'

She showed no surprise or even disappointment, but said lugubriously, 'I was afraid He didn't. But what am I to do?'

'It seems to me the only thing to do is to give the money back to the person it belongs to.'

'But what shall I say? It's such a loss of face!' I knew that, and wondered how I would have acted in similar circumstances. But I had no suggestion to make but the obvious one: 'I don't see what you can do but just tell him the truth.'

So that, more or less, is what she did, and it all worked out very well, for Mr. Li was so pleased to see his money again that he congratulated her on her honesty and said she was a credit to the doctrines preached at the Gospel Hall.

That little incident formed a bond between Mrs. Yen and me and although, wisely, she did not consult me on practical matters, it was a different thing when it came to moral or spiritual issues. So when her neighbour's granddaughter was in danger of being taken by a guerilla officer to become his second wife, and she saw a way of saving her, Mrs. Yen came to ask my advice.

'Pao Chen is the same age as my Dzan,' she told me. 'She's always lived in our courtyard with her grandmother, and she's like a daughter to me. But she's got a father, and he keeps an inn in the country, and it was while Pao Chen was staying with him that this guerilla officer saw her. He's taken a fancy to her. He's got a wife already—they both smoke opium.' She lowered her voice and continued, 'They're a bad lot of men, these guerillas.' I knew that a large contingent of them had come into our part of Henan. Ostensibly they were fighting for their country, harassing the enemy, but in reality they were skirmishing about in the No-Man's-Land between the Chinese Nationalist's garrisons and the Japanese, extorting money from wealthy landlords, holding people for ransom, abducting village girls. Everyone was in fear of them. Mrs. Yen knew it but she continued, 'I've nearly got Pao Chen engaged to a young man who lives near us.' Mrs Yen was an experienced middle-man in matrimonial matters. She said, 'If it goes through I could save her. But this officer, Captain Fong ... My family's afraid of what he would do, and told me to keep out of it. If the guerillas get up against me ... What ought I to do, Teacher?'

My reaction was prompt and decisive: 'Don't touch it, Mrs. Yen. You don't want to get up against the guerillas! Keep out!' The words were in my mind, ready to spring to my lips, but they were never uttered, for something happened. I don't know how to describe it except that I suddenly became aware of being silenced by a power greater than my own as the thought of Pao Chen, whom I had never even seen, came to my mind. This unknown girl was not only in danger of being forced into a life of grief and shame but also into a life that would ruin her morally. To leave her in the hands of that opium-smoking guerilla officer was equivalent to handing her, body and soul, to destruction. Here in this little room her fate, as it were, was to be decided.

'What shall I do, Teacher?' Mrs. Yen was asking. And I knew that one day I would have to give account to God for the answer I gave to this woman.

'Mrs. Yen,' I said, leaning forward. 'You've got to save that girl.'

So that is what she tried to do. Mrs. Yen succeeded in completing the arrangements for Pao Chen to be betrothed to the young man, then helped to smuggle her, with her grandmother and the young man as escort, away from the city. The young man's parents took fright after that, and fled, too, but Mrs. Yen could not flee. How could she leave her home, her husband, her son and his family and her unmarried daughter to their fate in order to save herself?

The net was tightening. The guerillas, confident of their strength, moved into the city, making their headquarters in a large courtyard right opposite the police station. No-one dared oppose them. There were rumours of what was happening to a lad they had kidnapped, whose ransom had not been paid: 'His leg's broken . . . they're a bad lot of men.' The whispers went round, then silence fell. I did not really know much of what was going on, so when, one day, a frightened white-faced girl came hurrying on to the compound and told me the guerillas had arrested Mrs. Yen, tied her hands together and marched her up to their headquarters, I was furious.

How dared they treat poor, honest old Mrs. Yen as though she were a criminal, and imprison her in a courtyard that was not even the acknowledged place for dealing with civic offences! Where was the justice in such an act? In a white heat of righteous indignation, and without stopping to think what I would do when I got there, I stalked along the street and down to the guerilla headquarters with Mrs. Han (courageous woman) by my side. We were admitted by the soldier on duty without a word. As a Westerner and the national of an allied nation I had 'face'—and I daresay that on this occasion I looked as though I was prepared to use it. We were directed into the very room where Mrs. Yen was standing, hands tied behind her back. A young soldier was lounging against the wall.

He looked thoroughly scared when I demanded to know how he *dared* treat this old lady in such a fashion. He wasn't in charge of the affair, he told us. Kong *Tai-tai*,* wife of the senior officer, was in charge. Still carried along on the wave of my indignation, I demanded to see Kong *Tai-tai*. She turned out to be a girl in her early twenties, sitting beside a charcoal fire in a bowl in the middle of a large room with a couple of beds in it. She rose with a polite smile when she saw me.

'You've come, Teacher?' she said. 'Please sit

*A respectful title for a married lady.

down.' Stools were brought for Mrs. Han and me
to join her by the fire and, as we exchanged the
usual polite preliminaries of conversation, my
indignation oozed away, and I realised that there
was nothing at all that I could do. I had no authority and no power. As I sat there, waiting for an
opportunity to plead Mrs. Yen's case, all I could do
was to pray silently, as I knew Mrs. Han was doing
too. I won't go into details as to what turns the
conversation took except to say that when I said,
'Kong *Tai-tai*, have *you* got a mother?' quite suddenly her attitude changed. She was silent for a few
seconds, then told one of the soldiers standing in
attendance to go and unloose Mrs. Yen and bring
her in to sit with us. And when I asked that Mrs.
Yen be allowed to come back with me to spend the
night in the Gospel Hall, she agreed, on condition
that she returned next morning.

Next day Captain Fong arrived—a tall, dark-
eyed ruthless-looking man. Mrs. Yen was sent for
and Mrs. Han and I went with her. I listened for a
long time as he and Kong *Tai-tai* discussed Mrs.
Yen's affairs, making a show of trying to find out
just where the culprit's fault lay and explaining that
as a foreigner I really did not understand Chinese
customs. Captain Fong said that Mrs. Yen had
interfered in other people's business and had
forced the engagement of Pao Chen against her
father's wishes and that now the girl had disappeared and she was responsible. She must find
the girl and return her to her father. If she failed
to do that, she would be punished. What punishment she would suffer was not specified and no
one enquired.

The atmosphere was sinister. There was a young man in the room whom I had seen the night before and whom Mrs. Yen evidently knew. He was sitting on the edge of one of the big beds, apparently quite free to come and go, but two or three soldiers were between him and the door, and his eyes had the sharp, wild look of a trapped animal. Every now and then he surreptitiously rubbed his wrists. I did not grasp the significance of what I saw then—it was only later I learned from Mrs. Yen that he had been kidnapped the previous evening, strung up by his wrists, and only lowered on the promise of a large sum of money.

It was not so easy to get permission for Mrs. Yen to spend the night again at the Gospel Hall. Captain Fong was evidently unwilling to let her go and it was not until Kong *Tai-tai* had gone and spoken to him hurriedly in a low tone that he gave a grudging consent. But Mrs. Yen must not leave the Gospel Hall and must return as soon as she was sent for next morning. The next morning, she was sent for early; Mrs. Han and I went with her but we were not allowed to remain.

Captain Fong was quite polite to me. He said he was afraid he was delaying me from my affairs at home. When I said no, I was in no hurry, he observed that he himself was rather busy that day. I'd been in China long enough to realise that etiquette was being stretched but I still sat on, with an absent-minded expression on my face. Then I remembered that my sole purpose in coming to China had been to warn men everywhere to repent and believe the Gospel, and that my responsibility to this guerilla officer was not the less because the occasion did not seem very propitious for making known the truths of God's judgment and also His mercy. To do Captain Fong credit, he listened with more interest and courtesy than might have been expected. Yes, he said, he had heard some of this before. What I said was quite right. Then, after a brief silence, he spoke again, very politely and very distinctly, 'Teacher, please go now. I want to interrogate Mrs. Yen.'

I did not fully realise the significance of the word 'interrogate' then; even if I had, I doubt whether I would have acted any differently. I was afraid that if I ignored again that deliberate, repeated request to leave, I should lose what little influence I had. What if I were ordered off the compound and refused re-admission, leaving Mrs. Yen without even the prospect of the little help I could give?

'All right, I'll go,' I said, rising to my feet. 'I'll be back this afternoon Mrs. Yen.' So Mrs. Han and I withdrew, and desperately I sought for a way to deliver Mrs. Yen. Should I go to the *Yamen*?[1] Useless, I was told. The *Hsien-chang*[2] there couldn't do a thing to control the guerillas. The police? Why, they knew pretty well everything that was going on—they were right opposite—but they dared not stir a finger. Eventually I went to see Deacon Liong, thinking he might have some advice for me. We sat in the dark little room at the back of his shop, and in his impassive way he outlined the situation.

'There is one thing you could do,' he said. 'You

---

1. Chinese mandarin's official residence.
2. Head official in the *Yamen*.

could go to the officer in the Nationalist garrison in Shenkiu, and because you have 'face', as a Westerner, he would have to do something. The guerillas would have to obey him, and Mrs. Yen would be freed.' He paused for a minute, then went on to present the other side of the picture.

'But when it was all over, in a few months' time, the guerillas would come back and take their revenge on Mrs. Yen . . .' We looked at each other silently for a few moments, then I rose to leave. There was no need to say any more. The thought of those reprisals was sufficient. There was nothing I could do.

'We will pray for Mrs. Yen,' he said quietly as we parted, and I knew he would do so.

When I got back to our compound I was told that a man had arrived with the news that Mrs. Yen was being tortured, but if I would pay the sum of 200 dollars it would be stopped. There was no question in my mind as to what my reply should be. I knew that if missionaries started paying out ransom money for church members, there was no knowing who would be kidnapped next or what it would lead to.

'No,' I said firmly. But the thought of Mrs. Yen being tortured was unendurable, so Mrs. Han and I again went to the guerilla headquarters.

Amazingly we were admitted, and taken to the very room where Mrs. Yen was sitting limply on a chair. One look at her told us she had been beaten, for her face had bruises, her cheekbone was grazed and her eyes were dark with pain. In a few brief sentences she told us what happened. The interrogation had not lasted long. Where was Pao

Chen? She did not know. The girl had gone off with her grandmother, she did not know where.

Then she must find her! How could she find her? She would not know where to begin.

Then Captain Fong had ordered that her wrists should be tied together, the rope thrown over a beam in the ceiling, then pulled.

So there she had hung, her toes dangling half an inch from the ground, while they beat her around the head. And under the anguish of that torture, she had said she would give her own daughter, Dzan, in marriage to the Captain instead of Pao Chen.

I went and sat beside her feeling numbed, unable to speak, as she went on talking in short, disconnected sentences.

'But I can't give her . . .

'I'll never give her . . .'

She spoke dully, her eyes dark and burning.

'I thought to myself, why was I suffering like this? It was for those three people. They've got away free. I'm suffering to save them.' She paused for a moment, then went on. 'And I thought of Jesus. I'm suffering for those three people, but He suffered for the whole world.'

Mrs. Han and I sat without moving. It was as though the shadow of a cross had stolen slowly across us as, behind the swollen, bruised face of that Chinese peasant woman, we saw Another Face. Many times we had read the records of the crucifixion but never before had we had so practical a demonstration of what it cost Him to save us as when we saw a dim reflection of His agony in the eyes of Mrs. Yen.

I'm finding it difficult to write this letter, trying to condense into a few lines an experience which it took me seven chapters to cover in a book I wrote about Mrs. Yen nearly forty years ago, called *Beaten Gold*. I have it on my lap before me now, reminding me of things I had forgotten as we sat with her that day in the guerilla headquarters—things such as the arrival of an elderly countrywoman who had walked forty *li** to see her daughter.

'She works for Kong *Tai-tai*,' she told us, adding in a lowered voice, 'They took her away by force.' But the girl herself looked cheerful enough in her smart bright blue jacket, laughing and talking to a soldier lounging against the door. Whatever may have been her first reactions, she seemed well satisfied with her life now.

'They're wicked people,' her mother continued in an even lower whisper. 'White powder . . .'

White powder. So there was drug smuggling, too, as well as ransom money?

'. . . and brothels,' in a murmur from Mrs. Yen, whose sharp ears had missed little.

There came the falling of darkness; the lighting of flickering oil lamps; the comings and goings of soldiers; a couple of men with provisions dangling from the ends of their carrying poles; then Mrs. Yen's sudden statement, 'Life and death are in this night.'

I remember the atmosphere of fear; ropes hanging down from beams; soldiers out to extort some money on their own account—business more easily accomplished after dark.

*A third of a mile.

My prayer was quiet and urgent; that this night, too, Kong *Tai-tai* would allow Mrs. Yen to come back with me. A soldier remarked that Kong *Tai-tai* was out at a feast, would be very late returning, as she was staying on to play mah-jong. I sat on stolidly, indicating that I was prepared to wait, no matter how long.

Eventually, Kong *Tai-tai* returned. She was surprised to see me there. First, she politely refused to allow Mrs. Yen to return with me; then with a sudden change of mind, she gave the permission, adding, 'But she must come back early in the morning. Captain Fong is going to take her with him to the country.'

So that was what he planned to do. Mrs. Yen had said he could marry her daughter Dzan and he evidently intended ensuring that she did not get out of it. Once out of the city Mrs. Yen would be entirely at his mercy with no-one to interfere, and unless the binding engagement contracts were duly signed. . . . torture!

That was the situation that faced us as we walked back through the dark streets. And that is why, sitting shivering in bed, unable to pray, I opened my Bible where the bookmark was placed at Jeremiah chapter 33 and started to read: 'Moreover, the word of the Lord came unto Jeremiah the second time, while he was yet shut up in the court of the prison, saying, Thus saith the Lord, the maker thereof, the Lord that formed it, to establish it; the Lord is His name . . .'

It seemed so far removed from our present extremity. I felt like turning to another portion, but read on doggedly, and my eyes fell on the

words, 'Call unto Me, and I will answer thee, and
show thee great and mighty things, which thou
knowest not.'

I stared at them and, as I did so, they seemed to
penetrate my numbness. I sat up in bed, still shivering slightly. With my open Bible on my knees, I
closed my eyes and clasped my hands tightly
together.

'O God,' I said aloud, slowly and deliberately. 'O
God, here it is in Thy word. Thou hast said "Call
unto Me and I will answer thee, and show thee
great and mighty things, which thou knowest not."
And now, Lord, I'm doing it. I'm calling unto
Thee.' Then, raising my voice, I cried as though
determined that He should hear. 'Oh God, save
Mrs. Yen, in Christ's Name. Amen.'

I closed the Bible, blew out the light, and lay
wide awake until the morning. There was nothing
more that I could do. God had said, 'Call,' and I
had done it.

20

Dear Edward,

I finished the previous letter last night, and as the tempo of this story changes at the point I left off, it seems very suitable to start on a fresh note this morning. And that fresh note must be the observation that God often works so quietly and unobtrusively that we fail to recognise His ways at all. The dramatic, the sudden, the violent impress us but not His skilful working in what appears to be the normal course of events. He seems to work in context, with complete understanding of local customs and conditions. Looking back on the events of the day following my desperate response to those words 'Call upon Me, and I will answer thee,' I find myself smiling with amusement at the way all our problems were eventually solved in a thoroughly Chinese-y manner.

The day started with the arrival of someone to escort Mrs. Yen back to the guerilla headquarters. A short time later Mrs. Han came along with two little parcels of sweet cakes carefully wrapped up in red paper. To my amazement she informed me that Captain Fong had sent them to me with his compliments.

'What's he giving me these for?' I asked her, bewildered. Cakes and compliments! I suspected there was a catch in it, but Mrs. Han assured me quite calmly it was just Captain Fong's expression of good will.

'What am I supposed to do now?' All I needed to do was write 'many thanks' on one of my cards in acknowledgment and give it to the servant to hand to him, she said. Conscious once more that I had completely failed to understand the subtleties of the oriental mind, I did so, thereby demonstrating that we had parted on friendly terms and had nothing to fear from each other.

Meanwhile Captain Fong was treating Mrs. Yen quite politely, as became a future son-in-law and, instead of making her walk, had ordered a wheelbarrow for her. He was taking her into the country, about forty *li* out of the city, he said. He was in good spirits, and strode on ahead, out of the West gate, little knowing that the word of authority had already been spoken in heaven, and that he was walking to his own confusion. How was he to know, with the whole vast plain before him, that when he took the path to the south-west it would lead to the very place in which his prisoner had been born and brought up?* And when he stopped at the inn and ordered rooms for the night, in the village of Hwang, little did he know that word was rapidly spreading among the Hwangs of what was happening to one of their members, to whom about half the population was related in some form or other;

*I can't vouch for the accuracy of the whereabouts of this place.

that already one of them was walking towards the home of a Hwang who was an official of some importance in the Nationalist government and who happened to be back in his native village on a brief visit.

The Hwangs, like most other families, were composed of a few wealthy and influential people and a lot of poor and unimportant relations. Mrs. Yen, of course, belonged to the latter category and, beyond receiving certain advantages in the matter of gleaning at harvest time, could expect little benefit from being related to the Hwangs of higher rank. But the situation she was in now put things in a different light. She was a Hwang and so was the official of some importance. However remote the relationship, family loyalty demanded that he should intervene on her behalf. And as his position with the Nationalists gave him 'face' which a guerilla officer was bound to respect, he was in a position to do so.

So he intervened.

I heard about it from Mrs. Yen herself when, quite unexpectedly, she turned up a couple of days later. It was Sunday, and I found her sitting in her usual place on one of the benches in the church-cum-barn, having arrived early for the service.

'Mrs. Yen!' I gasped. I could scarcely believe what I saw and behaved in a most un-Chinesey manner—rushing up to hug her, half sobbing, 'You're back! You're safe!'

'Don't, Teacher,' she said, somewhat embarrassed, and when I asked her what had happened, she told me quite unemotionally. The influential Hwang had come to the inn to visit Captain Fong who, of course, had welcomed him politely. They had sat together, chatting, sipping tea and nibbling peanuts, and the influential Hwang in the course of conversation had mentioned the matter of Mrs. Yen.

'This old great-aunt of mine who is with you, my wife would like to see her,' he had said. 'She wants her to stay for a day or two. It is too much trouble for you to have her here.' And although Captain Fong had assured him that it was no trouble at all, the word of the influential Hwang had prevailed, and when he'd sauntered away Mrs. Yen had trudged stolidly behind him, to spend the night in the security of his home. Her deliverance from further torture at the hands of Captain Fong had come about just as simply as that. But if the influential Hwang had not happened to be in the district at that time, or if Captain Fong had gone to any other area on the great plain but the one he unwittingly chose, how different it would all have been!

Not that it was the end of the affair, of course. Mrs. Yen still had to be released from her promise to give Dzan as a second wife to Captain Fong and to ensure that no reprisals would follow later on. How that was brought about, I have no idea. Undoubtedly middle-men were recruited to engage in delicate discussions, suggestions and arguments; and probably some money changed hands. It took some weeks to bring the matter to a satisfactory conclusion. But eventually a feast was given at which the influential Hwang and Captain Fong were the guests of honour, and for which all that was required of Mrs. Yen was that she should foot the bill. She was very thankful that it had been quietly agreed that wine should be provided, not 'white powder', which was so much more expensive. The feast made it evident that the whole matter was over and that Mrs. Yen need fear no reprisals. It nearly ruined her financially, but when it was all over she invested in a large print New Testament which she could not afford. She was determined to make good this time. She would learn to read, and she would read the Word of God, the God who had so remarkably delivered her out of her distresses.

The story had quite a happy ending, too, for after some months the guerillas left the neighbourhood altogether, and Pao Chen, the girl for whom Mrs. Yen had suffered so much, returned, well and happy, with her grandmother, her husband and a new-born baby. But by that time the famine was on us. And that is another story.

21

Dear Edward,

I have seen many harrowing pictures of famine-stricken people on the television in recent years, and somehow they seemed quite different from those in the famine we lived through in Henan, China, in the early 1940s. Hundreds of thousands of people must have died in it. Henan is thickly populated, and the famine was severe, made all the worse, of course, by the cutting off of supplies due to the war. Yet it came on us so imperceptibly that Doris and I were unaware of it at first.

It started with a poor harvest. With our English background, it did not occur to us, or at any rate to me, that a bad harvest would seriously affect anyone but the farmers. Prices might rise a bit, but that would be all that the rest of us would know about it. So we thought. The price of grain was as general a topic of conversation in Henan as was the weather in England, so we were accustomed to hearing remarks about its having gone up a cent or come down a cent. But as I walked through the markets that autumn I began to realise that people were talking about it in a different way. It was not only the price that they referred to, but the shortage.

'We haven't got enough grain,' they murmured. Then, more anxiously, 'We haven't got enough grain till the next harvest.' And as time went on; 'We shall starve . . .,' and finally; 'We shall die . . .'

And they did die. Quietly, in their homes.

But before that began to happen I had noticed a change in the streets. Everybody walked more slowly and the bearers of burdens were disappearing. There were fewer men with heavy loads swinging from their carrying poles, or being pushed on wheelbarrows. They had not the strength for the tasks and, in any case, fewer people could afford to employ them. Eventually there were none to be seen except the water carriers. Everyone needed water, so money must be kept for them.

Then there were the beggars. Beggars were a common enough sight in the China of those days and, unlike the pitiable, often repulsive looking beggars of India, they were almost an accepted part of the community, dressed like everyone else, though naturally shabbier. The insignia of their profession was an earthenware food bowl to receive any pieces of bread or scrapings from cooking pots that came their way, and a stick to beat off the dogs. Most households had a dog trained to bark at and even attack unannounced visitors unless called back by their owners. So beggars had to be on their guard. Not everyone was prepared to 'do good deeds' by giving them something, thereby gaining merit, and when beggars were not tolerated, the dogs were not called back. But as the famine increased, there was a subtle change in the beggar community. Parents with insufficient food to feed their children sent them out to hang around the courtyards of wealthier neighbours or distant relations. They wouldn't openly beg for themselves and there were limits to the extent they could trade on family or neighbourly relationships in 'borrowing' what they were likely never to return. But for the children it was different. A hungry child at the kitchen door when a meal was being prepared was not likely to be ignored.

'They'll give a little to a small child,' the parents said hopefully. 'If only the children can get enough . . .'

So it went on. The beggars, some of whom had come earlier from districts that were hit by famine before ours, became too weak to walk around. They crept out of the shacks where they slept, to lie here and there by the side of the road, moaning to the passers-by for just one thing: 'Bread! Bread!'

It was during this period that I read in one of the few newspapers to get through to us of such bumper harvests in North America that mountains of wheat had been burned for economic reasons. That news item made a deep impression on me, and still does when I think of it. Wheat to burn in some places, thousands dying for want of it in others. It challenges me as I think of the plentiful supply of all my material needs in the comfortable position in which I find myself in my old age. It challenges me as I look at the row of Bibles on my shelf, several different translations, and remember that there are fellow believers in places like China who have not so much as a portion of the Word of God in their possession. And it challenges me as I remember that there are millions in the world today who have never even heard the Gospel of Jesus Christ.

I am reminded that to whom much has been given much will be required, and I wonder how I shall measure up in the day of reckoning . . .

But to return to the famine, as it affected us in Siangcheng. Doris and I were already learning to live with inflation. As soon as our remittances arrived we would lay in stores of basic necessities like fuel, grain, oil, salt, rather than keep cash in hand, for money was losing its value all the time. Our remittances came quarterly, and we never knew how much they would be, with exchange rates fluctuating and the war affecting Mission finances. Luxuries like coffee and sugar were ruled out, of course, but we always had sufficient for our needs, which we soon learned were not as great as we had once thought them to be. But there was not much left over and there was little enough we could do to help others.

However—there was something. Unexpectedly a small allocation of famine relief money was granted to us, and we discussed its use very earnestly with the deacons.

Should it be used for Christians only? No: it was decided that as the money had been given to help the most needy, irrespective of their faith, it wouldn't be right to give preferential treatment to our own people.

Should it be used to help a few people effectively or many superficially?

'Most people will have ways of getting a little food, but for some of them it won't be enough. If we can help them eke out what they can get, we may help more people to stay alive,' the deacons said. The daily distribution of a little food would be the best way to do it. Deacon Liong, who studied these things, said there was more concentrated nourishment in an egg than anything else, but it was argued that a bowl of thick, hot porridge would be more satisfying. The idea of handing out a daily egg to the needy was abandoned in favour of a bowl of hot porridge per person per day, to be ladled out to those who came for it early each morning.

It may sound strange to you, but those months in the famine were among the most satisfying of my whole life. I have tried to analyse the reasons, and I think they can be summed up in the one word 'fellowship'. Primarily there was the sense of fellowship with God. I knew I was where He intended me to be, living among the poor just as His Son had done, and I wouldn't have exchanged places with a princess, for the quiet joy that consciousness gave me. Secondly there was the fellowship with the Christians in Siangcheng, as we lived through the famine together. And there was the satisfaction of being able to do something practical, little as it was, to alleviate suffering. That daily allocation of porridge to the hungry did as much for me, though in a different way, as it did for those who received it.

We had a routine to which we stuck rigidly. Early every day the few of us who lived on the compound met for Bible reading and prayer together. This period lasted about an hour, during which one of the women slipped out and got the fire going and the water boiling in the great cook-

ing pot, ready for the carefully measured supply of
flour and millet and salt to be stirred in. Then Mrs.
Han stood by the pot, ladling a scoopful into each
bowl held out to her. Gratefully the recipients
sucked in cold air with the hot porridge, licking the
bowl when all had been consumed, departing
rather reluctantly—some of them to spend the rest
of the day begging.

One incident during this period stands out in my
memory so distinctly that I can visualise it even
now. A prayer meeting was in process. We were
gathered in one of the little side rooms between the
guest hall at the front and the compounds at the
back. There were only a few of us, and as someone
was praying aloud I heard the familiar cry of a
beggar: 'Bread! Bread!' Looking through the glassless window frame, I saw a boy of about twelve
years old walking past, and it was his cry that
arrested me. It was different from the hopeless
moan of the beggars in the streets. This boy was
walking with purpose, and the desperate yet
imperative note in his voice moved me to action.
Hurriedly I slipped out of the room and followed
him, calling him back. He was dressed quite well—a
cap with ear flaps on his head, though his clothes
were getting shabby—and he begged me urgently
to give him food. He was pleading, not for himself
but for his mother who was too weak to move. If he
could not get something for her to eat she would
die, he said.

His urgency was irresistible. The prayer meeting
had to go on without me. I beckoned to Mrs. Han
and she slipped out, too. We got some food
together and went back with the boy to see his

mother.

She was lying on a ragged wadded quilt on the floor of a cart shed, and we learned that she and her husband and their little son had come from another district, even worse hit by the famine than Siangcheng. But her husband had died, she and the boy had had to fend for themselves, and now she was too ill to move. The boy had done what he could; gathered sticks and made a fire to try to warm her and then gone off to beg for food. He was desperate but determined. 'Bread! Bread! Give me bread!' His mother's life depended on him.

It is probably unnecessary to report that although many, many died in the famine, that boy and his mother came through it. We saw to that! Strangely enough, I can recall very little else about them. What I have always remembered was the urgency in that cry, so different from the unexpectant moaning of the beggars in the street. I have sometimes thought that much of our half-hearted praying is like the passionless pleas of those sighing beggars. It was the importunity in the cry of that boy that moved me to action. I think there must have been the same note in the voice of blind Bartimaeus that brought Jesus to a halt as He was passing through Jericho.

He is the God Who hears the cry.

22

Dear Edward,

It was just about the time the famine started that we received a letter which galvanised me, as missionary in charge in Siangcheng, to reluctant action. I had been feeling weary after six years in China without a proper holiday, and with no prospect of one in the foreseeable future. The Japanese had already attacked U.S. bases in the Pacific, bringing the States into the war against them, and many of our colleagues were now in Japanese internment camps. A furlough at home was out of the question with the Second World War raging in Europe. I remember one day thinking to myself:

'Well, I can keep going the way we are, just jogging along like this—but I couldn't rise to making a fresh effort.' We had a routine which, because of its regularity, had become undemanding. This letter challenged me to the very thing I had felt I could not do.

It came from Mission headquarters, which had been moved from the port of Shanghai on the east coast to the city of Chungking, a thousand miles inland to the west, which the retreating Chinese had made their wartime capital. The Mission Directorate was imparting to all of us who were scattered throughout free China a renewed vision of a truly indigenous church. This is what we should be aiming at getting established. Not a church in China that was dependent on western leadership and support, but a Church that was self-governing, self-propagating, and self-supporting: three Selfs.

(Even as I write these words I have to smile at the way the Communist Government has adapted to suit its own purposes the principle that had been clearly defined in missionary circles decades before. The name given to the state-controlled Church in China today is 'Three Self Patriotic Movement.')

There was nothing new in the idea. It was something that had been impressed on us right from the start of our missionary careers. The difficulty had been in its practical outworking. We were from the energetic West, we had come to live among the Chinese for the sole purpose of preaching to them the Gospel and teaching them to be disciples of Jesus Christ, and it was natural for us to go ahead and do it. When people were converted, and little groups of believers formed into churches, the missionary still instinctively took the lead and, often enough, the Chinese were content to follow. And since, in most cases, the people were poor, financial support for the work and for the provision of premises as places of worship were still coming largely from Mission sources.

The tendency with most of us missionaries was to accept the *status quo*, and the directive from

Chungking was designed to jerk us out of it.

'Evangelize—through the Church,' was the gist of its message, and it provided just the spark of inspiration needed to infuse new life into our task. Some of us had taken the admonition to leave church leadership to the Chinese so seriously that we were in danger of doing nothing at all, for fear of interfering. For me, the issue hadn't been difficult. As missionary in charge in Siangcheng, I had explained that I would devote myself to the women's work and occasional visits to the outstations, as I felt that church business and the leading of Sunday services should be in the hands of men, not women. I am afraid this apparently right-minded modesty was largely due to a natural disinclination for administration and public speaking. I was only too happy to leave such matters to the deacons and the resulting dichotomy between them and me might have continued to the end had it not been for the directive from Chungking.

This directive aimed at reassuring us missionaries that the vision of the evangelisation of China, which had brought most of us to the country in the first place, had not been lost sight of in the emphasis on an indigenous church. The task must be continued but the time had come for it to be done not independently but with the local church as the vehicle. Our job was to inspire the churches with which we were working to take the initiative; and some practical suggestions were made as to how we could set about it.

Without those practical suggestions I, for one, would not have known where to begin, for the directive, as it affected me, meant not only inspiring the deacons with an increased sense of responsibility for evangelism, but also encouraging them to provide their own place of worship instead of meeting in premises rented by the Mission.

I wondered how they would react to the suggestions I had to put forward. Very apprehensively, I asked if we could have a committee meeting.

I need not have worried. Looking back, I marvel at the perfect timing of things for all of us in that little church in Siangcheng. We had gone through a lot together, what with the ever-present threat of a Japanese advance, the tensions of the guerilla occupation and the food shortage. The experiences were bringing home to us the uncertainty and impermanence of our earthly existence, and I think we were ready for the challenge to direct our energies in an new way towards establishing God's kingdom among men right where we were. At any rate, that first committee meeting was more encouraging than I had dared to hope, with the deacons nodding in agreement as I shared some of the contents of the directive from Chungking. Especially there was the inspiration of the formation of an organisation to link together all the C.I.M. churches in the province of Henan, for mutual help and encouragement and the provision of evangelists and Bible teaching. It was an organization within the Chinese churches, with Chinese—not missionary—leadership and this put them on their mettle. Rather like children who are discovering that they can walk and want to do so unaided, the deacons were quite eager to go ahead along the lines suggested, particularly in the matter of getting their own church building.

We arose from that committee meeting with a new sense of purpose and with a warmer feeling towards each other. We agreed that we must have another committee meeting—to discuss matters further and to pray. And so things got started. The more committee meetings we had, the fonder we got of each other; and the fonder we got of each other, the more committee meetings we had. At one time we seemed to be having them every other day. The warmth and enthusiasm was communicated to the church members and, through the hard days of the famine, money was given, often at great sacrifice, to the fund for a church building of their own.

The day came when Doris and I were invited to go along the street and see the property that was being bought. It was quite a small courtyard of low buildings on all four sides of it with the usual heavy wooden doors and glassless window frames. Only one building boasted a tiled roof; the others were merely thatched. One of these buildings was to be the church. It was to be made large enough to accommodate about a hundred people by the simple but somewhat risky expedient of carving two arches in the wall that helped to support the roof, thus making two rooms into one. Doris and I looked on rather dubiously as this was being done, fearful of a complete collapse of wall and roof, but no such catastrophe occurred, and the deacons were well satisfied with the result.

Meanwhile, the famine was coming to an end at last, with a good sweet potato crop and spring vegetables to tide us over till the grain was reaped.

Life returned more or less to normal. There were rumours that the Japanese were preparing for another advance, and one evening Dr. Wang, who had friends among the military officials, came to see us and warn us that this time it was likely to be permanent.

'Don't risk remaining here too long,' she said. 'But if you don't get away in time, you can come with me and my family. We shall go into the country. Where we go, you shall go. Where we sleep, you shall sleep. What we eat, you shall eat.' She spoke in her slow deliberate manner, and we were touched, for we knew she meant what she said.

We had a letter from Mission headquarters, too, explaining that it might be necessary for us to move to Chowkiakow, forty miles to the west, to avoid being cut off by a Japanese offensive. But we had no definite instructions to do so and we had lived with alarms for four years now. The more immediate matter of the removal of Mrs. Han and her daughter, along with all the church furnishings, to the new premises claimed our attention along with preparations for the very first Sunday service in the new church.

It was an historic event. Although the day dawned wet and windy, the place soon filled up with men and women who looked around the freshly mudded walls with a kind of proprietary interest. In some ways the place compared unfavourably with the old one for it was much smaller and more congested. But it was their own, bought with their own money at the height of the famine; and, as I stood with a little group of them that

Sunday morning, I knew the Lord was there.

It was without any premonition of threatening clouds that I turned as someone spoke my name, and found Deacon Liong standing beside me.

'Teacher Dong,' he said in a low, but very clear voice. 'Here is a telegram for you.' He looked down at me impassively, but there was something about his manner that arrested me. Telegrams were rare, and as he held this one in his hand he asked, 'Shall I read it to you?' He knew I would have difficulty in deciphering the hasty scrawl. 'Yes, please.' I said. Again in that low, clear voice, he read to me the message it contained.

'Situation serious. Proceed with baggage to Chowkiakow immediately.'

I ought not to have been unprepared, for we had had those warnings; but, all the same, it came as a shock. I stood quite still for a moment, then said quietly, 'I'd been afraid of this.'

A man standing by asked anxiously what it meant, and quickly I murmured, 'Don't say anything.' That this should happen on the very first Sunday when the service was to be held on the new church compound! 'We mustn't let anything disturb them—not today.' I turned back to the little group with whom I had been talking, and walked away with them into the chapel.

Deacon Liong turned away impassively, too. A year ago I would have thought he did not care but I knew him better now. There was a wordless understanding between us to avoid any emotional demonstration of distress or alarm to spoil the joy of this day. All the same, as I sat among the women in the back rows, I found it no easy matter to control the conflicting thoughts of my mind and listen to the sermon. There would be so much work to do, and I wondered how soon 'immediately' could be.

After the service there was, of course, a committee meeting. Still I remained silent about the telegram. Not until various comments had been made about the arrangements for the service, and plans outlined for the future, did Deacon Liong look across at me and ask if I had anything to say, adding quietly, 'You'd better tell them your news, Teacher.'

So I told them. Teacher Way and I had received instructions to evacuate Siangcheng immediately, for fear of a Japanese advance that would cut us off; but we had been instructed to go to Chowkiakow, only forty miles away. Deacon Liong added reassuringly that there had been these rumours before; the teachers would probably be back again in two or three weeks' time, he said.

But as I went to bed that night, it was with the conviction that tomorrow would see the end of my service in Siangcheng. The thought was solemnizing. The books on this part of my life were closing. It would only remain, on the Day when they were opened, to give an account of what had been committed to me.

23

Dear Edward,

I don't know how to condense into a thousand or two words what filled a book forty years ago when I wrote about our last day in Siangcheng. Everything had to be cleared, the premises emptied, our stuff disposed of except what personal possessions we could get onto a couple of wheelbarrows or strap on the carriers of our bicycles. But all that was incidental. What really mattered, what filled the day, was the people: the people who came to do what they could to help and to say goodbye; the people with whom our lives had been so closely interwoven for years, and who, we realized, we would never see again.

It started with Deacon Hsiao's arrival. Alert and capable, he attended to the Famine Relief grain. It must all be distributed before we left, and I turned instinctively to him for that. Firmly putting aside his own affairs, he was in and out of the compound most of the day, making lists of the neediest people, weighing the grain, distributing it. He was unusually quiet, and when he had finished he came and said, 'I'm going back now, Teacher. If there's anything else I can do for you, send over at once. I shall not be far away.' We looked at each other silently then, for we knew it was goodbye. I wished I could think of some last word for him. Pastor Gee and Pastor Fee, the missionaries before me, had both given him the text—'Be thou faithful unto death, and I will give thee the crown of life'—as they were leaving. It had made a deep impression on him. But I seemed tongue-tied. Perhaps after the four years of our fellowship in the Gospel there was no need for further words.

'Thank you,' I said. He bowed and went away.

Then there was Mrs. Deng who hawked needles and other odds and ends to keep herself and her child alive, and had occasionally sold things for me or Doris when our funds were low. She came along for that purpose now; strong, reliable, ready to raise what money she could to provide for the uncertainties of the journeys that lay ahead of us. Picture frames, ornaments, crockery, clothing; she'd pick them up and ask, 'How much do you want for this, Teacher?' and off she'd go, time and again, to return with the money.

'I'd have died in the famine if it hadn't been for that bowl of porridge each morning,' she told me more than once. 'There's nothing that can't be gone through. Look at what the Lord has brought me through!' Mrs Deng had no idea what she meant to us, that last day in Siangcheng.

Mrs. Hsaio had no idea, either. She had been one of the first to hear the news, her husband having told her after the committee meeting, and she had come round, eyes red with weeping, to whisper softly, 'Teacher! You're going away . . . Oh, I wish you could live *for ever* in Siangcheng!' That unusual display of emotion was strangely comforting. It is so soothing to be loved!

Mrs. Han expressed her love in a different way. During the day she had been as fully occupied as we were, sorting her things, preparing for her move to the two little rooms where she was to live with her daughter on the new church premises. But in the afternoon, she came through the gate into our compound with Widow Wang, as she had come so many times before, but this time it was for a final, private visit. As our eyes met, she broke into a wailing cry, such as I had only heard once before, at the funeral of her father-in-law. Doris hurried forward to lead her gently to a chair, murmuring words to soothe her but I stood with my head buried in my hands, unable to speak.

So the day passed. Arrangements had to be made for a hasty departure next day; decisions had to be made about what we could take and what we must either sell or give away; items of furniture were sold to neighbours who got wind of what was happening; and, through it all, there was a little stream of Christians who had heard the news and came to say goodbye: Ma Tzu Meng, a well educated young man from a wealthy family, and New Covenant, a robust peasant about his own age; Li *Tai-tai*, strangely subdued, with a little group of women from the Street of the Oil House, and some men from the South Road: a peanut seller, a stocking maker, an elderly scholar, and an official in the city workhouse; Blind Joy, the beggar-girl married to a blind man about three times her age; Deacon Fan, who helped Deacon Hsaio with the Famine Relief distribution; Deacon Liong who, seeing the completeness with which we were disposing of everything, said rather reproachfully, 'It looks as though you hope you won't return, Teacher Dong.' We were giving the lie to his reassuring comments about being back in three weeks.

'It's not that I *hope* I won't return—I *fear* I won't return,' I answered. For I knew it was the end.

A twelve year old schoolboy who had recently been baptized came too, and Mrs. Han's schoolgirl daughter slipped in after dark, without her mother. Last of all came Dr. Wang, and Doris and I sat down with her rather soberly, knowing we would never do so again. Our times of intimate fellowship had not been many, but occasionally the Manchurian doctor, an exile from the home of her youth, had come to spend an evening with us; and the quiet talks over the supper table, the reminiscences, the unemotional intimacy of those evenings, had bound us together in a way that only exiles can know.

'My heart is very sorrowful,' she said. 'I know you ought to go. I should be worried if you did not go, for the situation is really serious this time. But my heart is very sorrowful.' She drew some money from her pocket, laid it on the table.

'This is the money for some of your crockery that I have bought,' she said 'and here is a little—only a very little—to help towards your travelling expenses.' We talked together for a short while, then she rose to go and we went with her, holding aloft the flickering oil lamp to cast a dim light over the bricked paths, through the compound, through the church and along to the street door.

'When you have gone,' said Dr. Wang in her

quiet deliberate voice. 'I shall never come to this place again. Goodbye, Teachers. I shall not come to see you to-morrow morning.'

'No, Dr. Wang,' we said, 'Please do not come.' Then, the last words, the Christian farewell—'The Lord be with you.'

Dawn. Quick, last minute packing. Big Sister Lee foreseeing needs, hurrying to meet them. Deacon Hsaio arriving—were the Teachers ready for breakfast? He had insisted that he and his wife should supply it. Hasty distribution of bundles specially prepared for Mrs. Han, Widow Wang, and Big Sister Lee.

Arrival of New Covenant to see to the loading of the wheelbarrows and march alongside them all the way to Chowkiakow. Final instructions for the distribution of furniture and remaining possessions. The group of people who had come to say goodbye crowding into our little dining room and overflowing into the bedroom, for a last prayer together. Out into the little garden, all stamped down and forlorn-looking now. Never again would I see Sister Lee squatting under the shady acacia tree, preparing vegetables for the midday meal. Never again would I see the Bible class girls with their straight black bobbed hair, slim and dainty in their long gowns, wandering around looking at the flowers and smelling the roses. Never again would I see the men who came to the Sunday afternoon Bible class, filing slowly but purposefully into the little dining-room, their Bibles tucked under their arms . . .

'It's getting late—we must go . . .'

I had just crossed the threshold of the chapel in my hurried walk towards the street door, when time suddenly stood still. The benches had gone, the pulpit had gone, only a few posters, too torn to be worth removing, remained on the brick walls. All had been conveyed to the new church building. Never again would I see the blue-garbed throng of men and women gathered there for worship on Sunday morning, or sit with the little group that circled round in the centre of the hall to remember the Lord's death, when sometimes we had all but seen Him helplessly nailed to the cross, dying for us.

I had just crossed over the threshold in my hurried walk towards the front hall and the street door, when God spoke to me.

It was an experience I will never forget. I heard nothing, but I knew He was speaking, as my mind was flooded with one sentence which completely submerged all the busy thoughts and conflicting emotions of sorrow and excitement that had been filling it. Just as it had been flooded with verses about angels on that memorable day in Taikang, just as it had been flooded with the command not to resist when the brigand had broken into the out-station chapel at midnight, so a simple sentence from one of the parables in Matthew chapter 25 flooded my mind now. It was a word of commendation, the 'Well done' spoken to the servants who, when their master called on them to give account of the money he had entrusted to them, had traded profitably.

There was such grace in the words, such un-merited favour, as to bring tears to my eyes and halt me in my path. I stopped dead. It seemed too good to be true. In spite of all my failures and foolishness, in spite of my impatience and faithlessness, I'd made the grade. I felt like a student anxiously scanning the exam results who, wonder of wonders, sees his name on the pass list.

It would have been a relief to fling myself on my knees and give expression to my pent up feelings. But there was no place to obtain such privacy now and no time, either. The wheelbarrows had trundled off, Mrs. Han's daughter and Deacon Liong's son were waiting to push our bicycles out into the street and escort us down the familiar North Road with its avenue of old trees.

'Goodbye! Goodbye! The Lord be with you!' we called to our friends.

We passed through the north suburb with its stalls and inn benches. Mrs. Yen rose from her stool as she saw us coming and greeted us with the usual words, 'Where are you going, Teachers?'— adding with dismay, 'To Chowkiakow! Why? . . . Oh! I didn't know. No-one told me . . . You're going . . . Here, wait a minute!' Quickly she gathered up half-a-dozen round bread biscuits. She ran after us and thrust them into our hands, saying, 'Here, take these to eat on the way . . .' Standing there, looking at us, she reiterated, 'I didn't know, no-one told me you're going . . .'

Clear of the suburb at last, on the dusty track leading through the wheat-fields, we got off our bicycles, laid them down, sat on a mound by the side of the road, and buried our faces in our hands. Less than forty-eight hours earlier, we had been in the new church compound, completely unaware that we were so soon to be uprooted from the place and the people we had come to know so well. What lay ahead of us we did not know, but it was not so much the future that weighed on us, as the consciousness of those we were leaving behind.

'Lord! Bless them . . . Help them . . . Keep them . . . Thou art the good shepherd . . .'

After a while we got on our bicycles, and cycled away.

24

29 July 1987

Dear Edward,

Two and a half years have passed since we met in the Charing Cross Hotel and I told you I wouldn't write my own story. Well, as you will see, I have only covered a limited part of it, but this is how it seems to have come. In view of the reason for writing it at all, it probably deals with the most significant part. You may remember that when you broached the subject it was because of the China interest.

'There are so few people left who knew China before the Communists gained control,' you said.

Certainly, they had not gained control in the early 1940s. They had completed their Long March, and were entrenched in the northern mountains, biding their time; but when Doris and I cycled away from Siangcheng in 1943 we were scarcely aware of their existence. It was the wave of the Japanese armies spreading over all the areas where we Henan missionaries lived that had affected us. The journey to Chowkiakow was only the beginning of a much longer trek as we joined up with others and moved farther and farther westward. (It was at about this time that Glady's

214

Aylward was making her epic escape with all those children over the mountains, by the way. I met her not long afterwards, for the first time, in the city of Sian, where she told me of the way she had got to China across Russia and Siberia, and much more besides. This personal knowledge of her gave me confidence in writing *A London Sparrow* many years later).

I had been in touch with Mission authorities about going to the Tibetan border, and was told I could do so, but not until I had had a furlough. So I went to Mission headquarters in Chungking instead, where I got involved in editorial work before returning to England; by aeroplane to Calcutta, then by troopship to berth in the Clyde.

The tide of war was turning in favour of the Allies at last, and I remember listening in to the crossing of the Rhine and the final capitulation of Nazi Germany, and then to a most inspiring radio programme in which we heard the chimes of cathedral bells ringing out from all the liberated capitals of Europe.

That was followed, some time later, by the Victory Parade, as representatives of the armed services—the Navy, the Army, the Air Force, the Marines—went swinging down the Mall to take the salute as the King stood to acknowledge them. They were followed by a heterogeneous stream of others who had played their part, even risked their lives, in the dark days of the conflict—the medics, the nurses, the Red Cross, the Wrens and the WAAF, the Women's Voluntary Service and the air raid Wardens, and many more. The great moment for them all was when they came abreast of the

King and saw him standing there, saluting them—proud of them.

I listened in to that programme with deep emotion. The memory of it still stirs me. It seemed like a foreshadowing of the great Victory Parade when our King returns in glory. I want to be able to hold my head up in that Parade.

The dropping of the first atomic bomb on Hiroshima in August, 1945, not only marked the end of World War Two, as Japan surrendered unconditionally to the Allies, and ushered in a new era in world history as mankind entered the atomic age. It was also the signal for the Communists in North China to start moving.

By the time I got back to China, at the end of 1947, they were already overrunning the vast areas that the Japanese had occupied and any hope of missionaries returning to the province of Henan had to be abandoned. As for me, I set off for the Tibetan border, leaving Shanghai early one wet Monday morning in February, 1948, on the first lap of the journey. I travelled in a lorry containing three and a half tons of Bibles, one of a convoy of five vehicles—two lorries, two jeeps with trailers, and a saloon car. There were seven of us in the party—three Americans, two British, a Swede and a Chinese. We were bound for Chungking, 1,000 or so miles inland, and the month-long journey was sufficiently eventful what with hairpin bends and the lorry toppling over into the river to justify my writing another book: *Bible Convoy*.

And that was the last of my China experiences to appear in book form for a very long time. Although I travelled widely during the next three years—to Kangting on the Tibetan border, to Howhwan on a tributary of the Yangtze, to Lanchow on the upper reaches of the Yellow River, and to Ningsia on the border of Mongolia— nothing could be published about my travels, except in short articles in the Mission's magazine. The Communists were already established in Peking, the capital, and it was only a matter of time before they would be in control of the whole country. As citizens of the 'capitalist' nations of the West we were viewed with suspicion, even hostility, and we knew that anything appearing in print under our name could not only endanger ourselves, but also the Chinese with whom we were associated.

Even when the Mission drew out of China altogether, in 1951, our lips were sealed regarding what we had seen and heard. Our exit visas had been granted only on condition that Chinese friends resident in the country would stand guarantee for us. They, not we, would have to pay the price for anything detrimental to the Communists that we divulged. It was a most effective way of keeping us quiet, and explains why I did not even write *The Reluctant Exodus*, the story of how the several hundred of us all got safely out of China, until nearly thirty years after it had happened.

So back to England I came—and the curtain went down on China. Occasional snippets of news got through—of arrests, imprisonments, executions, the closing of churches and the persecution of Christians—but, as the years passed, a blanket of silence seemed to shroud the land. I was editing the

Mission's magazine by this time and, in an effort to maintain interest in the country, I ran a regular feature called 'Window on China', to which Leslie Lyall was the main contributor. It seemed all that I could do.

Then, one evening in 1970, I fell and fractured my arm and was taken to a local hospital. There I discovered, to my amazement, that practically all the trainee nurses were Chinese. True, they were from Malaysia, Singapore or Hong Kong, not from China, but there was no question about their race. Chinese girls, right on my doorstep! Had it not been for my fractured arm, I doubt whether I would have become aware of their existence. But, from that time on, I had a little stream of them coming to my terraced house in North London, to keep alive my love for the Chinese. Even where I am living now, in South-west London, I am within walking distance of the Chinese Overseas Christian Mission, founded in 1950 by a refugee from China, the Rev. Stephen Wang. Through the years, during which I have become absorbed in the writing of one book after another, China and the Chinese have been woven like a golden thread through the tapestry of my life. The monthly meeting for prayer for China that I attend is a *must* in my diary, and how I glow inwardly when the news from Henan is of spectacular church growth! There are more Christians in that one province now than there were in the whole of China when I left it in 1951!

It's time I finished this last letter and got it into the post to meet the publisher's deadline. I am aware that I ought to conclude on a picturesque or touching or challenging note. It would be very suitable, in view of what I have just written, if it were something about China, and I've been sitting quietly, letting my memory run back over my life, to see what comes to mind.

And what comes to mind just now is not China. As I grow older, I find that the most vivid experience, and the one that I remember most frequently, is the day in 1933, when I heard those words: 'Jesus Christ died on the cross to give you everlasting life, and all you've got to do is to accept it.' I never cease to marvel that it was as simple as that—and that it worked.

That was the day I started my pilgrimage. It will end when I see my master face to face.